THE SOCIAL ORGANIZATION
OF
DOCTOR–PATIENT
COMMUNICATION
Second Edition

edited by

Alexandra Dundas Todd

and

Sue Fisher

ABLEX PUBLISHING CORPORATION
NORWOOD, NEW JERSEY

Library of Congress Cataloging-in Publication Data

The Social organization of doctor–patient communication / Alexandra
    Dundas Todd and Sue Fisher, editors.—2nd ed.
        p. cm.
    Includes bibliographical references and index.
    ISBN 0–89391–699–4 (P).—ISBN 0–89391–694–3 (C)
    1. Physician and patient.   I. Todd, Alexandra Dundas.
II. Fisher, Sue, 1936–
    [DNLM: 1. Communication.   2. Physician–Patient Relations.   W 62
S678]
R727.3.S6   1992
610.69′6—dc20
DNLM/DLC
for Library of Congress   92–10691
                                                           CIP

Ablex Publishing Corporation
355 Chestnut Street
Norwood, New Jersey 07648

Table of Contents

Preface to the Second Edition: Power and Resistance   *v*
    Sue Fisher and Alexandra Todd

Physician's Foreword   *ix*
    Howard Beckman, M.D.

Introduction: Communication and Social Context—Toward Broader
    Definitions   *1*
    Sue Fisher and Alexandra Dundas Todd

**Part I: SOCIOLINGUISTIC AND COGNITIVE APPROACHES
TO DISCOURSE**

  1 Three Types of Interference to an Effective Exchange of Information
      in the Medical Interview   *17*
    Roger W. Shuy

  2 Doctor/Mother/Child Communication: Linguistic Analysis of a
      Pediatric Interaction   *31*
    Deborah Tannen and Cynthia Wallat

  3 Hearing Is Not Believing: Language and the Structure of Belief in
      Medical Communication   *49*
    Aaron V. Cicourel

**Part II: THE PRODUCTION OF DOCTOR–PATIENT
COMMUNICATIONS**
A Social Accomplishment

  4 The Laying on of Hands: Aspects of the Organization of Gaze,
      Touch, and Talk in a Medical Encounter   *71*
    Richard M. Frankel

  5 On the Work of Talk: Studies in Misunderstandings   *107*
    Marianne A. Paget

  6 "Ask Me No Questions..." An Analysis of Queries and Replies in
      Physician–Patient Dialogues   *127*
    Candace West

Structure and Structuring

7   Doctor Talk/Patient Talk: How Treatment Decisions Are Negotiated
       in Doctor–Patient Communication   *161*
    Sue Fisher

8   A Diagnosis of Doctor–Patient Discourse in the Prescription of
       Contraception   *183*
    Alexandra Dundas Todd

Power and Resistance

9   Policing the Lying Patient: Surveillance and Self-Regulation in
       Consultations with Adolescent Diabetics   *213*
    David Silverman

10 Nice Doctors and Invisible Patients: The Problem of Power in
       Feminist Common Sense   *243*
    Kathy Davis

11 Exploring Women's Experiences: Power and Resistance in Medical
       Discourse   *267*
    Alexandra Dundas Todd

12 Reflections on Gender, Power, and Discourse   *287*
    Sue Fisher

Author Index   *301*

Subject Index   *305*

Preface to the Second Edition
Power and Resistance

The 1960s and 1970s were good times for sociological theory. There was increased interest in macro theories—Weberian, Marxist, and neo-Marxist—as well as micro theories—ethnomethodology and cognitive, interpretive, and existential sociology. As the 1980s approached, the emphasis shifted and became more integrative. In 1983 when this volume first appeared, we were interested in the relationship between social structure and social interaction. We conceived and published this book to examine this relationship.

At that time, very few sociologists were studying how language was used, and those few who were all too often ignored social structure. They treated language as if it occurred in a vacuum, as if everyone had equal access to conversational resources regardless of their institutional affiliation, class, race, or gender. Power was not a feature of their analyses. Those sociologists who addressed institutional arrangements, who took power as a central feature of their analyses, all too often dismissed mundane everyday interactions as theoretically uninteresting. Communication between doctors and patients seemed an ideal site to explore the relationship between social interaction and social structure, to explore the relationship between power and its social accomplishment.

We are still concerned with these issues, but today, nearly a decade later, our focus has shifted once again. The original chapters in this volume, each from its own disciplinary perspective and each in its own medical context, questioned the prior constraints of language studies. In so doing they expanded our understanding of the ways people communicate in social situations. Today social theory is opening concepts like social structure and power to similar questioning. Where once these concepts called up an image of a monolithic entity, of power wielded by corporate bosses, government heavies, or in our case doctors, today we are being asked to see these concepts in more particularistic ways. Once again communication between doctors and patients seems an ideal site to explore the relationship between social structure and social interaction now redefined, to see how power is exercised and resisted, how social structure is implicated and transformed as doctors and patients communicate.

PLAN OF THE BOOK

The chapters collected here represent the shifts discussed above. Although the order has been changed, most of the chapters in the first edition remain. In addition, we are adding four new pieces to illustrate current debates on power and resistance. The chapters are arranged in two parts.

Part One is devoted to sociolinguistic and cognitive approaches to doctor–patient discourse. The chapters by Shuy (Chapter 1) and by Tannen and Wallat (Chapter 2) analyze the patterns of talk that are produced by the situational demands of the medical setting. Cicourel (Chapter 3) provides a detailed examination of the interplay of clinical reasoning and language use in the organizational context of health care delivery.

Part Two examines the production of doctor–patient communication and is divided into three sections. Section One addresses the social production of doctor–patient discourse. Each of the three contributions relies on the context of the doctor–patient relationship for discussion, but does so differently. The chapter by Frankel (Chapter 4) uses the doctor–patient relationship as a set of boundary conditions within which to analyze how doctors and patients produce medical discourse. Paget (Chapter 5) and West (Chapter 6) make the relation between language and context more specific by suggesting that language use in the medical setting is micropolitical in its asymmetry: It both reflects the larger structural context and helps to sustain that context.

Section Two examines the relationship between social structure and social interaction more specifically. It contains chapters by Fisher (Chapter 7) and by Todd (Chapter 8). They continue the trend established earlier by combining methodological strategies, moving toward a more reflexive analysis.

In Section Three, the four new chapters explore the relationship between power and resistance. David Silverman (Chapter 9) examines an adolescent diabetic clinic and displays how in this clinical site, doctors are practicing a gentler, more humane, patient-centered brand of medicine. While it is just this shift, from a doctor-centered to a patient-centered clinical practice, that many reformers have been calling for, Silverman argues that neither greater attention to the social psychological aspects of health care nor a more humane clinical practice create much change. Social control, while subtler, is no less present, and medicine is in some ways even more individualized. He concludes that change can only come about through practical struggles, through subjects who act.

Kathy Davis (Chapter 10) addresses just such subjects. She examines medical discourse between "nice doctors" and normally "invisible patients". Acknowledging the asymmetry between the participants, she makes patients' strategies for resistance visible. She argues that concentrating empirically on patients' strategies provides a way to rethink power and resistance while avoiding monolithic, top-down analysis of power and oppression. Both Silverman and Davis, albeit from different theoretical starting points, talk about interactions between *nice* doctors and their patients. Both conclude that even with nice doctors practicing humane medicine or patients who resist, the symmetrical context of medical practices does not change. Alexandra Todd (Chapter 11) and Sue Fisher (Chapter 12) take up this discussion from a somewhat different perspective. They take as their central question: How can patients be seen as subjects who act, who resist, without blaming those who fail to resist or those whose resistance fails? Todd examines doctor–patient discourse and interview data to capture women's experiences. She analyzes women's voices exploring the active-passive continuum as well as the commonalities and diversities among women. Fisher reexamines data from a paper written with Todd and an earlier chapter in this book. She argues that if resistance is analyzed in the context of a continued commitment to a reflexive relationship between social structure and social interaction, we come perilously close to blaming the victim. But alternatively, if power works through a discourse which constitutes doctors and patients as social objects, and change is the responsibility of subjects who act, we come perilously close to obscuring the structural context of power and losing the impetus for social action. Clearly debate on power and resistance has just begun.

Sue Fisher   *Alexandra Todd*

Physician's Foreword

Traditional physician training consists of four years of medical school and between three and eight years of postgraduate residency training, depending on the technical demands of the specialty selected. That process of training, with its attendant night calls, sleep deprivation, emergency room trauma, endless ward rounds, and continuous pressure to perform is a powerful, often harrowing experience. Its influence on the development of a trainee's attitudes towards illness, health care, and people is profound. For me, three aspects of this period, the time when a medical student is "molded" into a clinician, were most remarkable.

Most obvious was the degree to which I was allowed to view, influence, and truly feel the spectrum of human emotions that patients and their families experience during the course of an illness. I was called upon to pronounce people dead and often, in the middle of the night, to inform spouses, parents, and children of their loved one's death. I was asked to help decide if heroic support systems were a justifiable or excessive use of technology, and I had to counsel and attempt to comfort patients anguishing over a decision regarding a treatment option. But, I also experienced the joy of delivering to patients the news that their biopsy results showed no cancer or telling children that their parent was out of danger.

These extraordinary responsibilities led me to question the second critical aspect of training—the absence of formal education, discussion, and recognition of these emotionally influential issues. Learning to handle these emotions and interactions was considered experiential; learned by trial and error. Observation of my interviewing and behavioral skill, or criticism to improve the approach to psychosocial problems was largely neglected. Each house officer, then, with the limited skills of a novice in a field, and sporadic support, was forced to develop a framework for coping with illness, death, depression, responsibility, and interactional competence. At least, in part, I believe that this type of training milieu resulted in the physician's inattention to psychosocial skills, which has received so much criticism recently. Learning the importance of factors that had "no medical relevance" was the third key aspect of training. These factors continually disrupted my "real' work, confused my plans, and continually frustrated me. Patients would not do what I told them; families suspected my motives; patients, when discharged from the hospital, would tell the nurse at the front door that they had nowhere to go, or the resources needed to provide quality care were not available. Indeed, the very factors that seemed to predict final outcome had little to do with the biomedical science taught in medical school and traditional postgraduate training. Clearly, the currently accepted biomedical approach to illness and medical training does not meet the resident's or society's current needs.

Fortunately, recent history has changed some of this story for current medical students and postgraduate trainees. In 1977, Engles excited concerned physicians by proposing the biopsychosocial model of care. He suggested that all factors influencing a person within his or her environment need be considered to most productively identify and evaluate a patient's concern, provide for ongoing preventive services, and successfully treat illness. It is just this expanded framework that allows physicians to extend their interests, responsibilities, and goals to include the influence of psychosocial factors on the diagnosis and treatment of illnesses. The issues that I struggled with as a resident may now be seen within a "legitimate" model of health care delivery and be openly discussed, researched, and taught. To accomplish this expanded task, both patients and providers need to be educated in these new roles. Patients must learn that they can demand expanded services from providers, and providers need to learn new skills in behavioral medicine—cultural aspects of care, the existence of alternative explanatory models of disease, and methods to improve and criticize their interpersonal communication skills. These require a re-exploration of the goals of hospital and office practice, the effect of interactional structure on these goals, and the study of all the issues that influence the delivery and quality of care. To accomplish these tasks, interdisciplinary teams of anthropologists, sociologists, economists, political scientists, linguists, and consumers must work with providers of services.

I have been fortunate over the past three years to work with such a team of social and behavioral scientists as part of a primary-care internal medicine training program with faculty team members representing the disciplines of social work, nursing, sociolinguistics, psychology, and medicine. We are attempting to train quality internists in the context of the biopsychosocial model of care. Using such a team, we are teaching residents to improve their verbal and nonverbal communication skills. We are developing an appreciation of the impact of psychosocial events, cultural values, and explanatory models in the construction of relevant treatment plans. Our residents are learning to assess family supports, financial barriers to care, and the secondary gains of illness. Using the nursing perspective, we are emphasizing education and counseling of patients, allowing them to more effectively co-participate in their care.

My experience suggests that the improvement of the health care delivery system rests in the ability of social, behavioral, and biological scientists, as well as patients, to value each other, collaborate in research, and develop creative investigations that explore the biopsychosocial model of care and encourage humane clinical practice. Volumes such as this begin such a process.

Howard Beckman, M.D.
Wayne State University
Department of Medicine

Introduction: Communication and Social Context — Toward Broader Definitions

Sue Fisher and Alexandra Dundas Todd

It is a commonplace assumption in social and behavioral science that communication, broadly defined, and social life are inextricably linked. Language has been called the single distinguishing element of humandkind—a unique communication code has been the tool used to fashion the many varieties of human society throughout the species' existence.

Language, it is claimed, accomplishes social action. It then becomes important to students of society to understand the relationship between language and action—to understand the forces that shape language use as well as how the language we use brings about social ends.

There are several academic traditions in which the connection between language and social context has been explored; anthropology, linguistics, and philosophy among the most notable. This book examines communication, verbal discourse in particular, between doctors and patients, continuing the tradition and extending it for sociology.

Our goal is an exploration of some intricacies of communication and language use between physician and patient. The articles collected here detail how doctor and patient communicate, that is, how they exchange (or fail to exchange) information. Some contributors concentrate on talk, with detailed word-by-word analysis; some on the interplay of talk and other communication modalities;

some on the reciprocal effects of the doctor's clinical reasoning, the patient's cognitive processes, and language use; some see parallels between subtle structural arrangements in the larger society and doctor-patient discourse; still others address the consequences of doctor–patient talk exchanges. What is common to these articles is that they explore the relationship between language and context. The data that support the analyses and perspectives of the authors document the doctor–patient relationship in its various settings, be it in a private-practice office or a clinic's examination cubicle.

In this introduction we briefly examine some major threads in the long-standing discussion of the interrelatedness of language and social context. In our overview we emphasize that language and social action are themselves produced in a cultural milieu, and suggest ways of extending the notion of context to further an understanding of the reflexive relationship between language and the social world. The complementarity of language and social action on the one hand and social structure and behavior on the other draws attention away from utterances exchanged in a vacuum to the context in which they occur, and back again to language.

OVERVIEW: CONTEXT AND LANGUAGE

Sociological approaches to language share one thing; it is allowed that context influences discourse. But, as we will see, definitions of context range from the level of language itself—the doctor's and patient's speech acts—to the level of interaction between doctor and patient, to the organization of both the profession of medicine and Western health care institutions, as well as to the structural arrangement of society. The source of this diversity is severalfold.

Philosophers of language, exemplified in the works on ordinary language by Ludwig Wittgenstein, John Austin, and John Searle, provide the beginnings of the sociological language-context "connection." The later work of Wittgenstein (1953) has had a major influence; he does not directly discuss context, but his preoccupation with language *use* as central to meaning and human activity lends itself to sociological insights. Wittgenstein challenged the philosophical tradition that considered only the referential function of language, that sees words as simply standing for, representing, things in the world—which is a passive understanding of language. Rather his interest was in what words *do* and how they are *used*—an active rendition of language. The question Wittgenstein raises, then, is not "What is 'power'?" but "What does 'power' mean?" or "How is the word 'power' used?" The implications of this perspective, despite Wittgenstein's lack of focus on it, is that context, implied in an understanding of meaning and use, is vital for an understanding of language.

Austin (1962) and Searle (1969) develop a theory of language as a part of a general theory of action. Speech acts are activities through which participants in interaction construct a social context. To speak an utterance is to carry out an act. To use an often-cited example, the utterance *I promise* is a speech act that accomplishes promising. Language *is* action, and as such it occurs in a social context. Thus a contextual world of normative internalized rules is assumed, even though Austin and Searle leave it implicit and unexplored as did Wittgenstein before them. But, by shifting the focus to what the utterance *does* for speaker and hearer, a framework is created within which to analyze language as a socially organized event with normatively ordered patterns of social interaction. Searle develops these patterns into speech act theory. It is this—the examination of the "work" of speech utterances—that provides an empirical handle for sociologists to study language in social settings.

The field of linguistics provides a very different picture. Structural linguistics, using an empirical analysis and rigorous methods of verifications, concentrates on "surface" utterances. For Noam Chomsky (1965), as with the linguists who worked before him, the sentence was the unit of analysis. However, unlike earlier linguists for whom meaning or usage in language was seen as unknowable and thus unresearchable, Chomsky created a revolution for psychology and linguistics. He posited a relationship between linguistic forms/utterances (surface structure/performance) and the internal processes that produce them (deep structure/competence).

Others building on Chomsky's model, although often disagreeing with it, sought to introduce an analysis that was more contextual, one that would display how performances are patterned by the external situation. Anthropologists and sociolinguists (e.g., Hymes 1962; Labov 1972), using ethnographic descriptions, have displayed how people talk differently in different situations; they have shifted the analytic focus from context-free internal processes to context-bound external factors as the mechanisms from which to draw our understanding. Imbedded in these works is a grounding for the detailed study of the social production of language.

There are interesting parallels between the recent history of linguistic thought and the development of sociological theory. Large-scale sociological studies have treated the external world as a "fact" and taken for granted the activities of the co-participants that produce and sustain the larger society. In the past decade or two, some sociologists have examined the interactional activities that produce social facts (see Garfinkel 1967), and more recently there has been a movement in sociological theory to bridge the gap between the external social world as given and the social production of that world by people. It is on this work that the discussion of a reflexive relationship between context more broadly defined than heretofore (in sociology) and language rests.

SOCIOLOGY: STRUCTURE AND ORGANIZATIONS

It is well within the sociological tradition to analyze the organizational and structural factors that impinge on the social facts of the doctor-patient relationship. Structurally, as Scully (1980) points out, "Health care is a vivid microcosm of inequality, American style." There is a dual health-care delivery system in the United States; one for those of lower income (primarily nonwhite, elderly) and one for the more well-to-do. This duality recapitulates the class composition of our society. The Ehrenreichs (1970) argue that the tremendous profit for all the participants in the health-care-delivery system—the corporations that produce drugs and medical supplies, the insurance and nursing home industries, as well as hospitals and doctors—gives them a vested interest in maintaining the system as it is. There is also a monopoly that influences the legislative process. The American Medical Association and the medical corporate establishment have powerful legislative lobbies that have been successful in resisting and limiting change. Equally important, if not more important, is the medical monopoly. Medical providers have the institutional authority to control medical skill, technology, and knowledge; they have the power to channel and limit public access to services and information.

This structure is mirrored in the organizational factors that shape the health-care delivery system and are equally resistant to change. Freidson (1970) suggests that a defining feature of a profession is its autonomy. The profession of medicine is one of the most successful in achieving this autonomy and establishing the freedom to work without outside regulation. It is only physicians who have been vested with the responsibility of monitoring one another's performance. This organizational structure reinforces the performances of procedures for profit rather than the performance of procedures for health. The medical consumer, unlike the consumer of any other product of service, has a very small voice in determining health care practices or policies.

There is a critical literature that outlines in great detail the flaws in the health-care delivery system, their roots in the structure of society and their manifestation in the organizational arrangements of the field of medicine (see Waitzken and Waterman 1974; Navarro 1973; Ehrenreich and Ehrenreich 1970). There is a smaller, but growing, body of literature that addresses the manifestation of sexual discrimination in medical practice and medical institutions (Scully 1980; Ehrenreich and English 1978; Seaman and Seaman 1977). It is argued that the structural bias of sexism is maintained, or perhaps sustained, in the male-dominated medical profession and contributes to the medical care women receive.

There is also an empirical literature that describes medical interactions in great detail. Each of these positions reflects a slice of the social world of medicine. Rarely does one level of analysis incorporate the offerings from other levels. Although some sociologists discuss broad structural arrangements, others concentrate on organizational contexts and still others focus on the interaction between individuals in the setting. Few use more than one perspective. The chapters in this book move toward a convergence, either explicitly or implicitly, by focusing on the social organization of language.

CULTURE: CONTEXT BROADENED

The role of belief systems, attitudes, and values and their integration with health care remain unexplored. This level of ideas provides doctors with a view of themselves and their profession that colors their medical practice and supports the status quo, despite increasing external and internal questioning and criticism. Further, most patients have (unwittingly) learned the same set of cultural beliefs and as a consequence accept the medical definitions of their health, their bodies, and their needs even when these run contrary to their best interests. These shared assumptions and expectations—a world view—need to be included in a definition of context when discussing a theoretical framework for examining doctor–patient discourse (as would nonshared assumptions in discussing cross-cultural discourse, medical or otherwise). It is to this that we now turn.

The role of ideas in influencing behavior has a long tradition in the history of Western thought. This tradition is evident in the idealism of Plato and in Weber's analysis of the influence of religion on social structure. Greta Lerner, in a recent interview (Stimpson 1981), points out that structural and organizational arrangements cannot be the end point of analysis. She argues that there are cultural, or meta-structural, issues that also need to be considered, suggesting, as did Weber, that the Protestant Reformation was one such change in world view that impacted every level of Western life. Daly (1978) argues that patriarchy is also a meta-structural issue—a world view, an idea—which can shape social reality and social life. The rise of the modern scientific world view in Western society (Wright 1982; Todd 1982; Ehrenreich and English 1978; McKeown 1976) provides another idea that shapes our everyday lives as well as the practice of medicine.

Cultural (or meta-structural) arrangements play a major role in any medical system. However, this influence is, for sociologists, a background connection that is difficult to observe directly, especially when one recognizes the practical aspects of medicine and the "abstractness" of belief systems. Nevertheless an exploration of the system of beliefs that affects our everyday lives holds the potential to enrich our database. Structural and organizational extensions of context are to some degree observable in doctor–patient communication. Although "culture" is not as directly observable, the medical event becomes much more understandable when relations among abstract world views, more concrete structural and organizational contingencies, and medical discourse are considered.

This strategy is, after all, part and parcel of scientific investigation. The material world is understood through theoretical constructs. For example, physicists have posited the theory of electron spin to account for the basic structure of matter. Electron spin is not directly observable, but as an organizing concept it has explanatory power to account for observable relations at the molecular level. In a similar manner, transformational linguists posit the notion of deep structure and similar conceptual schemata to account for the underlying regularities of language. A deep linguistic structure, which can never be observed directly, is postulated as an assumption that leads to the production of data. Data, in turn, substantiate the value of the assumption and indeed have led to a revolution in the understanding of language acquisition. Deep structure, like electron spin, is an inference from the material world, a move in the language game of linguistics provided by the overarching theoretical framework. This is also the case in other social sciences. We do not directly observe social class or stratification, which are also conceptual strategies like deep structure, provided by the theoretical framework of which they are a part. What we observe are their artifacts, if you will. Electrical energy, language, and social class are all very real parts of the material world. The models of electron spin, transformational grammar, and social stratification provide theoretical paradigms for understanding experienced phenomena. It is in this spirit, then, that we suggest that sociologists need to consider the beliefs that participants bring to an encounter. It can only enrich their analysis of medical communication.

A caveat, however: Mapping doctor–patient communication becomes increasingly difficult as we escalate the levels of abstraction from interaction and organization to structure and culture. We have found no concrete solutions to the problem we raise, rather we offer some observations and suggestions.

It is not new to sociology to say that "ideas" or world view impinge on behavior. Mindful of this tradition it seems reasonable to suggest that they impact on the doctor/patient relationship as well. Scholars date the arising of our European scientific explanatory system—a world view—to the sixteenth and seventeenth centuries. By the nineteenth century, abstract ideas inherent in this world view were beginning to have practical consequences. In the twentieth century these ideas have been incorporated into the fabric of Western society. One aspect in particular, the notion that the conscious mind can be understood as separate from the mechanical body, has influenced medical theory and practice (McKeown 1976; Wright 1982; Todd 1982).

Two ideas, the pathological, germ theory of illness, and the fragmented, mechanistic approach to the body have multiple concrete expressions in the delivery of health care. If mind and body are divided, then concrete, scientifically valid, pathological agents are assumed to cause illness. If these agents cannot be found, the medical problem is described as "functional" (nonorganic) and the patient's trouble is seen as psychological. The very structure of the medical profession, organized as it is by parts of the body, reflects a mechanistic view focused on disease rather than health or prevention: obstetrician/gynecologists take care of women's reproductive organs, urologists take care of urinary tracts, cardiologists take care of hearts, and so on.

Technology provides another example of the relationship between ideas and practice. As Reiser (1978) points out, technological development has redefined the doctor–patient relationship and estranged medical providers from their own understanding of illness. The stethoscope, microscope, ophthalmoscope, and X-ray technology draw physicians away from relying on their natural senses and distance their direct contact with patients.

Reiser was talking about the nineteenth century, but the same claims could be made about the fetal heart monitor today or forceps yesterday (Ehrenreich and English 1978). They are technological developments that redefine ideas about childbirth, have direct consequences for the delivery of health care, and are observable. These mechanical devices managed and understood by medical providers become influences on and shapers of illness and medical practice.

CONTRIBUTION OF FEMINIST STUDIES

Similar threads in the development of modern medicine have been examined with regard to women's general and reproductive health care. Analyses of the structure and organization of Western medical institutions provide ways of understanding the development of the practice of a male-dominated profession. Tremendous profits are possible for the medical industry when ideas about normal, healthy aspects of women's lives from menstruation through menopause are redefined and placed in the disease-oriented medical model, under the auspices of a predominantly male-governed profession unrestricted by outside regulation. The values toward and institutional definitions of women one learns as a member of this particular society—patriarchal values and attitudes—also play an important role in the medical treatment of women. It is to this point that many feminist scholars have addressed their arguments.

From this perspective it is argued that to the degree that discrimination toward women is pervasive in our society, it is also deeply embedded in the field of medicine (Scully 1980; Ruzek 1978; Ehrenreich and English 1978). This argument is extended by others who see sexist practices as micropolitical—they both reflect and act to reinforce sexism in society (see Henley 1977). During the last decade there has been a resurgence of these views in scholarly work. The rise of the male-dominated, profit-oriented medical profession is, as Barker-Benfield (1976) points out, related to an overall trend for men to take over the control of women—their sexuality and reproduction. This idea had practical applications in the practice of medicine arising in the nineteenth century, chief among which was the institutionalization of surgery for psychological disturbances and sexual "disorders." The disorders included hysteria, ineptness as a wife, or an interest in women's rights. Cliterectomies and other sexual surgeries were done in an attempt to control such deviance.

The practice of having what is normal and healthy defined and treated as a disease or deviant by doctors continues today. Menstruation is dirty, the curse, and in need of medical treatment (Delaney, Lupton, and Toth 1976). Menopause is potentially carcinogenic, hazardous to women's health, and in need of medical management (Culpepper 1978). Birth control and birth are increasingly medicalized. Birth control is defined as a medical concern, researched, controlled, and distributed by the medical profession, while birth is treated as yet another surgical procedure (Gordon 1974; Arms 1975). Surgery on women—hysterectomies, mastectomies, and Caesarean sections—has reached epidemic proportions with growing evidence that it is often unnecessary (Dreifus 1977). Estrogen replacement therapy is the medically accepted treatment for menopause, yet lately it has been widely criticized as carcinogenic. Estrogens, also found in the birth control pill, can cause far-reaching, often life-threatening, medical problems. It is an estrogen in Diethylstibestrol, prescribed extensively for pregnant women in the 1940s and 1950s, that has been shown to be a cancer-causing agent for the daughters (and more recently sons) of the women who took it (see Seaman and Seaman 1977 for a fuller discussion of estrogen-related diseases).

Sexism—a set of ideas that negatively defines women—can also be seen in the female images in drug company advertisements. Women are depicted as suffering from primarily psychosomatic rather than organic problems. Traditional sex roles are reinforced—males are portrayed as the doctors, females as the nurses and patients. The female patient is more often than not portrayed as an anxious housewife and as a burden to her husband and doctor. Anxiety is medicalized and tranquilizers are the cure (Prather and Fidell 1975).

These activities are prevalent in medical education as well. Howell (1974), former Associate Dean of Harvard Medical School, conducted research that reports degrading attitudes toward female medical students and patients held by their professors and doctors. In a study of gynecological texts, Scully and Bart (1973) found condescending attitudes toward women, as well as dated and sexist information about female sexuality, anatomy, and physiology. Women's bodies were defined in terms of their relationship to men. Scully (1980) finds that what is evident in medical school continues in the training of gynecological residents, and Fisher (1979, 1982) finds that it continues into medical practice as well.

The literature on women and health is steadily growing, providing insights into the treatment of women by the medical profession. This work, however, like the work of macro sociologists, often lacks empirical demonstration—what actually transpires between doctor and female patient as they communicate in the medical setting.

On the other hand, although it is logical to extend context to include structure, organization, and culture, there is very little empirical work by micro sociologists that does so.

The most notable exception so far is work on talk. In this work, gender differences in forms of talk (proportions of tag questions, intensifiers, and the like) and in the ways men and women talk with each other have been investigated (Lakoff 1975; Eakins and Eakins 1978; Miller and Swift 1977; Thorne and Henley 1975). Similar differences in talk have been pointed out by those studying language in organizational settings (see Mehan 1979; Griffin and Humphrey 1978; Fisher 1982). What this boils down to is that asymmetrical interpersonal relationships direct the ways talk is used to accomplish organizational events.

SUMMARY AND CONCLUSIONS

We are suggesting that structure, organization, and culture are features in our commonsense knowledge and as such form aspects of context that are realized in language use. Language use, in turn, helps to sustain these aspects of context—a reflexive and complementary relationship.

Philosophers of ordinary language have made context the keystone in their understanding of meaning. Searle and Austin added the notion of action—that language accomplishes interactional work. The thread of discovery that extends from traditional linguists through sociolinguistics makes context an empirical topic, enabling an analysis of the social production of talk. Anthropologists and sociologists examining the delivery of health care have extended the notion of context to organizational and structural levels of analysis. In a similar way, scholarship in the history of social thought and in feminist issues has laid a firm foundation for a consideration of the impact of ideas on societal arrangements, institutional organizations, and interactional accomplishments.

The movement from a concern with "organization," "structure," and "culture" to "interaction" and "communication" means bridging what has been called the macro-micro gap. From the macro perspective this has long been allowed for theoretically. Such social thinkers as Marx, Weber, and Durkheim, from various perspectives, explored the connections between larger structures in society and individuals' actions. Although these thinkers neither researched these issues empirically nor provided theoretical or methodological outlines for doing so, their work, nevertheless, lends itself to a reflexive analysis.

More recently, Habermas (1970, 1976) most explicitly describes a theoretical connection between social structure and social interaction: Human beings share an intersubjective repertoire of skills for communicative interaction (language seen as shared practices following the later Wittgenstein). Forester claims that critical theory obviates the macro-micro distinction by providing a structural phenomenology. He says:

> It is a phenomenology because it attends to the skilled and contingent social construction and negotiation of intersubjective meanings...; it is structural because it attends equally to the historical stage upon which actors meet, speak, conflict, listen or engage with one another. (Forester 1981:2)

This structural phenomenology, he argues, is consistent with speech act theory. Had Searle used "coercing" instead of "promising" as his paradigmatic case, the political significance of speech acts might be more evident (Forester 1981:3).

We would agree that critical theory has the potential to bridge the gap between social structure and interaction; however, unlike Forester, we do not think the phenomenological side of the equation has been developed in sufficient detail—there is no theory of interaction. The interactional side of the Habermas equation is, in reality, but a revision of speech act theory. Concentration on single utterances or units of action does not allow for analysis of the *social* production of communication across the flow of the interactional event. Further, this approach lacks a solid foundation of evidence on which to ground a careful description of talking and acting in medical practice.

From the interactional perspective, the perceived gap between social structure and interaction has both a theoretical and a methodological component. There has been an attempt to demonstrate empirically how larger social structures, particularly organizational structures, interface with how people behave and make sense of one another's behavior in face-to-face encounters (see Cicourel 1975; Mehan et al. 1981). The argument is that a theoretical mistake is made if social structures and the effects they have on people's lives have an existence attributed to them independent of people's observable behavior.

For these researchers, a theoretical interest goes hand-in-hand with a search for research methods and a theory of interaction that can document how members categorize the world as well as how they socially enact and accomplish meaning. And, because much of human interaction is verbal, several language-based methodological strategies—sociolinguistic, discourse, and conversational analyses as well as speech act theory—are used to do a detailed study of the event as it is accomplished by the situated activities (talking and acting) of the participants in particular social contexts, for example, in classrooms or medical examining rooms. The unit of analysis is the *event*. The focus is on interaction (usually captured on audio- or videotape) and the data are analyzed to find systematic patterns of routine behavior generated by the interactional and communicational work of co-participants in these situations—these are the structuring activities that assemble the social reality of the medical encounter or of classroom events.

We believe that these linguistic strategies and the theory of interaction they support have the potential to yield a view of the interactional patterns across participants, settings, organizational contexts, as well as the potential to display structural and cultural arrangements. Although the potential exists and is addressed by those who work in this area, the articulation of a thread that runs through and connects all of these levels of analysis needs to be examined in greater detail.

REFERENCES CITED

ARMS, SUZANNE
  1975   *Immaculate Deception.* New York: Bantam Books.
AUSTIN, J.L.
  1962   *How To Do Things With Words.* Cambridge, Mass: Harvard University Press.
BARKER-BENFIELD, G.J.
  1976   *The Horrors of the Half-Known Life.* New York: Harper Colophon.
CHOMSKY, NOAM
  1965   *Aspects of the Theory of Syntax.* Cambridge, Mass.: The MIT Press.
CICOUREL, AARON V.
  1975   Discourse and text: Cognitive and linguistic processes in studies of social structure. *Versus: Quaderni de Studii Semiotici* 12:33–84.
  1982   Notes on the integration of micro and macro levels of analysis. IN *Advances in Social Theory and Methodology: Toward an Integration of Micro and Macro Sociologies.* K. Knorr-Centia and A.V. Cicourel, Eds. Boston: Routledge and Kegan Paul.
COLLINS, R.
  1982   Micro-translation as a theory-building strategy. IN *Advances in Social Theory and Methodology: Toward an Integration of Micro and Macro Sociologies,* K. Knorr-Centia and A.V. Cicourel, Eds. Boston: Routledge and Kegan Paul.
CULPEPPER, EMILY
  1978   Exploring menstrual attitudes. IN *Women Look at Biology Looking at Women,* M.S. Hennifin, et al., Eds. Cambridge, Mass.: Schenckman Publishing.
DALY, MARY
  1978   *Gyn/Ecology: The Metaethics of Radical Feminism.* Boston: Beacon.
DELANEY, JANICE; MARY JANE LUPTON, AND EMILY TOTH
  1976   *The Curse: A Cultural History of Menstruation.* New York: New American Library.
DREIFUS, CLAUDIA, ED.
  1977   *Seizing Our Bodies.* New York: Vintage.
EAKINS, BARBARA W., AND R. GENE EAKINS
  1978   *Sex Differences in Human Communication.* Boston: Houghton Mifflin Co.

EHRENREICH, BARBARA, AND JOHN EHRENREICH
  1970 *The American Health Empire*. A Health-Pac Book. New York: Vintage.
EHRENREICH, BARBARA, AND DEIRDRE ENGLISH
  1970 *For Her Own Good*. Garden City, N.Y.: Anchor/Doubleday.
FISHER, SUE
  1979a Women, surgery, and the negotiation of identity. Paper presented at the
         Meeting of the Southern Sociological Association, April.
  1979b The Negotiation of Treatment Decisions in Doctor/Patient Communications
         and Their Impact on Identity of Women Patients. Doctoral dissertation,
         University of California, San Diego.
  1982   The decision-making context: How doctors and patients communicate. IN
         Linguistics and the Professions, Robert J. Di Pietro, Ed., pp. 51–81. Norwood,
         N.J.: Ablex.
FORESTER, JOHN
  1981   Critical Theory and Organizational Analysis. *Working Papers in Planning*.
         Ithaca, N.Y.: Department of City and Regional Planning in conjunction with the
         Program in Urban and Regional Studies, Cornell University.
FREIDSON, ELIOT
  1970   *Profession of Medicine; A Study of the Sociology of Applied Knowledge*. New
         York: Dodd, Mead.
GARFINKEL, HAROLD
  1967   *Studies in Ethnomethodology*. Englewood Cliffs, N.J.: Prentice-Hall.
GORDON, LINDA
  1974   *Woman's Body, Woman's Right: A Social History of Birth Control in America*.
         New York: Penguin.
GRIFFIN, PEG, AND FRANK HUMPHREY
  1978   Talk and task. IN *The Study of Children's Functional Language and Education in
         the Early Years*, Peg Griffin and Roger Shuy, Eds. Final Report to the Carnegie
         Corporation of New York. Arlington, Va.: Center for Applied Linguistics.
HABERMAS, JURGEN
  1970   Toward a theory of communicative competence. IN *Recent Sociology, Number 2:
         Patterns of Communication*, Hans Peter Dreitzel, Ed. New York: Macmillan.
  1976   Some distinctions in universal pragmatics: A working paper. *Theory and
         Society* 3:155–167.
HENLEY, NANCY
  1977   *Body Politics: Power, Sex and Nonverbal Communication*. Englewood Cliffs,
         N.J.: Prentice-Hall.
HOWELL, M.C.
  1974   Sounding board: What medical schools teach about women. *New England
         Journal of Medicine* 291 (August):304–307.
HYMES, DELL
  1962   The ethnography of speaking. IN *Anthropology and Human Behavior*, Thomas
         Gladwin and William C. Sturtevant, Eds., pp. 13–53. Washington, D.C.:
         Anthropological Society of Washington. (Reprinted in *Readings in the Sociol-
         ogy of Language*, Joshua A. Fishman, Ed., pp. 99–138. The Hague: Mouton,
         1968.)

LABOV, WILLIAM
  1972 *Sociolinguistic Patterns*. Philadelphia: University of Pennsylvania Press.
LAKOFF, ROBIN
  1975 *Language and Woman's Place*. New York: Harper Colophon.
MCKEOWN, THOMAS
  1976 *Medicine: Dream, Mirage or Nemesis?* London: Nuffield Provincial Hospitals
        Trust.
MEHAN, HUGH
  1979 *Learning Lessons: The Social Organization of Classroom Behavior.* Cambridge,
        Mass.: Harvard University Press.
MEHAN, HUGH, ET AL.
  1981 Identifying handicapped students. IN *Politics and Education: Organizational
        Analysis of Schools and School Districts*, Samuel S. Bacharach, Ed. New York:
        Praeger Press.
MILLER, CASEY, AND KATE SWIFT
  1977 *Words and Women: New Language in New Times*. Garden City, N.Y.: Anchor.
NAVARRO, VICENTE
  1973 *Health and Medical Care in the U.S.: A Critical Analysis*. Farmingdale, N.Y.:
        Baywood.
PRATHER, JANE, AND LINDA FIDELL
  1975 Sex differences in the content and style of medical advertisements. *Social
        Science and Medicine* 9:23–26.
REISER, STANLEY JOEL
  1978 *Medicine and the Reign of Technology*. London: Cambridge University Press.
RUZEK, SHERYL BURT
  1978 *The Women's Health Movement*. New York: Praeger.
SCULLY, DIANA
  1980 *Men Who Control Women's Health: The Miseducation of Obstetrician-Gynecolo-
        gists*. Boston: Houghton Mifflin.
SCULLY, DIANA, AND P. BART
  1973 A funny thing happened on the way to the orifice: Women in gynecological
        textbooks. *American Journal of Sociology* 78: 1045–1050.
SEAMAN, BARBARA, AND GIDEON SEAMAN
  1977 *Women and the Crisis in Sex Hormones*. New York: Bantam.
SEARLE, JOHN
  1969 *Speech Acts*. London: Cambridge University Press.
STIMPSON, CATHERINE R.
  1981 Gerda Lerner on the future of our past. Interview in *Ms.* 10 (September):50–52;
        93–95.
THORNE, BARRIE, AND NANCY HENLEY, EDS.
  1975 *Language and Sex: Difference and Dominance*. Rowley, Mass.: Newbury
        House.
TODD, ALEXANDRA DUNDAS
  1982 The Medicalization of Reproduction: Scientific Medicine and the Diseasing of
        Healthy Women. Doctoral dissertation, University of California, San Diego.

WAITZKIN, HOWARD B., AND JOHN D. STOECKLE
  1976   Information control and the micropolitics of health care: Summary of an
          ongoing research project. *Social Science and Medicine* 10:263–276.
WAITZKIN, HOWARD B., AND BARBARA WATERMAN
  1974   *The Exploitation of Illness in Capitalist Society.* Indianapolis: Bobbs-Merrill.
WITTGENSTEIN, LUDWIG
  1953   *Philosophical Investigations.* London: Basil Blackwell & Mott.
WRIGHT, WILL
  1982   *The Social Logic of Health.* New Brunswick, N.J.: Rutgers University Press.

Part I

SOCIOLINGUISTIC AND COGNITIVE APPROACHES TO DISCOURSE

1

Three Types of Interference to an Effective Exchange of Information in the Medical Interview*

Roger W. Shuy

The application of linguistic knowledge to another field, such as medicine, involves the bringing and sharing of organizational concepts and analytical techniques. Just as the physician can look at a person's body or an X-ray of that person's body and tell a great many things about that person that the medical layman could never see, so the linguist, in observing medical communication, or records of that communication, can determine a great deal about the communication that the linguistic layman could never hear. The physician's eyesight and the linguist's hearing are not necessarily any better than those of the laity. What is different is simply the organizational concepts and analytical tools provided by their disciplines.

Because health is so apparent to everybody, so crucial and so focused, the expertise of the physician is easily perceived. At the opposite end of the spectrum is language. Not many people are aware of it as they use it. Language is a given, a thing so natural that we are not even aware of it. We learned it early— by the age of three or four. For this reason, language seems to be trivial as an adult tool. Yet the more we learn about language, the more critical it becomes.

* This was originally presented as a paper of the same title at the meeting of the Society for Computer Medicine, Atlanta, 1979.

In the area of medicine, a great deal hinges on small, unperceived differences in the assumptions and communication between physician and patient. Interference to a successful communication between physician and patient can be found in three areas: the obviously different uses of jargon or vocabulary; the less obvious cross-cultural differences involving terminology, attitudes toward illness, and social distance; and even less obvious—only recently discovered by linguists as a structured concept and organizational principle of face-to-face interaction—the structure of the discourse itself. This chapter addresses these three areas of interference to an effective exchange of information in the medical interview.

JARGON OR VOCABULARY

From a linguist's perspective, vocabulary is the most trivial aspect of language study. In physician–patient communication, it is the most obviously repairable problem, provided it is noticed and understood. The usual reaction to the medical jargon issue is to wring one's hands in embarrassment. The public, including physicians, seems to believe that jargon is bad and that it should be avoided at all times.

A linguist's view is quite different. Jargon is perfectly acceptable and useful *within the groups that know it*, as a kind of shorthand code to well-known concepts and things. When jargon goes wrong is when it is used *outside* the group that knows it, resulting in either a lack of comprehension for the outsider or a social one-upmanship on the part of the insider. This principle is a common one in language study. Linguists call it code-switching. The language code used with one group, though perfectly appropriate there, becomes inappropriate for another group either in understandability or through creating social distance. What medical personnel need to learn is not to avoid jargon at all times but only to avoid it when talking to nonmedical people.

This realization, however, leads to still other, more complex language problems. Strategies for making the in-group information available to the out-group are very complicated and, in general, not well conceived. Most people are not taught how to communicate the significant aspects of their field to those who do not know their field. This is, of course, as true for linguists, lawyers, theologians, and teachers as it is for physicians. Our problem is not only to know our field but to communicate it to those who need it.

Physicians have felt the need to communicate their knowledge considerably less than those in most other fields, largely because their clients are often in trouble or pain and willing to be told rather than eager to know. As client relationships go, that of doctor and patient is maximal for control and minimal for needing to learn how to communicate information to the client.

The second, largely unrecognized aspect of the interference of jargon or vocabulary is that it is not just the physician who uses jargon. The patient may also have a medical, social, or regional vocabulary that is at odds with that of the physician. In all the medical interviews that I have taped and analyzed for their communicative content, the clear expectation is that the patient adjust to and acquire the language of the physician. At no time is it appropriate for the doctor to talk like the patient.

This is, perhaps, not surprising; but what is surprising is the general lack of awareness that the physician should develop what linguists call a *receptive competence* to patient language. This means only that doctors should not attempt to speak it but that they should learn to understand it. The principle is similar to that of a parent trying to understand their teenager's jargon. They would sound foolish if they tried to speak it, but they certainly ought to understand it. The contrast between receptive and productive competence in language is an established tradition in language study and it seems particularly appropriate here as well.

Because more has been written about the problem of jargon and vocabulary in doctor–patient communication (e.g., Boyle 1970; Haberman 1970; Kimball 1971) and because this is the most obvious aspect of interference to a clear exchange of information, I will not deal with it further here, but will move, instead, to the less obvious areas.

CULTURAL DIFFERENCES

Elsewhere I have discussed some of the problems involved in the delivery of medical service to minority patients (Shuy 1976). It is clear from the research conducted at the Georgetown University Hospital that minority speakers put on their very best (standard) language when they go to the doctor. Our tape-recorded medical interviews done with vernacular Black-English-speaking patients revealed that they refrained from dialect forms in many parts of the interview, but returned to those forms once they became involved in narrating some very personal aspect of their lives, which might well be considered by them to be the nonmedical part of the interviews, such as the following (italics indicate dialect forms):

DOCTOR: Does Mr. Jones work?
PATIENT: He *work* manually. He *work* at the courthouse downtown.

The patients who speak vernacular Black English also used their dialect when their effort to describe something became so intense and focused that they forgot their resolve to talk like the doctor:

DOCTOR: [discussing chest pain] Even under your arm?
PATIENT: Yes, in this arm here and it, and like when I wake up, I *can't hardly* hold it, you know. It *go to sleep*...

DOCTOR: Is this—does it hurt?
PATIENT: Yeah, and then I, you know, when I try to use it it *feel* like it goes dead and *don't have no* feeling in it.

In our research, however, it is safe to say that very little vernacular dialect was employed by the patients, despite the many indications that they use it habitually in other contexts. Most vernacular dialect features that are not vocabulary differences (*high blood pressure* for *stroke, runny bowels* for *diarrhea*), however, are not likely to cause problems in comprehension. The pronunciation and grammar of vernacular Black English differ from Standard English, but not to the extent that would create gaps in understanding. What does happen, however, is that the person who hears a vernacular dialect spoken tends to devalue the speaker of that dialect. Consciously or unconsciously, dialect speakers tend to get worse treatment, wait longer for service, are considered ignorant, and are told what to do rather than asked what they would like to do. Therefore, the effect of the patient's vernacular dialect in the medical interview is a potential source of interference to the effective exchange of information.

STRUCTURE OF DISCOURSE

The third and least obvious type of interference to an effective exchange of information in the medical interview stems from the structure of discourse itself. It is not difficult to think of words when one thinks of communication, but it is apparently quite difficult to realize that there are intricate structures at work at the discourse level as well. By discourse, I mean units of language larger than a sentence.

In normal conversation, for example, there are patterns of discourse that involve marking sequences, such as openings, closings, and continuation markers. Conversations don't just happen. They get started; and we have structured, predictable ways of doing this. Nor do conversations just continue on their own.

There are predictable, structured ways of providing cohesion to a conversation. One strategy is that of anaphora: a systematic referencing system that languages have that keeps the characters clear in past, present, or future reference. Another strategy involves the use of sequence markers such as *first, next, another way, my third* point, and so forth. Such markers point ahead and backward at the same time, providing a place of reference for the listener and a sense of where we are in the conversation.

In addition to these sequence markers, normal conversation also has other important structures. We all know that conversations have topics. Otherwise there would be no conversation at all. Topics can be identified and separated from one another by at least three criteria:

1. Subject matter differences.
2. Prosodic differences from the previous topic (that is, a change of intonation, rate of speech, or pauses).
3. The internal cohesion of the topic (that is, the sequencing markers noted earlier are found within a topic—it is opened and closed and internal anaphora referencing is complete within that unit).

Once topics in a conversation are identified and set off by the above structural criteria, it becomes possible to see a pattern that is not normally noticed. Of particular interest in most conversations is who introduces the topic, who switches it to another topic, how an introduced topic is responded to by other participants in the conversation, how interruptions take place, and many other things.

It has been necessary to describe some of the structural elements of a normal conversation to show how physician–patient communication works. It should be clear, first of all, that the doctor–patient medical interview is not normal conversation. It is instructive, in fact, to note *how* this interview is not normal conversation. For one thing, in normal conversation, there is an expectation of balanced participation. Not only are the participants expected to talk in about the same quantities, but they are also both expected to introduce new topics and to respond to the topics introduced by the other speaker. If there is no response, there is no conversation. Nor does a normal conversation contain only questions by one speaker and answers by the other. When this happens, we have an interview. The rules of interruption are also different in the medical interview from those of normal conversation.

The point of this discussion about normal conversation is simply this: Patients are used to engaging in normal conversation. Seldom are they used to being interviewed. Just as small children bring only their own experience and knowledge with them when they go to school for the first time, so patients bring with them only their own experience and knowledge about talk or conversations when they come to the doctor. Both the young child going to school and the patient going to the doctor bring along a great deal of fear. But what they have to call on is only their own past experience.

The child going to school soon learns that the teacher can interrupt him or her but that he or she had better not interrupt the teacher. The child also has to learn that the teacher is in total control of the class and that substantive topics are introduced only by the teacher. And, in fact, as children learn these discourse rules of the classroom, their own classroom speech is modified accordingly. Children who are perceived as troublesome are often those who have unconsciously made use of conversational rules that are perfectly acceptable elsewhere but not acceptable in the school. The application of this comparison of the child and the school should be apparent in the physician–patient medical interview.

ANALYSIS OF MEDICAL INTERVIEWS

To determine whether or not there is interference from the relaxed, normal conversational rules to the rules of the medical interview, I have begun to analyze the discourse patterns of the latter. The remainder of this chapter describes this analysis. Three medical histories conducted at Georgetown University Hospital will be cited. These three tape-recorded interviews of working-class women were selected because they exhibit a range of the physicians' interview styles. The analysis is not intended to characterize the field of medicine as a whole nor to praise or criticize the physician who conducted them. I intend only to demonstrate how the structure of discourse works in a medical interview and to suggest how knowledge of this structure might lead to modification of technique. The discourse areas to be addressed are as follows: topic introduction, topic response, topic recycling, and sequence marking (cohesion).

Topic Introduction

It is not surprising that in a medical interview that clearly follows a visible written questionnaire format, there is a rather rigid topic introduction sequence. However rigid that format may be, one startling conclusion faced me at the end of my examination of some 100 interviews: It would be very difficult to reconstruct the written questionnaire on the basis of the tape-recorded interviews. Whereas there may well be logical topics suggested in the written interview schedule, not all interviews cover the same topics and by no means are all questions covered consistently across all interviews. The range of variability was, in fact, gross.

As to who introduced the topics of discourse, one doctor introduced all 11 topics in the interview. Another doctor introduced 11 out of 12 topics, and the third introduced 5 of 7. It is expected, of course, in an interview setting, as opposed to a normal conversation, that the interviewer will introduce most of the topics. It is interesting, however, that the third physician conducted his interview in a style more characteristic of a normal conversation. His friendly, kidding style made the patient comfortable enough to introduce a new topic twice during the interview. The second physician recycled one topic three times (topics 4, 7, 9) and another topic twice (topics 7 and 9).

Figure 1 displays the topic introduction and recycling structure for the three interviews under discussion. The three interviews differ from normal conversation to different degrees and in different ways. The third interview is most like predictable conversation and least like an interview. It would not be difficult to say that this interview was the most relaxed and the one in which the participants are most equal. As is characteristic of most conversations, the participants both evidenced some control. An interview is characterized by a lack of total control on the part of the person being interviewed.

FIGURE 1 Topic Introduction and Recycling in Three Medical Interviews

Topic #	1	2	3	4	5	6	7	8	9	10	11
						Interview 1					
DOCTOR:	Past care	Demographic background	Body background	Family background	Marriage background	Diseases	Operations	This pregnancy	Past pregnancies	Left overs	Frame: close
PATIENT:											
						Interview 2					
DOCTOR:	Frame: opening		Demographic background	Body background	Marriage background	Family background	Body background	Family background	Body background	Diseases	Past pregnancies
PATIENT:		Pills									
						Interview 3					
DOCTOR:	Frame: openings	Body & family background		Explains treatment		Diseases	Frame: close				
PATIENT:			Body background		Complaints						

The paradigm case of interview control may well be the appearance of witnesses in a trial. There the witnesses, even expert witnesses, do not have control. They are at the mercy of the attorneys who interview them. If witnesses do introduce a new topic, it is quickly deemed out of order or nonresponsive. Thus, the nature of the interview restricts the communicative freedom of the respondents.

If the desire of the physician is to make the patient comfortable, to reduce anxiety, thereby increasing the probability of acquiring complete and accurate information about that patient, it seems evident that the interview style will be modified to be more conversational and less like an interview. Physician 3 does this best here. Physician 2 makes one small movement in that direction by recycling topics. Topic recycling occurs in normal conversations but in ways not exactly parallel to Physician 2's use of it here. In fact, he appears to be picking up on things he overlooked the first time around rather than trying to be more conversational. Physician 1 apparently follows the written script religiously.

Topic Response

Once a topic is introduced, it is necessary to do something with it. The conversational pattern can expand on the topic, amend it, and argue with it but cannot ignore it. If the topic is ignored, the conversation moves on quickly to something else or else it dies. In a medical interview, the rules are somewhat different. In the most rigid interview, the patient is not expected to expand, amend, or disagree with the topic. Nor can the patient ignore it. The only conversational strategies left for the patient are to request clarification, interrupt, pause, express hesitation or uncertainty even in the presentation of a response, agree, or respond directly. Our three interviews evidence all of these patient strategies.

The usual requests for clarification result from a lack of clarity or specificity on the part of one of the speakers. In the three interviews analyzed here, patients made all the requests for clarification. For example:

DOCTOR: Any German measles?
CLIENT: Uh, is that one of the childhood diseases?

The usual response to a request for clarification is to clarify. This particular physician chose to be vague in response.

DOCTOR: Uh, like sometimes; sometimes no.

Undaunted by this lack of clarification, the patient proceeded to admit to having something.

PATIENT: I had some kind of measles.

To this, the doctor defined this kind of measles for her:

DOCTOR: You had regular measles.
PATIENT: Right.

This request for clarification was handled very badly by the physician. In fact, rather than clarifying, he actually defined the type of measles for her, sight unseen and concept unknown. In desperation, the patient agrees with the doctor that her measles were not German, although there is nothing in the text to indicate that they were or were not.

This tendency of the physician to label the injury or disease, whether it was clearly that injury or disease or not, is seen again in the second interview, where the doctor asks:

DOCTOR: And have you ever had an accident, breaking an arm, break a leg?
PATIENT: Not broken but, I, when your arm is in a sling, that means it's not broken, it's not always knocked out of place. This was when I was a child.
DOCTOR: It was dislocated.
PATIENT: Well, right, dislocated.

In contrast with these requests for clarification, which actually yield diagnostic labeling rather than understanding, is the request made by the patient in the third interview. This was the comfortable, conversational interview, and the patient's question is greatly different from the others:

PATIENT: What do you mean?

This question is direct and secure. It actually challenges the doctor to be clear. It is, in fact, hardly a request at all. It is more an imperative to be clear or specific. It fits the conversational style, not the interview style. It is asked in a way that reveals that the patient has a right to know.

Interrupting, another characteristic of normal conversation, is also a topic response. People interrupt for a number of reasons: impatience, boredom, irritation, or eagerness, to name a few. The usual pattern in conversation is for the dominant party to interrupt the passive speaker. In the case of interviewing, however, where the dominant speaker is in total control, the need to interrupt to establish power is less apparent. In addition, the entire point of the interview is to solicit information from the other person. If the patient is not allowed to finish a sentence, then the purpose of the interview is thwarted. For this reason, we find very few instances of doctors interrupting patients.

There are, on the other hand, frequent interruptions of the doctor by the patient. Of great interest, however, is that in interruptions, there is always a brief period of simultaneous speaking, quickly followed by the cessation of talking by one of the two speakers. In such cases, we refer to this as prevailing or declining. The prevailing speaker, the one who wins out, whether the interrupter or the interruptee, is the dominant speaker. In each case in which the patient attempts to interrupt the doctor in our data, the doctor prevails and the patient's interruption, for all practical purposes, loses out. For example:

DOCTOR: Your last menstrual period was the twenty-seventh of
PATIENT: $\begin{bmatrix} \text{July} \\ \text{Yeah} \end{bmatrix}$ . . .
DOCTOR: . . . of last year, so you're due in April?

In this case, the patient's overlap, *yeah*, is ignored by the doctor, who goes right on with his sentence. This was the only type of interruption discovered in our data. If the physicians in our study had been concerned enough to attempt a more conversational interview, they might have considered the possibility of attending to the patients' overlaps and interruptions and perhaps even let the patient win one once in a while.

Pauses and hesitations are another topic response strategy found in normal conversation. If participants do not wish to commit themselves immediately, they have, at their disposal, the right to pause. (Up to 4 or 5 seconds is permissible; beyond that is awkward.) When a speaker pauses for an inordinate length of time—say 10 or 15 seconds, the conversational awkwardness causes the first speaker to begin speaking again. It is as though the pausing speaker has relinquished his turn. In general, the longer the pause, the more awkward things become.

In the case of interviews, long pauses are expected and permitted by the interviewer, the dominant party. This is because the interviewer has the agenda, the clipboard, the questionnaire. The interviewer is the one doing the thinking. The interviewee is only responding.

In the medical interviews studied here, I found, as predicted, long pauses by the physician that were respected and left silent by the patients. The more interesting case is what happened when the patient left long pauses to the doctor's questions, for example:

DOCTOR: What type of pills are those?
PATIENT: [13 second pause] [gets pills out and shows them to doctor].

Later, in the same interview, the doctor permits the patient to pause for 10 and 14 seconds, clearly unable to specify how long ago something happened or what a treatment was. In normal conversation, the dominant speaker would put both at ease by offering some words, not just stark silence.

Closely related to pausing, which can indicate uncertainty of some sort, is the use of what linguists call lax tokens. These are certain response words—such as *yes, no,* and *what*—for which English has variations called lax tokens. These lax tokens are *uh-huh* for *yes, huh-uh* for *no,* and *huh* for *what.* There are others as well, but these are the most common. Lax tokens are commonly used in intimate speech events as a kind of informal code. But when they are used cross-socially, as by lower status people to high status people, their use becomes more complex. Here they can be used to indicate a level of uncertainty, a phenomenon I noted in an earlier paper as negative weakening (Shuy 1976). For example, to a series of related questions that move from easy to difficult, early-on clear responses, such as *no,* gave way to lax tokens as uncertainty grew. This is not to say that all *huh-uh* responses are uncertain, but it is clear that, on the whole, *huh-uh* is a less reliable negative response than *no.*

More recently, Jefferson (1978) pointed out that two-syllable lax tokens, such as *uh-huh* and *huh-uh,* which contain reversed stress patterns, are sometimes deliberately reverse-stressed to be even less clear. Thus the negative, *huh-uh,* normally stressed in the first syllable is stressed in the second syllable, making it ambiguous with the lax token for "yes," *uh-huh,* which has inherent second syllable stress. The principle, in short, is similar to that of the person whose spelling is so poor that he or she resorts to sloppy handwriting or abbreviations to cover up this inadequacy. Note this exchange about the patient's reaction to penicillin:

DOCTOR: No reaction at all?
PATIENT: Huh-*uh*.

And later:

DOCTOR: Have you been constipated during this pregnancy at all?
PATIENT: *Uh*-huh.

Both of the above lax token responses are stressed in reverse of their usual manner. Both are at least suspect in their accuracy.

Sequence Marking (Cohesion)

The sequence marking of the medical interviews show many of the same characteristics found in interviews of all types. In these interviews we find openings, closings, and transitions between topics.

Openings. The opening of some interviews requires a great deal of justification about why the person is being interviewed, what will be done with the information, assurance of anonymity and so forth. The medical interview requires none of this because it is perfectly obvious why the interview is taking place and the patient is too helpless to have an opinion about what will be done with the data. Two of the openings were simple, "How are you today?" This would be perfectly adequate in most circumstances. One patient took it as a greeting ritual, the other as an inquiry about her health. The third physician disambiguated the opening by asking, "How are you feeling? Pretty good?" The medical interview can be cold and frightening to a patient. If the goal of the physician is to make the patient comfortable, a bit of personal but interested and relevant chitchat, whatever the cost in precious time, is advisable. The patients are familiar with normal conversation openings that stress such chitchat. The medical interview would do well to try to move closer to a conversational framework.

Closings. All three interviews contain clear closing statements by the physician. Human life seems to require a ritual goodbye, and when we examine how these rituals work, we learn that they are quite complex. There is often a pre-close that occurs well in advance of the final close. At a cocktail party, for example, one gives pre-closing signals to one's host and hostess well in advance of one's departure. Phrases like "It's getting late" or mumbling about the baby sitter in a way that can be overheard by the hostess are ways of carrying out the pre-close.

Physician 1, for example, pre-closes, then returns to some leftover unfinished business:

DOCTOR: That's just about all, I guess, that I need to ask you. You haven't had any problems with any dizziness, have you?

Two questions later, the doctor wraps it all up by repeating that these are all the questions he has to ask right now and he introduces the physical examination to the patient as a closing for the interview.

The second physician was more clearly final and offers no pre-closing at all. He simply concludes with, "OK, I think we're about ready to uh, do the physical." Physician 3 is, as usual, more conversational and less ritualized in his closing: "Let me talk to you when you're squared away." Of the three interviews, the first was more like the structure of conversation in that it offered pre-closing signals that the end was near. The third was more verbally conversational in that the words were ones that could easily be found in real conversations. If the goal of the medical interview is to make the patient comfortable and to reduce the mismatch between speech familiarity and the terse interview, physicians would do well to use the more conversational structure and verbiage.

Transitions. In normal conversation there is often an effort to create transition between topics. If the conversation has been serious and intense, there is often a recognized need to offer more light, social, chitchat as a transition to the next serious topic. In that the medical interview is, technically, nothing but seriousness, the interview can become rather heavy unless there is some light talk occasionally. In our three interviews, such talk exists in three quite different ways. Physician 1 is serious and businesslike. He makes transitions between topics with little more than an introductory *OK*. In two topics (topics 2 and 6), he uses the agenda organizer as his transition: by this I mean the recitation of what he is doing, a kind of metacognitive behavior. For example, as a preface to topic 2:

DOCTOR: Uh, this morning what I'd like to do is just ask you a few questions; more than a few questions really . . .

Again, as a preface to topic 6,

DOCTOR: Now what I would like to do is, uh, uh, I'm going to ask you a series of diseases, OK?

There are no other transitions in this interview. Everything else is a stark leap to the next topic.

Physician 2 makes transitions with hesitation markers and positive place holders. He uses noises like *uh* and *ah* along with positive terms like *OK, Okie Dokie, alright* and time sequence terms like *Now, and,* and *uh*. A place holder simply refers to a word uttered for no other reason than to hold a turn until the speaker's mind cranks up enough to ask the next question. There is little lightness or social interaction in Physician 2's speech, but there is, at least, a conversational intonation to accompany al this heavy seriousness.

Physician 3 is at the opposite end of this continuum. He is conversational throughout, actually making transition unnecessary. His style, of course, is least intimidating and most friendly. This is not to say that all medical interviews should be light and gay. But, if one goal of the interview is to make the patient comfortable by matching the predictable expectations of conversation rather than the sterility of interview, then some heed could be paid to learning how to create and use transitions between topics effectively as a means of putting the patient at ease.

CONCLUSION

The effective exchange of information in the medical interview has at least three major components. This chapter mentions but does not explore in detail the components of jargon and cultural differences. The third component, the structure of discourse, is a recently developed adjunct of the mixture of several disciplines, including linguistics. The interference of the interview framework on a society that is more comfortable with the discourse structure of conversation tells us one very important thing about how to make patients more comfortable.

If patient comfort contributes to improved accuracy of information exchange, and everything points to the fact that it does, then there are clear steps that can be taken to move in that direction. This chapter analyzed three representatively different medical interviews to point out some of the dimensions of variability currently in practice. But even from these few instances, it is possible to suggest clear changes in interview practice.

REFERENCES CITED

BOYLE, C.M.
  1970 Differences between patients' and doctors' interpretations of some common medical terms. *British Medical Journal* 2:286–289.
HABERMAN, P.W.
  1970 Ethnic differences in psychiatric symptoms reported in community surveys. *Public Health Reports* 85:495–502.
JEFFERSON, GAIL
  1978 What's in a nyem? *Sociology* 12(1):135–139.
KIMBALL, C.P.
  1971 Medicine and dialects. *Annals of Internal Medicine* 73(1):137–139.
SHUY, ROGER W.
  1976 The medical interview: Problems in communication. *Primary Care* 3(3):365–386.

2

Doctor/Mother/Child Communication: Linguistic Analysis of a Pediatric Interaction*

Deborah Tannen and Cynthia Wallat

Evidence from recent studies of beliefs, expectations, and communicative interaction associated with health care indicates that there has been a steep rise in consumer dissatisfaction with professional clinical practice and that patients and healers differ in their thinking about and response to illness (Kleinman 1980). This chapter demonstrates the theoretical and practical significance of moving beyond the well-attested conclusion that conflict exists. It explores the consequences of these differences in beliefs and expectations for a medical interview and examination, yielding an explication of how communication works and does not work and how meaning gets encoded in and decoded from talk in medical settings. An analysis of communicative demands arising in the interaction between physician and parents is needed to judge the practicality of laws and regulations aimed at "maximizing" family participation in societal institutions, including health care systems.

* We are grateful to the staff of the Child Development Center and to Jody's family for their generous cooperation and support. We especially appreciate the extra time taken by the mother and doctor to participate in the replay sessions. This is a significant revision and expansion of our "A sociolinguistic analysis of multiple demands on the pediatrician in doctor/mother/patient interaction" in *Linguistics and the Professions*, Ed. Robert J. Di Pietro, Norwood, N.J.: Ablex, 1982.

Kleinman, a medical anthropologist and practicing physician, argues (1980) that systematic analysis of doctor/patient relationships provides a strategic site for studying social development. In all societies composed of different social groups, different professions, different families and individuals, there is an amalgam of modern and traditional beliefs, values, and expectations "held together in varying patterns of assimilation, complementarity, conflict, and contradiction. . . . It is [therefore] not surprising that health care systems provide some of the sharpest reflections of the tensions and problems of social development" (Kleinman 1980:37).

Kleinman further argues that the currently prevalent biomedical model has no means for taking into account how patients and healers deal with different perspectives on health and illness and therefore has little to say about the core tasks and relationships that constitute clinical care. Other physicians and medical clinicians (Gallagher 1978) have also called for new theoretical perspectives. Studies of what a family doctor does (e.g., Fabb, Hefferman, Phillips, and Stone 1976) indicate that the core clinical functions taught in family medicine programs place demands on physicians' communication and interpersonal skills (e.g., interviewing, conducting physical examinations, using diagnostic procedures, recognizing problems, selecting appropriate treatments, assessing progress, explaining preventive methods, and displaying medical competence). Pediatricians are among those calling, for example, for research that recognizes that "in family practice understanding of different levels of communication and the different mechanisms by which we communicate is especially important" (Bryan 1977:102).

THE STUDY

The research discussed in this chapter focused on the problem of what processes make possible or interfere with successful exchange of information in a medical setting that includes a mother, child, and pediatrician. What is the result of conflicting demands for information during a pediatric interview and examination? The pediatrician's diagnosis depends on the parent as a source of information about the child's medical history (which the parent may or may not have). This parent is concerned with prognosis: information she believes (rightly or wrongly) the pediatrician may have concerning the child's future condition.

This study was part of a broad research design developing a methodology for identifying and analyzing interrelations between individuals, social settings, and social development. Following recent pioneering studies in sociolinguistic microanalysis (Gumperz 1972, 1977), the first step in the project was to obtain video recordings of naturally occurring medical interviews and examinations.

We began working with the Georgetown University Child Development

Center, a division of the Department of Pediatrics at the Georgetown University Medical Center. The Child Development Center is an exemplary interdisciplinary training service and research facility constructed with funds provided under PL 88-164 to help children with developmental disabilities.

We analyzed a series of videotapes made by the Child Development Center documenting examinations and interviews with a nine-year-old physically and (somewhat) mentally handicapped child, whom we shall call Jody, and her parents and two sisters. The tapes include initial interview of both parents with a coordinator; examinations by a psychologist, social worker, occupational therapist, physical therapist, nutritionist, speech pathologist, audiologist, dentist, educational advisor, and pediatrician; home visits by two nurses; a staff meeting at which the staff reported their findings to one another and agreed on recommendations; and a meeting at which the staff presented and interpreted their findings for the parents (called a "parent interpretive").

The primary focus of our analysis was the pediatrician's examination of the child in the mother's presence. Where relevant, we refer to interaction in other settings. Within the pediatric examination transcript, we focus on talk about two recurrent themes that were of significant concern on the parents. One was the presence in the child's brain of a recently diagnosed arteriovenous malformation and associated hemangiomas (bruise-like marks) on her face.[1] The second theme was the child's raspy breathing at night, which the parents feared indicated she was having difficulty breathing.

Our analytic procedure consisted of (*a*) previewing and repeatedly viewing videotapes of interactions across the 14 situations described, (*b*) carefully transcribing interaction segments from the pediatric examination/interview and selected excerpts from other tapes, as they bear on talk being analyzed in the pediatric examination, (*c*) microanalyzing transcribed segments, (*d*) playing back the tapes with the mother and pediatrician in separate interviews. (For detailed presentation and discussion of procedures and implications for linguistic and communication theory see Green and Wallat 1981; Tannen 1983; Wallat and Green 1979.)

Our analysis shows that the pediatrician balances multiple and sometimes conflicting demands, addressing three audiences, each of which is involved in at least three "frames" associated with distinct footings (Goffman 1979) marked by use of identifiable linguistic registers. In addition, the pediatrician suppresses her emotional responses and monitors the amounts as well as impact of information she imparts.

---

[1] *Hemangioma* is a congenital anomaly or tumor—a mass composed almost entirely of capillary type vessels, blood filled channels. Hemangiomas occur anywhere in the body, but are most frequently noticed in the skin. *Arteriovenous*: relating to both an artery and vein. (*Stedman's Medical Dictionary*. Baltimore, Md.: Williams and Wilkins Co., 1972).

Conceptual and Theoretical Orientation

Our theoretical and methodological framework is in the tradition of sociolinguistic microanalysis developed by Gumperz (1977, 1982; Gumperz and Tannen 1979) and extended by others (Green and Wallat 1979, 1981; Tannen 1983; Wallat and Green 1979, in press). This research focuses on linguistic and paralinguistic cues and their use in interaction, as ways of conveying meaning and of identifying contexts. Theoretical foundations are provided by frames theory.

The major premise underlying these investigations, as well as the present one, is that miscommunication occurs in all institutional settings. Kleinman's (1980) observation of the complexity of social and cognitive constructs operating in medical settings highlights the need to examine what participants actually do and say in pediatric contexts.

Past work (Tannen 1983) shows that a binary distinction between understanding and misunderstanding in communication is idealized. In actual interaction, speakers and listeners achieve varying degrees of understanding of each other's intentions and linguistic devices. To communicate, speakers signal *how* they mean what they say and how ideas are related to each other by use of linguistic and paralinguistic devices, such as tone of voice, pitch, loudness, rate of speech, and lexical choice. Any such device can fail to establish rapport, distance, or whatever its user intends when listeners are not accustomed to its use for that purpose. This occurs not only among speakers of different languages but also, as demonstrated, among a half-dozen friends, all native speakers of English, during a Thanksgiving dinner at one friend's home. Each participant used a unique combination of linguistic devices that constituted individual style. When those devices were similar to those used for similar purposes by others present, communication among them was smooth. When the devices used by one or more participants differed from those expected by one or more others, communication was disrupted or even obstructed.

These processes obtain in doctor/patient interaction as well. Studies of interaction depend on the observer's ability to identify and explicate both the message (that is, communicative content) and the metamessage (Bateson 1972), communicated through intonation and nonverbal cues (the metamessage refers to communication about the relationships between participants, and how the message is to be taken, which is understood from the *way* something is said). To understand more about family/professional interaction, we must identify first how such devices as overlap, pace, stress, pitch, silence, gestures, and use of certain topics tend to cluster and, second, the interpretations that individuals construct, modify, or suspend during interaction in medical settings.

Gumperz sets out this method in the following terms:

> The natural unit for such conversational analysis is the interactional exchange or sequence of two or more utterances, not an isolated utterance . . . Two questions are

relevant in the analysis (1) What is meant by the exchange? What does it reflect about the speaker's state of mind and his relationship to the [other]? (2) By what verbal devices are the relevant effects obtained? Are there any special features of style, pronunciation or vocabulary, which are significant? (Gumperz 1972:222)

Thus characterization of doctor/mother/child interaction depends on analyzing processes of interpretation of others' linguistic and paralinguistic cues. The pediatric examination/interview represents the brief interaction of three individuals, each bringing to the encounter unique communicative habits growing out of at least the following "frames" or "structures of expectations" (Tannen 1979):

1. Conversational style (individual and social differences in ways of signalling meaning in conversation).
2. Shared history (previous interactive experience among and between participants).
3. Personal history.
4. Expectations of the situation (including effects of the immediate environment).
5. Role expectations of self and others.

All of these dimensions are dynamic. At any one time, one or more of these potentially conflicting demands, or differing ways of fulfilling them, can contribute to, complicate, or override the health objective of the examination/ interview.

The Frames Approach in Analysis of Pediatric Interaction

Tannen (1979) reviews and integrates notions of frame, script, and schemata, which have been important in recent theory in a number of fields including linguistics, cognitive psychology, anthropology, sociology, and artificial intelligence. This and subsequent work (Tannen in press) suggest that there are two notions of frames that have been developed: one interactive and one pertaining to knowledge structures. Both will be drawn upon in the present study.

The interactive notion of frame, found in theoretical work in anthropology (Bateson 1972; Frake 1977) and sociology (Goffman 1974), as well as in the anthropological linguistic notion of speech activity as used by Gumperz (1977), refers to the superordinate message (or metamessage) about what activity is being engaged in when words are uttered in interaction. The frame is the definition of what is going on, without which no message could be interpreted.

Participants identify frames by recognition of familiar linguistic and behavioral routines, as well as conventionalized use of linguistic and paralinguistic features—in other words, what you say *and* how you say it. Goffman's (1979) characterization of changes of frame within an interaction, which he calls *footing*, figures in our analysis of the demands on the doctor in the pediatric examination. For example, we find that the pediatrician signals, by the way she talks, which task she is engaged in and hence which "footing" she is maintaining within the examination/interview (for example, examination or friendly conversation or demonstration for trainees).

The knowledge structure notion of frame, found in theoretical work in cognitive psychology, artificial intelligence, and linguistics, has gone by various names, including *scripts* (Schank and Abelson 1977), *schema* (Chafe 1977; Rumelhart 1975), in addition to frame (Minsky 1975). This notion of frame refers to knowledge structures in the minds of participants—sets of expectations that people have for other people, objects, settings, and the structure of interaction. For example, in the conversation discussed in this chapter, the pediatrician asks whether the marks on the child's forehead and lip have changed in size. How she asks the question and the fact that she asks it grow out of her association of the marks with the arteriovenous malformations in the brain; she understands that both are malformations of blood vessels. It is clear, however, from the way the mother talks about them both in this setting and in other settings (with the coordinator in the initial interview and with the social worker) that the mother is not associating the blue marks on the child's face with the dangerous arteriovenous malformation in the child's brain. For her, the hemangiomas are associated with a cosmetic frame: concern with the child's appearance.

Both the interactive and knowledge structure senses of frame account for the demands on the pediatrician in the interview/examination. Without a theory of frames, it is easy to see that the doctor deals with three audiences: the child, the mother, and the video camera and crew. This could lead to a general statement that there are multiple cognitive and social demands on the pediatrician when others beside the patient are present.

But if one views the interaction recorded on the videotape from the viewpoint of frames, we see that the demands are even more complex, for the doctor approaches each audience in several different ways. In other words, each frame operative in the interaction entails its own set of cognitive, linguistic, and social demands *for each interactant*. A brief sample of the frames we have identified highlights the complexity of the demands operative on the pediatrician in this setting (Table 1).

What appears on the surface as similar activities can grow out of different frames and hence represent different cognitive and social demands on the doctor. For example, the pediatrician examines the child. At one point she examines the child's stomach; at another she examines the skin behind her ear. Both seem to be parts of the examination frame. But only one is. The examination of the child's stomach is part of the standard pediatric evaluation, which the pediatrician must remember to perform and report for the training audience. (This may make little sense to the mother, who has not noted any problems in that area.) But when the pediatrician looks behind the child's ear, she is interrupting her

TABLE 1 Communicative Demands on Pediatrician Seen as Frame-related

Frame	Child	Mother	Video camera/crew
		Audience	
Management of social situation	Entertain child	Establish rapport with mother	Ignore camera & crew
Pediatric examination	Examine child, following preset examination structure	Ask mother for information that may be relevant to child's condition	
Training videotape	Be an exemplary pediatrician	Be an exemplary pediatrician	Monitor readiness of crew; Report findings for future trainee audience
Consultation with mother	Hold child in readiness; Examine child to answer mother's questions	Answer mother's questions; Suppress emotions; Blunt impact of diagnosis on mother	Ignore camera & crew

examination to check out something the mother has asked about and to allay the other's (unfounded) fear that there may be a connection between the skin eruption and the child's cerebral palsy, because both show up on the same side of the body (evidence of the mother's frame for the illness).

Each of the frames shown in Table 1 (and co-occurrent demands) entails ways of behaving that potentially conflict with demands of other frames. For example, entertaining the child, the doctor may lose time needed for the examination. Reporting findings to a camera requires a succinct and direct summary of findings. This may conflict with establishing rapport with the mother and will certainly conflict with the need to blunt the impact of findings for the mother's benefit, in a setting in which the doctor is not at leisure to counsel the mother at length. Finally, during time spent answering the mother's questions, the child may become restless, making the examination more difficult.

We have found identifiable linguistic and paralinguistic correlates to these frames. The sections that follow describe our analysis and findings.

Shifting Frames in the Pediatric Examination. In the 20-minute exam, the pediatrician directs 19 questions and 46 comments to the mother; directs 29 comments to the training audience; and fields 18 questions and 26 comments from the mother. At best, these complex and varied demands burden the pediatrician's attention and cognition. In some cases, the demands clearly conflict.

The following excerpt illustrates such a conflict. The pediatrician has explained to the mother that the child's breathing sounds noisy because of weak muscle control, a direct result of the cerebral palsy. Then she returns to the examination, resuming a running commentary of what she finds, directed to the video camera apparently for training purposes. (The examination and reporting represent double frames.) After this, the pediatrician begins engaging the child's attention, using a "teasing" register that is part of the "management" footing geared to the child, to move onto the next phase of the examination in which she looks at the child's ears.

The mother, however, is operating in only one frame: consultation with the doctor. Probably reacting to the pediatrician's shift in frame signaled by the use of teasing register with the child, the mother interjects another question related to earlier questions she asked about the child's breathing. For the mother, this represents no shift in frame. For the doctor, however, the mother's question is an interruption of the examination sequence and requires a sudden shift in focus or break in frame, to return to her consultation mode. The pediatrician stops the examination, turns away from the child, purses her lips, and covers the ophthalmoscope (ear light) with the palm of her other hand, the only time she evidences (and it is ever so slight) the strain placed on her by frame shifting.[2]

DOCTOR: Jody?...I wanna look in your ears...Jody?
MOTHER: This problem that she hás,...is not...interfering with her breathing, is it?
CHILD: Hello. [Spoken to Doctor's earlight]
DOCTOR: No.
MOTHER: It just appears that way?

---

[2] The following transcription conventions are used.
...half second pause. Each extra dot represents another half second pause.
á marks primary stress
′ marks high pitch on word
. sentence final falling intonation
, clause-final intonation ("more to come")
? yes/no question rising intonation
: lengthened vowel sound. The more :s, the longer the sound is held.
/   / inaudible or uncertain transcription
acc spoken quickly
⌈ Penned brackets connecting lines show overlapping speech.
⌊ Two people talking at once.
Penned brackets with reversed flap ⌉
                                    ⌊ indicates latching (no pause between speaker turns).

DOCTOR: Yes. It's very...it's...really...it's like flóppy you know and that's why it sounds...the way it is.

MOTHER: She worries me at night.

DOCTOR: Yes.

MOTHER: Because uh...when she's asléep I keep checkin' on hér so she doesn't⌉

DOCTOR: ⌊As you know the important⌉

MOTHER: ⌊I keep thinking

                         DOCTOR: [chuckle-------

she's not breathing properly.]

DOCTOR: As you know, the impórtant thing is that she dóes have difficulty with the use of her muscles.

        MOTHER: mhm

The pediatrician is balancing three frames: managing the child, examining her, and demonstrating for the video audience. The mother's question introduces the fourth: consultation.

Even when there is no conflict, balancing and shifting among three audiences and at least four frames in a single setting has significant cognitive, social, and emotional consequences. This kind of complexity is not evident from a content analysis of interaction but is made visible by sociolinguistic microanalysis.

Linguistic Evidence for Registers Associated With Frames. The pediatrician addresses each of her three audiences in a different linguistic register; that is, she switches among three distinct codes, each with its own intonation, voice quality, lexical and syntactic structures, and content, as illustrated in the following transcript excerpts.

When talking to the child, the pediatrician uses the classic features of "motherese" (Newport, Gleitman, and Gleitman 1977): high pitch, elongated vowel sounds, sing-song intonation, teasing. For example, while examining the child's ear through an ophthalmoscope, the pediatrician teases, and the child responds with delighted laughter:

DOCTOR: Let me look in your ear. Okay? Do you have a monkey in your ear?

CHILD: [laughing] No::::.

DOCTOR: No::::? . . . Let's see . . . .I . . see . . . . . . a ′ birdie.

CHILD: ⌈[laughing] No::.   acc....]

DOCTOR: ⌊[smiling] No.

Immediately after this, with no perceptible break in timing, the pediatrician turns her body toward the camera and says, with only a slight stumbling in the quick repetition of "are":

DOCTOR: Her canals are-are fine, they're open.

This is an example of a pattern of speech recurrent throughout the examination: a running account of the procedures performed and resultant observations. This register constitutes 29 of the pediatrician's comments during the examination and is characterized by easily observable paralinguistic and nonverbal cues: flat intonation, rapid rate of speech, relatively low pitch, and absence of marked facial expressions and gestures. All these cues give this register an unmistakable character that we call "reporting."

Talk uttered in this register is generally directed toward the video camera, though the pediatrician's gaze may be elsewhere. She apparently has the training audience in mind, and her comments during playback confirm this hypothesis. It is clear that the mother perceives the special cues associated with this register, as none of her comments or questions is interjected when the pediatrician is talking in this register.

Thus the mother perceives that the reporting register signals a frame that excludes her as a participant. This finding correlates with an intriguing observation by Cicourel (1975) in his work on medical interviews. Cicourel draws attention to the question of how physicians distill concise statements relevant to diagnosis as written in medical records, from fragmented and nonsequential spoken discourse at the interview. Though his primary interest is in comparing spoken discourse (face-to-face conversation) during the interview with written text (the physician's written report summary), Cicourel's data include a spoken report that was produced when a faculty supervisor entered the room in which a third-year resident was conducting an interview with a 15-year-old patient, his mother, and an uncle who was acting as interpreter for the Spanish-speaking patient and mother.

Although the transcript of this interview does not include paralinguistic features, precluding conclusion about whether or not the resident's oral summary sounded like what we call reporting register, it is interesting that the family members did not interject any comments during the report, even though the rest of the interview was characterized as problematic and noisy. Even a direct request for confirmation by the resident elicits a minimal response from the uncle, who at other times is a voluble participant in the interaction. It seems likely that the resident's spoken summary is indeed an example of a reporting register. This would account for the fact that the patient and his family did not participate; they perceived the way the resident delivered this report as a change in frame and consequent footing.

Cicourel notes the similarity between this spoken summary and the one later written by the resident. This finding supports our hypothesis that the reporting register reflects the doctor's diagnostic frame and that paralinguistic features are a way of observing shifting frames.

In our data, then, the pediatrician uses motherese when talking to the child; reporting register when performing diagnostic procedures; and, finally, a register that sounds very much like everyday conversation when she talks to the mother.

The following example shows the pediatrician shifting among these three registers. She is examining the child's throat:

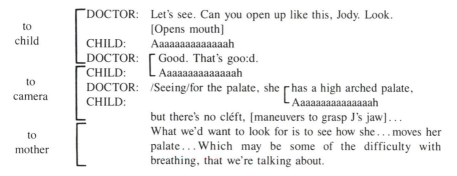

to child	DOCTOR:	Let's see. Can you open up like this, Jody. Look.
		[Opens mouth]
	CHILD:	Aaaaaaaaaaaaaaah
	DOCTOR:	Good. That's goo:d.
to camera	CHILD:	Aaaaaaaaaaaaaaah
	DOCTOR:	/Seeing/for the palate, she has a high arched palate,
	CHILD:	Aaaaaaaaaaaaaaaah
		but there's no cléft, [maneuvers to grasp J's jaw]...
to mother		What we'd want to look for is to see how she...moves her
		palate...Which may be some of the difficulty with
		breathing, that we're talking about.

First the pediatrician looks inside the child's throat—an endeavor requiring some maneuvering, especially since Jody has cerebral palsy and hence poor muscle control. After the doctor succeeds in looking in the child's throat, she reports her findings to the camera, using the reporting register. Then she gradually shifts her gaze and addresses the mother to explain how these findings relate to the child's noisy breathing, a matter the mother expressed concern about during the preceding interview.

Before we leave our discussion of these three registers, we would like to comment further on the reporting mode. Obviously, most pediatric examinations are not carried out in the presence of a video camera. Nonetheless, it is our hypothesis that the reporting register makes observable a cognitive process that is always present in the examining doctor's consciousness, by virtue of the diagnostic process. The doctor must follow a set of procedures prescribed by medical training. Furthermore, any professional acting in a professional role must refer for a behavioral model to his or her perception of the expectations of colleagues. In other words, the professional has a "frame" or set of expectations (Tannen 1979) for behavior in this role and setting. This is similar to Goffman's (1959) notion of "team" as the basic unit of analysis in human interaction and underlies Bucher and Stelling's (1977) analysis of professional socialization among doctors.

The use of a reporting register by medical professionals, a natural consequence of such professional demands as training, diagnosis, and report, may have significant implications for doctor/patient communication. That the mother in our study never initiates interaction with the doctor when she is operating in this mode is a suggestive finding.

Thus, the reporting register may reflect what Cicourel calls "sets of schemata or islands of informational content" growing out of "the influence of the physician's prior training and concern with specific issues or problems that could help explain the patient's condition" (1975:46). This phenomenon is related to our notion of knowledge structure frames as well: the sets of associations that the physician expects that lead her or him to ask questions and answer questions one way rather than another, which Cicourel calls *elicitation frames*. Note, however, that this use of "frame" is very different from both our interactive notion of frame as signals of the metamessage and our knowledge structure notion of frames as cognitive schemata.

Emotional Demands

Another demand on the pediatrician is to conceal her emotional response during the examination/interview. Whereas an emotional response to a medical problem might be appropriate when expressed by a friend, it is quite another matter coming from a doctor, because the point of reference differs. When a friend responds emotionally to a medical condition, the negative evaluation is interpreted as relative to good health. A doctor's reference, however, is assumed to be a range of examples of bad health. Hence, an emotional reaction from a doctor implies that this is a terrible condition relative to the great number of terrible conditions the doctor has witnessed.

The pediatrician in our data clearly seeks to avoid such implications. She repeatedly stresses during the interview/examination that Jody's condition is "normal" and "common" for a child with cerebral palsy. Here again, the Child Development Center's complete set of videotapes is an invaluable resource. In the examination/interview, the pediatrician seems relatively unconcerned about the danger of the arteriovenous malformation in the child's brain. She explains in simple language and with graphic gestures that the arteriovenous malformation is an abnormal blood vessel connection that puts pressure on the brain, causing the child's seizures. The mother asks,

MOTHER: I often worry about the dánger involved too ——➤
DOCTOR: Yes
MOTHER: cause she's well I mean like right now, ... uh ... in her present condítion. I've often wondered about how
               DOCTOR: mhm
dangerous they they are to her right now.
DOCTOR: We:ll ... um ... the ónly danger would be from bléeding. ... Fróm them, If there was any rúpture, or anything like that which ´ cán happen. ... um ... thát would be the dánger. ... fór that. But they're
               Mother:mhm
... mm ... nót going to be something that will get worse as time goes on.

MOTHER: Oh I see.
DOCTOR: Buy they're just thére. Okay? [returns to exam]

The pediatrician minimizes the danger of the arteriovenous malformation by using a syntactic construction with "only": "the only danger." She stresses the positive side, that "they are not going to... get worse." She uses fillers ("um," "hm"); repetition and paraphrase ("bleeding," "rupture"; "the only danger," "that would be the danger"; "they're not going to... get worse," "they're just there"); conditional tense (*would* in "the only danger *would* be from bleeding," and "that *would* be the danger"); and buffer language ("or anything like that").[3] All this linguistic evidence of (a) the pressure of cognitive processing in verbalizing the diagnosis; (b) the need to monitor the diagnosis, which is not yet complete; and (c) the desire not to upset the mother. The pediatrician does not yet have all the relevant medical evidence; she is in the process of formulating hypotheses about the child's condition. Furthermore, she does not have time to prolong the digression from the examination to deal with the mother's emotional response to information she receives.

The effects of these production demands on the pediatrician's discourse have important implications for the mother's participation and response. (Too often analysis focuses on one or the other.) The halting quality of the pediatrician's discourse (a) mitigates the effect of the information conveyed on the mother and (b) leaves plenty of space for the mother to insert further questions if she feels the need.

As can be seen from the earlier segment, the mother and the pediatrician often interrupt each other and finish each other's sentences, using overlap in a cooperative way (Tannen 1983). There is nothing in the pediatrician's delivery, bearing, or tone that communicates noticeable distress or concern. She, herself, on viewing the segment during replay, expressed surprise at her use of the word "only" and at the effect of her words on the mother, who, she commented, seemed visibly reassured, despite the ominous message conveyed.

The pediatrician's deep concern about the danger of the arteriovenous malformation is evident in her report to the staff. At the end of the staff meeting, she returns to the issue of the malformation and stresses that she would like to communicate with the child's regular doctors, follow her condition, and make sure that the parents get necessary counseling—in an appropriate setting. Following is an example from her comments at the staff meeting:

DOCTOR: [portion omitted]... uh: I'm not sure about how much counseling has been
            dóne,... wíth these parents,... around. .the íssue... of the a-v malforma-

---

[3] We have coined the term *buffer language* to characterize what has been called "empty language," because such words and phrases serve a purpose, as demonstrated, and therefore are not empty.

> tion. Mother asked me questions, . . . about the operability, inoperability of it, . . . u:m which Í was not able to ánswer. She was tóld it wás inoperable, and I had to say well yes some of them are and some of them aren't. . . . And I think that this is uh . . . uh . . . an important point. Because I don't know whether . . . the possibility of sudden death, intracranial hemorrhage, if any of this has ever been | discussed with these parents,

The terms "sudden death" and "intracranial hemorrhage" contrast sharply with the words used in addressing the mother ("bleeding," "rupture"). In addition to lexical choice, there is a difference in syntactic structure: "the possibility of . . . " vs. "the only danger would be . . . ". The former asserts the danger, while the latter conditionalizes and thereby mitigates the danger.

The pediatrician's speech in the staff setting is faster and more assertive; it is not characterized by the hesitation and circumlocution that were seen in the segment addressed to the mother. Furthermore, when she says, "sudden death, intracranial hemorrhage," she uses listing intonation, indicating that these are two of a series of dangers, in direct contrast to the use of "only." The doctor's deep concern is apparent throughout. It seems clear that, when talking to the mother during the examination of the child, she was monitoring her comments so as not to cause alarm before she had all the relevant information and in a setting not designed to accommodate the mother's reaction.

CONCLUSION

Public opinion, now reinforced by law and the goals of the medical professions themselves, contributes to a general call for parent involvement. But what research there has been has focused on measuring outcomes in terms of children's development. Until now, as Merton has observed, there has been no analysis of the demands on professionals created by parent involvement. As Merton points out, in the absence of such studies, the behavior of medical professionals is "condemned or applauded . . . (or) morally judged, not systematically investigated" (1976:39).

We have suggested that a sociolinguistic analysis of actual interaction in a pediatric setting can furnish such investigation. We have demonstrated that preliminary analysis in this paradigm has shown the complexity of cognitive, social, and emotional demands on the pediatrician posed by parent involvement in the examination of the child. Other findings of our preliminary analysis suggest the direction for continued investigation: (a) overlapping, competing, and possibly conflicting frames operating for all participants and (b) the possibility of misunderstanding resulting from choice of phrasing, intonation, and other linguistic and paralinguistic cues that result from differing expectations in this setting as well as individual and social differences in conversational habits that arise in all interpersonal interactions.

The process of interaction in a pediatric setting is an instance of face-to-face interaction, subject to all the pitfalls and successes of that process, as well as an instance of a particular kind of event, structured by the requirements of participants and their expectations and associations. In our analysis, we have dealt with exemplary participants—a staff of professionals who are highly trained, compassionate, and sensitive to issues of parent and community involvement. They are not constrained by inordinate financial or time limitations and have at their disposal the superior facilities of the Georgetown Medical School and the Child Development Center. The parents are intelligent, articulate, and very concerned, and they provide for the child a financially and emotionally stable family. Our analysis turns up no deficiencies in the behavior of participants. We are engaged, rather, in uncovering processes inherent in the structure of the interaction in particular and communication in general. These are forces at work that can at times create problems in the best of all possible pediatric worlds.

REFERENCES CITED

BATESON, GREGORY
  1972 *Steps to an Ecology of Mind.* New York: Ballantine.
BRYAN, THORNTON E., ED.
  1977 *Academic Missions of Family Medicine.* Washington, D.C.: National Institute of Health. (U.S. Government Printing Office DHEW Publications No. (NIH) 77–1062).
BUCHER, RUE, AND JOAN G. STELLING
  1977 *Becoming Professional.* Beverly Hills, Calif.: Sage Publications.
CHAFE, WALLACE L.
  1977 Creativity in verbalization and its implications for the nature of stored knowledge. IN *Discourse Production and Comprehension,* Roy O. Freedle, Ed., pp. 41–55. Norwood, N.J.: Ablex.
CICOUREL, AARON V.
  1975 Discourse and text: Cognitive and linguistic processes in studies of social structure. *Versus: Quaderni de Studi Semotici* 12:33–84.
FABB, WES E.; MICHAEL W. HEFFERMAN; WILLIAM A. PHILLIPS; AND PETER STONE
  1976 *Focus on Learning in Family Practice,* Melbourne, Royal Australian College of General Practitioners, Family Medicine Programme.
FRAKE, CHARLES O.
  1977 Plying frames can be dangerous: Some reflections on methodology in cognitive anthropology. *The Quarterly Newsletter of the Institute for Comparative Human Cognition* 1:1–7.
GALLAGHER, EUGENE B., ED.
  1978 *The Doctor-Patient Relationship in the Changing Health Scene.* Washington, D.C.: U.S. Government Printing Office. (DHEW Publications No. (NIH) 78–183)

GOFFMAN, ERVING
  1959   *The Presentation of Self in Everyday Life*. Garden City, N.J.: Anchor.
  1974   *Frame Analysis*. New York: Harper & Row.
  1979   Footing. *Semiotica* 25:1–29. (Reprinted in his *Forms of Talk*, Philadelphia:
         University of Pennsylvania Press, 1981)
GREEN, JUDITH, AND CYNTHIA WALLAT
  1979   What is an instructional context? An exploratory analysis of conversational
         shifts across time. IN *Language, Children, and Society,* Olga K. Garnica and
         Martha L. King, Eds., pp. 159–188. New York: Pergamon.
  1981   Mapping instructional conversations: A sociolinguistic ethnography. IN *Eth-
         nography and Language in Educational Settings*, Judith Green and Cynthia
         Wallat, Eds., pp. 161–205. Norwood, N.J.: Ablex.
GUMPERZ, JOHN J.
  1972   Sociolinguists and communication in small groups. IN *Sociolinguistics*, B.
         Pride and Janet Holmes, Eds., pp. 203–224. Baltimore: Penguin.
  1977   Sociocultural knowledge in conversational inference. IN *Georgetown University
         Round Table on Languages and Linguistics 1977: Linguistics and Anthropology*,
         Muriel Saville-Troike, Ed., pp. 191–211. Washington, D.C.: Georgetown
         University Press.
  1982   *Discourse Strategies*. Cambridge: Cambridge University Press.
GUMPERZ, JOHN J., AND DEBORAH TANNEN
  1979   Individual and social differences in language use. IN *Individual Differences in
         Language Ability and Language Behavior*, Charles J. Fillmore, Daniel Kempler,
         and William S-Y. Wang, Eds., pp. 305–325. New York: Academic.
KLEINMAN, ARTHUR
  1980   *Patients and Healers in the Context of Culture*. Berkeley: University of
         California Press.
MERTON, ROBERT K.
  1976   *Sociological Ambivalence and Other Essays*. New York: The Free Press.
MINSKY, MARVIN
  1975   A framework for representing knowledge. IN *The Psychology of Computer
         Vision*, P.H. Winston, Ed., pp. 211–277. New York: McGraw-Hill.
NEWPORT, ELISSA L.; HENRY GLEITMAN; AND LILA R. GLEITMAN
  1977   Mother, I'd rather do it myself: Some effects and non-effects of maternal speech
         style. IN *Talking to Children: Language Input and Acquisition*, Catherine E.
         Snow and Charles A. Ferguson, Eds., pp. 109-149. New York: Cambridge
         University Press.
RUMELHART, DAVID E.
  1975   Notes on a schema for stories. IN *Representation and Understanding*, Daniel G.
         Bobrow and Allan M. Collins, Eds., pp. 211–236. New York: Academic.
SCHANK, ROGER C., AND ROBERT P. ABELSON
  1977   *Scripts, Plans, Goals, and Understanding: An Inquiry into Human Knowledge
         Structures*. Hillsdale, N.J.: Lawrence Erlbaum.
TANNEN, DEBORAH
  1979   What's in a frame? Surface evidence fo underlying expectations. IN *New
         Directions in Discourse Processing*, Roy O. Freedle, Ed., pp. 137–181.
         Norwood, N.J.: Ablex.

1983   *Conversational Style: Analyzing Talk Among Friends.* Norwood, N.J.: Ablex.
In press   Frames and schemas in sociolinguistic analysis of pediatric interaction. *Quaderni di Semantica.*
WALLAT, CYNTHIA, AND JUDITH GREEN
    1979   Social rules and communicative context in kindergarten. *Theory Into Practice* 18(4):275–284.
    1982   Construction of social norms by teacher and children: The first year in school. IN *Socialization for Children in a Changing Society*, Kathryn Borman, Ed., pp. 95–119. Hillsdale, N.J.: Lawrence Erlbaum.

3

Hearing Is Not Believing: Language and the Structure of Belief in Medical Communication*

Aaron V. Cicourel

Medical interviewing and history-taking provide us with a fairly self-contained social context for understanding complex interactions between personal beliefs, organizational role behavior, and how experiences and events are interpreted and summarized in bureaucratic settings. The doctor's abstract written summary enables us to link a prior local context of social interaction to a formal record. The way that doctor–patient discourse is transformed into a legal–medical text can tell us something about the way health care delivery occurs in formally organized settings. But doctor-patient interviews and history-taking also reflect larger societal patterns of information control and social stratification.

The doctor and patient, as speakers and listeners, must be able to create and construct coherence with and from each other's speech. Language use becomes central to the identification of fragments of discourse or text that contain uniform

---

* This is a revised and expanded version of a paper presented at the 6th World Congress of the International Association of Applied Linguistics, Lund, Sweden, 1981, and published in the proceedings: *Studia Linguistica* 35, 1981. The medical information used was obtained as part of a larger study of a gynecological oncology clinic. I am grateful to Dr. Sue Fisher, a former student, for her help in obtaining the interview materials. The analysis of these interviews and my own interview with the patient are entirely my responsibility. I am grateful to Dr. "B" for his generous help.

references, or the way a referent is expressed in one part of a long dialogue and then suspended, but subsequently resumed (Grimes 1981; Jones 1977; Reichman 1978).

When a physician sees a patient, he or she may have some general idea of what seems to be bothering the patient. If the patient has been referred by another doctor to a specialist, then the specialist begins to hypothesize immediately about possible alternatives. The hypotheses will include several levels of conceptualization, including content about basic science, basic clinical science, and clinical experiences, and will interact with the physician's general but not expert knowledge about sociocultural and psychological issues. The physician's changing knowledge base guides the kinds of questions asked.

In this chapter, I use a single case of a patient with seemingly parallel but conflicting beliefs about her diagnosis and treatment and the cause of her illness. The discussion of these beliefs illustrates theoretical and methodological issues associated with the way we make inferences about referential uniformity, conformity, content, and coherence in different parts of discourse or textual materials.

The medical interview is of value to the social or behavioral scientist interested in medical communication because it highlights conditions that exist in the study of discourse but that are not always addressed. For example, the patient cannot always remember details or the sequence of events. The patient may mislead the interviewer by the description he or she gives. The physician may interrupt the patient frequently to pursue a given topic while being told extraneous and seemingly irrelevant information, all the while seeking to remember if each answer is adequate and if a sequence of events is clear. The physician and social or behavioral scientist face similar problems: how to make visible those aspects of discourse and textual materials that seem to be intended, implied, or misleading. The doctor and patient must also maintain aspects of politeness, interest, and expertise.

Memory and language limitations of the patient and the doctor are unavoidable aspects of the study of discourse. The knowledge base or beliefs of the patient can be a significant limitation for answering the physician's questions, just as the doctor's limited knowledge of sociocultural and psychological issues can lead to a failure to recognize nonmedical problems that affect the illness. These problems are sometimes ignored when we code interview or textual materials only for their content while being indifferent to memory and language limitations inherent in creating and sustaining or changing beliefs, or summarizing complex experiences and events.

The medical history enables us to examine a text that is traceable to previous social interaction. In this way the medical history affords us a rare glimpse at some of the reasoning processes and aspects of the knowledge base of those who contributed to the content and form of a text and how beliefs are linked to language use, emotions and feelings, and reasoning in complex sociocultural environments. This chapter examines contrast between a notion of hypothesis-testing we would attribute to the doctor and patient and the notion of beliefs as reverberating or semiclosed systems in which reasoning, feelings, emotions, and value-laden goals and ideas can be resistant to change.

We can simplify the contrast by reference to two idealized notions. The first refers to a comprehensive process that is analogous to hypothesis testing, evaluation of goodness of fit, and parameter estimation, where the subject must learn to integrate different sources into hierarchically organized schemata so as to be successful at problem-solving tasks (Rumelhart n.d.). This view of comprehension is a form of literacy we learn in school, but it begins with the socialization process. The ideal of beliefs that can resist change begins with a preschool oral literacy socialization period that is not displaced by but interacts with the formal literacy learned in school. The idea of a legal-rational bureaucracy epitomizes the exercise of efficient problem-solving, while the ideal of a close-knit community dominated by common-sense reasoning or concrete thinking and beliefs that resist modification is often associated with a notion of tradition-oriented forms of social organization.

The medical interview and history reflect aspects of these two forms of literacy: The physician recodes the often ambiguous, rambling interview language into abstract categories that facilitate and depict efficient problem-solving; patients use a particular or restricted semantic domain to represent the beliefs they employ and create about their illness. These beliefs often run counter to the doctor's views.

COMPARING THE DOCTOR'S PROGRESS NOTES
WITH THE INTERVIEW

I use a case of a patient referred to a gynecological clinic of a teaching hospital to illustrate the recoding process used by the physician in his attempt to understand the patient's illness. Although this case history is not typical of the many cases I have observed, the confusions and misunderstandings that occurred are common in the delivery of health care, even if the details are not as dramatic as in the case discussed.

The doctor's progress notes (or brief history) are contained in Figure 1. The information on the patient's age, weight, and blood pressure were not part of the interview but were taken by the nurse before the patient was seen by the physician. The doctor's notes (lines 2–4, Figure 1) reveal that the patient has been a widow for nine months and is depressed. She had seen an internist four months earlier because of vulva irritation and was started on 1.25 mg. of Premarin (EST or estrogen), which she stopped because of breast soreness.

Wt: 146 B/P 112/64 3/21/77: Age 62   1
Widowed 9 mos. - depressed. Saw internist 4 mos. ago because of vulva   2
irritation - started 1.25 mg. *Premarin* → breast soreness, so stopped EST   3
On estrogen for 7-8 yrs. up to 4 yrs. ago. 1.25 mg. then 0.625 mg. at Phipps'   4
Clinic - Mammogram - fibrosis (1971) - reduced dose of *Premarin*.   5
General: (1) Large cyst L kidney known for many years.   6
Has had 2 kidney stones - age 21 & age 59 - passed spontaneously,   7
Has "kidney infections" of 2-3 years,   8
(2) Acute glaucoma- surgery 12/75 at UCLA (R eye) - needs for both eyes,   9
2 children (ages 27-son, 23-daughter)   10
Surgery: Skull fx age 10, Appendectomy age 17, T&A age 8-9   11
PH: Diphtheria age 5   12
Systems Review: D arrhythmia recently - Takes Inderal p & n almost every   13
night.   14

FIGURE 1   Doctor's Written Progress Notes

Medical Interview (Segment 1)
Each dot = 1 second pause

DOCTOR:	What can I do for you?	1
PATIENT:	Well, uh, I was concerned about, uh...last	2
	summer, I guess, I-I was having a problem in the	3
	uh...uh, I guess w-what you call the bulk of	4
	the outer uh part of the organ. There's like,	5
	paper thin uh cuts, just a little bleeding. And	6
	finally when I went to have my checkup, which	8
	was uh...about 3 months ago, my internist	9
	asked me if I'd had a paps, test and I hadn't	10
	so he took one and he said uh my uterus was	11
	kind of spongy, and also I had uh, very low,	12
	I was very low in hormones, and he-uh-the	13
	estrogen	14
DOCTOR:	mh	15
PATIENT:	the count was so low he said I didn't get it so he	16
	put me on uh...oh, uh on the estrogen pills.	18
	Now, about four years ago when I went through	19
	Phipps, uh, they had cut me down to a half	20
	and I still was getting alot of uh swel-swelling	21
	and soreness in my breasts and they took a	22
	mameograph that time and they told me to get	23
	one about every six months, but, I sort of took	24
	myself off the estrogen and found that I didn't	25
	have any of that feeling, so I've been off of it,	26
	and uh that's what-I didn't realize when first	27
	my husband died nine months ago, but still,	28
	anybody'd just look at me and you know I'd	29

just be...be uh the bereavement. I don't   30
know. I uh never used to be like that...   31

I tried to guess the doctor's inferences about the patient's remarks by comparing the progress notes with the original interview material. The opening line of the medical interview is a question by the doctor or a "request" for the information that can be used to help the patient. We assume the patient is being invited to supply information that will clarify the kind of help the doctor can provide. Knowing that a physician is asking the question enables us to view the doctor's opening remark as a routine way of eliciting information from the patient. Thus, knowledge about the organizational or bureaucratic setting enables us to process considerable information in a matter-of-fact way.

The physician's progress notes (which were handwritten at the time of the interview) in Figure 1 (line 2) refer to the patient as "widowed 9 months - depressed." Lines 27–31 of the medical interview (transcript above) provide information about the husband's death nine months earlier and also give indirect information that could be linked to the physician's inference that the patient was depressed. The patient remarks, "I didn't realize when first my husband died nine months ago, but still, anybody's just look at me and you know I'd be...be uh the bereavement. I don't know. I uh never used to be like that..." This implies that perhaps there is a link between her present condition and her husband's death: She has felt like a different person since her husband's death. Her manner of talking could be perceived as emotional and confused. But the patient's thinking and her occasional emotional displays should not be viewed as an indication that she is disturbed or impaired in her ability to conduct daily affairs and meet serious obligations.

The progress notes reflect several key topics and state that the patient saw an internist four months earlier because of vulva irritation. The patient mentions seeing her internist "about 3 months ago" instead of the doctor's recording of "4 mos." The physician's reference to "vulva irritation" summarizes the patient's problem of "the bulk of the outer uh part of the organ. There's like, paper thin cuts, just a little bleeding." The patient elaborates in lines 8–18: She says "finally when I went to have my checkup," as if to say that the checkup was to confirm the problem. The confirmation of a problem is suggested by noting that the internist had asked if she had a Pap smear test. The results of the test are not reported but there is a reference to the patient's uterus being "kind of spongy" and her being "low in hormones."

The doctor's progress notes (Figure 1, lines 2–3) state that 1.25 mg. of Premarin was started four months earlier by an internist, but we do not know if this may have been a result of (Medical Interview, lines 12–18) the patient's uterus being "kind of spongy" or her being "low in hormones" or the vulva irritation. The doctor's notes (lines 2–3) imply that 1.25 mg. of Premarin was started four months earlier and then stopped because of breast soreness.

The patient (lines 19–26) refers to a visit to Phipps (clinic) four years earlier when, she states, an unknown dosage of estrogen was reduced to one-half. She also reports taking herself off the estrogen because of "...swel-swelling and soreness in my breasts..." The doctor's subsequent notes and the patient's remarks indicate she was on estrogen during the visit to the clinic four years earlier.

Another physician reading the progress notes could infer that the internist had prescribed 1.25 mg. of Premarin four months before the present visit and that the patient had terminated the treatment because of swelling and sore breasts. The patient's narrative up to this point describes two different time periods.

As the interview continues (lines 32–38) the patient mentions four time periods; 11 to 12 years ago, 4 years ago, the previous summer, and 3 months before the present interview. The physician's progress notes (lines 4–5), Figure 1) state that the patient began taking estrogen "for 7–8 yrs. up to 4 yrs. ago." The notes imply that the dosage was initially at 1.25 g. and then reduced to 0.625 mg., or half dosage. The doctor picks up on the visit to Phipps Clinic four years ago (lines 32–34, Medical Interview, Segment 2) to ask about the length of time the patient had been taking hormones.

Medical Interview (Segment 2)

DOCTOR:	Now, four yrs. ago when you were taking the	32
	hormones, uh...you were going to Phipps	33
	Clinic, how long did you take the hormones	34
	before-I mean, had you taken them for a	35
	number ⌈of years?	36
PATIENT:	⌊I had been taking them.	37
	Yes, probably about...8, 7-8 years...	38
DOCTOR:	And that was the purple one?	39
PATIENT:	That was the yellow one to start with, and then	40
	the purple one when they cut me down.	41
DOCTOR:	Do you know whi-which hormone you were taking?	42
PATIENT:	So I (?) the yellow one, the orange,	43
	yellow one.	44
DOCTOR:	Have you ever taken a different dose from that?	45
PATIENT:	Well, uh, at Phipps they had uh, subscribed	46
	half that dose, the little brown one I believe. .	47
	uh . but as I say, I don ⌈'t...	48
DOCTOR:	⌊But that still caused	49
	breast probl ⌈ems, too, hmm?	50
PATIENT:	⌊Hmm-hm. I mean, I just stopped	51
	taking them and I hadn't been back for a test	52
	or anything, but my breasts are back to normal	53
	and I q-quit those things...	54

The patient's responses (lines 40–41, 43–44, and 46–48) to the physician's questions (lines 39, 42, and 45,) refer to the color of the pills as a means of identifying the dosage. Yellow seems to be associated with 1.25 mg. of Premarin, while purple or brown seems to represent half of this dosage. The same conclusion is reached and noted in Segment 1 of the interview transcript; the patient took herself off the estrogen four years earlier because of their negative affect on her breasts.

The physician's reconstruction of the patient's remarks is also evident in the way the mammogram is noted in line 5 of the medical history notes, although the patient mentioned this point earlier in line 23. The notation of "fibrosis (1971)" (line 5, Figure 1) seems to be an inference that an examination of the breasts indicated a fibrous condition and hence the reason for the mammogram. But the date is confusing because the patient stated the mammogram was taken four years earlier at Phipps Clinic, making the year 1973, not 1971.

The physician notes the reduced dosage of Premarin in lines 4-5 of the medical history progress notes, but the patient had already given this information earlier (lines 19–24).

The physician makes many inferences about medical conditions based on particular lexical items and phrases in the patient's indirect remarks. For example, there is a reference to the patient being depressed, establishing the dosage of the Premarin by trying to clarify the color of the estrogen pill taken, and perhaps we can assume that a mammogram had been ordered because of the fibrous condition of the patient's breasts. But the patient's rambling and sometimes emotionally confused style of speaking also leads to errors of fact; it was difficult for the physician to establish certain facts and to clarify ambiguous statements by the patient as when dates are not recorded as stated by the patient or events are transposed because of contradictory dates.

Reports of patient dissatisfaction with how physicians elicit information and ignore the patient's perspective are common in daily discussions by lay persons and are also openly discussed in medical school classes and in the literature on doctor–patient communication. When a physician pursues what he or she believes are good guesses about what occurred or is happening to the patient, many symptoms are ignored, some are misunderstood, and others become reinterpreted to fit the doctor's prior and emergent knowledge base or schemata. Some of the ignored or misunderstood or reinterpreted information may (as in the present case) be reexamined and corrected during subsequent visits and because of a physical examination and laboratory tests. The physician's perspective may be at variance with what the patient thinks is happening.

The brief review of the medical history and medical interview discussed thus far does reveal a few differences in the physician's and patient's attempts to understand past events. The language they use reflects the two forms of literacy alluded to earlier: the physician recodes the patient's often ambiguous rambling, and somewhat emotional language into fairly abstract categories; the patient's unclear or particular or concrete terms are converted into crisp and explicit medical terminology, interpretations, and factual statements. The two forms of literacy imply modes of thinking that are different.

The reference to two forms of literacy as reflected in the surface forms of language, paralinguistic, and nonverbal displays that occur during social interaction can be described as different linguistic registers. (Tannen and Wallat 1982 and this volume). Tannen and Wallat note how a pediatrician can address three audiences with different linguistics registers. The three codes used by a pediatrician addressing a training audience in pediatrics, a mother, and the mother's child each have their own particular intonation, voice quality, content, and lexical and syntactic structures. The use of different registers presumes that each listener may be capable of comprehending one or more specific domains of knowledge, while at the same time revealing the pediatrician's professional competence, and the pursuit of different goals for each audience. The professional-bureaucratic setting, therefore, makes different and specific demands on the physician's and patient's information processing abilities and also constrains the kinds of responses that can be expressed.

A medical interview can touch on many topics, and several of them can be associated with disturbing or emotionally charged conditions. The physician must, therefore, be sensitive to a social context that can change momentarily, depending on how the doctor seeks to pursue and control the interview and the kinds of topics introduced by both participants.

BELIEFS ABOUT ILLNESS AS DEPICTED IN THE PATIENT'S NARRATIVE ACCOUNTS

The patient's doubts about the physician's diagnosis and beliefs about her illness were expressed to the doctor, and they were still present 16 months after her initial visit. Although the patient was told that laboratory tests confirmed that she required an operation to remove a cancerous uterus, she was convinced that her illness was linked to visits to her husband while he was dying of cancer of the pancreas some two years earlier. This belief can also be linked to information from the mass media, how the physician discussed her illness with her, and an impersonal bureaucratic procedure used by the hospital to inform patients about the results of a Pap smear test. My discussion is based on rather lengthy tape-recorded information. To save time and space, I will paraphrase the extensive narrative materials but will provide two brief portions of the transcript.

My interview with the patient provided an opportunity to reconstruct a set of beliefs about her illness. We do not know if the beliefs reported to me during our exchange 16 months after her initial visit to the gynecologist existed at the time of her original interview with the physician, but she did express many doubts to the doctor about the accuracy of the diagnosis and the necessity of the operation. The first interview did not provide an occasion for the patient to speak about her husband's illness and how it might be connected to her problems. When she expressed doubts about her illness during subsequent visits to the gynecologist, the doctor made several attempts to explain the nature of her illness. During our interview 16 months after the initial visit, the patient complained about the way the doctor related to patients, yet she was quite insistent that he perform the surgery and expressed her complete confidence in the gynecologist's medical competence. She always kept her appointments and pursued a course of treatment that lasted several years with the gynecologist.

The belief that she did not have cancer and that the operation may have been performed on the wrong person seems to have existed in parallel (or perhaps in partial interaction) with the belief that she and her children had contracted cancer from a "contagious" husband who had died of cancer nine months before her first visit to the gynecologist.

Patient's Reconstruction 16 months after Initial Interview
Each dot = 1 second pause

PATIENT:	I had two thoughts, was this somebody else's	1
	letter stuck in my envelope, or uh...or was	2
	that normal and somebody in, along the line	3
	somewhere said it wasn't normal, and I, as	4
	I say, then I, I just didn't know what to	5
	think. When you get, open up a letter like	6
	that...see...it's a shock particularly I	7
	think I hadn't gotten over the shock of my	8
	husband's death yet and all this kep, came	9
	upon me.	10
RESEARCHER:	Okay...okay...and you did speak to	11
	the doctor....	12
PATIENT:	Apparently he said something to them, so	13
	I'm getting a date on it now but still as you	14
	see I don't have a name on it.	15
RESEARCHER:	Yeah.	16
PATIENT:	What's so hard about typing in a name?	17
	I think this is an important procedure that	18
	we do these Pap tests and I think	19
RESEARCHER:	yes	20
PATIENT:	they should be	21
RESEARCHER:	I agree	22
PATIENT:	covered well instead of just haphazardly.	23

The interview I conducted 16 months after the patient's first visit to the gynecologist began with a surprise. She confronted me with a report from the hospital laboratory that had arrived when the patient was in the hospital recovering from surgery. There was no date on the letter and only a stamped signature of the gynecologist. The envelope was dated May 3, 1977. The patient's remarks in the transcript indicate that she assumed that perhaps a mistake had been made. Her remarks (lines 1–5) are not clear (first she stated that someone's letter had gotten into her envelope), but we could infer that the patient was also thinking that perhaps her Pap test was normal "and somebody in, along the line somewhere said it wasn't normal." The patient seems to have assumed that there had been a bureaucratic mistake, and this led her to question the original diagnosis and the subsequent operation.

The letter with the report of a "normal" Pap smear test was labeled as a "shock" by the patient and reminded her of the "shock of my husband's death." When the patient states (lines 9–10), "and all this kep, came upon me," we can infer that the letter with the test results brought forth previous doubts about her illness, the justification for surgery, and renewed thoughts about her husband's death. The interview continues with an exchange over the way the patient came to choose her physician and remarks about why she wanted private hospitalization instead of gong to a military hospital.

The patient then began talking (lines 24–34) about the Pap smear test done during her first visit to the gynecologist and then being told over the telephone that she had cancer. The implication here is that the discovery of her cancer seemed not to be important because she was still so upset over her husband's death.

Patient's Reconstruction 16 months after Initial Interview (cont'd)

PATIENT:	. . . But, uh, Dr. B. gave me the examination,	24
	and took this Pap test and then I don't	25
	remember, it wasn't very long after he called	26
	me and he, on the phone, and he said	27
	that . . . uhm . . . uhm . we found cancer	28
	cells. Or cancer, cancer cells, I don't	29
	remember just how he said it, and of course	30
	I was, as I say, still in shock from my	31
	husband's death. It didn't phase me that I	32
	had cancer at the time. It didn't, I, it didn't	33
	register. I just asked him what comes next.	34
	But, he mentioned prior to this, that if there	35
	was anything, and I don't know why, we were	36
	talking about if there was anything. This,	37
	what, as Dr. B. brought up. I stopped to	38
	think why was that brought up; I can't	39
	remember, but, uh, that he would then take	40
	a D and C. But when, when he called me,	41
	he said there would be no need for a D and	42
	C, that there was definitely cancer. . . . and	43
	so he would take a biopsy . . . and he took a	44

	biopsy...and told me that there was. I	45
	guess, and uh, as I say, I got the two kind of	46
	mixed up because, uh, he called me and asked	47
	me to come in for a biopsy and (not?) do	48
	a D and C, and then he said there was no	49
	need to do a D and C. That there was, that	50
	it was definite. So I went to see my intern,	51
	internist, and he said well....uh...what	52
	did he say? He said something about, he said	53
	he must have really hit a particular spot	54
	where it started because, I guess, according	55
	to him, and he had taken a Pap test prior	56
	to that about four or five months before that.	57
	An then, uh, I think it was uh, probably a	58
	Class 2 or something and I had a little	59
	infection that he was treating but, uh...I	60
	was uh...sort of going fairly early so just to	61
	double check and talking to this widow, she	62
	thought so much of Dr. B. that she, she	63
	said go see him you'll feel better if you do.	64
	But, uhm, then reading that letter I thought	65
	well, something got mixed up there. Maybe	66
	somebody is walking around with cancer	67
	and I didn't have it. I, all this was going	68
	through my mind, you know...	69
RESEARCHER:	All right, but that was going through your	70
	mind after you came out of the hospital in	71
	terms of the letter. . is that right?	72
PATIENT:	Well, uh...my friend said, why don't	73
	you double check with another doctor.	74
RESEARCHER:	Oh, I see.	75
PATIENT:	And I said, I'm just so mixed up now, I'm,	76
	I, I said.... if I need surgery, I would	77
	want Dr. B. to do that (?), I've heard he's	78
	such a good surgeon. So, even my internist	79
	said that he's probably done 2,000 of them	80
	so don't worry about your surgery. You'll	81
	be all right (laughs). So, I got that....	82
	part, but, I, I, no, I kind'a went into it not	83
	sure that I had cancer.	84

The patient's remarks are difficult to interpret. In lines 35–38 she states, "But, he [the gynecologist] mentioned prior to this, that if there was anything, and I don't know why, we were talking about if there was anything. This, what, as Dr. B brought up." The "prior to this" could have been an attempt to reference the physician's concluding remarks of the first interview in which he told the patient, "well...from uh...uh standpoint of uh, a gynecologist, I think everything is, is really pretty good." But there is no mention in the first interview of the D & C (dilation and curettage of the uterine cervix) that the patient mentions in line 41 of this segment. The patient may have thought that the D & C and the letter from the hospital meant that she had a fairly benign condition. Between 21 March 1977, the date of the first visit, and 25 March 1977, the date of the second visit, the physician had called the patient and told her that her Pap smear was abnormal and that she was to come to the clinic for biopsies. The physician also implied that if the biopsies were negative, she might also come in the following week for a D & C.

The patient confuses two telephone calls from the physician and several visits with the physician (lines 41–50). During the 25 March 1977 visit with the physician the patient was reminded of the doctor's telephone call and the possible need for a D & C. At the same visit, the physician performed the biopsies. On 28 March 1977, the physician entered a note in the patient's chart and confirmed (as a result of biopsy findings) an adenocarcinoma suggested earlier by the Pap smear. He called the patient and explained that the D & C would not be necessary and she should come in for a visit as soon as possible. The patient returned on 30 March 1977 and was again told about the results of the biopsies and that a D & C was not necessary. The physician repeated many of the questions asked during the first interview, including a review of previous estrogen taken and the sequence of steps that resulted in her coming to the gynecologist.

The patient did not remember the sequence of events clearly. She confused the first interview and the first telephone conversation with a second and third interview and a second telephone conversation. The information she received from the first interview suggested that there was nothing serious involved. The abnormal Pap smear results based on the first interview led to a call by the physician telling the patient that a D & C might still be in order while also stating that biopsies should be performed. The patient continued to maintain her belief that her condition was not serious, even after a second visit to the physician on 25 March 1977 when the biopsies were performed. The doctor's second telephone call on 28 March 1977 and interview with the patient on 30 March 1977 failed to convince her that the diagnosis of cancer was the result of appropriate medical practice. The patient was still confused in July 1978 when I interviewed her at home (lines 24–50).

The remarks in the second part of the reconstruction suggest a series of confusions that began with the initial interview and physical examination. The gist of the confusion is an apparent discrepancy between the physician's remarks of the seemingly routine nature of her condition and the progressively serious consequences that led to the operation for the removal of her uterus. The confusion is evident in the remainder of this segment when the patient retells how she went to see her internist (lines 51–60) to tell him the results of the biopsies. The implication is that she may have returned to the internist because she doubted the validity of the gynecologist's tests because the internist had told her previously that an earlier Pap smear was "probably a Class 2 or something and I had a little infection that he was treating but..." (lines 58–60).

The patient had made her original appointment to see the gynecologist because she wanted a specialist to give her a second opinion, "just to double check" what the internist had told her. The internist presumably believed that the biopsy done by the gynecologist was taken at precisely the right place (perhaps because of luck as we read the patient's accounting of things), as if telling the patient how to interpret the gynecologist's diagnosis.

In lines 58–69, the patient briefly indicates how she was looking for a second opinion to the internist's treatment of her infection, and then returns to the letter she received about the normal Pap smear test after returning from the hospital. Her remarks (see also lines 81–84) again imply that perhaps there had been a mistake, that she did not have cancer and that someone else does have cancer who does not know it. There is an implication that the biopsies were also incorrect.

The details of this case are lengthy, and I only want to sustain the present discussion long enough to give some closure to the nature of the patient's beliefs about her illness.

When I asked the patient what she tells people who ask about her illness, she was able to articulate an answer indicating that she had cancer in the lining of her uterus. She added that she tells this to people with some doubt "because there's that 'if' in my mind."

The patient's doubts about her illness seem clear. Yet she was able to provide me with considerable medical information many months after her surgery. This information about her condition was obtained from the gynecologist and contradicts her repeated remarks that the doctor had not provided her with adequate explanations about the necessity of the operation and what was to be done during surgery. The patient did not understand the significance of the dilation and curettage procedure. She interpreted the mention of it to mean that something fairly routine was to be done if all the tests proved negative. The patient seems unaware of the diagnostic importance of a D & C, if performed, for confirming problems and not simply a procedure that implies a fairly benign conclusion to her gynecological troubles.

The patient seems to reject the test results, reminding the interviewer of the way her lab tests are reported by the hospital. The patient's selective use of information contrasts sharply with the fact that she was aware of many of the factual explanations and data given to her by the physician. Throughout my contact with her, the patient displays a reverberating or semiclosed belief system that acknowledges the existence of information that another observer (the physician, the researcher) can view as contradictory but that the patient sees as consistent or correct. The patient's own narrative remarks reveal an awareness of knowledge or information we interpret as contradictory. The hypothesis testing that occurs, if this is an appropriate way to talk here, seems to have as its goal the maintenance of beliefs that remain immune to information or knowledge that contradict them or that would force significant changes in them.

The patient's suspicion about her own cancer must be contrasted with her views of cancer in general and her belief that "maybe, the cancer is contagious and nobody warned us, and my, me dear son, he always kissed his dad on the forehead and, un my uh daughter did too, and you know that last three weeks or so, they really perspire and I wonder if the germs don't come out with the perspiration." The fear is that perhaps the entire family had contracted cancer from the husband because of the possibility that pancreatic cancer is contagious. There is another reference to the possibility that leukemia is also contagious.

The patient suggested that her son's current urological illness may be linked to her husband's cancer. The patient also stated the daughter had a problem, and noted elsewhere in the interview that the daughter had "a lump" on her neck. The patient's belief about cancer being contagious, therefore, combines several family conditions that lend coherence to her account.

It is difficult to pinpoint the origin of the patient's beliefs about cancer. The reconstructions that are elicited in my interview with the patient 16 months after her initial interview with the gynecologist are based on the assumption that her internist did not seem concerned with the results of the Pap smear test he ordered, treating her problem as a local infection. From the patient's viewpoint, a diagnosis of endometrial cancer, despite the biopsies, was perhaps difficult to understand because she thought the gynecologist, after the initial interview, had mentioned that things appeared normal. The patient seemed to confuse the two telephone calls made by the physician. In the first call, a D & C was mentioned as an option; in the second call, a D & C was ruled out because the biopsies confirmed the presence of cancer.

The patient viewed the bureaucratic practice followed by the hospital at the time of the patient's visits—sending test results without the patient's name on the letter itself—as support for her belief that perhaps she did not have cancer (having received a normal report) and that the wrong person had received the operation. The patient also thought that the nature of her illness had not been explained adequately. But, this was contrary to the facts.

The hospital records and our tape-recorded sessions of several physician-patient interviews indicated that the doctor had explained why the D & C would not be necessary. The physician also explained the nature of the patient's illness. The doctor also discussed the patient's illness with her family. He was well aware of the discrepancy between the patient's views of her illness and his own views. She believed he had not pursued the matter. What is unclear is why the patient sought a second opinion from the gynecologist but then seemed not to accept it emotionally, despite following his instructions for the operation. Instead, she seems to have linked what she thought was benign diagnosis by the internist to her claim that the gynecologist mentioned the option of a D & C.

We could speculate that the patient had acquired the belief about cancer being contagious during her husband's illness, and that this motivated her to seek a second opinion, despite the internist's diagnosis that her condition was benign. The patient's belief system seems to contain two independent and parallel focuses. On the one hand, she believes cancer is contagious and that she and her children probably contracted the disease from her husband. On the other hand, she seems to have linked the internist's benign diagnosis to the gynecologist's remark at the close of the initial interview and physical examination that she seemed to be in good condition, with her claim that the gynecologist had told her of an option of a D & C, and a receipt of a normal Pap smear report from hospital upon returning home from surgery. These latter conditions and her contention that the gynecologist failed to explain her illness and the operation led her to the conclusion that she did not have cancer and that perhaps the wrong person had received the operation and treatment.

CONCLUSION

Belief systems can be described as sets of schemata or mental models about the nature of the events, objects, or situations we confront in our everyday lives that do not always interact with one another to form clearly integrated and hierarchically structured higher level abstractions or predications that are updated as new or contradictory information is received. A selective use of information seems to occur, despite the possible existence, in other domains of knowledge, of contradictory or inconsistent information. People often use these mental models to understand their everyday experiences and the complicated factual information that must be processed when formal modes of communication and content are encountered. We need to understand the extent to which beliefs can resist new or contradictory information and how the thinking employed contrasts with thought processes used in problem-solving tasks where consistency and coherence are said to be central aspects of a decision.

In the medical case, the perceived or estimated possible outcomes or consequences of an operation are not clear and usually differ for the patient and physician. Professional-bureaucratic settings refer to goals, intentions, procedures, and possible consequences in a language and mode of thought that are not easily understood by patients or clients. The patient faces a decision problem, and may have a definite preference; but the professional-bureaucratic context can influence the preference by the way the problem is framed (Tversky and Kahneman 1981). Patients may or may not be aware of alternative frames and their possible effect on the options perceived to be open to them. Inconsistencies may not be perceived, and this can lead to routine misunderstanding between professional or technical personnel and the patient. The values, beliefs, habits, and personal characteristics of the patient as decision maker may not be known to the professional; or only become partially known during the course of several encounters over a considerable period of time.

The patient's beliefs about cancer and her illness in the case discussed here display particular forms of speech and reflexive or self-conscious thoughts about her experiences and perceived factual information. But these beliefs do not seem to be integrated vis-à-vis contradictions that we can perceive as researchers, and the beliefs do not seem driven by an executive control system that continually integrates incoming information across existing schemata to form hierarchies of clearly defined domains of knowledge. Instead, the integration of information and the resolution of conflicting data seem to occur within parallel belief structures or schemata, despite several attempts by the physician to correct apparent misconceptions about the significance of a Pap smear test, a D & C, and the findings of biopsies.

We have a contrast between the patient's beliefs about illness and its causes, and the formal discussions presented by the physician. The cultural conceptions making up the patient's belief systems interact with and incorporate the factual knowledge presented by the physician.

The contrast between the patient's and the physician's knowledge can be clarified by extending D'Andrade's (1981) notions of abstraction by recoding and content based abstractions. D'Andrade discusses the difference between a computer program that requires a high degree of precision, an exact and unambiguous specification of the steps that must be taken to complete a task, and humans who often describe how to do a task incompletely and ambiguously.

In the case of a computer program, what is being accomplished does not have to be stated clearly or represented in the program, while humans often refer to what is to be accomplished in detail. The key difference between what is done to program a computer and the way humans are taught to do something is that computers usually involve abstraction by recoding into a formal system at every level, while humans normally learn in interactional settings where there is group or cultural guidance. Human problem-solving is characterized as highly local and content-specific, while computers follow global and formal strategies. Humans usually code information within a particular semantic domain, but they can also learn to recode a problem into a different symbol system.

The notion of abstraction by recoding can involve a market transaction recoded into a formal symbol system like algebra. But we can also refer to situations in which a person's legal, medical, tax, or insurance problem is recoded into a professional or bureaucratic symbol system. The professional-bureaucratic setting tends to follow, at least officially, an abstraction by recoding principle when dealing with patients or clients. The patient or client primarily employs a content-based abstraction strategy when interacting within a professional–bureaucratic organizational setting. This content-based abstraction principle invariably includes feelings and emotions professionals seek to minimize when they interact with patients and clients. The physician's medical history reflects the abstraction-by-recoding strategy inherent in the way technical-legal documents are written for professional-bureaucratic communication and record keeping.

The patient is exposed to mental models based on abstraction processes that emphasize a repertoire of patterns or configurations that can be applied to a wide number of situations. D'Andrade (1981) notes that these patterns are coded within the particular semantic domain at hand or content-based abstraction. But the physician is accustomed to recoding the patient's speech acts into a different symbol system that employs formal language abstraction and an external memory like dictionaries for medical terms, textbooks, laboratory reports, and X rays. These two forms of literacy are often found in their more idealized forms in casual discourse and in computer programs that try to simulate real-world human processes and objects. In everyday circumstances, the two forms of literacy interact, and one is favored over the other according to their implementation by persons assuming particular social roles in various organizational or institutional settings.

The patient finds it difficult to follow the physician's language and often tacit or even explicitly specified symbolic recoding. The patient's literacy or rationality, even if he or she is highly educated, is no match for the physician's language and external memory system, a system that is constantly being updated if the doctor is able to keep up with new developments in medicine.

Whenever we must confront formal bureaucratic procedures, we must face persons who have become expert in recoding information into different symbol systems. Our dealings with physicians, lawyers, dentists, accountants, or other professionals or technicians often means interacting with someone under circumstances where there is an inequality of power. We must often rely on forms of reasoning and emotion that interact or blend into one another and that seem to be orthogonal to the recoding operations that formal bureaucratic faces and procedures force us to confront.

In this chapter, I have briefly illustrated the bureaucratic recoding operations of the physician by reference to the way the progress notes summarize the actual medical interview. This recoding seldom makes visible the patient's perspective. Yet the doctor may be aware, as in the present case, of the patient's views about her illness. The postoperative interview with the patient months later illustrates her views and beliefs about the illness. A brief analysis of the research materials suggests that the notion of two forms of literacy can help us clarify the way cognition and language use are central to our understanding of the social structure of health care delivery, especially if we recognize the important role played by the organizational setting.

A common consequence of asymmetrical communicative power is misunderstanding. The professional-bureaucratic setting creates informational constraints and resources for the doctor, but tends to weaken the patient's communicational capabilities. When a person believes their ability to express their views, feelings, and emotions is constrained by the organizational setting, they are likely to generate doubts about what they are told, despite a desire to adhere to the trust that is presumed to be routinely attached to doctor–patient communication. The patient may harbor doubts about the doctor's assessment of his or her condition yet continue to return for visits and follow a course of treatment. Physicians may worry that the patient will take themselves off a course of treatment, not continue to take prescribed medication, and perhaps not return for routine visits or call when specific symptoms appear. The socially organized context of doctor–patient communication, therefore, provides us with a microcosm of the kinds of misunderstanding that is inherent in complex societies where persons must rely on different uses of literacy to comprehend and deal with different forms of technology that can affect their lives.

REFERENCES CITED

D'ANDRADE, ROY G.
  1981   The cultural part of cognition. *Cognitive Science* 5:179–195.
GRIMES, J. E.
  1980   Context structure patterns. IN Nobel Symposium on text processing. Stockholm: in press.
JONES, L. K.
  1977   *Theme in English Expository Discourse*. Lake Bluff, Ill.: Jupiter Press.
REICHMAN, R.
  1978   Conversational coherency. *Cognitive Science* 2(4):283–327.
RUMELHART, DAVID E.
  n.d.   Understanding Understanding. Ms.
TANNEN, DEBORAH, AND CYNTHIA WALLAT
  1982   A sociolinguistic analysis of multiple demands on the pediatrician in doctor/mother/child interaction. IN *Linguistics and the Professions*, R. J. Di Pietro, Ed. Norwood, N.J.: Ablex.
  1983   Doctor/mother/child communication: Linguistic analysis of a pediatric interaction. IN *The Social Organization of Doctor–Patient Communication*, Sue Fisher and Alexandra Dundas Todd, Eds., pp. 203–219. Washington, D.C.: The Center for Applied Linguistics.
TVERSKY, A., AND D. KAHNEMAN
  1981   The framing of decisions and the psychology of choice. *Science* 211:453–458.

Part II

THE PRODUCTION OF DOCTOR–PATIENT COMMUNICATION

A Social Accomplishment

4

The Laying on of Hands: Aspects of the Organization of Gaze, Touch, and Talk in a Medical Encounter*

Richard M. Frankel

The task of translating medical knowledge into medical practice is a major problem in the relationship between technological advance and the everyday world of social activity. This is particularly true in the area of ambulatory or primary-care practice because the range of diagnostic problems encountered is less obviously disease-dependent compared with inpatient or specialty care practice.[1] Also, the organizational settings for recommending treatment are often remote from the actions or treatments recommended. Taking pills, giving oneself an injection, and monitoring bodily processes are all examples of the

* Grateful acknowledgment is made to Winifred von Ehrenburg for her assistance in editing this manuscript. Helpful comments and suggestions were also provided by George Girton, Charles Goodwin, Doug Maynard, Eliot Mishler, Tracy Paget, and Candace West.

[1] Primary care as defined for purposes of health manpower legislation includes family practitioners, internists, and pediatricians. A recent National Academy of Sciences Institute of Medicine study (1978) defined primary care in terms of the scope, character, and integration of services provided. The Institute of Medicine study provides a broader framework within which a number of different types of providers may be said to be delivering primary-care services. General and family practitioners, internists, pediatricians, and obstetrician-gynecologists were described in practice content, however, as most likely to fit the definition of a primary care provider.

temporal disjunction between communicating medical advice and acting on it in some subsequent social and linguistic context.[2]

From a conceptual perspective, the incorporation into clinical reasoning of complex social and psychological factors (including work and family environment), health hazards (like chronic tobacco and alcohol use), and positive participation in health care (via maintenance, screening, and prevention programs) has multiplied the bases from which questions of health and illness *as well as* disease may be considered topics of appropriate clinical concern.[3] On the practical side, increasing the range of legitimate complaints by expanding their logic of explanation to include both biological and social factors highlights the fact that much of the *practice* of medicine, whatever its bases of inference for clinical decision making (also perhaps irremediably) consist of a concrete set of communication tasks accomplished within the constraints of an ongoing temporal and sequential order.

This study focuses on a stretch of interactive behavior as it unfolds between a pediatrician, his young patient, and the patient's mother. Both the encounter and the fragment analyzed were selected because they typify routine elements of care. The patient has no disease and care is not being sought for an existing problem. This type of encounter is what is referred to medically as a "well-child visit." The particular portion of the visit to be analyzed is similarly routine and involves a close-order description of the verbal, visual, and tactile elements of communication that emerge as the pediatrician completes the history-taking phase and initiates the physical examination by "laying on hands"—touching the patient.

The purpose of analyzing routine elements of communication between physicians and patients is to focus attention on the sorts of generalized rules of

---

[2] The most widely researched dimension of this problem is found in the large but by no means conclusive literature on adherence/compliance in which rates of failure to follow recommendations have been shown to vary anywhere from 30% to 90%. Although it is tacitly argued among researchers that failure to follow recommendations represents a gap in the physician's ability to extend his or her influence on patient's behavior outside of the office, the actual social and linguistic conditions under which such failure occurs are poorly known and have rarely been investigated. Much of the data in this area are limited to responses to questionnaire items and stimulated recall of events associated with issues of adherence/compliance. Unfortunately, such cognitive measures offer little empirical insight into the scenes, settings, and interactions that produce failure to follow medical recommendations. Stone (1979) comes closest to acknowledging this problem in his review of research efforts in this area.

[3] Recent statements in medicine (Eisenberg 1977; Engel 1977) and medical anthropology (Fabrega and Van Egeren 1976; Kleinman 1980) have suggested the need for more broadly based definitions of health and illness than are currently available in western-style biomedicine. Several different frameworks have been proposed including the biopsychosocial, biobehavioral, and ecological. Each has been claimed as a new model of health care and offers an expanded theoretical conception of the role of cultural, ecological, and behavioral factors in defining disease, illness, diagnosis, and treatment.

social conduct that instantiate a medical encounter from beginning to end. Unlike the rules of biological and chemical action systems, which are fixed by definition, communication rules are shared and, therefore, always open to problems of meaning and interpretation. The differences in scope and responsibility that these two conceptions of action embody have important consequences for the ways health care is conceived and carried out.

Several preliminary remarks are in order to make clear why the study of communicative interaction is pertinent to ambulatory care. First, unlike biological and chemical action systems in which the criteria of assessment are hard and fast (e.g., lithium chloride is *always* lithium chloride regardless of its country of origin), social action systems can and do behave quite differently under different circumstances.[4] For example, gazing at or away from one's interlocutor while conversing can produce different interpretive consequences depending on the sex and cultural backgrounds of the participants. These differences arise even when the structure and duration of mutual gazing are exactly the same.

Second, the logic of social interaction is different in kind from the laboratory "gold standard" or the idealized diagnostic decision-making tree, both of which serve as predetermined canons of practice for increasing the predictive accuracy of naming or treating pathological conditions. Viewing medical care by reference to the rules of social conduct not only makes interpretive variations and asymmetries from either perception of the relationship possible, it ensures that mutual participation becomes an essential property of the consultation process. Thus, the physician's belief that a patient is angry or denying his or her condition has another interpretive dimension in which the patient's own definition or intentions come into play. Patients may believe, rightly or wrongly, that it is the *physician*, not themselves, who is denying them access to expressing their true or immediate feelings. Thus, the cultural view of social action, in which each party contributes but does not fully control outcomes, raises the issue of multiple realities or frames of reference as a continuous feature of medical care.

Third, despite the range of differences and interpretation that are possible in developing social relations, medical encounters are real-time sociolinguistic events in which "progress" (i.e., movement from beginning to end) at any particular point in time is dependent on the local work of a speaker and hearer who negotiate and ratify each other's actions as meaningful. The fact that meaning emerges through coordinated action provides the analytic rationale for

---

[4] Biological and chemical facts are not always free from social or contextual interpretation. Eric Cassell, M.D., in his course for second-year students at Cornell Medical School entitled "The Uses and Functions of Language in Medicine" cites the case of a South American patient who has come to the United States to obtain American lithium because she is convinced that it is more effective than the same drug manufactured in her own country. Her belief makes up an important part of the reason she has sought care in the U.S. Thus, although lithium chloride always *is* lithium chloride, the context in which it is named may produce differing, and in some cases conflicting, interpretations.

investigating the claim that much of ambulatory practice consists of concerns and problems that arise and are managed at the level of discourse.

A concern for understanding the effects of communication context on ambulatory care is not simply idle academic curiosity. Recent results from the 1980 National Ambulatory Medical Care Survey (NAMCS), an ongoing study of all office-based visits in the United States, indicate that the bulk (51%) of care provided was for conditions that were identified by the participating physicians as either "no problem," or "not serious," that is, non-disease-based. Further, fewer than one in five visits were reported as "serious," or "very serious."[5] Even if one takes the cautious stance of disqualifying all instances of serious disease as a criterion for determining the extent to which language and social interaction function in the ambulatory arena, an impressive number of patients seeking care, 290,680,000 of an estimated 577,000,000, appear to be "healthy," i.e., nonsymptomatic.

What these findings suggest is that disease is neither the only nor the major reason for seeking care. What remains to be established is the nature of those concerns that fall outside the biomedical definition of disease and their "fate" in terms of current standards of practice for diagnosis and treatment. I suggest that social interaction and, more particularly, an understanding of the relationship between speech exchange and other communicative modalities may be used to explain the process and outcome of routine health care.

Methodologically, this line of argument runs counter to a widely held view that advances in medicine are marked by developing more precise technologies for controlling biological and chemical action systems. It could equally well be suggested that an understanding of the cultural medium through which ambulatory care is delivered represents a significant potential for improving health on a national or societal level.

A NOTE ON METHOD

In January 1976, the National Center for Health Services Research (NCHSR) created the Work Group on Education for the Health Professions. The task of this group was to suggest research directions that would best evaluate the effectiveness of education in he health professions in terms of benefits to the health status of Americans. After meeting extensively for more than a year, the group concluded that the paucity of useful knowledge in this area could be explained by a central theme of discontinuity between the modes of educating health

---

[5] Statistics for diagnostic and therapeutic services (NAMCS) are equally impressive. Approximately one out of every ten ambulatory visits concluded with no diagnostic services having been provided. And, in terms of treatment, one out of five patients seen required no therapeutic services whatsoever.

professionals and the day-to-day practice of health care delivery. Three areas of discontinuity in training with direct consequences for the nation's health were identified:

1. The experiences and needs of patients and populations are not effectively related to how health professionals practice;
2. What health professionals do in their practice does not sufficiently influence the content of professional education;
3. What is learned in professional education about the public's health and illness is not generally applied in professional practice.

The issues raised by the NCHSR Work Group are instructive in pointing out the current lack of fit between methods of educating health professionals and subsequent professional practice. As already suggested, part of this problem may stem from an overemphasis on the technological aspects of medicine, high-lighted by hospital-based training, which in the long run is unrepresentative of the actual office-based practice settings most physicians enter. A second part of the problem may be the lack of a concrete understanding of what actually constitutes daily physician professional practice. Again, this raises the question of *knowledge,* as an abstract conceptualization of the accumulated skills and training of the provider, and *performance*, as the concrete enactment of an encounter between him or her and persons seeking care.

In addition to the contrast between the different institutional settings in which medicine is taught and then practiced, it is important to ask more basic questions about the research methods used to investigate medical work. For example, it is important to know whether researchers focusing on reasons for seeking medical care implicitly adopt the same biologically based criteria used by providers to assess problem severity. If so, this potentially introduces a type of "professional-ist bias" on the part of the researcher who defines the range and import of problem severity from only one end of what has been defined as a negotiated relationship.

A problem of similar dimensions has recently been reported by several authors (Atkinson 1978; Douglas 1967; Sacks 1966a) who have re-analyzed Emile Durkheim's classic sociological study of suicide.[6] It is pointed out by these authors that in relying on "official statistics," Durkheim uncritically accepted a diverse set of coroners' interpretive practices, which biased his conclusions in at least two ways. First, since the coroners' records themselves were assembled in different geographic regions, under differing circumstances of knowledge and

---

[6] Similar questions of methodological adequacy have been raised in studies of record-keeping practices in an outpatient clinic (Garfinkel 1967); educational counseling interviews (Erickson and Shultz 1982); classrooms (Mehan 1979); and police treatment of juvenile delinquents (Cicourel 1968).

expertise, using different methods of interpretation, the claim of correspondence between them and actual rates of suicide is questionable. Second, by using such statistics as themselves matters of fact, Durkheim's estimation of rates of occurrence was biased toward the institutional values and norms of those doing the reporting. It is probable that the attribution of suicide as a cause of death in some cases differed according to the local practices of reporting and the social standing of the coroners involved; in addition to these local variations, a number of potential suicides probably escaped detection because they were marginal or did not properly "fit" the established criteria for category inclusion.

Methodologically, the point to be made here is that Durkheim's use of "official statistics" to investigate differential rates of suicide failed to take into account the orders of commonsense reasoning that stood between his theory and the data on which his theory was based. In so doing, Durkheim settled for a commonsense definition of the very problem he set out to investigate. The analogy for researching problems of ambulatory medical care without taking into account our cultural and institutional presuppositions about the nature of patient concerns is, of course, that we run the same risk of adopting problem definitions both independently and in advance of those concrete occasions of interaction in which they emerge and are negotiated. In other words, we risk duplicating rather than explicating the objects of research.

In sociological circles, at least, there is a pervasive tendency to adopt problem definitions because they are obvious to begin with. For instance, we need not generate an independent criterion for identifying one-leggedness as a type of visible stigmata; we simply recognize it. Research based on such readily recognized features of the social order are common. The question is, How do we, as analysts, separate what we know and recognize about a phenomenon from what we wish to investigate? Zimmerman and Pollner (1970) referred to this problem as one of confusing the topic of an analytic investigation with the commonsense resources, such as ordinary language, that supply the materials for that topic.

Another way of formulating the problem is to ask, What is the analytic purchase gained by using one set of language processes (e.g., commonsense recognition of deviance as a criterion for its definition) to investigate another set of language processes (the influence of father's education on adjustment to one-leggedness)? Zimmerman and Pollner's point is to challenge the use of accepted facts as a conventional basis for theorizing in the social sciences and to underscore the analytic importance of distinguishing between conventions and the cultural practices that underlie and support them.

If it is true, or at least analytically plausible, that we use commonsense cultural knowledge to furnish a basis for our theorizing about the world, and if it is also true that as analysts we use language to investigate language, then the question of routine or conventional behavior becomes a major topic of inquiry because the same commonsense cultural organization furnishes both the dramatic and the continuing background against which contrast or change appears.[7] (In a world of one-legged individuals, in a hospital ward let us say, one-leggedness is not an a priori basis for identification as deviant. In such a world, two-leggedness may be defined as strange and out of place.) We may discover, as a result, that the dramatic and the routine are not only equally worthy of study but that both are necessary ingredients in training health care professionals.

For the current topic under investigation, "The Laying on of Hands," the methodological implications are clear. Although the miraculous powers of touch have been chronicled from the days of the physician-kings (who could heal by touching a supplicant and signing the cross) through more modern versions, which attempt to describe the healing nature of the physician's touch, the methods employed have been largely historical; the term "touch" in this context is being used more as a metaphor for describing the larger process of healing and recovery than concrete occasions of interaction.[8]

This metaphor has been extended in sociological practice as a theoretical argument that states that physicians in this culture are unique among professionals, in part because even though they are nonintimates, they are permitted

---

[7] This issue has recently been raised in the field of animal ethology. Many early ethological studies, it appears, focused on such *dramatic* problems as how members of a troop of monkeys display cohesion in the face of attack or incursion by predators. Other studies have dealt with the adaptive significance of aggressive behavior within a troop by noting that within a group challenges and threats are rarely fatal for either of the challengers. The problem with this sort of theorizing about behavior based upon fear, fright, or alarm, according to Van Hooff (1967), is that it tends to neglect the situation for action when the troop is at rest, that is, when individuals who will aggressively challenge one another in one set of circumstances will *routinely* approach and come into prolonged contact (during sleep for example) with one another in other circumstances. The analogy to human social conduct is obvious. Any truly comprehensive theory of behavior must account for both dramatic states (activities during arousal) *and* background states activities during which individuals are routinely brought into relationship.

[8] The most often cited relationship between touching and healing appears in references to "the placebo effect," which is defined as the alleviation of symptoms through agents or agencies that do not by themselves alter chemical or physiological processes in the body. A good review of various placebo effects and the ways in which they have been investigated can be found in Liberman (1963). Specific connections between the situated or "communicationally based" nature of the physician's touch and its healing consequences are difficult to find. Bruhn (1978:1471) is typical of the idealized (historical) stance that has been taken in attempting to develop the concept of the healing touch. Thus, "patients' reactions to the doctor's touch or lack of it are influenced to a great extent by the expectations patients have when they seek out a doctor...they hope the physician will give them 'a clean bill of health,' and a 'pat on the back,' i.e., a form of blessing or will advise them of aspects of their health that warrant close scrutiny, i.e., a form of therapy or preventive medicine. All [kinds] of patients expect some form of healing or laying on of hands by the physician. Thus, while touching has diagnostic value for the physician, touching has therapeutic value for the patient."

bodily access and contact with their clients. Despite this assertion, there are surprisingly few reports on how instances or episodes of contact in the medical encounter are actually organized and managed.[9] As a matter of method, it seems worth investigating some actual instances of touching and their relationship to other communication modalities such as gazing and speaking as a means of uncovering the features of social interaction that make touching a mundane, rather than miraculous, achievement of routine medical encounters.

Finally, by focusing on routine as well as dramatic forms of communication, we can study the role of visible behavior in social interaction. Analysis of the rules that underlie and guide visible activity in its own terms may provide understandings with direct relevance for both the actors and the settings in which they are involved.

Having raised the possibility that studies of institutional arrangements often leave unaddressed more fundamental questions of how social performance is coordinated in time and space, let me introduce some general considerations of the problem of evidence from an interactional point of view. This will be approached in two ways. First, through an analysis of the results of experimentally disrupting the conventional relationship between looking and talking, it will be shown that shared norms guide participants' understanding and interpretation of events as they emerge in interaction. The goal here is to demonstrate that communication is both collaborative and provides visible grounds for interpretation, in some cases despite the intentions or motives of a speaker. Second, by considering the interactive structure of a phase transition in a naturally occurring pediatric encounter, it will be shown that the same shared rules that guide interpretation may also be used as the basis for strategic management of another's behavior. In this case, it will be proposed that the pediatrician's knowledge of the rules of visual attention successfully allow him to shape the character of the patient's coparticipation as the physical exam begins, by limiting the available options for appropriate response. In this second effort, the goal will be to demonstrate that speaker and hearer mutually monitor and regulate each other's behavior from moment to moment. The overall relevance of this finding for medical work is that it establishes the need to discover what the basic units of social participation in the consultation process are, and with that knowledge to build a description of the systematic influences of social context on the character of health and health-related interactions.

---

[9] Emerson's (1970) report on how issues of deference and demeanor produce conflicting role demands for the gynecologist, whose activities in other circumstances might be labeled as sexual or intimate, comes closest, perhaps, to representing individual action in communicational terms. Although Emerson's focus is on the meaning of events for individuals, it is also clear that she is more concerned with the symbolic products of communication than the actual heard and seen properties of the communication process itself.

EXPERIMENTING WITH LOOKING AND TALKING IN INTERACTION

Much of what has just been claimed is abstract and speculative; therefore, a return to a more concrete focus on interaction will be useful. This section describes the results of an experimental procedure designed to illuminate the relationship between presuppositions and action by altering a conventional background in interaction, the relationship between speaking and looking.

Psychologists, such as Argyle and Cook (1976), have attempted to describe the relationship between speaking and looking. They have developed several theories to explain why gaze is distributed both differentially between speakers, and differently under different speaking conditions. Kendon (1967) posits that gaze plays a major role in regulating the exchange of speaking turns in conversation. Kendon notes that speakers tend to look away as they reach a turn's completion, while hearers tend to shift their orientation from looking away during the speaker's turn to looking toward the speaker at its completion.[10]

Argyle and Dean (1965), on the other hand, report that gaze during talk is associated with interpersonal attraction and claim that the more one party looks at the other, the more regard he or she has for the other. Jellison and Ickes (1974) and Exline (1974) discuss looking and its absence and how they relate to power. They claim that looking is distributed differentially, with more powerful members of an interaction looking less at less powerful members than the reverse.[11] This same principle is the basis of what Chance (1967) termed "a structure of attention" for animal species, where less dominant members of a herd will distribute comparatively greater visual attention to a dominant male than is given by that male in return.

Although these studies have contributed tremendously to understanding problems based on frequency of gaze, it is clear from them that gaze is not an absolute or invariant phenomenon; that is, it does not always "mean" the same thing wherever and whenever it occurs.

Most of what is known about the relationship between gaze and talk is based on isolated judgments of their co-occurrence over a delimited and sometimes experimentally manipulated stretch of talk.The results are then correlated with theoretical propositions about their meaning and significance. The problem with

---

[10] Apparently this pattern is connected with a redundancy in the turn transition system that provides both verbal (prosodic features such as intonation and turn terminal glides) and visual (both parties shift gaze and assume "new" positions) clues to the nature and timing of the actual transition.

[11] Mutual gaze has also been related to aggression in animal and human-animal interaction—see Exline and Yellin (1969). In humans, it is the basis of a form of "friendly" aggression known as a "hard stare" and "staring down" another person; see Exline 1974.

drawing inferences about meanings from frequency counts that move across individuals and situations is that the basis of expert knowledge of the culture comes from the researcher and his or her viewpoint rather than from the participants (users) themselves. All questions of meaning as the negotiated accomplishment of interacting parties are lost when features of a setting, such as gaze, are collected into a single contrast set of present-absent. This sort of procedure cuts off all reference and access to problems of production internal to the particular societal arrangement at hand, in this case the meaning gaze or its absence has as an emergent phenomenon within discourse.

Much of the research on gaze and its relationship to talk seems based on a conventional presupposition that assumes rather than explicates the dynamic range of functions gaze may play in the making of meaning. Much like the sociologist who sets off to investigate deviance with the criterion for definition already in hand, so many researchers investigating gaze seem to assume that gazing and speaking stand in static relation to each other. This means that changes in one communicative domain do not or should not affect meaning or significance in the other. This is not necessarily the case, as we are about to see.

As indicated above, little research emphasis has been given to the relationship of gaze and talk as constituting rather than inherently containing meaning. A few recent studies (Frankel 1982; Goodwin 1978) have begun to look at gaze behavior as it relates to speech production on a moment-by-moment basis. Goodwin, for example, posits that gaze is a conventional necessity in some speaking situations for establishing the status of another as a co-recipient. His analysis of the production of a single sentence dramatically illustrates how a speaker, failing to gain eye contact with an intended recipient, can modify the emerging speech stream to make it relevant to a second candidate recipient and, failing to gain eye contact with an intended recipient, can modify the emerging speech stream to make it relevant to a second candidate recipient and, failing to gain eye contact in this circumstance, to a third. What is remarkable in Goodwin's analysis is that the same emerging sentence produced unsuccessfully for two previous candidate recipients can be modified in its course to maintain its ongoing coherence and relevance for each of the candidate recipients involved.

In a study of the interactive behavior of autistic children, Frankel (1982) illustrated how a set of conventional presuppositions about eye contact in question-answer sequences interfered with language training tasks. Frankel found a pattern in which the mother of a 16-year-old autistic boy repetitively attempted to engage her son's visual attention through the use of requests containing such pro-term references as *what's this?* or *what is it?* In normal conversation such requests operate explicitly to solicit information and implicitly to solicit visual attention. The "cost" of using requests with implicit as well as explicit functions is that it requires shared knowledge, which may move beyond the interactional competence of the autistic child. The resulting confusion is often disastrous to the goal of the lesson, namely, increasing the child's vocalization skills.

The degree to which gaze may be involved as a matter of obligation or sanction is just beginning to be explored. One technique for investigating the dynamic relationship between the conventional orientations of different communication modalities is through what Garfinkel (1967) has termed a disruption experiment. Such procedures are designed to expose the conventions of social organization through deliberately violating them. In the case of looking and talking, two general rules of appropriate behavior for corecipients may be readily noted. First, it is conventionally appropriate in this culture for listeners to attend to the speaker visually from time to time. Second, when attending behavior is present, it is conventionally appropriate to direct it toward the speaker's face. By designing an experiment that violates these two norms, it should be possible to discover more about the nature of the rules they violate and more about the culturally appropriate practices that inform them.

Violating the Rules of Gaze and Talk

As a class exercise, 175 graduate sociology students at a large state university in southern California were assigned the task of engaging in two violations of visual behavior according to the following instructions:

1. While in the course of face-to-face interaction with another, begin to direct your visual attention over the left or right shoulder of your interlocutor. Continue to maintain this position for a minimum of 10 consecutive speaking turns, engaging your recipient as normally as possible and as if nothing unusual or out of the ordinary were happening. Record your observations.
2. While in the course of face-to-face interaction with another, begin to direct your visual attention toward any body part of your interlocutor, except the head or facial region. Maintain this position for a minimum of at least 10 consecutive speaking turns, engaging your recipient as normally as possible and as if nothing unusual or out of the ordinary were happening. Record your observations.

Results

In the first condition (− gaze), the response was nearly uniform. By the fifth conversational turn, nearly 80% of the experimenters reported that their interlocutors had shifted their own visual focus and had initiated a glance in the direction of the experimenter's gaze. By the tenth conversational exchange, an equal number of interlocutors had produced a verbal account or formulation of the experimenter's activity as having violated or in some way altered the conventionally appropriate rules for talking and looking. Typical responses were as follows:

Example 1
In a bookstore, I asked the saleswoman which Saul Bellow novels she had in hard cover and started a conversation about his newest novel. She was very polite and concerned with trying to figure out what I wanted. Four or five turns into the conversation, she turned around to see what I could be looking at and simultaneously asked me if there was something else she could help me with. I replied there was nothing else I needed so she then directed me to browse, noting that if I needed assistance she would be happy to oblige.

Example 2
My boss was just preparing to leave and I cornered him and we began to speak about the World Series. He responded immediately by looking down the hall to see what I was staring at; when he saw nothing, he looked back and resumed our conversation. Approximately three turns later, he said, "What the hell are you looking at Mike?"

Example 3
The group on which I carried out this exercise was composed of nine women attending a Girl Scout meeting and seated in a circle. I began to stare at the molding on the window in back of the organizer while she was speaking to the group. Within a minute or two, the women seated to her immediate right and left began to glance up to see what I was looking at. This created a chain reaction, and everyone in the room, except the organizer who was still speaking on Girl Scouting, glanced up to see what the other women were looking at. At this point, the organizer said, "I wish you would all pay attention because this is very important," then continued to speak and I continued to stare at the molding. After making a few more comments on scouting, she stopped talking and looked over her shoulder at the window. She then turned back to the group and said, "You know we're going to get drapes in here after we get all the paneling up." I smiled at her.

In addition to producing effects on the locus of visual attention, the absence of gaze had demonstrable effects on both the topic and direction talk. For instance, while topical cohesion is maintained in Example 1, the experimenter does note that his interlocutor was overly polite and solicitous in her offers of assistance. Whether this is a consequence of the experimental procedure is difficult to establish without additional information. The second and third examples are much clearer, for in both the experimental procedure is explicitly formulated and introduced as a new topic. In these two cases, violations of a norm may be said to interrupt discourse organization by becoming its focus.

It is also interesting to note the contrasting formulations offered in Examples 2 and 3. In Example 2, the experimenter's boss was unable to find a visual warrant for the attention being paid outside the dyad. In lieu of finding such a warrant through self-inspection, the experimenter's co-recipient requests, perhaps demands, to be supplied with an accountable basis for its occurrence. Such a demand implicitly acknowledges the experimenter's right to monitor the dyadic visual space, but only on the condition that another mutually acknowledgeable site of attention is present. In this sense, the interlocutor's response is operating as a potential warning to the experimenter about what constitute appropriate foci of interaction.

The last example illustrates the same process of searching for a violation, and even formulates the problem in terms of a corrective, "I wish you would all pay more attention," which focuses on a general dispreference for attentional shifts in meetings or circumstances in which one speaker addresses a group of recipients. The case is interesting for it also illustrates the ability of the speaker to find a warrant for the gazing activity, even where none is intended. It is not simply that the experimenter has shifted focus that is of concern to the speaker, but that the focus must involve some problem or delict that will account for the shift. In this case, it is the need for new curtains and speaker's formulation of this need as appropriate in general, but not at this moment, that is evidenced in her response.

In the second condition (+ gaze, but − appropriate gaze site), the results were similar and also demonstrate the disruptive effects of altering the site of gazing activity during conversation. Again, in about 80% of the cases, a verbal account or formulation that attempted to "make sense" of the behavior had surfaced by the tenth conversational exchange. Three typical responses follow:

Example 1
The second exercise was designed like the first, but instead of looking over the subject's shoulder, I stared at a female friend's stomach. We were sitting on a couch, both in comfortable positions. As I fixed my gaze on her stomach, her first reaction was to pull her knees up on the couch, folding her hands over her stomach. She next pulled her jacket to cover her stomach and finally said, "Tom what's the matter?"

Example 2
For the second part of the exercise, I decided to stare at the left shoe of a woman with whom I was conversing. When she became aware that I was staring at her shoes, her first reaction was to move her feet under her chair. However, I could still see her left shoe, so I continued to stare. She then tugged at her skirt—conversing all the while as if nothing out of the ordinary was happening—in an unsuccessful attempt to cover her feet up. Finally, she looked down at her feet to discover why I was staring at them. At this point she said, "They really are scuffed aren't they?"

Example 3
My 5-year-old nephew approached me and asked if I would set up his train set for him. I looked at his feet the whole time and he immediately squatted over to check his shoestrings to see if they were tied. After he had checked, he asked me to set his train up again as I agreed to [do] it for him, and it was then he began to stare at my shoes. Later he wanted to play the "looking at the feet game" again.

As in the first condition, a range of responses may be noted. Example 1 illustrates the same unsuccessful search for a delict and a request/command for a suitable warrant for explaining the presence of the experimenter's gaze. Example 2 also demonstrates that the product of a search initiated by a recipient's "deviant" gaze may provide its own warrant. The response, "They really are scuffed aren't they?" formulates the experimenter's gaze as having been directed and warranted by some unusual characteristic of the scene (i.e., scuffed shoes). In this case, the search for a delict to account for the experimenter's behavior has been satisfied, in the form of a "found" relationship between the experimenter's behavior and its presumed motivation.

Examples 1 and 2 both point to an intervening step between the identification of an item of attention and its appearance in discourse. This step consists of a nonvocal attempt to remove the offending or attractive item from the visual field. In Example 1, this step consists of pulling up the knees, folding the hands over the stomach, and covering the body with an article of clothing to reduce visibility at the locus of attention. In Example 2, it consists of attempting to hide the feet and reduce body visibility by tugging at the skirt. In both cases, some attempt is made at "correction" or amelioration of the problem before it is announced. Example 3 is notable, for it formulates the deviant activity in terms of its appropriateness to a particular form of structured exchange (i.e., a game). It is perhaps typical of young children in interaction with adults to treat otherwise deviant behavior as nonserious (i.e., game-like) and to act on that basis.

Two observations are pertinent in discussing the results of this disruption experiment. First, gaze behavior may affect discourse by shifting the immediate focus of attention within which talk is occurring. Second, under some circumstances, such shifts may interrupt discourse by becoming its topical focus. What this experiment demonstrates is that meaning in social interaction is negotiated, and that communication elements like gaze vary according to the social and conversational contexts in which they occur.

A NATURALLY OCCURRING EXAMPLE IN PHYSICIAN–PATIENT INTERACTION

Michael is a normally healthy six-year-old boy who has been brought to his pediatrician for a routine checkup. He has visited the pediatrician before, and is familiar with some of the ground rules for a routine checkup. Michael's caretaker, his mother, is also familiar with the general organization of such encounters.

Michael's pediatrician is an established private physician who has been in practice in the Boston area for some 20 years. He has agreed to allow a researcher with a videotape machine to record the interactions between himself, his patients, and their caretakers. For the particular encounter reported here, the researcher and his equipment are present in the examining room. Bias introduced by the presence of the camera and an operator is probably of minimal relevance to the stretch of interactive behavior reported.[12]

The larger segment of interaction from which the analysis is drawn includes an opening sequence, a short exchange with the patient, a history of current concerns from the mother, and a portion of the physical examination. A verbal transcript of this segment is included as Appendix B. The sequence of analytic interest occurs at the transition between the mother's history and the beginning of the physical examination.

Phase transitions are of general interest for the ways in which interactional boundaries are signaled, negotiated, and re-established among co-participants. For our purposes, the significance of shifting from a history-taking to a physical examination phase is that it marks an expectable location in the encounter during which the physician may "officially" engage in acts of touching, probing, and palpating the patient's body. Far from being miraculously organized, the touch that begins the physician's physical examination is highly conventional and *forecast* by reference to its location within the encounter structure. Its achievement, however, may be quite complex by virtue of the competing communicational modalities that may come into play as touching occurs. More specifically, as physician and patient engage each other, elements of vocalization, gaze, and touch may occur simultaneously, leading one to ask whether there is any systematicity to these events and their management.

The analysis will proceed as follows: Each line of the verbal transcript has been numbered and will be referred to for locating the stretch of talk under consideration. In addition, the videotape from which the verbal transcript was made is enumerated so that each frame of video material is identified with a unique number code. Because video images are created at the rate of 60 fields per second, each second of the encounter is temporally organized into 60 discrete units.[13] Frame numbers will be used to designate moments in time that are of analytic or descriptive interest. Reproductions of actual video frames accompany the text.

We may begin by noting the gross shifts that have occurred before the physician's initiation of physical contact at line 72. Apart from the fact that a request for action has been issued in line 65 about climbing onto the examining

---

[12] Kendon (1979:19–20) suggests that the presence of recording equipment, although it may initially be oriented to by one or both parties in an encounter, characteristically becomes a routinized element of the social scene and does not interfere in any significant way with parties' willingness or ability to interact.

[13] This method is far more sensitive to micromomentary shifts in gaze, and the like, than for example, Kendon's (1967) one, which sampled interaction at the rate of every half second. Similarly, film studies such as Condon and Ogston (1971) are based on units of $1/24$ of a second between frames. For a good discussion of the relative merits of sound film and videotape methods see Kendon 1979.

table, there is little vocal evidence that a physical examination is under way. That is, there is no vocal announcement that a physical examination is being conducted. It may be assumed that both parties are aware of the fact, and on this basis no "verbal" announcement need be given.

There is evidence that a change in organizational formats has taken place, however. This change may be noted in three different ways. First, before the phase transition, the physician has engaged in a variety of speech acts—queries, assertions, compliments, and so on—with both the patient and his caretaker. After the transition has occurred, the physician addresses only the patient and does so using only one type of speech act—queries. Second, the physician, who has been a recipient of and respondent to queries (line 13) and stories before the transition, is the sole initiator of conversation after the transition. And finally, the queries the physician initiates after the transition are tied to one another and form a cohesive topical focus. Thus, given the type and closeness of topical connections of the utterances from line 74 to 103, there is some vocal evidence to suggest that a structured unit or phase composed of physician-initiated questions and patient responses is in operation. Sacks (1966b) has referred to these sequences as question chains, and their operation has been noted as common in interviews, interrogations, and classrooms.[14]

The questioning chain itself provides further evidence that marks the transition and indicates that multiple orders of activity are ongoing. Consider the physician's "Oka:y," which begins line 74 of the transcript. Sacks (1966b), Schegloff and Sacks (1973), Jefferson (1978), and others have pointed out that lexicals—such as *okay, alright, well,* and *so*—are commonly used to signal a disjunction between a previous state or topic of talk and an upcoming one. In analyzing closings, for example, Schegloff and Sacks note that in shifting from the "business" of a telephone call toward its closing, such items can be used by a speaker as a test or "last call" for topic continuation. If no more topical material is forthcoming, closings will begin. The work of these items seems to be that of setting off one type of speaking activity from another.

In another context, Erickson (1975) noted a close order relationship between topical junctures and large-scale shifts in proxemic behavior. While topic shifts do not require proxemic shifts in any strict sense, Erickson does note that such junctures are rich locations for changes in postural configurations. The physician's use of "Oka:y" in line 74 is well fitted to marking a shift in vocal activity. Its positioning after a request for action that has produced large-scale postural

---

[14] See Frankel (In press) for an extended analysis of the chaining phenomenon in physician-patient discourse, where it appears that systematic constraints limit the distribution of particular turn-types to particular speakers. Thus, Frankel found, for example, that physicians initiated 99% of the questions asked in 10 routine encounters. Patients virtually never initiated questions or utterances operating as first pair parts. West (this volume), in a similar study, found that physicians initiated 91% of all questions in her sample of family practice physicians.

changes also suggests that nonvocal as well as vocal behaviors are being coordinated by the physician's discourse. It is proposed that the physician's "Oka:y" announces the beginning of the examination phase of the encounter and thereby signals that all subsequent vocal and nonvocal behaviors belong or are related to that phase. The physician's utterance establishes an "official" beginning to the examination.

Plate 1 is a photographic reproduction of video frame 8048. In terms of vocal behavior, frame 8048 occurs just after the physician has completed his vocal disjunct, "Oka:y." Nonvocally, the physician has been engaged in adjusting a piece of equipment (an ophthalmoscope), moving it from its position behind and to the right of the patient (from patient's point of view) to a new location next to the patient. In the course of this adjustment, the physician has touched the patient on the thigh (frames 7658–9704) while laughing simultaneously with his caretaker (lines 69–70). In addition, at frame 7928, approximately one second before the announcement of an "official" initiation of the examination phase, the physician apparently grasps one or both hands of the patient and begins to examine it or them.[15] The fact that some form of touching is already in progress at the point of announced transition and that it precedes the announcement by only one second suggests a close order coordination between vocal and nonvocal modes of communication. What is this order, and what are its consequences for the interaction?

Notice the visual orientation of each of the parties to the interaction in frame 8048. The patient, who at this point is being touched by the physician, has his head and eyes cast down in the direction of the physician's hands. The conventions that relate attention to body contact from a stranger or near stranger make his orientation expectable. In this culture it is conventionally appropriate for one party (the patient) to visually monitor the hands of another party (the physician) as they approach, make contact, and explore visually accessible parts of the body. The physician's gaze in frame 8048 is focused on the patient's body and most probably on the hand or hands that are in his grasp. Together, the physician and patient compose a joint focus of attention on the body parts that are in mutual contact. Both are oriented and perhaps obliged by convention to focus on an attentional site of mutual interest.

The patient's caretaker is in the role of an onlooker to the scene. She has observed but has not participated vocally in the interaction since line 62, the beginning of the re-alignment process. At frame 8408, the caretaker continues to observe, focusing her visual attention on her son. Her facial expression exhibits a

---

[15] Although the actual position of the hands on the body is not observable given the particular field of focus at that moment, it is possible to discern a slight torso shift on the part of the patient at frame 7920. This shift and the accompanying behaviors of the physician and patient suggest that frame 7920 is the point at which initial contact is made.

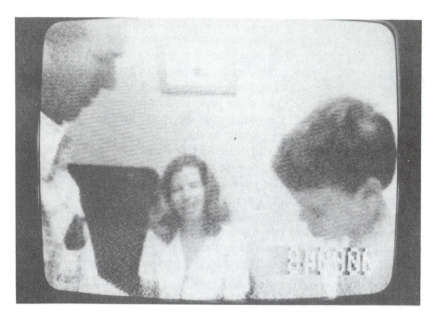

PLATE 1   Initiation of Physician's Speaking Turn (Frame 8048)

smile. The smile is potentially "carried over" as a response to the physician's previous utterance, an ironic noticing of the patient's posture in climbing onto the examining table, and about which both parties have engaged in a colloquy by laughing together (lines 69–70).[16] Thus, while involved visually with the current state of her son's interaction with the physician, she is simultaneously displaying a response to a previous sequence of activity in that interaction. As an onlooker,

---

[16] Among the postural and gestural accompaniments to speech, the smile is unique in its ability to reference previous items and sequences of talk. Most gestures and postures will be read for their relevance to the local interactional environment in which they occur (lexical, phrasal, and, at most, turn-sized components); smiles may be read for their relevance to turns or exchanges that are comparatively distant in conversational time, having already occurred and been acknowledged. In general, one finds that there is a principle of nondisorderability that characterizes the relationship between gestures, postures, and facial expressions, etc., and the conversational milieux in which they appear. Apparently, although talk both signifies and is itself an action, nonvocal activity, at least when it occurs in the environment of talk, takes on its sense from its local environment and not by historical reference, i.e., reference to prior turns. Scheflen (1973) claims that in certain forms of pathological behavior, schizophrenia, for example, certain postural configurations are recurrent as thematic structures of communication. In this sense, a particular gesture or posture may play an identifiable role in the communication process and may even be recognizable as the point at which the patient recurrently lapses into bizarre or inappropriate behavior. This may be a special case in which a particular combination of gestural and postural elements combine to yield a patterned display with historical and signaling significance. For routine, nonpathological behavior such

PLATE 2   Completion of Physician's Speaking Turn (Frame 8178)

she may be characterized as engaged in displaying multiple involvements in the interaction.[17]

Plate 2 is a photographic illustration of frame 8178, the completion of the physician's speaking turn (line 74). Several interesting relationships may be noted. First, by the time the physician's turn at talk has completed, he has shifted the site of his looking from the patient's hands to his face. The actual shift occurs vocally at frame 8135 at the beginning of "this" in the utterance, "What grade did yo:u ih- were you in ➤this last year." (The arrow pointing upwards marks the point at which the physician begins gazing toward the patient.) The shift on the physician's part is consistent with Kendon's (1967)

---

specific historical coincidences seem far less apparent. Interlocutors are not in the first place assessing one another's behavior for signs for psychopathology. The gaze violation experiments reported earlier are relevant here, for it will be recalled that interlocutors relied on the rational character of the other's glance or gaze as tied to something of interactional relevance, e.g., a more interesting element of the environment in the case of staring over the shoulder and the search for a personal delict in the case of gazing at a body part, before any challenge to the potential for deviance occurred. So, too, in normal discourse, gestural and postural displays are conventionally affiliated as constituents of the scene as it is emerging rather than being judged for their prior or future relevance to the ongoing character of the discourse.

[17] Scheflen (1973) has an extended discussion of the use of multiple involvements as a psychotherapeutic and diagnostic tool.

During Physician's Speaking Turn: Line 74

Gaze of Phys:	O	O	O	O	O	O	X	X	X
	Oka:y, what grade did you ih- were you in						this past yea:r.		
Gaze of Pt:	O	O	O	O	O	O	O	O	O

FIGURE 1   Diagrammatic Representation of Gaze Behaviors of Physician and Patient

observation that a speaker will generally return his or her gaze to a listener at, or just before, points of turn transition.

We can represent the relationship between vocal and gaze behavior as follows: O represents looking away, and X represents looking toward the speaker.[18]

Notice that although the physician and patient have shared a mutual focus at the beginning of the physician's speaking turn, by its completion, at least one member of the dyad, the physician, has begun to shift his visual orientation from the hands of the patient to his face. Recall that the conventions of appropriateness to a query may involve direct and indirect requests for action. During the physician's turn, which initiates a new phase of the encounter at the same time that it requests information, the patient displays no shift in visual orientation whatsoever and continues to stare throughout the turn at what has been a site of continuing visual attention, the physician's hands.

The caretaker's orientation in this frame has shifted only slightly. While her gaze is directed toward her son throughout the physician's speaking turn, her mouth, which exhibited a smile in frame 8048, is closed in frame 8178. The mouth closure occurs in exact synchrony with the completion of the physician's speaking turn, which suggests a finely calibrated order of participation between the caretaker and the ongoing speech activity.

Plate 3 is a photographic illustration of Frame 8223, approximately six-tenths of a second after the completion of the physician's speaking turn. At this point, neither the physician nor the caretaker appear to have changed significantly in affect or orientation. The patient's visual orientation has changed dramatically, however. Where the patient's gaze had been focused on the physician's hands in the previous plate, it is now quite clearly oriented toward the face and eyes of the physician. The physician and patient now appear to be in direct eye contact, having thus established another site of mutual focus and attention.

The patient's shift begins at frame 8198, approximately three-tenths of a second after the completion of the physician's speaking turn. In conversational

---

[18] This form of transcription for gaze was developed by Charles Goodwin and is reported in his seminal paper, "The Interactive Construction of a Sentence in Dialog" (1979).

PLATE 3   Transition Between Physician's Speaking Turn and Patient's Reply (Frame 8223)

terms, this is a region that Sacks, Schegloff, and Jefferson (1974) have characterized as "transition relevant." It is that point in the ongoing construction of a sequence type or dialogic unit at which a recipient is conventionally obliged to furnish evidence of his or her participation in speech exchange by formulating an appropriate response. Such responses are constrained by both issues of content (i.e., an appropriate response to a question is an answer) and timing (i.e., in a sequence type such as question-answer, the first part of which has just been completed, it is both relevant and appropriate that the second part, if it is to occur at all, should do so as soon upon the completion of the first as possible).[19]

---

[19] Failure to respond to a complete sequence first pair part produces a noticeable absence in the conversational flow which, in turn, initiates a sequence designed to "repair" the delict. See Schegloff, Jefferson, and Sacks (1977).

A: Are you going tomorrow night?
              (1.5)
A: Jo:hn?
              (1.0)
A: Jo::hn.
B: Huh
A: I asked you if you're going tomorrow night

Where visual appropriateness is an issue as well, often the case in conversations between parents and children, a form of sanction may also be applied.

Thus, there are strong grounds for arguing that the patient's shift in orientation that begins at frame 8198 and ends at frame 8223 is directly relevant to the now completed speech organization (turn) produced by the physician.

One way to characterize this relationship is to say that in the course of producing an appropriate response to a sequence, first pair part, visual attention has come under conversational control. This is to say that the patient's visual attention to the physician's hands, both before and during the physician's speaking turn, is no longer appropriate given his obligation to produce an answer here and now. And it is the turn transition region that transforms the *option* of shifting gaze at any point during the physician's turn into an *obligation* containing both visual and vocal requirements.

It is thus by reference to a rule for vocal behavior constraining the time order relationship between a sequence first part and its response *and* an orienting rule requiring a response plus visual orientation that we arrive at the conclusion that the patient's behavior at frame 8223 is both relevant and appropriate to the features of conversational organization. Visual attention has been recruited into the organization of conversation by the rule, When making a response to a query in sequence initial position, it is relevant and appropriate to look at the face of your interlocutor. Failure to do so will be read or interpreted as a violation (e.g., as resistance or an attempt to avoid embarrassment or shame), and will be treated in much the same manner as gazing over the shoulder or at the body of one's interlocutor. Such familiar phrases as "look at me when I'm talking to you" and "don't try to avoid the issue by hiding your head in shame" bear witness to the natural occurrence of these violations.

There are two final pieces of evidence that bear on this point, but first let us be clear about what has just been asserted. My purpose thus far has been to develop a characterization of the constitutive elements of social organization which co-participants in social interaction orient to and acknowledge, routinely. My basic premise has been that various forms of interactional participation (e.g., talking and touching) are independently organized but related by convention. The focus of interest has been the role of gaze in those situations in which competing warrants for visual attention are present. Thus far, it has been shown that, unconstrained by the presence of talk, gaze in the presence of touch monitors touch. Gaze in the presence of touch and talk seems to behave quite

---

Mother:	Chris
	(1.6)
Mother:	Chri:s
	(1.3)
Mother:	What's this Chris.
Child:	Euhh
Mother:	Chris look at me when I'm talking to you

differently; its presence or absence is rapidly and preferredly made relevant to conversational structure.

It seems to be the case then, that conversational structures, such as queries, could be used strategically if the goal of a co-conversationalist was to shift visual attention from one modality (e.g., touch) and establish its relevance to another (e.g., talk). This line of analysis seems to offer a strong possibility for characterizing the behavior of the physician toward the patient.

As previously established, the physician's use of queries from the point of phase transition onward seems to constitute a natural unit or pattern. It is of interest that the reference for each of the physician's queries locates action outside of the context of the current encounter and the ongoing touching activity. It is also of note that each of the queries comes quite soon after the completion of the patient's nonvocal or vocal response. As speech acts, queries have already been implicated in constraining the orienting behavior of their recipient. It will be argued that the physician's questions represent an attempt to systematically divert the patient's attention away from the work of the hands, using the conventions of conversational organization.

At least partial evidence for the power of these constraints to recruit and maintain orienting behavior comes from an examination of Plate 4, which is a photographic illustration of frame 8665 and represents the conclusion of the entire exchange unit begun with the physician's initial query. The realization of this exchange unit is complex and will not be dealt with in detail here. Briefly, between the completion of the physician's initial question and the patient's affirmation by a vertical shake of the head, two intervening sequences have occurred. The first is an interruption of the patient's initial response (Plate 3) to the physician's query, delivered while the patient is shifting gaze from the caretaker back to the physician. The patient has engaged his caretaker in a nonvocal sequence which recovers the vocalization, "Kindergarten?"[20] The sequence is complicated by the fact that the patient's answer is ambiguous in at least two respects: Without a targeted recipient, "Kindergarten?" is equally hearable as the answer to the nonvocal prompt of the caretaker or as a response to the physician's initial question. The net result is a further elaboration of the sequence to clarify the status of the patient's response.

We can see from this illustration that Goodwin's (1979) *speaker-based* rules for achieving co-recipiency work both ways. Not only do speakers need mutual gaze to identify hearers, but the relevance of a response to more than a single

---

[20] Jefferson (1972) has described a base unit type that she characterizes as a "side sequence." Side sequences have the property of intervening disjunctively in an ongoing sequence while still allowing that sequence to continue normally after the side sequence has been completed. The "embedded" side sequence described here may be unique to children, for it involves a co-conversationalist beginning a reply to a previous speaker, interrupting that reply to engage with another party altogether, and returning conversationally to complete the original response.

recipient suggests that hearers need to secure a speaker's gaze, as well, to be able to respond appropriately. In this case, the physician's response to an utterance lacking a clear-cut orientation is to introduce a disambiguating query: "Were you in kindergarten?" Plate 4 represents the situation just after the patient produced an acknowledgment that completes the entire elaborated sequence. The entire exchange unit is displayed in Figure 2.

What is notable at the completion of this sequence in Plate 4 is the return of the patient's gaze to the area in which the physician's hands are continuing to probe. It is as though the obligation to look when responding to the physician's query is exhausted once a sequentially complete response has been provided, at which point the patient is free to return his gaze to another warrantable site of attention (in this case, the hands). This is particularly fascinating because the shift in the patient's gaze is timed exactly with the completion of his turn and of a complex exchange unit.

A similar sequence without embedding occurs at lines 82-84 of the transcript. At frame number 8831, the physician initiates a second elaboration on the topic of kindergarten, the first having been a simple yes–no question: 'hh Didju like it?,." The second query, "Whatij- whatija *do* the:re," requests a formulated response. Again, during the time the question is being asked, the patient begins to reorient by re-establishing mutual eye contact with the physician; he continues to maintain that eye contact during the entire length of his response. And again,

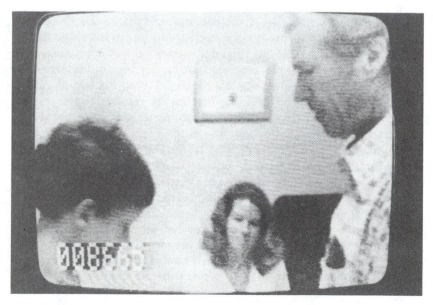

PLATE 4   Completion of Patient's Response (Frame 8665)

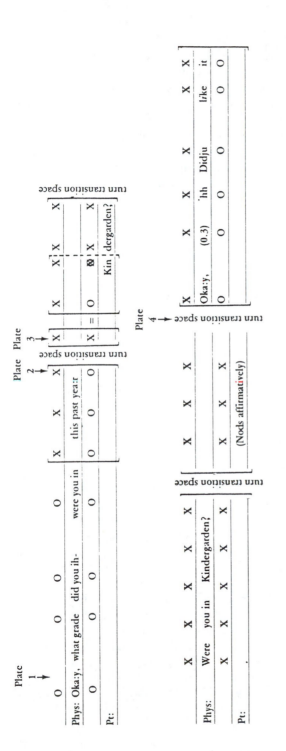

FIGURE 2 A Diagrammatic Representation of the Complete Exchange Unit

Legend

Plate 1 = frame 8048 Physician turn initiation
Plate 2 = frame 8178 Physician turn completion
Plate 3 = frame 8223 Patient's initial response
Plate 4 = frame 8665 Patient's completion

Transcription conventions

X = gazing toward
O = gazing away
Ø = transitional state

as in the initial example, once a complete response has been produced, the patient returns his gaze to the physician's hands.

One begins to sense a pattern in which the physician is using the questions to direct the visual attention of the patient away from the work of the hands and to the task of conversing. It also seems that as quickly as the patient's obligations to attend are exhausted, his attention returns immediately to monitoring the work of the hands. It is against this background of ongoing manual activity that a sequences of questions, topically connected, and also locating action references outside of the immediate scene, is being used strategically by the physician to create an alternative focus of attention for the patient. By relying on the cultural conventions that organize gaze and touch in the presence of talk, the physician produced a set of constraints whose effect is to limit the distribution and location of the patient's visual attention.

SUMMARY AND CONCLUSION

This investigation developed a descriptive account of the basic interactional mechanisms involved in an episode of touching during a routine pediatric examination.

Touching is a complex communicational phenomenon involving aspects of affect, orientation, and attention. Touching is also a constitutive phenomenon, which is to say that its meaning is always contingent on a background that furnishes both a texture and rules for deciding the appropriateness of an action in any given situation. Holding the elements of gaze and talk constant in an experimental manipulation of these background conditions provides further evidence for the assertion that meaning in social interaction is both contingent and negotiated. This line of reasoning argues against the principle of inherency or correspondence in which names and objects are seen to stand in a one-to-one relationship. It argues instead for a view of action that is interpretively based and cannot be removed from the particular contexts in which it occurs.

A theory of meaning based on the contextual particulars of social interaction has special relevance for the study of physicians and patients in relationship. The notion of meaning as an interactional accomplishment, for example, locates physicians and patients as members of a culture demonstrating their competencies as speakers and hearers of a language; not as (biologically) independent entities engaged in the mechanical process of information transfer. That status, power, and control may be facets of a relationship is far less important conceptually than recognizing the mutual interdependence of inputs and outputs (e.g., identification and treatment of an illness) in a system that is socially, as opposed to biologically or chemically, defined. The value of an interpretive view in medicine is that it radically transforms the nature of the physician's participation in the health care encounter from an objective, dispassionate giver of advice to an interactional partner who actively participates in the social construction of illness, its treatment, and outcome. By analyzing "unremarkable" stretches of videotape such as the one studied here we can begin to develop an understanding of medicine as an extension of, not an exception to, the social organization of everyday life.

The analysis itself offered an opportunity to study a routine event in the organization of the medical encounter, the beginning of the physical examination. In contrast with methods based on historic or synoptic metaphors, the analytic task was conceived as an attempt to describe the interaction rules linking participants to one another in real time and space. Unlike most casual conversations (between nonintimates) that do not include nonrestricted touching of body parts, the beginning of the physical examination was found to be separated linguistically from other portions of the encounter. More important, vocal and nonvocal activities were coordinated in a way that systematically partitioned the patient's attention away from one locus of action, palpating the body, to another, a smoothly flowing conversation about school.

That two activity systems within a single encounter could exist simultaneously is not surprising; human beings seem eminently capable of conducting themselves in sets of multilayered activities. Of more significance was the finding that precise coordination and transformation of the patient's attention to the physical exam were achieved as the physician introduced particular conversational structures, i.e., queries, into the stream of behavior. Thus an important nonmedical question concerning the interrelationship between vocal and nonvocal activities was answered. In a situation such as a medical encounter where information is being sought in a number of modalities simultaneously, attention appears to move hierarchically from one site to another depending on the type of sequential structure involved. In the case of the physical examination under study, it was found that touching in the absence of talk creates a locus for attention at the touching site. In a situation in which talk and touching occur simultaneously, however, conversational structure seems to take precedence by transforming both the site and the obligation of a listener to attend to the speaker's face.

What has been learned that is of value for physicians and their training? In a practical sense, the analysis of this short pediatric transaction seems trivial because neither its content, direction, nor meaning were problematic to begin with. On the other hand, some practical information about the conduct of a routine physical examination has been generated and can serve as a baseline for educational and teaching purposes. More generally, having isolated a specific location that is characteristic for all such encounters permits the spectrum of behaviors that occur in one or several practice types or settings to be compared or contrasted.

Focusing on what people actually do also has the benefit of demonstrating the orderly ways in which cultural or social expression is realized. In this particular case, the fact that the pediatrician used a specific linguistic format to partition the patient's attention does not exhaust the possible avenues in which appropriate communication should or must proceed. Other forms of linguistic expression, such as the use of declarative assertions or directives to elaborate on rather than restrict the patient's attention to a series of touches, are not only possible, but constitute a readily recognizable alternative style of pediatric practice. A contrast between OB/Gyn and pediatric providers on this communication dimension could lead to better strategies for teaching the physical exam so as to optimize the comfort of both the patient and the physician.

Recommendations based on this approach are not of the type that unilaterally assign value to one style of interaction or another. Rather, the value of a descriptive understanding of practice is that it provides alternative models of behaving appropriately in an encounter situation. Similarly, increasing physicians' awareness and sensitivity to the communicative dimensions of health not only increases the range of possibilities for participating in the delivery of care, it provides a link to the cultural contexts which make health and illness meaningful as experiences embedded in an everyday world. Given the large number of ambulatory visits that are of no concern medically, the addition of a number of options for broader participation in defining and responding to patient concerns offers the potential for reducing the gap between health care needs of the population and current standards of practice.

Finally, for the student learning to *do* medically relevant behavior, the analysis provides a grounded approach to learning about social interaction. It is unfortunate that in the teaching of medicine the social is often "lost" to the biological. To the extent that behavior, in particular the meaning of behavior, can be "explained" in causal terms, reducing the fit between foreground and background, between the concept of disease and a concept of the individual, it becomes a preferred mode of operation. As a consequence, the facts in a case often become more important than the person in the case. The social and its soft underbelly of meaning is cast to the side in training as a dimension of practice better left implicit and better left in the realm of the philosophical, not the practical.

Microanalysis of communicative interaction holds the potential for shifting the basis of what is known about physicians and patients in relationship from a currently underrepresented and ad hoc form of theorizing to a systematic search for the concrete bases of social behavior. By identifying both recurrent and emergent organizational patterns (i.e., by focusing *simultaneously* on the relationship between the expectable and the actual) a clearer, more fruitful picture of the "working" nature of communication in the context of medicine and social relations, in general, may be within our grasp.

REFERENCES CITED

ARGYLE, MICHAEL, AND MARK COOK
1976   *Gaze and Mutual Gaze*. Cambridge: Cambridge University Press.

ARGYLE, MICHAEL, AND JANET DEAN
1965   Eye contact, distance, and affiliation. *Sociometry* 28:289–304.

ATKINSON, J. MAXWELL
1978   *Discovering Suicide: Studies in the Social Organization of Sudden Death.* Pittsburgh: University of Pittsburgh Press.

BRUHN, JOHN G.
1978   The doctor's touch: Tactile communication in the doctor–patient relationship. *Southern Medical Journal* (Birmingham, Alabama) 71(12):1469–1473.

CASSELL, ERIC
1978   The Use and Functions of Language in Medicine. Audiotaped lectures of a course for second-year medical students. Ithaca, N.Y.: Cornell University School of Medicine.

CHANCE, MICHAEL
1967   Attention structure as the basis of primate rank orders. *Man* 2:503–518.

CICOUREL, AARON
1968   *The Social Organization of Juvenile Justice*. New York: Wiley.

CONDON, W.S., AND W.D. OGSTON
1971   Speech and body motion synchrony of the speaker hearer. IN *The Perception of Language*, David L. Horton and James J. Jenkins, Eds., pp. 150–173. Columbus, Ohio: Charles Merrill.

DOUGLAS, JACK D.
1967   *The Social Meanings of Suicide*. Princeton: Princeton University Press.

DURKHEIM, EMILE
1951   *Suicide*. New York: The Free Press.

EISENBERG, LEON
1977   Psychiatry and society: A sociobiologic synthesis. *New England Journal of Medicine* 296:903–910.

EMERSON, JOAN
1970   Behavior in private places: Sustaining definitions of reality in gynecological examinations. In *Recent Sociology No. 2: Patterns of Communicative Behavior*, Hans Peter Dreitzel, Ed., pp. 73–97. New York: Macmillan.

ENGEL, GEORGE L.
1977   The need for a new medical model: A challenge for biomedicine. *Science* 196:129–135 (April 8).

ERICKSON, FREDERICK
1975   One function of proxemic shifts in face-to-face interaction. IN *Organization of Behavior in Face-to-Face Interaction*, Adam Kendon, Richard M. Harris, and Mary Ritchie Key, Eds., pp. 175–187. The Hague: Mouton.

ERICKSON, FREDERICK, AND JEFFERY SHULTZ
1982   *The Counselor as Gatekeeper: Social Interaction in Interviews*. New York: Academic.

EXLINE, RALPH
    1974   Visual interaction: The glances of power and preference. IN *Nonverbal Communication: Readings with Commentary*, Shirley Weitz, Ed., pp. 65–92. New York: Oxford University Press.

EXLINE, RALPH, AND A. YELLIN
    1969   Eye contact as a sign between man and monkey. Paper presented at symposium on nonverbal communication. Nineteenth International Congress of Psychology, London.

FABREGA, HORATIO, AND L. VAN EGEREN
    1976   A behavioral framework for the study of human disease. *Annals of Internal Medicine* 84:200–208.

FRANKEL, RICHARD
    1982   Autism for all practical purposes: A microinteractional view. IN Special Issue of *Topics in Language Disorders*, J. Duchan, Ed., 3(1):33–42.
    In press   Talking in interviews: A dispreference for patient-initiated questions in physician-patient encounters. IN *Interactional Competence*, George Psathas and Richard Frankel, Eds. New York: Irvington.
    Forthcoming   Microanalysis and the medical encounter. IN *New Directions in Ethnomethodology and Conversation Analysis*, D. Helm, W.T. Anderson, and A.J. Meehan, Eds., New York: Irvington.

GARFINKEL, HAROLD
    1967   *Studies in Ethnomethodology*. Englewood Cliffs, N.J.: Prentice-Hall.

GOODWIN, CHARLES
    1979   The interactive construction of a sentence in natural conversation. IN *Everyday Language: Studies in Ethnomethodology*, G. Psathas, Ed., pp. 97–121. New York: Irvington.

JEFFERSON, GAIL
    1972   Side sequences. IN *Studies in Social Interaction*, David Sudnow, Ed., pp. 294–338. New York: The Free Press.
    1978   Sequential aspects of storytelling in conversation. IN *Studies in the Organization of Conversational Interaction*, Jim Schenkein, Ed., pp. 219–248. New York: Academic.

JELLISON, J.M., AND W.J. ICKES
    1974   The power of the glance: Desire to see and be seen in competitive and cooperative situations. *Journal of Experimental Social Psychology* 10:444–450.

KENDON, ADAM
    1967   Some functions of gaze direction in social interaction. *Acta Psychologica* 26:1–47.
    1979   Some theoretical and methodological considerations of the use of film in the study of social interaction. IN *Emerging Strategies in Social Psychological Research*, G.P. Ginsberg, Ed. New York: John Wiley.

KLEINMAN, ARTHUR
    1980   *Patients and Healers in the Context of Culture: An Exploration of the Borderline Between Anthropology, Medicine, and Psychiatry*. Berkeley: University of California Press.

LIBERMAN, ROBERT
    1963   Analysis of the placebo phenomenon. *Journal of Chronic Diseases* 15:761–783.

MEHAN, HUGH

1979 *Learning Lessons: The Social Organization of Classroom Behavior.* Cambridge, Mass.: Harvard University Press.

NATIONAL ACADEMY OF SCIENCES, INSTITUTE OF MEDICINE

1978 *A Manpower Policy for Primary Care*, IOM, Publication #78–02. Washington, D.C.: Author.

SACKS, HARVEY

1966a The Search For Help: No One To Turn To. Doctoral dissertation, University of California, Berkeley.

1966b Unpublished lecture notes, winter quarter. University of California, Irvine.

SACKS, HARVEY; EMANUEL SCHEGLOFF; AND GAIL JEFFERSON

1974 A simplest systematics for the organization of turn-taking for conversation. *Language* 50:696–735.

SCHEFLEN, ALBERT

1973 *Communicational Structure: Analysis of a Psychotherapy Transaction.* Bloomington: Indiana University Press.

SCHEGLOFF, EMANUEL; GAIL JEFFERSON; AND HARVEY SACKS

1977 The preference for self-correction in the organization of repair in conversation. *Language* 53:361–382.

SCHEGLOFF, EMANUEL, AND HARVEY SACKS

1973 Opening up closings. *Semiotica* 8:282–327.

STONE, GEORGE C.

1979 Patient compliance and the role of the expert. *Journal of Social Issues* 35(1):34–59.

U.S. DEPARTMENT OF HEALTH, EDUCATION, AND WELFARE

1982 1980 summary: National ambulatory medical care survey. *Advance Data* No. 77 (February 22).

VAN HOOFF, J.A.R.A.M.

1967 The facial displays of catarrhine monkeys and apes. IN *Primate Ethology*, Desmond Morris, Ed., pp. 7–68. London: Weidenfeld and Nicholson. [Also Garden City, N.Y.: Doubleday Anchor, 1969]

WEST, CANDACE

1983 'Ask me no questions...': An analysis of queries and replies in physician-patient dialogues. IN *The Social Organization of Doctor-Patient Communication*, Sue Fisher and Alexandra Dundas Todd, Eds., pp. 75–106. Washington, D.C.: The Center for Applied Linguistics.

ZIMMERMAN, DON, AND MELVIN POLLNER

1970 The everyday world as phenomenon. IN *Understanding Everyday Life: Toward the Reconstruction of Sociological Knowledge*, Jack Douglas, Ed., pp. 80–103. Chicago: Aldine.

APPENDIX A
Transcribing Conventions

The method of transcription employed here was developed by Gail Jefferson, at the University of California, Irvine, in the course of collaborative research with the late Harvey Sacks. The transcription system is intended to act as a guide to speech production activities as they occur on a micromomentary scale.

Dr: [Right]
Pt: [[And] if there's anything

Pt: No (0.3 an' nothing since]
Dr: [Not all all]

The onset of simultaneous speech is indicated with either a double or single left-handed bracket depending on where it occurs. Double brackets are used to indicate simultaneous turn beginnings; single brackets indicate interruption or overlap of ongoing speech. Single right-handed brackets indicate resolution points for simultaneous speech.

Pt: Something I wanna / / do]
Dr: That's the whole-]

(1.3)

An alternate method of indicating overlap is the use of double oblique lines at the point of overlap or interruption.

Numbers in parenthesis indicate pauses or breaks in speech production and are indicated in tenths of seconds. Pauses are marked both within and between speaking turns.

.?,?,

Punctuation marks are used to indicate intonation and not grammar. A period indicates a sharply falling intonation; the question mark a sharply rising intonation. Commas and question commas (?) indicate intonational blends, = slightly rising or slightly falling intonation.? = moderately rising intonation

Pt: 'hh U:hm the: uh: (0.5) the back

Colons indicate a sound stretch or prolongation of an immediately prior syllable. Each colon represents one-tenth of a second.

Dr: That's the whole-

A hyphen indicates that immediately prior syllable has been cut off.

Dr: Y' put half a' pound on this time. =
Pt: = I don't know what tuh

Equal signs are used to indicate that no discernible time has elapsed between the completion of one speaker's utterance and the beginning of another.

'hh hh

Breathing patterns are signified using hh's. A period followed by *hh*'s marks an inhalation; *hh*'s alone stand for exhalation.

APPENDIX B
TRANSCRIBED FRAGMENT OF PHYSICIAN/PATIENT/
CARETAKER INTERACTION

Physician:	How (de doo)	1
Caretaker:	hHi	2
	(0.4)	3
Patient:	Hi?,	4
	(0.3)	5
Physician:	( )we come with uh (0.2) equipment.	6
Caretaker:	uh hih-hih	7
Physician:	Waddaya think a this Michael.	8
	(2.1)	9
Physician:	⌈(Guess) the last time I say yuh you had a sore throat.⌉	10
Patient:	⌊(Awright) ⌋	11
	(0.4)	12
Patient:	Know what?,	13
Physician:	What.	14
Patient:	I got-a five swimming race ribbons (0.8) from Saturda:y hh	15
Physician:	Fi:ve,	16
	(0.5)	17
Patient:	Five swimming ribbons on/ /e wz white] hhh an one's blu::e	18
	'n I got three:: (0.3) red ones.	19
Physician:	Ribbons.]	20
Physician:	Isn't that gre:at.	21
Physician:	Wadda all those colors mea:n.	22
Patient:	Sekkint, first, third, (1.0) Right Mo:m?	23
Caretaker:	Right	24
Physician:	That is just fi:ne, you must be a very good swimmer	25
	(1.0)	26
Physician:	Good.	27
Patient:	An 'm gunnuh swim(.) in the finals,	28
Physician:	Yer goin' 'a swim?, (0.9) or that was the finals.	29
	(1.0)	30
Patient:	It wasn't. right Mom?	31
	(yes)	
Caretaker:	Saturday (it is)	32
Physician:	Saturday's coming up, =	33
Caretaker:	= Muh hmh	34
	(0.6)	35
Physician:	W/l you really-look ez if you've been gitting some sunshine,	36
	you've got a ta:n (0.8) and you must hev alot of fun swimming.	37
	(0.4) Isn't that great.	38
Patient:	Uhm-d'you swim practice very often?	39
	(0.7)	40
Patient:	Right mom,	41
Caretaker:	Muh hmh.	42
	(0.5)	43

Physician:	Swim every da:y?	44
	(1.3)	45
Physician:	Really,	46
Caretaker:	Mmh hmh ( ) goes every day ( ).	47
Physician:	W-how's he been.	48
Caretaker:	Super. He started t' get the sniffles this morning.	49
	(0.7)	50
Caretaker:	Hehhh hah hh hh hh/ /hm 'hh uh-heh 'hhh]	51
Physician:	⌈(Well)	52
Physician:	⌊Let's hope it's our(.) our our not so] warm weather.	53
	somethin thet - nothing too bad. = D'he act at all sick.	54
Caretaker:	No:h he's n- u-h however on Wednesday he was around a boy that	55
	was sick that hed 'hh an infected ear an throat, en everything.	56
	that we found out about forty five minutes afterwards his mother	57
	mentioned 'hh thet he'd had an infected everything.	58
Physician:	hmh	59
Physician:	Well now hez uh-I saw 'im in Ma:y, hez he had any trouble	60
	since then.	61
Caretaker:	No: he's been fine.	62
Physician:	Good.	63
	(0.3)	64
Physician:	Michael?, c'n you climb up here,	65
	(8.2)((rustling sounds))	66
Physician:	Wanna hang yet feet over here so thet I c'n- (0.4) I think yer	67
	comfortable in (lotus position) but Im' not.	68
Physician:	Huh huh-huh	69
Caretaker:	Heh heh heh	70
	(0.6)	71
Physician:	'hhh Makes my (.) toes ache (0.4) lookin' at cha	72
	(1.0)	73
Physician:	Oka:y, what grade did ju ih- were you in this last yea:r.	74
	(3.7)	75
Patient:	Kindergarten?	76
	(0.4)	77
Physician:	Were you in kindergarten?,	78
	(0.6) ((Nods head affirmatively))	79
Physician:	Oka:y, (0.3) 'hh Didju like it?,	80
	(0.6) ((Nods head affirmatively))	81
Physician:	Waddij- waddijuh do ther:e.	82
	(0.8)	83
Patient:	We did lots a' things like we painted picture::s 'n stuff.	84
	(1.0)	85
Physician:	(Mm)hmh	86
	(0.8)	87
Physician:	Remember the name of yer schoo:l?	88
	(2.1) ((Patient nods affirmatively))	89

Physician:	What w'z the name of yer school,	90
	(1.0)	91
Patient:	Avalon.	92
	(0.3)	93
Physician:	Avalon.	94
	(1.0)	95
Physician:	"N that's I think a very nice place. (0.4) had lots of trees around there didn't they?	96 97
	(0.4)	98
Physician:	°Mmh hmh	99
	(1.0)	100
Patient:	En they got little toy:s 'n stuff down on the playground	101
	(0.3)	102
Physician:	°Mmh hmh	103

5

On the Work of Talk: Studies in Misunderstandings*

Marianne A. Paget

A stretch of talk from a medical encounter follows. The typescript preserves fine details of the speaking practices of an internist and his patient. They met three times in the early months of 1972 in a large, university-affiliated clinic to discuss her medical problems. Each of their encounters was ambiguous and unresolved. Each encounter exuded misunderstandings. Their talk was awry with disagreements, odd semantic constructions, radical breaks and shifts in discourse topics, and allusions to an operation that were not clarified.

The central tension of their talk was created by the physician's assessment: that her basic health was good and that the problem was her "nerves." But throughout their meetings, she reported a number of minor and serious symptoms that challenged his assessment.

The transcript (see page xx) reads vertically as well as horizontally, because speech is produced in small bundles of considerable interactional and interpretive significance. These bundles are often phrases or clauses like "I wan yuh tuh sit straight" or "sit facing me." Sometimes, however, they are single words like "no" or nonlexical speech sounds like "ohhh" or "ahhh."

* Research on which this chapter is based was supported by an NIMH Postdoctoral Training Fellowship in the Department of Psychiatry, Harvard Medical School. The tapes used come from a study of information control conducted by Howard Waitzkin and John D. Stoeckle. This research was first presented at a roundtable in medical sociology at the 49th Annual Meeting of the Eastern Sociological Society, March 16-18, 1979, in New York City. Peter Finkelstein, Richard M. Frankel, Leslie L. Howard, and Elliot G. Mishler were very helpful in its preparation.

The organization of the transcript facilitates reading fine details of each participant's speech production in the presence of and in reaction to the other. Pauses within a turn at talk are marked by periods, each period representing a tenth of a second. Pauses between speakers are in parentheses. Interruptions that indicate a struggle for control between them are identified by brackets. Many other transcript notations are explained in Schenkein (1978:xi–xvi).

This stretch of talk and others from the same series of interviews will be used to examine the speaking practices of physicians, particularly their practices of questioning patients. A diagnosis is not just an abstract thing connected with a nomenclature and a theory of disease entities, although it is that, too. It is not just a term on a medical chart or a record, although virtually an infinite number can be found there. A diagnosis *is* a feature of the organization of talk, and its production is continuously realized in that talk. This analysis will focus on questioning practices because these practices often construct the meaning of a patient's illness.

D: I wan yuh tuh sit straight. . . .
     no
     sit facing me
                        (3.4)
     d yuh wear a hat by preference
     or yer having anything wrong with yer
     scalp
                        (0.8)

P: oh
                               I'm I'm I wear it cuz its co:ld
                               but *I* ha *I* I-my sc*alp* is a littabit
                                 [   ]
D: *oh* oh °yeah
P: my sc*alp* is getting all *abra*sions on it
                               fer some *crazy* reason or other
                               [
D: w'l let me jus have a look
                              . .

     take it off jus fer a second
        [
P: look at tha- look at this . uh .
     uh   ths- I can't even (man-)
                               I can't even bleach my *hair*
                               I don kno-I dunno if they're still there
                               but last week it ws all *r:ed*
                               it was
                               [
D: no:h
                               it looks pretty clean

P: yeah
                                                            tha-wha- my barber js
                                                                           [
D: there's a little bit
          of dandruff there
          but that's about all
P: yeah
D: alright putcher hat down
                     [   ]
P: °m °husba °thinks
                                        (0.8)
D: y'll be more comfortable °without °it

In the excerpt above, which opens the first of three encounters, this physician
introduces a topic with a compound question, "d yuh wear a hat by preference or
yer having anything wrong with yer s*calp*." He apparently observed that this
patient, a woman in her mid-40's, is wearing both a frock, in preparation for an
exam, and a hat.

The topic (her hat and scalp) is explored through a series of turns at talk in
which each participant responds to the other's utterances. She answers both of
his initial questions. "I'm I'm I wear it cuz its co:ld," is her response to his first
question, and "but *I* ha *I* I-my s*calp* is a littabit my s*calp* is getting all *abra*sions
on it fer some *crazy* reason or other," is her response to his second question
(Shuy [1974] discusses the common medical practice of asking two questions at
once). Her response is complex because it projects an act. Implicitly, it requests
that he examine her scalp, and it is heard that way. The physician responds. He
both says, "w'l let me just have a look," and looks (Churchill 1978; Labov and
Fanshel 1977; Sacks 1972; Sacks, Schegloff, and Jefferson 1974; Searle 1969).
His looking is captured in their talk's silence of almost two seconds, in his
assessment, "no:h it looks pretty clean," with which she agrees, and in his
related observation that "there's a little bit of dandruff there," with which she
also agrees. This discourse topic comes to its close with his request that she put
her hat down and with his connected politeness, "y'll be more comfortable
°without °it." His next request introduces a new topic, "now let me see yer
throat."

The excerpt is a microparadigm of the pattern of this physician's and patient's
talk, for he continuously directs their talk. Through questions and other
"requests" for action, and sometimes through commands, he introduces,
develops, and dissolves discourse topics. (Questions are, in fact, "requests" for
action. They are used to carry on interactional activities, such as clarifying,
assessing, complaining, and explaining.) Abrupt breaks or shifts often appear in
their discourse, and the physician, too, initiates these shifts and breaks. She
helps develop their talk by responding to his questions and his other "requests"
and, sometimes, by suggesting and expressing her own concerns. But often he

ignores her concerns, which also contributes to the developing discontinuities in the movement of their talk.

The exchange continues:

```
D:   now let me see yer throat
                                          (7.8)
     uh have the teeth been remo:ved
     that were in question
P:                                    no:
                                      my mouth is drivin me cra:zy
                                      (. . .) in fact when I:
                                      sleep with my head over here
                                      or my head inclined on the side. . . . .
                                      m- my whole mouth hu:rts
                                          (0.6)
D:   w'l I would hate t have them remo:ve
               [   ]
P:             ohhh
D:   any more teeth
     without bein sure
     thet they were the cause of something
               [   ]
P:             ahhh
                                          (0.6)
P:                                    o:h I kno:w it
                                      but what m I gonna do
D:   w'll let's look straight
                                          (5.6)
```

His utterance, "w'l I would hate t have them remo:ve any more teeth without bein *sure* thet they were the cause of something," is representative of the abrupt shifts that occur in their talk. His utterance does not develop her reply, "my mouth is drivin me cra:zy." He does not ask how long her mouth has been bothering her, how often if happens, or when she last saw a dentist. Instead, he shifts ground. The utterance contains an unmarked pronoun "them," which has no previous referent in their talk, and suggests that "them" may have removed teeth unnecessarily.

A discourse analyst must continuously confront ambiguities that arise in the highly contextual features of talk and its unfolding ellipses (Garfinkel 1967; Goffman 1976). In the previous exchange, "them" is a reference to unknown dentists who removed some of her teeth, which the physician noticed while examining her mouth. His insinuation that some of her teeth may have been removed unnecessarily is the first of several insinuations about her past care. (His use of unmarked pronouns will recur.) She hears the suggested uncertainty about the appropriateness of removing some of her teeth and responds, "o:h I kno:w but what m I gonna *do*." He replies with a command, "w'll let's look straight."

The physician's failure to respond to her question again shows the discontinuities of their talk. And, his impoliteness captures a pattern of dominance (his) and subordination (hers) as it is being constituted in their conversation. Throughout their exchanges, however unconnected his utterances are with what has gone before, they will be supported. Even when appearing with unmarked references like "them," they will be developed. She will reply. Very often, however, her inquiries will go unsupported and unclarified. (See Mishler 1975 and 1978 for an analysis of the role relations created by questioning and Waitzkin, Stoeckle, Beller, and Mons 1978 for an analysis of physician control of information in medical interviews.)

Politeness forms like "ok" "yeah" and "thanks" occasionally follow responses to questions or other requests. They acknowledge a response. But politeness forms are frequently deleted from discourse. They are almost entirely absent from the speaking practices of the physician in these encounters.

THE VICISSITUDES OF DISCOURSE

Questioning patients is the most common method of acquiring information about illness. Questions create a reservoir of usable knowledge in responding to illness. In an analysis of the talk of British general practitioners and their patients, Byrne and Long (1976) report that patient care takes place as a series of discourse exchanges that last on the average of eight minutes. They reviewed 2,500 tapes. In eight minutes, physicians attempted to establish rapport, discover the reason for a patient's visit, verbally and physically examine the patient, discuss the patient's condition, establish a treatment plan, and terminate the exchange.

Questioning practices will be the focus of *detailed* attention here because of a discovered problem in the talk of this physician and patient. This woman is a postoperative cancer patient, concerned about the spread of her cancer and about her survival. Yet, across their three encounters, her condition as a cancer patient and her fear that her cancer would metastasize were never introduced as discourse topics. Her condition became apparent in the course of a close analysis of their talk, including increasingly detailed transcriptions of their encounters.

Oblique references to her recent surgery appeared in their first exchange: scar, tumor, surgery, and remaining kidney. These oblique references, however, were not connected with her recurrent expressions of pain. The physician assessed her many symptoms and complaints, her anxieties about what was happening to her body, and her fear of her death as signs of a neurotic depression. He continually assured her that her basic health was good and that the problem was her nerves.

Instead of discussing her concerns about cancer they talked about a virus, persistent pain in her mouth, her teeth and gums, a sinus condition, her nerves, her visits to other physicians and to dentists, medical procedures she has undergone in the past or may undergo, medications that she is taking or might take, plans for new tests, additional visits, her weight, consultations with other physicians for a cyst on her face, and eyeglasses.

Medical audiences are able to hear the talk's oblique references to surgery as a "conversation" about a cancer operation. Especially important in confirming this impression are references to procedures that were undertaken three months earlier by another clinic where her surgery was performed, among the procedures, an angiogram. References to these procedures appear on the third tape. The existence of cancer was independently corroborated through questionnaires that were collected in the course of the original study and made available to me.

Because this woman's condition as a cancer patient was never discussed, her essential concern about its recurrence could not be addressed. More fundamentally, her continued symptoms, persistent reports of pain, anxieties about her health and health care could not be referred, or, at least as the discourse developed, *were not referred* to her experience of cancer. Both the referents to her cancer and the implications of the experience were lost in the discourse. Instead, her symptoms were referred to her nerves.

She was reassured that her basic health was good. For example, the physician said, "I'm . sure that yer basic health is good," and "w'l yer eventually gonna have to be::convinced of it or you won't be well," and "yuh got to feel it deep down *in* (0.6) so that yer (1.6) you have a chance to recover completely." Their exchanges became marked by her struggle to resist his diagnostic assessment that the problem was her nerves and by her effort to clarify the meaning of her symptoms.

Because her condition as a cancer patient was never addressed, I will explore its exclusion by following allusions and oblique references to it in their first encounter. Each knew that she had cancer, and each knew that the other knew, and each also knew that these oblique references recurred without achieving expression. Attention will be given to *how* discourse topics are established and developed, because, although this topic was not developed, many, many others were.

Excerpts from the early phase of the first encounter will be used because it is in the early phase, the physical examination phase, that the physician begins to formulate his diagnosis that the problem is nerves. An excerpt that stands as their first major exchange on the problem of her nerves will be presented. Preliminary exchanges, along the way of that assessment, will also be presented. Then, a second assessment of her health will be displayed. The unspoken topic, cancer, hovers on the verge of expression in the questions she asks. Discontinuities in the discourse are noted throughout the analysis. These discontinuities continuously capture asymmetries in questioning and answering practices that shaped the meaning of her illness. All excerpts are from the physical examination phase of their encounter. How far into the exchange the excerpts occurred is noted at the beginning of each excerpt.

3 1/2 minutes

(3.6)

P: I'm one person haf so:
darned many com:pl*aints*
n not bein anything
I mean y know
(n the past few months)
          [

D: ((noises))
hold it

(1.0)

there has to be
some explanation
but it doesn't ((noises))

(3.1)

it doesn't haftuh be::
a dise:ase
in order t organize
        [

P: oh I'm not lookin fer a *dire* disease

(0.6)

y know
°or °anything °like °that
I'm not lookin for anything
         [
        ((noises))

(2.6)

In this exchange, this physician interrupts her, a characteristic discourtesy that will recur. "Hold it," he commands. The examination is captured in a silence, and he begins to speak, while examining her: "there has to be some explanation but it doesn't ((noises))." Again, the exam is captured in a silence, then, "it doesn't haftuh be::a dise:ase." This is his first suggestion that a disease may not be the cause of her pains. It is a kind of initial offering and it will be followed by others. It comes as an expansion of a developing discourse topic, her many complaints, and there "not bein anything." The physician's speech carries an emphasis on "be" and "disease," and emphasis is important in hearing. It invokes special notice in the melody of talk. Such emphasis, here the elongation of sound, can be translated as "hear what I am saying under this accent, it doesn't have to b*eee* a dis*eease*" (see Gunter 1974).

Several of her own utterances carry accents: "complaints" and "dire." She hears his emphasis and interrupts to say that she is not looking for a "dire disease." Her speech continues very softly, "°or °anything °like °that." Her interruption signals her sensitivity to the idea of disease. It does not expand on the other part of his offering, that pain may not be caused by a disease. Soon she will ask about the pain in the area of her scar.

5 minutes

```
                                    (6.1)
P:                                      °oh that °hurt
                                    (0.6)
D:   where. .
     oh that's in the scar
                                    (0.6)
P:                                      °right in here
D:   yeah
        [
P:      o:hh is that in the scar
D:   that is the scar
P:                                  I::. . . .
                                    it is
D:   noh that-
                                    (0.8)
P:                                  is it- is that- I had-. . . .
                                    is that supposed to hurt like that
                                    from a (. . .)
                                            [
D:                                  it. .occasionally it does for
     quite awhile
             [   ]
P:           o::h
D:   that does not represent anything wrong
     that's because when they make a scar
     as big as that
     it has to cut nerves
P:                                  o:h it-
                                    but it didn't hurt me until this week
                                    (0.6)
D:   well
                                    (0.6)
P:                                  ahuh
                                        [    ]
D:                                  let's see
                                    (0.6)
P:                                  o::h
D:   now breathe
                                    (4.1)
```

This exchange refers to pain that is located in the course of his examination of her back. "°Oh that °hurt." "Where (0.2) oh *that's* in the scar." "O:hh is that in the scar." "That *is* the scar." "Is it-is that-I had-(0.4) is that supposed to hurt like that from a (. . .)." Her question is interrupted in its course, and its last component is lost. The physician assures her that occasionally such pain continues for quite a while, an ellipsis of "quite a while after an operation." "*That*," he continues, "does *not* represent anything *wrong*." "O:h it-," she says, "but it didn't hurt me until this week."

"But" signals a disagreement with his assessment that "*that* does *not* represent anything *wrong*," and that disagreement is developed in her statement, "it didn't hurt me until this week." His response, "well," is a token of his recognition that she has disagreed. And her response, "ahuh," reaffirms her position against his reservation. These are small, delicate signs of a continuously developing conflict about what is wrong with her. He says, "Let's see," and dissolves the topic in the exam.

6 minutes

(3.4)

```
D:   how good is ye:r win:d
     can you: . carry bundles
     n walk up a hill without being
     short of breath
     or do you
          [
P:        no I can't even climb up a flight of stairs without gettin
                                        completely exhausted
                              (0.6)
D:   now do you have any pain under this . .
     . . kidney
                              (1.2)
P:                                        sniff
                              (0.6)
P:                                        ahhh
D:   there
P:                                        not when you touch it
                                          bt I've ben havin
                                          [         ]
D:                                        Whistling
P:                                        pain in that area
                                          [   ]
D:                                        fine
     you do have pain in this area . . . . .w'l that's too soon y see
          [                                                    ]
P:               o::h yeah o:h that hurts right there
D:   that's too soon to tell
     anything about that
```

```
P:                                      HHH
                          (1.0)
P:                                      how about in he:re
                          (0.6)
D:    tch no wait a sec-
      we're gonna do that later=
P:                            =o:h ok HH (heh)
```

This excerpt also occurs while he is examining her back. It begins with two questions and introduces a new discourse topic, her breathing. She answers his questions. But her response is not acknowledged. Acknowledgment has two forms. A response may be acknowledged either explicitly with a token like "oh" or "yeah" or implicitly by developing the content of what has just been said (i.e., "how often do you experience exhaustion" would constitute an implicit acknowledgment). Here, neither one form nor the other occurs.

Instead of developing her reply—that she can't climb a flight of stairs without becoming exhausted—the physician begins a new discourse topic: "now do you have any pain under this (0.4) kidney." His failure to develop a discourse topic he has introduced constitutes an inattention to the semantic sense of what she has said about her exhaustion. And his inattentions will recur. In recurring, they will leave some of her responses hovering without development.

Once again, the exam is captured in a silence. Then this patient says, "ahh" and he "there" and she "not when you touch it bt I've ben havin pain in that area." He whistles across part of her statement and says "fine," then he summarizes, "you do have pain in this area." In close synchrony with the semantic sense of his summary, she says, "o:h *that* hurts right there." He continues "w'l that's too soon y see that's too soon to tell anything about that." She exhales loudly.

"Anything about that," of course, refers to the unspoken topic and to the possibility that her cancer may return. Her noticeable exhalation suggests that she has heard that it is too soon to tell. The exam is again captured in a silence between them. The many silences that punctuate their talk during the physical exam suggest its preeminence as an activity; and the many characteristic interruptions that return their talk to the exam emphasize the exam's importance. It is an activity in which his power is expressed.

Next she suggests, "how about in here." He "tchs" the beginning of his utterance in response, and says, "no wait a sec- we're gonna do that later." He will, over the course of their encounters, "tch" at the beginning of many utterances and "w'l" at the beginning of others. Both "tch" and "w'l" become ongoing tokens of his disapproval (Pomerantz 1975).

In the course of the physical examination, he asks about her family, "d y have any problems in yer home with yer (1.2) husband or your marriage or is that . . ." This topic appears without previous reference in their talk. Although the question has no discourse history and comes without prefatory notice as a question, she responds to it, and to a number of related questions. She repeatedly supports the development of discourse topics and activities, however unconnected they are. Here, his inquiry moves progressively away from her recent surgery.

9 minutes

(17.1)

D: d y have any problems in yer home
        with yer . . . .
        husband or your marriage
        or is that

                   (2.1)

P: ahh. . . . . . .
                         no I haven't actually had . .
                         problems
                         my husband is quite. . . .
                         perturbed that I uh. . . . . .
                         in the past. . . . .
                         four or five months
                         that I'm not. . . . . .
                         gettin any *bet*ter. . . . . .
                         an. . . .
                         y know he's
                         °I'm °not °a °happy °person °to °be
                         °with

                   (1.4)
                         ut I-
                         be*fore that* I hadn't uh. . . . . .

D: there were no problems before that
               [
               ((sounds of blood pressure being taken))
P: w'll there were domestic . p-problems
                         (. . .)
                  (1.2)
                         I uh (. . .)
                  (4.1)

D: ((sounds of blood pressure being taken))
    [
   d y think yer *were* having more than average problems
   or probably less

                  (1.6)
P: uhm
                  (2.0)
                         maybe I was havin abit mo:re
                         than the average person. . . . . . .
                         not from the marriage itself
                  (2.0)

the marriage is a good marriage

(2.0)

    (. . .)

      [

D: It isn't anything enough tuh

yer marriage   threaten

(1.4)

P: right no:w I think its getting so:

                           [

                           ((noises))

if I don't get. . . . . .

something done

about my ph(h)ysical condition. . . . . .

uh about my *out*look

uh I don't doubt but what-

I I (think) I want to feel better

I I was-a. . . .

very active person. . . . . .

had many interests

n many hobbies

n. . . .

I loved to do things with the children

n with my husban

n. . . . . .

uh I I still *do*

but I find that I just

haven't got the . . . .

stamina. . . . . .

tuh tuh do it. . . . . . .

which is *crazy*

       [ ]

D: uhm

P: because I think I have when I start

t do it. . . .

n then I just fall apart

(0.6)

D: now big breath

The question on her family life, on problems in her home with her husband, or her marriage, is not fully formed. It contains an "or is that" and a pause of two seconds. She responds across the awkwardness of the question and its shape, and her response stumbles over its course, "ahh (0.8) no I haven't actually had (0.2) problems my husband is quite (0.4) perturbed that I uh (0.6) in the past (1.0) four or five months that I'm not (0.6) gettin any *bet*ter (0.6) and (0.4) y know he's °I'm °not °a °happy °person °to °be °with." The repeated hesitations in her speech here display reflection. Pauses occur within phrases and clauses as well as between them, for example, "my husband is quite (0.4) perturbed that I uh (0.6) in the past (1.0)." For a discussion of long stretches of searching speech see Paget (1981a, 1981b, and 1982).

"That" in her utterance "but I- be*fore that* I hadn't uh" refers to the past four or five months. He develops the topic: "There were no problems before that." "That" again occurs, but here it does not refer to the past four or five months; this physician is not probing the problems with which she and her family have lived in the two months before her operation and the three since; he is probing the time before that. She responds, "w'll there were domestic . p-problems (. . .)." There is a pause, then, "I uh (. . .)" and her talk falls away in silence. Her reticence here is noticeable and is strongly heard.

What is less noticeable is the shift away from the past four or five months of her life to the months before them. While taking her blood pressure he asks, "d y think you *were* having more than average problems or probably less." The talk now has moved entirely away from the most recent events in her life. The discourse topic developing is the problem of her marriage before her cancer operation, not the problems that can be produced by that operation. The "or" in his question in this cycle is one of his regular speaking practices. He asks questions, often in the form of either/or, which forces a choice.[1] She stumbles on.

Then, unexpectedly, he returns the discussion to the present with "it isn't enough tuh thr*eat*en yer marriage." "It" refers to what was before the past four or five months. He means what was before the past four or five months "isn't enough tuh thr*eat*en yer marriage," now, is it? She responds, "right no:w I think its getting so:." Her response again stumbles on across a number of pauses and hesitations. And, it contains considerable feeling. No acknowledgment occurs. "Now big breath," he says.

Across the talk's breaks, across the recurrent discontinuities in the development of topics, acorss the unmarked and unreferenced terms in his questions, she makes sense of what he says and asks. But in ignoring her replies, he makes a kind of non-sense of her talk, for his responses to her replies often do not develop what she has said but dissolve her answers back into the exam. Her talk goes without exploration often; her physical condition, her exhaustion, her anxieties about her health hover without clarification or resolution. The microparadigm of the movement of their talk is captured recurrently in these excerpts. The physician controls their discourse. His control inhibits expression of her concern about her experience of cancer.

---

[1] This analysis has focused on the sequencing and semantic sense of questioning practices rather than on the kinds of questions asked. Closed, rather than open-ended, questions are common here and in medical practice generally. See, for example, chapter 5, Byrne and Long (1976).

10 minutes

                                                    (1.0)
D: w'll has it possibly occurred to you
    that with all the troubles
    that yer . . . .
    body has gone through
    that yer nerves *have now got* to the
    point
    where they suffer
    an where you need help to get yer
    nerves re*stored*

                                                    (1.6)
P: uhh. . . . . .
                                          yes I- I *think* I'm abit nervous. . . . . .
                                          I I I don't see whatchu mean
                                                      [
D: I ha- I don't I didn't mean overtly
    nervous
    I meant that- that. . . . . .
            [ ]
P: no
D: yer nerves have suffered
    tuh the point that they could be
    producing some of these pains

                                                    (1.0)
D: be*cuz I* don' believe you've got a *new tu*mor
    ev'ry p*lace* you have a new pa:in
    I wouldn't *think* of it
    [
P: I'm not lookin for a new tumor

                                                    (0.6)
P: no sir I never said that
                                                      [
D: and I don't
    think- no I know you didn't
    and I don't think there's anything *bro*ken
            [   ]
P: °okay
D: where yer having the pains

                                                    (0.6)
D: I *do* think there were nerves cut where you had yer s*car*
            [   ]
P: it's right there right there
                                                    (2.6)

"Have now got" carries strong stress, and it expresses, across the obliqueness of the form of this utterance, his assessment that her nerves have now gotten to the point where they suffer and need assistance. She, again, and quite characteristically, answers his questions, "yes," and observes that she is a little nervous, and she continues, "I I I don't see whatchu mean." He interrupts to say that he does not mean overtly nervous. He explains that her "nerves have now suffered tuh the point that they could be producing some of these pains."

This is his most explicit communication of the functional basis of some pain. After a pause of a second, he adds, "be*cuz* I don' believe you've got a *new tu*mor ev'ry *pla*ce you have a new pa:in." And he then adds softly, "I wouldn't think of it." And, in its course, she hears his reference to a new tumor and says that she is not looking for a new tumor, "no sir, I never said that." He continues his assessment and, hearing her response, he acknowledges that she never said that.

The synchrony here and the semantic sense of their utterances across the interruptions is rare. Here, they each hear and acknowledge that they have heard the other, and each thus knows and understands that "she never said that" and that she "is not looking for a new tumor." He acknowledges his understanding with, "I know you didn't." She responds to his acknowledgment with, "okay."

Her statement that she is not looking for a new tumor echoes an earlier response: that she is not looking for a dire disease. And it comes with a "no sir," which somewhat sardonically suggests his power as it is continuously being realized in their exchanges.

His observation, "I don't think you have a new tumor every place you have a new pain," finds its sense as a reference to her cancer, as does her retort, "I'm not looking for a new tumor." His expansions, "I don't think there's anything *bro*ken where yer having the pains," and "I *do* think there were nerves cut where you have yer s*car*," are clarifications of his point of view. And his reference to scar once again alludes to the incision for which the scar stands.

"It's right there right there" follows along. She will often point to areas of pain. The silence that follows signals the exam once again and suggests that he may be looking where she has pointed.

It is important to remember that these excerpts are taken from the first encounter, which continued for more than 15 more minutes and that two additional exchanges occurred between this physician and patient. The talk presented represents a stretch of their discourse in its first phase. Yet these excerpts are not intended as mere illustrations. They capture the course of a conversation filled with misunderstandings.

The meaning of this patient's illness is constructed by the physician as her symptoms and pains are separated from her experience of cancer and progressively connected with her nerves. And her illness as nerves is continuously confirmed by her nervousness. More fundamentally, the meaning of her illness is continuously constructed in what he sees, asks, and hears.

The small increments of the construction of her illness take shape both in the questions he asks and the discourse topics he develops, as well as in the questions he does not ask and the discourse topics he does not develop. The direction of his questioning is always away from her experience of cancer, and their "talk" about her cancer always obscures her experience of cancer. The unmentioned discourse topic that hovers is progressively disconnected from her anxiety, and her "complaint" finally comes to antedate her experience of cancer and be the "real" source of her symptoms. (Later he will say, for example, "you: been through (0.6) anxiety of havin:g this complaint for so long without anybody finding a reason for it an then ha:ving a m-major surgery.") All the while, each knows that the other knows that she has had cancer. The physician's progressive formulation of the problem as a matter of nerves produces continuous tension and conflict between them, and this, too, confirms her nervousness.

The patient participates in the development of the discourse process by answering questions and, sometimes, by expressing her own concerns. Although not as an equal, she contributes to the ongoing misunderstandings between them. She, too, speaks only of the scar and the tumor in their first encounter. She is both afraid to express her fear of the spread of cancer and afraid to ignore the possibility. She tries furtively to discover how a clinician thinks, to catch the truth of her circumstances, across the unspoken fear between them.

A final excerpt follows. In this exchange, the physician again says that he can find nothing wrong. She begins to ask about the scar. Softly she says, "°that's °the °scar," and then a series of questions about her condition, "do y think maybe the uhm (0.6) do y think maybe this kidney is is *uh* (0.4) overloaded or something," "oh they removed an adrenal gland," "HHH I dunno. I'm thinking maybe it's a ho:rmone deficiency or something." Two of her questions are interrupted in their course and the third seems not to have been correctly heard. All her questions refer to the impact of her operation on her health. He looks at the scar and inquires about the other end of it and says, "it's beautiful surgery."

14 minutes
D: *well.* . . . . .
     I feel *noth*ing. . . .
     in yer abdomen. . . .
     that's *wrong*

                                    (3.1)
     I don't feel any arteries that are too big
     n I don' feel any lumps
                                    (2.0)
P: °that's °the °scar
                                (0.6)
D: see the scar is
P: do y think maybe the uhm. . . . . .
                                do y think maybe this kidney is is *uh*. .

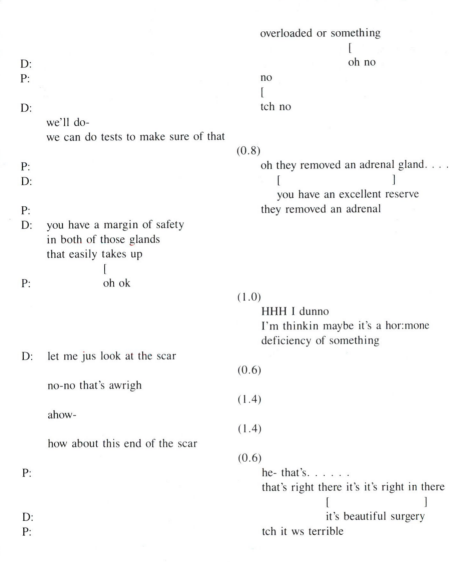

```
                              overloaded or something
                                  [
D:                                oh no
P:                       no
                         [
D:                       tch no

        we'll do-
        we can do tests to make sure of that
                              (0.8)
P:                            oh they removed an adrenal gland. . . .
D:                                [                    ]
                                  you have an excellent reserve
P:                            they removed an adrenal
D:   you have a margin of safety
     in both of those glands
     that easily takes up
                [
P:              oh ok
                              (1.0)
                              HHH I dunno
                              I'm thinkin maybe it's a hor:mone
                              deficiency of something
D:   let me jus look at the scar
                              (0.6)
     no-no that's awrigh
                              (1.4)
     ahow-
                              (1.4)
     how about this end of the scar
                              (0.6)
P:                            he- that's. . . . . .
                              that's right there it's it's right in there
                                  [                    ]
D:                                it's beautiful surgery
P:                            tch it ws terrible
```

THE WORK OF TALK

This analysis has focused on questioning practices because questions often introduce, develop, and dissolve topics. Although this physician's questions introduced, developed, and dissolved many topics, one topic was ignored: this woman's experience of cancer. In their three exchanges on her medical problems, no question ever addressed her experience of cancer.

Although a number of her questions gained their sense as references to her experience of cancer, her questions never lead to the establishment of her experience of cancer as a discourse topic. As the meaning of her experience of cancer became lost in their talk, its significance, in connection with her symptoms and pains, also was lost. The early establishment of a diagnostic assessment that the problem was her nerves, and her sense that there was something wrong, provoked continuous tensions between them. Furthermore, as already noted, her nervousness continuously confirmed his diagnosis that the problem was nerves.

Discourse is both spoken and heard, and the interpretive sense conversationalists make of their evolving talk is carried not only in the movement of their talk on a series of discourse topics, but also in the semantic sense of what is said and heard. Inattention was a serious problem in the taped exchanges of this physician and patient. The many discontinuities in their discourse, only a few of which have been reported here, suggest that he was not listening. Many of her replies were not clarified, and almost all of her answers were not acknowledged. His interruptions suggest that what she said was not very important to his understanding. He relied continuously on his observations and his questioning strategies, and his questioning strategies did not clarify the meaning of her symptoms and pains but continuously confirmed his observations of her nervousness. Furthermore, he failed to remember that cancer is not merely a "thing" to be excised by a medical procedure.

He spoke to her as though she were an anatomical display. "Yer nerves have now got to the point where they suffer." "Y got pretty good (0.2) teeth n joints." "It's beautiful surgery."

Talk, when it is serious rather than casual, is as much as it is anything at all a labor of understanding, of listening and interpreting, of clarifying and acknowledging what has been said, and responding. It is an interactionally constituted activity sustained by conversationalists. The form and substance of serious talk is shaped by a dialectic of questioning and answering, and requesting and responding, and explaining and responding. And, in its course, the dialectic of talk realizes the many asymmetries that constitute the dialectic.

It was their talk's pervasive tensions and disharmonies that awakened my puzzlement about their discourse, the sharp contrast between what she said and what he heard. An impression of radical misunderstanding led me to increasingly fine transcriptions of their talk, for on the surface these tapes do not reflect the problems of a "postoperative" cancer patient, they reflect the problems of a hypochondriacal woman of 45 being assured recurrently that her health is good and that the problem is her nerves.

In their second exchange, which occurred one month later, they discuss other physicians who have, in the past, also told her that the problem is her nerves. Some, she reports, suggested that without even bothering to examine her. One had given her Valium surreptitiously. As she said, angrily, the same thing is happening again; for although she was given Valium and told that the problem was her nerves, she also had a tumor. "How," she asks at one point, "do you explain that?" Her question goes unanswered. Their talk focuses on a virus, her sore throat, the pain in her mouth, her visits to dentists, to other physicians, medical procedures she has undergone or may undergo, medications she has taken or is taking. She complains of persistent back pain. And she says that she is afraid. He assures her that her basic health is good.

Their third exchange occurred one month after the second. Almost half their talk is about the pain in her mouth, her dental care, and the medications she has received from another physician, including Valium and Prednisone. She complains that she is gaining weight and thinks that Prednisone is causing that. Prednisone is a corticosteroid, producing many serious side effects. It is most commonly used to control the pain of rheumatoid arthritis, and although she reported many pains, joint pain was not among them. She complains again of back and abdominal pain. They discuss the possibility of X-rays, and the kinds of X-rays and medical procedures she has undergone in the past. She says that she does not want to die. He reassures her that her health is good. Once again, at the end of their third encounter, he tells her that the problem is her nerves.

This analysis has not investigated this physician's intentions. I suspect that he would not have chosen so cruel an outcome of his encounters with this patient. In good faith, he taped their meetings as a participant in a research study. He, therefore, was unaware of his manner. This analysis has, however, addressed the question of *how* their talk developed. What this physician might have intended does not seem as relevant, in understanding their discourse, as how their talk proceeded, and how, as a series of turns at talk on discourse topics, it shaped the meaning of her illness. It was not his intentions that shaped their discourse; it was his questioning practices. It was not his intentions that shaped the meaning of her illness; it was his inattentions. And, in any case, it is not the intentions of physicians that are at issue here; it is how a discourse process expresses and realizes the work of medicine, for the work is in the talk and the talk is a realization of the work. The discourse of physicians and patients is controlled by physicians who, in asking questions, "request" that patients respond on specific topics. And the development of discourse topics is also controlled by physicians, who, with each successive question or request, shape the meaning of what is said.

This physician reported his diagnosis on a questionnaire called "Physician Questionnaire Concerning Specific Patients." It was as follows: "(*1*) depression, conversion symptom, (*2*) status postnephrectomy for a hypernephroma, 1971." He also reported that he was certain of his diagnosis. This patient also answered a questionnaire. Like so many physicians, she said, this physician told her that there was nothing wrong when she had cancer. She also said that since their last exchange, she had gone to another hospital where she was told that she has cancer of the spine. No further information is available on this woman and her search for care.

REFERENCES CITED

BYRNE, PATRICK S., AND BARRIE E. L. LONG
1976   *Doctors Talking to Patients*. London: Her Majesty's Stationery Office.
CHURCHILL, LINDSAY
1978   *Questioning Strategies in Sociolinguistics*. Rowley, Mass.: Newbury House.
GARFINKEL, HAROLD
1967   *Studies in Ethnomethodology*. Englewood Cliffs, N.J.: Prentice-Hall.
GOFFMAN, ERVING
1976   Replies and responses. *Language in Society* 5:257–313.
GUNTER, RICHARD
1974   *Sentences in Dialog*. Columbia, S.C.: Hornbeam Press.
LABOV, WILLIAM, AND DAVID FANSHEL
1977   *Therapeutic Discourse: Psychotherapy as Conversation*. New York: Academic.
MISHLER, ELLIOT G.
1975   Studies in dialogue and discourse: II. Types of discourse initiated by and sustained through questioning. *Journal of Psycholinguistic Research* 4:99–121.
1978   Studies in dialogue and discourse: III. Utterance structure and utterance function in interrogative sequences. *Journal of Psycholinguistic Research* 7:279–305.
PAGET, MARIANNE A.
1981a   The ontological anguish of women artists. *New England Sociologist* 3:65–79.
1981b   Experience and the construction of knowledge. Unpublished paper (revised October 1982), 38 pp.
1982   Your son is cured now; you may take him home. *Culture, Medicine and Psychiatry* 6:237–259.
POMERANTZ, ANITA
1975   Second Assessments: A Study of Some Features of Agreements and Disagreements. Ph.D. dissertation, School of Social Science, University of California at Irvine.
SACKS, HARVEY
1972   Transcripts of unpublished lectures. School of Social Science, University of California at Irvine.
SACKS, HARVEY; EMANUEL SCHEGLOFF; AND GAIL JEFFERSON
1974   A simplest systematics for the organization of turn-taking in conversation. *Language* 50:696–735.
SCHENKEIN, JIM, ED.
1978   *Studies in the Organization of Conversational Interaction*. New York: Academic.
SEARLE, JOHN R.
1969   *Speech Acts: An Essay in the Philosophy of Language*. Cambridge: Cambridge University Press.
SHUY, ROGER W.
1974   Problems of Communication in the Cross–Cultural Medical Interview. *Working Papers in Sociolinguistics* 19.
WAITZKIN, HOWARD; JOHN D. STOECKLE; ERIC BELLER; AND CARL MONS
1978   The informative process in medical care: A preliminary report with implications for instructional communication. *Instructional Science* 7:385–419.

6

"Ask Me No Questions..."
An Analysis of Queries and Replies
in Physician-Patient Dialogues*

Candace West

A few years ago, *Sixty Minutes* presented a televised story on adults who had developed cancer of the lymph nodes from X-ray treatments received in early childhood. One of the mothers interviewed on the program said that her child (now an adult) had been given extensive X-ray treatments for what was characterized by the family physician as a "funny-sounding" cry. When pressed by the *Sixty Minutes* interviewer on why she had allowed her child to undergo heavy doses of radiation for such a minor matter, she protested, "You never questioned a doctor in those days. The pediatrician was God!"

"God," she implied, was someone not to be questioned. Questions and answers are, however, commonly regarded as an important means of exchanging information between people. The dialogue between a physician and patient would seem to provide a particularly important opportunity for an exchange of information, for here its presence or absence can have life-and-death consequences. From a pragmatic perspective, patients are the best sources of information on certain medical questions; certainly, they are physicians' only sources of information regarding the subjective experiences of their health and

* Grateful acknowledgment is made to Richard Frankel, Erving Goffman, Judy Martin, Wendy Martyna, Bob Pantell, Gilly West, and the editors of this volume for helpful comments on earlier versions of these ideas. For financial assistance with the study, I thank the Committee on Faculty Research and Junior Faculty Development Committee at UC Santa Cruz. Finally, appreciation is offered to the Department of Family Medicine, Medical University of South Carolina, Charleston.

127

illness. So, it is understandable that doctors would be predisposed to question their patients.

Patients, though, should be similarly predisposed. In the situation of a visit to the doctor, patients come to petition their physicians for information regarding their medical care—information only a physician can provide (cf. Parsons 1951). Thus, there are also pragmatic reasons for patients to question their physicians.

Although these practical considerations would seem to aid the flow of information between physician and patient, a growing body of research indicates that the information exchanged in medical dialogues is not always organized as a two-way "swap." For example, Korsch, Gozzi, and Francis (1968) found that mothers' questions to pediatricians are often ignored, given vague responses, or met with a change of subject by doctors. Wallen, Waitzkin, and Stoeckle (1979) report that less than 1% of total time in information exchange between patient and physician is spent on physician explanations to patients. And Frankel's (in press) analysis suggests that the majority of doctor-initiated talk consists of questions to patients. Patient-initiated utterances, in contrast, tend to be anything *but* questions. These findings led Frankel to conclude that the speech produced in doctor—patient "interviews" is far more constrained by utterance-type and speaker identity than in casual conversation.

Frankel's (in press) findings raise several important issues. Interviews are, by definition, prestructured states of talk, characterized by a relatively "fixed" order of turns people take, length of turns they take, and content of turns (Sacks, Schegloff, and Jefferson 1974). Therefore, it makes perfect sense that people talking in interviews would be alternating speaking turns made up of questions and answers (1974:710). Conversations, though, are characterized by variable turn order, turn size, and turn content, all of which are determined on a turn-by-turn basis. Thus, conversations present fewer restrictions on what can be said and how it should be said.

If doctor—patient dialogues are primarily interviews and only secondarily conversations, an open, two-way flow of questions and answers will be difficult to maintain. But, because conversation is a form of talk that is not prestructured, purely conversational medical encounters may be difficult to confine to the typical 15-minute appointment slots allotted in the physician's daily schedule.

To be sure, conversations and interviews are both forms of talk that fall along a continuum of lesser and greater prespecification. Each may contain elements usually found in the other. Thus, questions and answers may appear in a casual conversation, and sociable greetings and farewells may bracket what otherwise might look like an interrogation. The difference between these alternative forms of talk is, as Frankel notes, the degree they constrain the use of alternative utterance-types by speakers of different identities. For example, in sociable chitchat, "there is no necessity for one party to remain a questioner and another an answerer" (Frankel, in press). In a medical interview, however, we would expect to find an asymmetrical distribution of questions and answers between physicians and patients, with doctors initiating the questions and patients providing the responses.

My aim in this chapter is to provide an explicit empirical comparison of the initiation of questions and answers between patients and family physicians during routine visits to the doctor. To understand why patients might have difficulty posing questions to their physicians, even when their queries have a direct bearing on the state of their health. I examined the organization of questions and answers between physicians and patients and the consequences of these events for subsequent talk between them. My findings lend support to Frankel's (in press) claim that patient-initiated questions are "dispreferred" in medical dialogues. Further, I found structural evidence for this dispreference in the very organization of patients' questions and physicians' responses to them.

QUESTIONS AND ANSWERS

Establishing the status of a question as a question would seem an easy task. Any dictionary can provide a definition that concurs with common sense; for example, "An interrogative sentence calling for an answer; an inquiry" (*Funk and Wagnalls* 1964:1034), or "A sentence in an interrogative form, addressed to someone in order to get information in reply" (*The Random House College Dictionary* 1975:1083). Such seemingly self-evident definitions are not limited to dictionaries:

> Within much of linguistics...the single sentence, abstracted from actual occasions of its use, serves as the unit of analysis...the properties of questions are seen as the self-contained...linguistic products of an individual speaker, irrespective of the communication situation itself. (Frankel, in press: fn. 7)

Although analysts of texts may find that interrogative sentences form the building blocks of the questions they encounter, the researcher faced with actual instances of talk will be forced to acknowledge alternative units of analysis. People, in short, do not speak in the ways dictionaries prescribe. For example, exchanges between doctors and patients (and between conversationalists in general) contain numerous interrogative sentences along with their requisite answers (see the Appendix for transcribing conventions used here):

(Dyad 10: 152-154)
DOCTOR: Duh yuh ha:ve any *nu:mb*ness 'r *ti:ng*ling?
PATIENT: This- ha::n' stays numb all a ti:me.

But so too can one find interrogative items that do not properly qualify as sentences, and even these may elicit answers:

(Dyad 10: 156-158)
DOCTOR: Thuh who:le hand? 'R jis' *part* of it.
PATIENT: Muh fingers, mos'ly.

In this fragment, for example, "Thuh who:le hand?" becomes intelligible as a question in the context of the fragment just preceding it (i.e., the physician's query regarding numbness or tingling and the patient's response regarding the hand that stays numb all of the time). In itself, though, "The who:le hand?" does not constitute a grammatically complete sentence. So, it seems that questions do *not* require formulation as interrogative sentences to elicit answers from their recipients. Indeed, Sacks, Schegloff, and Jefferson (1974) propose that speaker turns at talk may be constructed of possibly complete words, phrases, clauses, or sentences, depending on their context. Given that a question is one utterance-type that may fill a speaker's turn, their proposal contradicts the usual dictionary definition: A sentence need not have been uttered for a question to have been asked.

Further, just as "less" will do, so will "more." Goffman (1981) notes that speakers may initiate a series of queries to conceal one item as an unobtrusive component in a larger sequence (:43). The resulting sequence may itself emerge as a whole, to which increasingly abbreviated answers serve as responses (Shuy 1974:21, cited in Goffman). Frankel (in press) finds a complementary phenomenon in the abbreviation of questions into smaller question particles within question-answer chains:[1]

(Frankel, in press)
A: Does anybody have tuberculosis?
B: No, not that I know of
A: Heart disease
B: No
A: Diabetes
B: No

Worth noting here is that only the first item in the series is formed with an interrogative intonational pattern. And yet, as parts of the whole, we have no trouble seeing "Heart disease" and "Diabetes" as items that require answers. Although intonational criteria are sometimes invoked to distinguish questions from other utterance-types, these grounds for distinction are shaky ones, at best (cf. Lakoff 1975:7). In doctor–patient exchanges, for example, queries may be intoned as assertions:

---

[1]Harvey Sacks first formulated the notion of a "chain rule" for questions in unpublished lectures given at the University of California, Los Angeles, 1966.

(Dyad 19: 548-550)
DOCTOR: .h An' yih been ha:vin' some i:tchin' in yer
          throat=
PATIENT: = Uh:, Uh-hu:h

And, answers may display question-intonational contours:

(Dyad 15: 466-468)
DOCTOR: °anything like tha:t?
                    (.8)
PATIENT: .h They *con*stuntly make that (.) cli:cking (.) cra:cking sou::n'?

Hence, there seem to be no ironclad intonational rules for differentiating questions from other types of utterances.

As if these conceptual problems with "questions" were not sufficient to discourage potential analysts, Schegloff and Sacks (1973) contend that the case for "answers" is still more obscure. They note, for example, that purely linguistic criteria (semantics, syntax, phonology, etc.) offer no unequivocal way to establish an utterance as an "answer" to a question. With minor variations in paralinguistic features, such items as "yeah," "uh huh," and "yep," often used to answer questions, may also be employed to show acknowledgment, agreement, or understanding of another's utterance (see also Jefferson 1973). Further, some questions (e.g., "D'yuh know what?") require subsequent questions (e.g., "No, what?") rather than statements in response.

The methodological difficulties posed by these considerations lead some researchers to abandon questions and answers as appropriate units of analysis:

> Our basic model for talk perhaps ought not to be dialogic couplets and their chaining, but rather a sequence of response moves with each in the series carving out its own reference, and each incorporating a variable balance of function in regard to statement-reply properties. (Goffman 1981:54).

Clearly, Goffman is correct in noting that there is no reason to hypothesize that conversation is composed of predetermined utterance-types. Statements, questions, and responses might all provide reasonable building blocks for a form of talk in which turn order, turn size, and turn content are all free to vary. For the analyst of physician–patient exchanges, however, "dialogic couplets and their chaining" are not so easily replaced by alternative analytical units. If this form of talk is in fact organized as alternating questions and answers, some means must be found to identify these and to distinguish them from other utterance-types.

Schegloff and Sacks (1973) propose that such utterance-types as answers to questions (or replies to summonses, response to roll calls, etc.) achieve their status as answers only through their placement following questions. As the second parts of *adjacency pairs*, the intelligibility of answers is *conditionally relevant* on the initiation of questions in the first instance. Thus, given the occurrence of a question, or first pair part, an answer, or second pair part, is then expectable. And, given the occurrence of a first pair part, the absence of a second pair part is notable.:

> We would expect that a Q followed either by silence or by talk not formulated as 'an answer' would provide the relevance and grounds for repetition of the Q or some inference based on the absence of an answer. (Schegloff 1972:77)

Thus, an answer ought to occur in the turn following completion of a question; and, if it does not, it may be seen as "officially" absent.

To be sure, the immediate adjacency of questions and answers is not always dictated by this model. For example, insertion sequences (Schegloff 1972) and side sequences (Jefferson 1972) can sometimes intervene between an initial question and its answer without severing the relationship of conditional relevance between them. Hence, requests for repetition or clarification may appear in the turn-spaces usually reserved for answers to initial questions:

(Dyad 11: 007-009)
DOCTOR: = 'Bout one
            fi:fty over ninedy. ⌈Uh-⌉
PATIENT: ⌊How⌋ in the worl' could she 'ave
            gotten tha:t?
DOCTOR: *Par*don me:?
                                        (.2)
PATIENT: How in the world could she 'ave gotten that?

Occasionally, one even finds protracted insertion sequences, in which the work of reiteration occupies several turn rounds:

(Dyad 09: 457-476)
DOCTOR: One-twenty-ei:ght over one-oh-six.
                                  . ((three lines deleted))
                                  .

                                  .
PATIENT: (°One-oh-eight?)
                                        (.4)
DOCTOR: Hu:m?
                                        (.2)
PATIENT: One-oh-eight?
                                        (.6)
DOCTOR: One-oh-si:x
                                        (1.2)

PATIENT: °Ah (men') thuh to:p nummer.

                             (.6)

DOCTOR: One *twen*ny eight.

                             (.)

PATIENT: °One *twen*ny eight.

                             (.)

DOCTOR: °Tha:t's about the same as normul (.8) (fer yu:h)

Yet, even where protractions occur, the conditional relevance of an eventual answer on the initial question can be observed. In the fragment just above, we can see the doctor's "One *twen*ny eight" as an answer to the patient's initial query, despite the layered reiterations between the two. Where side and insertion sequences occur, then, it is in the turn-spaces just following completion of those sequences that answers to initial questions ought to appear, or, if not, can be seen as "officially absent" (Schegloff 1968:1083).

A caution must be entered here. Schegloff and Sacks's (1973) analysis provides a clear distinction between the first pair part and second pair part of an adjacency pair, based on the respective temporal position of each component. For questions and answers, this distinction means that an answer must follow a question in time and sequential position. Goffman offers a somewhat related observation:

> Although a question anticipates an answer, is designed to receive it, seems dependent on doing so, an answer seems even more dependent, making less sense alone than does the utterance that called it forth. Whatever answers do, they must do this with something already begun. (1981:5)

We get a sense, then, that questions are forward-looking things, whose objects come recognizably next in a sequence. Answers, on the other hand, have a retrospective flavor, and their sense must be garnered from what has preceded them. Thus, the conditional relevance of answers on questions is not entirely reciprocal. Whereas answers depend for their intelligibility on questions having been asked, the reverse is not true.[2]

---

[2] Goffman (1981) is misleading here, I think. In reviewing Schegloff and Sacks's (1973:299) suggestion regarding the indexicality of answers, he contends:

> One problem with this view is that in throwing back upon the asker's question the burden of determining what will qualify as an answer, it implies that what is a question will itself have to be determined in a like manner...this formuiation leaves no way open for disproof. (Goffman 1981:51, n. 31)
>
>   . . .

However, for an unanswered question, "proof" is provided by the relevance of a repetition of the question "or some inference based on the absence of an answer" (Schegloff 1972:77). Thus, the

This fact recommends a serious reconsideration of some items that may be employed to build side and insertion sequences. For example, Schegloff, Jefferson, and Sacks (1977) observe that interrogative question terms (e.g., "Hunh?", "What?") may be used to initiate a repair or repetition of another party's previous speech object:[3]

(Dyad 08: 280-285)
PATIENT: Bo:y, that thing (is) col::e.
                                    (.6)
DOCTOR: *What*? ((pulling stethoscope away from one ear))
                                    (.2)
PATIENT: That- THAT STETHOSCOPE IS COL::E!
DOCTOR: AH'M SORRY.

Elsewhere, Jefferson (1972) notes that interrogatives employed in this fashion have prior objects as their "product items" and the selection of the prior object is done in the production of the interrogative. The answer to "Whut?" in this fragment is a reiteration of the utterance just preceding it. Thus. "Whut?" looks backward, not forward, in sequential time. Items that can be employed similarly include "Who?," "Where?" and "When?" (Schegloff 1977) and the more formal "Pardon me?" (see the fragment excerpted from Dyad 11, presented earlier).[4]

---

intelligibility of a question as a question does not rest entirely on the presence of an answer in the next turn-space. Of course, as Goffman argues, "When an intended question receives no apparent answer the asker will often let the matter pass, and so, although there is no phenomenal evidence of a question having been asked, it really has" (personal communication, October 7, 1981). Clearly, such instances are ripe for further empirical study.

However, for an unanswered question, "proof" is provided by the relevance of a repetition of the question "or some inference based on the absence of an answer" (Schegloff 1972:77). Thus, the intelligibility of a question as a question does not rest entirely on the presence of an answer in the next turn-space. Of course, as Goffman argues, "When an intended question receives no apparent answer the asker will often let the matter pass, and so, although there is no phenomenal evidence of a question have been asked, it really has" (personal communication, October 7, 1981). Clearly, such instances are ripe for further empirical study.

[3] The authors note that these question words are not always used to initiate repair of actual prior components of another party's speech object. For example:

(Schegloff et al. 1977:369, n. 15)
BEN: They gotta- a ga*r*age sale.
ELLEN: Where.
BEN: On Third Avenoo.

In this fragment, "Where" elicits something more than was present in the utterance preceding it. In my reconsideration here, I am only interested in initiations of repair directed toward actual prior turn components.

[4] Schegloff et al. do not include "Pardon me?" in their analysis of devices used to elicit repairs. From a linguistic standpoint, as Jorge Hankamer has pointed out to me, this device operates in

Schegloff et al. (1977) find some repairs are initiated by partial repeats of a prior trouble-source turn:

(Dyad 08: 035-042)
PATIENT: CAN YOU TELL- HOW SOMEBODY CUN EAT-
           EAT U:H- WHUT CHA EAT-EAT IN THE BLOOD?
                          (1.0)
DOCTOR: Can yuh tell *what* chat eat?
                          (.2)
PATIENT: Yeah!
                          (.2)
DOCTOR: We:ll, so:*me*times.

Other requests for repair combine "Y'mean" with some candidate understanding of the prior object (Schegloff et al. 1977):

(Dyad 10: 319-322)
PATIENT: An' ah cun take thi:s hand an' li:ft it, an' it duh'unt
           hurt.
                          (1.6)
DOCTOR: Yuh mean, when you *lif* the ar:m up, using yer
           other *han:d*? =
PATIENT: = Uh-huh.

Despite their variations in form, all of these devices share the retrospective quality of a search back to earlier items in a sequence. In this sense, requests for repair differ from other questions that might be asked: They look backward rather than forward in sequential positioning.

By this description, I do not mean to imply that a backward look will always locate some previous object that is "objectively" in need of correction. Schegloff et al. note that some repairs are initiated in the wake of error-free items and that "nothing is, in principle, excludable from the class 'repairable'" (1977:363). As we saw in an earlier fragment (excerpted from Dyad 09), repair-requests may themselves be followed by further requests for repair (e.g., "One-oh-eight?," "Hu:m?").

However, I would suggest that wherever they appear, requests for repair display a conditional relevance on the *existence* of a previous repairable. Schegloff (1981:fn. 23) provides a telling illustration of this point in a fragment of conversation in which one party "suspects" that the other has spoken:

---

slightly different fashion from "Who?" or "What?" (e.g., "Where?" might be reconstructed in sentential form as "Where did you go?"). From an interactional standpoint however, "Pardon me?" does at least the work of requesting repetition of a previous speech object. Hence, I include it in the general category of requests for repair in this analysis.

silence
A: Huh?
B: I didn't say anything.

Here, speaker B's denial ("I didn't say anything") displays its orientation to the circumstances under which A's "Huh?" *could* be relevant (i.e., if something had been said before its intonation).

For purposes of this chapter, note that two other classes of conditionally relevant question-types are routinely found in doctor-patient talk (and, for that matter, in casual conversation). One class might be termed "requests for confirmation of a prior item." Here, a declarative utterance type (such as an assertion) is coupled with "Y'know?", "Okay?", "Like...?" or "Right?" to stimulate an inquiry:

```
(Dyad 02: 027-028)
PATIENT:   It Hur:::ts, ok ⌈ay:?      ⌉
DOCTOR:                    ⌊°Mm-hmm⌋
```

In this fragment, which is by no means atypical, the request appears in tag-position and is overlapped by an acknowledgment token ("Mm-hmm"). But the acknowledgment token cannot legitimately be viewed as an answer to a question, for what would the question be? Instead, it seems that "okay?" provides an opportunity for the other to confirm or disconfirm some aspect of that to which it is appended. (Frankel (in press) provides an elegant analysis of how physicians use "Okay?" to solicit "last calls for information" from patients before moving to the next activities.)

Another class of conditionally relevant question-types is composed of objects elsewhere identified (Schegloff 1981) as markers of surprise (e.g., "Really?", "Oh Really?", "Izzatso?"). These markers typically appear in the wake of some bit of "news" delivery, where acknowledgment tokens might not provide sufficiently emphatic evidence of a listener's appreciation:

```
(Dyad 06: 228-230)
PATIENT:   Then muh wife sez she bihli:ves she might be
           pre:gnunt? h
                            (.6)
DOCTOR:   Ril:ley? h
                            (2.0)
PATIENT:   ⌈°So::      ⌉
DOCTOR:    ⌊She gon⌋ na come see me about it?
```

Here we see indication of the patient continuing ("So::") rather than responding to the physician's surprise marker. The patient's lack of response is understandable, since surprise markers employed with questioning intonations can only elicit confirmations or disconfirmations of the objects that preceded them (e.g., "Yes, really!" or "No, I was kidding!"). Even where responses to surprise markers may occur, then, we can see they will be oriented to previous objects in a sequence.

In the analysis that follows, I do not include conditionally relevant question types (requests for repair of a previous item, requests for confirmation of a previous item, and markers of surprise at a previous item) in the general category of questions that call for answers. As we have seen, such objects look backward rather than forward in sequential time, and hence they seem dependent for their sense on some equivalent of a first pair part.[5] Further theoretical grounds for separation of these items from the general class can be found in consideration of their answers. For example, when requests for repair are initiated in the turn-space following a question, the repair itself is a reiteration of the initial question:

(Dyad 08: 308-315)
PATIENT: YUH GONNA DO THAT WITH MUH- MY
          HU:RNEE TOO? ((the patient has perhaps had
          a hernia))
                                        (1.0)
DOCTOR: *PAR*dun?
                                        (.2)
PATIENT: YUH WAH- YUH WANNA SEE MY HURNEE
          ⎡TOO?⎤
DOCTOR: ⎣Ye ⎦ ah,

Here, failure to separate this patient's repair from his initial formulation would result in a tally that counted the same question twice. Similar results would follow requests for confirmation of a question—the initial question, if confirmed, would be tallied doubly.

An independent analysis of the distribution of conditionally relevant question types would be interesting, and is a challenging task for future research.[6] It is important, however, to distinguish such an analysis from the primary purpose of this chapter, the empirical description of the organization of question–answer sequences in physician–patient exchanges. An interview, for example, does not consist of alternating requests and repairs, but of alternating questions and

---

[5] I use "some equivalent" advisedly here, because my purpose is to suggest an analogy rather than an equivalence. Insofar as *any* prior utterance serves as a possible repairable, it is impossible to specify the first pair parts of repairables in advance of their occurrences.

[6] Meehan (1979) and Frankel (in press: n. 36, n. 15) take a first step in this direction, noting that where physicians ask questions using technical medical terminology, patients frequently request clarification and further information.

answers (Sacks et al. 1974). As we are now in a theoretically grounded position to identify these events, I move now to a description of the collection of materials in which they are located.

METHOD

Data analyzed in this chapter consist of 21 two-party exchanges between physicians and patients recorded in a family practice center in the southern United States. The physicians in these exchanges were residents in family practice, a medical specialty requiring a three-year residency program beyond medical school.[7] Typically, the physicians are in their late 20s to early 30s when completing their residencies. Seventeen of the exchanges involved white male physicians, and four involved white females.

Patients in these exchanges ranged in age from 16 to 82 years. They were from a variety of backgrounds, including professional, domestic, construction worker, and unemployed carpenter. Of the 21 dyads in this collection, 5 involved black females; 6, white females; 4, black males; and 6, white males.

All of these interactions occurred during actual physician visits, so they are not standardized according to duration of exchange, purpose of visit, or length of relationship between doctor and patient. The family practice center at which they were recorded has employed audio- and videotaping for several years as part of the ongoing training of residents. With their signed consent, patients are recorded, with their doctors, by means of ceiling microphones and unobtrusive cameras located in the corners of examination rooms. Thus, recordings were not produced for purposes of the present study, but they were subsequently transcribed for these purposes.

Transcribing was done according to a set of conventions modeled after those suggested by Jefferson (see the Appendix). The aim of this method of transcribing is to capture as close to a verbatim version of interaction as is possible, and hence to preserve the details of how something was said in addition to what was said. All of the recorded material was transcribed, but not all recordings captured entire exchanges. Sometimes, for example, tapes cut off the first few moments of greetings or last few moments of farewells between physician and patient. In all, the 21 recorded interactions yielded 532 pages of transcript.

Transcripts were then inspected, and instances of questions and answers were distinguished from other utterance-types using the criteria specified earlier.

---

[7] Two physicians who are not residents are included in this collection. One is an alumnus of the training program who still sees patients there after completing his residency four years ago; the other is a faculty member on the Center staff. In the analysis that follows, their exchanges with patients exhibit no marked differences from those that took place between patients and resident physicians.

With the exception of conditionally relevant question-types, all possibly complete questions and answers (including nonverbal responses) are included in these results, regardless of their content. Thus, head nods and head shakes were included as answers when they seemed to be treated this way by the parties involved. And, questions on matters other than medical treatment are also included for analysis. Obviously, the primary concern in procuring these data was the confidentiality of the physician–patient relationship. In the following analysis, identifying references to parties involved have been disguised, and fragments are offered for the reader's inspection only when the anonymity of speakers is ensured.

By now, it should be clear that this corpus does not constitute a random sample of physicians, patients, or doctor–patient exchanges. For example, my lack of control over such variables as length of interaction or degree of acquaintance between doctor and patient resulted in a nonstandardized final collection, which includes exchanges of various lengths between doctors and patients with different past contacts. Some were involved in well-established relationships of three years standing, while others were meeting for the first time. Some visits were devoted primarily to talk, while others included physical examinations.

Moreover, the family practitioners involved in these exchanges are completing their residencies in a relatively new field of medicine. Hence, they are neither well-established physicians of long standing, nor are they comparable in medical specialty to doctors studied in previous research (e.g., Frankel in press; Korsch et al. 1968; Wallen et al. 1979). To the extent that these factors are likely to influence my results, it is probably safe to surmise that their influence lies in a conservative direction. For example, these physicians are in a training program that emphasizes the importance of communication skills through the ongoing recordings of their interactions with patients. Further, their residencies are in a specialty that stresses that a doctor is "a personal physician, oriented to the whole patient, who practices both scientific and humanistic medicine" (American Medical Association 1964). In such a training program for such a specialty, we would expect to find heightened physician sensitivity to patients' questions and a greater likelihood of a two-way exchange of questions and answers between physicians and patients.

FINDINGS

My analysis begins by examining the overall distribution of questions between physicians and patients in this collection (see Table 1). In the 21 exchanges and 532 pages of transcript, 773 questions were observed. Of these, 91% (705) were initiated by doctors; 9% (68) were initiated by patients. Physicians asked as many as or more questions than patients in each dyad, and in 14 of the 21 exchanges, they initiated more than 90% of the total questions asked.

TABLE 1   Distribution of Questions Between Physicians
and Patients in 21 Medical Exchanges

Patient Identity and Age	Doctor-Initiated Questions % (N)		Patient-Initiated Questions % (N)	
White male, 16	100	(41)	0	(0)
White female, 17	100	(41)	0	(0)
Black female, 16	100	(38)	0	(0)
White male, 16	100	(37)	0	(0)
Black female, 31	98	(54)	2	(1)
Black male, 36	97	(37)	3	(1)
White male, 38[a]	95	(19)	5	(1)
White female, 82	95	(84)	5	(4)
White female, 36	94	(15)	6	(1)
White female, 32	94	(31)	6	(2)
Black female, 67[a]	94	(45)	6	(3)
Black male, 17	94	(64)	6	(4)
White female, 58[a]	92	(44)	8	(4)
White male, 36	91	(21)	9	(2)
Black female, 52[a]	89	(49)	11	(6)
Black male, 26	83	(15)	17	(3)
White male, 56	82	(23)	18	(5)
Black male, 58	72	(18)	28	(7)
White male, 31	70	(7)	30	(3)
Black female, 20	57	(4)	43	(3)
White female, 53	50	(18)	50	(18)
Total	91	(705)	9	(68)

Note: Dyads are hierarchically arrayed in order of increasing symmetry between physician and patient.

[a]This patient visited a female physician; others visited males.

Total numbers of questions display a broad range, with as few as 7 and as many as 88 questions initiated in a single exchange. Doctor-initiated questions seem to account for a greater proportion of the variation than do patient-initiated questions, with doctors asking as few as 4 and as many as 84 questions (in comparison to patients' range of 0 to 18 questions asked). However, neither sex nor race (of physician or patient) seemed to influence the distribution of questions between parties in this collection.

One possible avenue for further investigation is highlighted by the particularly marked asymmetries of question-initiation in exchanges between physicians and adolescent patients. Where teenagers were involved, we see that physicians asked 100% of the total questions in 4 cases out of 5. At the other end of the age continuum, a pattern is not so clear. The most symmetrical distribution of questions occurred between a physician and white female patient of 53 years. (In this dyad, each asked an equal number of questions.) Yet, the next most symmetrical exchange took place between a physician and black female patient who was 20 years of age. Thus, a clear trend toward increased symmetry of questions with greater patient age cannot be established here.

What can be established throughout these data is support for Frankel's (in press) claim that patient-initiated questions are disprefered in physician-patient interactions. Overall, we find that doctors ask the questions.

To be sure, interviews are constructed not merely of questions, but of questions and answers in alternating turns at talk. Of the total 773 questions asked in these exchanges, 96% (748) elicited answers. However, the proportion of physician-initiated questions answered by patients and the proportion of patient-initiated questions answered by physicians was not equal. Of the 705 questions doctors asked, patients answered 98% (689). Of the fewer (68) questions patients asked, doctors answered 87% (59). So, while questions do, in most cases, elicit answers from their recipients, patients answer doctors' questions more often than doctors answer theirs.

When Doctors Ask The Questions

When patients failed to answer their physician's questions, it was often under constraining structural circumstances. For example, when physicians chained questions together with no intervening slots for answers, the individual queries that comprised the chains frequently failed to elicit patients' responses:

(Dyad 05: 358-363)
```
DOCTOR:   NO:chi::lls?shakin' chi::lls?=
PATIENT:                        =  ⎡Don'-⎤
DOCTOR:                            ⎣high ⎦              fever?=
PATIENT:  =No:, jis-(.) slee:ping (.)alo:t (.) too:
                ⎡That-⎤
DOCTOR:         ⎣O    ⎦ kay.
```

Thus, in this fragment, if "chi::lls?", "shakin' chi::lls?" and "high fever?" constitute three separate queries, it is not clear to which, if any, of them the patient ventures a reply.

I also found constraints on patient answers constructed through physicians' not infrequent formulation of multiple-choice questions. For these queries, a bit more than "yes" or "no" may be called for. Yet the very design of the questions leaves little doubt as to how much more will be tolerated:

(Dyad 15: 038–049)
```
DOCTOR:   It's pai::n?= Or- or- or- or re::al weakness.=
          That=you're=discri:bing.=
          The=inabili ⎡dy=duh=come=up⎤    from
PATIENT:              ⎣Wea:knuss::.     ⎦
```

DOCTOR: a crou:ch.

                                                       (1.2)

PATIENT: ⎡Wea:knuss.⎤
DOCTOR: ⎢Ri:ght   ⎢
           ⎣((nodding))⎦

                                                       (.6)

DOCTOR: I:z yer ri:ght (.2) le:g (.2) strong enough tuh
           overcome the *pro:b*lum? = Or- (.4) or (1.4)
           ((tch)) d' yuh 'ave: the same knee problum on
                        yer ri: ⎡ght si:⎤ de
PATIENT: ⎣Ye:ah ⎦
           as well? =
PATIENT: = Bo:th sides.

Here, a series of "either/or" responses are embedded within the physician's
formulation of his questions (i.e., "*Pai::n* or *weak*nuss?" and "R:ght si:de or
bo:th sides?"). Further, the slots in which the patient's answers could come (and
should come, given the organization of adjacency pairs) are already occupied by
the physician's latched, forced-choice alternatives. In this way, the physician
limits both the placement and content of possible patient information responses.

Finally, I found that when physicians' "next" questions are posed over
patients' attempted answers to their "last" questions, incomplete answers often
appear within states of simultaneous speech. Elsewhere (West, forthcoming), I
note that physicians' interruptions of their patients are commonly constructed of
"next question–last answer" chains. Through the ongoing construction of these
chains, the conditional relevance of patients' last answers is structurally usurped
by physicians' next questions:

(Dyad 02: 85–99)
PATIENT: When I'm sitting *up*right. Y'know =
DOCTOR: = More so than
            it was even before?
PATIENT: Yay::es =
DOCTOR: = *Swel*ling 'r anything like that thet
            chew've no:ticed?
                                    (.)
PATIENT: Nuh:o, not th ⎡et I've *nod*i-
DOCTOR: ⎣TEN:::DER duh the tou⎦   ch?
            press:ing any?
PATIENT: No::, jus' when it's s- *si*::tting.
DOCTOR: Okay: =
PATIENT: = Er lying on it.
DOCTOR: Even ly:ing. Stan:ding up? walking aroun:d?

PATItENT: No: ⌈jis-⌉
DOCTOR: ⌊Not⌋ so mu:ch. Jis'-ly:ing on it.
            Si:tting on it. Jis' then.

In the fragment immediately above, the longest pause that ensues between a patient response and physician's next query is one tenth of one second. On two occasions, the physician's "next" utterance aborts the patient's completion of her answer to his "last" one. Through the staccato pacing of his questions and their incursions into the patient's turns, this doctor is demonstrating that a simple "yes" or "no" is all that he will listen to.

Of the 16 physician-initiated questions that did not elicit patient answers, 11 were positioned in chains and/or states of simultaneous speech in such fashion as to preclude slots for patient answers. Thus, patients' "failures" were in large part a product of the ways in which physicians initiated their questions.

When Patients Ask the Questions

As noted earlier, patient-initiated questions were relatively rare in the exchanges, comprising only 9% of the questions asked. Indeed, only 1 of the 21 dyads contained more than 10 patient-initiated questions, and that exchange exhibited more symmetry in the distribution of questions between doctor and patient than any other in this collection.

Given their scarcity, it is notable that patient-initiated questions failed to elicit answers from doctors more often than the reverse (13% versus 2%, respectively). More notable still is that the highest number of physician failures occurred in the exchange in which the patient asked most questions. Of the 9 questions not answered by physicians, 4 were initiated in this single exchange. So, the circumstances under which patients' questions fail to receive answers from doctors are potentially illuminated by a detailed examination of this exchange.

A precursor to one question in this dyad is first posed indirectly, and it does not get finished.

(Dyad 01: 615–626)
PATIENT: When *Tack*-o-cardia star::ts, have you god any goo:d sugges-like jus' now:,
          I- I suddenly felt sort of a .hh-
          hh (.2) *thing* starting in my throat, which is of'un a
                          (.2)
DOCTOR: Uh-does the (Mac Craw::: sa:w massage
          (do anything for)
          (work for) yuh sometimes?
          ((stroking his throat))
                          (.)
PATIENT: *Some*ti:mes.

Here, the patient's initial query is dropped mid-utterance and left hanging incomplete. It has, evidently, been recognized by the doctor, who offers a counter-question as a candidate "good suggestion" (albeit, one that works only "sometimes"). The side sequence that follows this exchange leaves further completion and elaboration of the initial query unfinished.

Shortly thereafter, we find the first "official absence" of an answer to a possibly complete question:

(Dyad 01: 634–640)
PATIENT: .h Well, I've be::n taking Did-jox-cin three times a
        day, though I understand juh can take it all on::ce, if
        you wan'. Is- Izat ri::ght?=
DOCTOR: =You've been taking
        point-one-two-five three times a day ev'ry day:,
        °right?
                    (.)
PATIENT: °Ye:ah.=
DOCTOR: =°O:kay ((makes a note))
               (1.0)

Again, an insertion sequence intervenes in the wake of the initial query, leaving it unanswered. Once the insertion sequence is completed, however, the patient begins a reformulation of her previous incomplete question:

(Dyad 01: 649–657)
PATIENT: *Yeah.* Uh- fou::r times a day fer tha:t, an' La:n-ox-cin
        I been taking three:: times a day. *So.* If I *start* into a::
        (.) ((leans back in her chair again)) into a- uh- ah: Pa-
        Pee Ay Tee:
                  (.8)
DOCTOR: How: long 'ave you been takin that = three times a
        day.
               (1.0) A long time?
PATIENT: Ye:ah ((nodding))

The question, once more, is left hanging, supplanted by a physician-initiated insertion. In the concluding states of *this* sequence, the patient reiterates her earlier completed but unanswered query:

(Dyad 01: 671–682)
DOCTOR: thet's high- hi:ghter thun the u:sual *dose*. (.) Fer a
        woman of yer si:ze.
               (.2)
PATIENT: °Mm. Wull- he'ad *to:le* me I could take all *three*: of
        thum at *on::ce*.
               (.)

DOCTOR: Ye:ah, yuh ca::n.
PATIENT: An' I thoud it'd be bedder duh space it ou:t 'n- it rilly
             doesn' make any diff'runce?

                            (.2)

DOCTOR: It- we::ll hh-hh Taking *tha:t* dose, ((pointing with his pen to the sheet in
             front of him)) I'd- I'd rather
             see yuh space 'em ou:t.

Note that a "straight answer" to this question is absent. The doctor does not
indicate that "it really doesn't make any difference"; on the other hand, he does
not indicate that it *does*. Instead, he offers his preference for what she ought to
do. ("I'd rather see yuh space 'em out.")

In the wake of this failure, yet another ensues:

(Dyad 01: 684-720)
PATIENT: Um-hmm:.

                           (.)

DOCTOR: Now: if =   ['e = wuz = taking-]
PATIENT: [Wull isn' it   ]   on my re:cord?
             ((she brings her hand down on the desk, index finger
             first, as if point)) when 'e had the le:vels mea-
             sured? ((pulls her hand back now)) it shou*::ld* be:

                          (1.0)

DOCTOR: ((flipping back through the pages in her file))
             Le:mme check.

                                        ((13 lines deleted))

DOCTOR: [No::]   [I *don't*]   see a dih-jox-cin level here
             anywhere.

                        (.6)

PATIENT: Wull *he's* had that taken, at *least twi::ce*, thet I
             rihmember.

                              . ((2 lines deleted))

DOCTOR: ((still rifling through her file)) Uh-hunh::
                        (2.4)

DOCTOR: Wuzzat in a *hosp*idul? you had it taken? ((still
             rifling))

                        .2)

PATIENT: *He:::re.* ((points over her shoulder to the door behind her))
                      (1.0)

PATIENT: At this cl:nic. ((brings her hand down again))
DOCTOR: Hmm::m, °Okay. ((still lifting page after page))

                      (6.8)

DOCTOR: Hm-um-um-umph! ((yawning)) 'Scu:se me, mm:

                     (12.0)

DOCTOR: We:ll. ((puts file aside and looks up)) I'd like tuh
          measure that tuh*da:*y an' see whuddit i:s, cuz I- like I
          sa:y, id i:::s (.) a higher than average dose.

The patient's query, "Wull isn' it on my re:cord?", is remarkable in a variety of
respects. It is formulated as a direct question (rather than a "tag," for example),
it interrupts the doctor's utterance, and it constitutes a challenge regarding the
manner in which her records have been kept. Moreover, when the physician fails
to provide a direct response ("I *don't* see a dih-jox-cin level here"), the patient
elaborates the query ("Wull *he's* had that taken, at *least twi::ce*"). Even at this,
after a considerable delay, the physician announces that he will himself take
another measurement—without ever having provided a direct response to the
patient's question.

    This patient's initially incomplete question (regarding her excessively rapid
heartbeat) is eventually answered by the physician, considerably later in the
exchange:

(Dyad 01: 749-760)
PATIENT: .hh Alright. SO if I fe- fee:l this coming on, an' I'm
          sidding up in a *pla:ne*, 'r I'm out somewhere in a
          ca:r, .h 'n I c ⌈an't lie dow- ⌉
DOCTOR: ⌊LIE:: DOW:N! ⌋
PATIENT: = Wull, spoze I can' lie *dow*:n
                              (1.0)
DOCTOR: 'F yuh can' ((tosses his head)) lie down, yih can' lie
          dow:n. =
PATIENT: = °Mm =
DOCTOR: = Uh::: si:t calmly, (.) an' take
          a Valium.
                              (1.0)
DOCTOR: An' the:n, I'd try thuh thro:at (craw-sage) massage firs'. Jis' keep it
          gen'rally steady fer about twenny-
          thirdy sekkins. 'F it doesn' - swi:tch within that time,
          try: th' other one.

Observe, however, it took the patient three tries to elicit an answer to the query.
When the physician's response finally emerges in the transcript, it appears more
than 100 lines from the patient's initial formulation of the question.

    Repeatedly in these excerpts, we see patient-initiated questions bypassed and
circumvented by physician-initiated activities (e.g., counter-questions to patient
questions and consultation of medical files). Circumvention requires a considerable amount of work in this exchange, because the patient is far more articulate
(by conventional standards) than many other patients. She uses medical
terminology in relatively sophisticated fashion; exhibits an active, sometimes

challenging curiosity about the state of her health; and consistently repeats her questions when they go unanswered. Yet she evidences *more* difficulty getting her questions answered than any other patient in this collection.

Though impossible to prove here, it may well be that this patient's assertiveness is associated with her difficulties. If physicians normatively ask the questions and patients normatively respond to them, a dispreference for patient-initiated questions may be reflected in this physician's reluctance to answer "too many" of them.

Stronger evidence of the dispreferred status of patient questions is provided by close inspection of the ways in which they are initiated. In the course of this analysis, I constructed a list of patient-initiated questions excerpted from their contexts. What is most striking in this list is the presence of marked speech perturbations in the objects patients used to pose their queries. For example, even in the dyad just examined, the onset of patient questions was routinely marked by hitches or stutters in the patient's production of an object:

(Dyad 01: 634)
PATIENT: I understand juh can take it all *on::*ce, if you wan'.
                 Is- Izzat ri::ght?

(Dyad 01: 649)
PATIENT: If I *start* into a:: (.) into a- un- ah: Pa- Pee Ay Tee:

(Dyad 01: 749)
PATIENT: So if I fe- fee:l this coming on,

Similar markings are apparent in other fragments we examined earlier:

(Dyad 08: 035)
PATIENT: Can YOU TELL- HOW SOMEBODY CUN EAT-
                 EAT U:H- WHAT CHA EAT- EAT IN THE *BLOOD*?

Of the total 68 patient-initiated questions, 46% (31) exhibited some form of speech disturbance in the course of their production. Simply put, patients displayed considerable difficulty "spitting out" their questions.

Their difficulties, however, exhibited no systematic patterns. In a few instances, stutters and hitches appeared in questions that might have been associated with patient anxiety:

(Dyad 18: 299)
PATIENT: Ah mea:n, i::s it *ri:ll* serious? Iz- izzit somethin' that
                 could-

(Dyad 07: 993)
PATIENT: Wull that- Is that nor:mul? I mean is tha:t oka::y?

But stutters also showed up in questions regarding matters of relatively little consequence to patients:

(Dyad 06: 051)
PATIENT: Wu- yuh can' take the thing ((a scab on his finger))
            off tuhda:y?

            (Dyad 09: 514)
PATIENT: Ah nodice' peepul put *salt* all ovuh theah body when
            theh wuh in thuh *steam* bath. S- Whut's that foah?
            duh yuh kno:w?

In some instances, stutters appeared to be linked to what Schegloff et al. (1977) term *self-repairs*. Repairs of one's own utterance may be initiated by dropping objects midway through production to substitute alternative formulations for them:
(Dyad 02: 232)
PATIENT: Was my blood pr- Wha' wuz my blood pressure *this*
            ti:me?

Here, for example, a possible question + assessment (i.e., "Was my blood pressure high?", "Was my blood pressure low?", "Was my blood pressure okay?") is replaced with a request for the information on which an assessment would be based. In another case of reformulation, a patient's own assessment is retracted for a request for the physician's opinion:

(Dyad 04: 002)
PATIENT: Ah had a couple of uh: nose: bleeds an': Ah guess
            meybe that's (1.0) .h wadduh yuh think tha:t come
            from.

Some stutters preceded self-corrections of "errors" in an object under production:

(Dyad 14: 712)
PATIENT: Wull *is iss a:ll due for-* from th' hear::t?

(Dyad 08: 308)
PATIENT: YUH GONNAD DO THAT WITH MUH- MY
            HUR:NEE TOO?

Other stutters preceded replacement of a speech object with the same object just suspended:

(Dyad 11: 595)
PATIENT: Whut would uh: keep- keep me from ha:vin' it flex?

(Dyad 01: 736)
PATIENT: Wh- when will yuh have the rihsul:lts (.2) the tes's
you'll have taken tuhda:y, tuh*mor*:row?

Thus, the items which followed a stutter did not necessarily correct anything.

In some instances, possibly "presumptive" questions were downgraded to less forceful queries:

(Dyad 18: 372)
PATIENT: Won' I- (.4) Wull I be gettin' a hot- ho:t pad from it?

On other occasions, the object that followed a hitch seemed a stronger formulation than that which preceded it:

(Dyad 04: 454)
PATIENT: Ah'm try:in' to: uh- .h ((clears throat)) i:s there:*any*
*oth*er type: that chew could u:h fi:gger aroun:' it?

Whether they were downgraded, upgraded, or regraded with the same stuff, patients' reformations all displayed the troublesomeness of asking doctors questions.

In all the exchanges in which patient-initiated questions were found (17 of the total 21), only one patient managed to produce her single question without a hitch:

(Dyad 05: 161)
PATIENT: Yeah:, y' get those 't drugstores?

In the case of every other patient who initiated questions in this collection, some (if not all) questions asked were marked by stuttering.

This finding does not mean that a singularly inarticulate group of patients was included in this database. To the contrary, even relatively articulate patients (e.g., the female in Dyad 01), whose speech production was fluent in other contexts, displayed noticeable hitches when asking doctors questions. What this finding seems to indicate is that patients also treat self-initiated questions as somehow problematic.

DISCUSSION

This chapter began with an anecdote illustrating the lofty heights inhabited by entities "not to be questioned." Recall that from one patient's perspective, both God and the family physician had achieved such exalted status. On the basis of findings reported here, I would have to conclude that some physicians indeed inhabit a privileged position (if not a state of grace) with respect to being questioned by their patients.

Of the 773 questions identified in 21 medical exchanges between patients and family practitioners, only 9% were initiated by patients. As noted earlier, these exchanges were recorded as they occurred during actual physician visits. So, they constitute neither a standardized nor random collection of doctor–patient interactions with regard to length of visit, duration of previous relationship or type of presenting complaint. Some physicians and patients had known one another for three years at the time of recording, while others met initially on this occasion. Some visits were routine checks for problems of long standing (e.g., diabetes or high blood pressure); others uncovered new complaints for the first time (e.g., following accidents or recently developed symptoms). Despite these variations, exchanges displayed a systematic and asymmetric pattern: Over-whelmingly, doctors asked the questions. The consistency of this pattern offers considerable support for Frankel's claim that patient-initiated questions are dispreferred in medical exchanges.

My findings further indicate that doctor–patient talk is more constrained by utterance-type and speaker identity than casual conversation, consistent with Frankel's suggestion to this effect. Not only do doctors ask the questions in these exchanges, but patients provide the responses to them. Thus, for example, patients answered 98% of the questions posed to them by doctors (689 of the total 705). But doctors, who were asked far fewer questions by their patients, also answered fewer of those they were asked (87%, or 59 of the total 68).

To be sure, the majority of patient questions *did* elicit answers from physicians in this study. And, in only 5 of the 21 total exchanges did physicians fail to answer patient-initiated questions. Therefore, it would be incorrect to conclude that patient questions were generally neglected by physicians in this collection. Whereas Korsch et al.'s (1968) findings indicated that patients' queries were commonly ignored, given vague answers, or met with changes of subject by physicians, my findings show most patient questions are answered.

Certainly, there are major differences in methods of data collection between these two investigations. Korsch and her colleagues recorded interactions in a large teaching hospital, and I collected tapes in a small clinic affiliated with, but geographically removed from, a medical university. While Korsch et al.'s research design treated mothers as patients in exchanges with pediatricians, my analysis was restricted to two-party interactions between adult patients (16 years or older) and family physicians. Thus, our methodologies are not strictly comparable.

Even so, there are parallels between our findings. In Korsch et al.'s survey of 800 patient visits, "10% of mothers asked no questions and an additional 27% asked only one or two" (1968:864). In my analysis of 21 exchanges, 19% of patients asked no questions of their doctors, and 29% asked one or two. In other words, 48% of these exchanges (10 of the 21) contained two or fewer questions initiated by patients. Moreover, in the single exchange that displayed a symmetrical distribution of questions between physician and patient (and contained the largest number of patient-initiated questions), I found the largest number of physician failures to answer questions asked.

This finding corresponds with results obtained by Wallen et al. (1979), who note that the patients who ask most questions are necessarily the ones to receive most explaining time (:145). Indeed, the dispreference for patient-initiated questions in medical exchanges may be displayed in physicians' reluctance to answer "too many" of them. In purely quantitative terms, then, the relative scarcity of patient questions and their lesser likelihood of being answered by doctors provides strong evidence in support of the notion that patient-initiated questions are not the preferred organizing devices for talk between physicians and patients in these exchanges.

Support for this notion was further garnered through qualitative analysis of the organization of doctors' and patients' questions. Doctors, for example, exhibited a tendency to formulate some questions in ways that limited patients' options in the placement and content of their answers. Where physicians linked single questions into chains, formulated multiple-choice queries, and initiated their next questions over patients' answers to their prior questions, patients were left with limited (or nonexistent) slots for answers. As other analysts (e.g., Frankel in press; Goffman 1981; Sacks 1966; Shuy 1974; Roy and Webb 1966) have noted, the construction of multiple-question utterance-types can itself place constraints on opportunities for answers. Hence, both the numbers of physician-initiated questions and the ways they are constructed display their orientation to a normative order of medical exchange in which physician-initiated questions are preferred.

As we have seen, even patients' questions exhibit this orientation. When patients posed queries to their doctors (which was rarely, to be sure), nearly half (46%) the questions they produced were marked by speech disturbances. Stutters preceded some questions that may have been anxiety producing for patients, but not all of them did. Although some hitches in speech preceded patient reformulations of questions, other "reformulations" turned out to be formulations of the very objects that were hitched. So, although repairs and reiterations displayed no consistent patterns according to what, if anything, they "fixed," they did provide considerable evidence of patients' difficulties "spitting out" their questions. Through the very talk they produce, patients seem to exhibit a dispreference for self-initiated queries.

Obviously, other activities are routinely conducted while doctors and patients converse. More than a few of these activities may be associated with the asymmetric distribution of questions and answers I observed. Diagnosis, for example, is often likened to hypothesis-testing, in which an ordered sequence of theories is subjected to an ordered set of proof procedures.[8] Thus, while talking

---

[8] An explicit comparison of diagnosis and hypothesis-testing is provided by The Royal College of General Practitioners' *The Future General Practitioner: Teaching and Learning* (1972: 21-47).

to patients, physicians attempting diagnoses may be simultaneously engaged in cognitive processing of information regarding their patients' states of health. From this perspective (in which information processing is conducted in deductive fashion), a patient's question may constitute an interruption of the physician's deductive thought process.[9] Of course, this perspective also assumes that the process of diagnosis occurs entirely within the physician's head, rather than emerging between doctor and patient in the course of interaction with each other.

Some might argue that the findings of this study might be explained through consideration of similar activities external to physician–patient talk. At this point in our knowledge, however, these "explanations" do not have the status of reasons but of hypotheses, needing exploration. I would suggest, therefore, that they might be more usefully employed as the bases for future inquiries than as explanations for results reported in this one.

The implications of these results also provide grounds for present speculation and future research. We can, however, indulge in some consideration of their potential import, given the context of the physician–patient relationship in the larger society. First, we can note that the production of a medical "interview" (i.e., an order of speech exchange in which doctors ask the questions and patients answer them) is a thoroughly interactional accomplishment. As we have seen, this order of affairs is not merely an outcome of patients' passivity, nor is it unilaterally imposed by domineering doctors. Rather, the observed dispreference for patient-initiated questions is *jointly* produced by doctors and patients through their talk with each other. Thus, not only do physicians structure questions that limit patients' options for answers, but patients themselves stammer when asking questions of their doctors. *Both* doctors and patients are implicated in the construction of the asymmetrical patterns we observe. So, as Frankel (in press) notes, "it would be inappropriate to view the issues of control and responsibility in the medical encounter as properties of individuals'. Instead, we are compelled to view such issues as micropolitical achievements, produced in and through actual turns at talk.

---

[9] Here, I am indebted to Judy Martin, M.D., for her critique of the assumed necessity for "systems reviews" through Yes/No questioning:

> It brings to mind Mary Daly's criticism (indictment? exorcism?) of Medicine and Gynecology—one of the characteristics of torture is that it's highly ritualized, to neutralize the horror. (Martin, personal communication, February 24, 1982).

Indeed, as Daly (1978) notes:

> The therapeutic curers of disorder impose a false order (meaning) upon the histories of their patients/clients. Vying with the unnaturalness of the lithotomy (supine) position, of The Pill, of exogenous estrogens, of cosmetic surgery, this physically disordering order decomposes and dismembers women's personal histories, recomposing them to match the monotonous beat of the Masters' metronome. (:282-285).

Second, we can note that physicians' and patients' evident preference for doctor-initiated questions is scarcely at odds with the presumed role of the physician in the larger system of social action. It is, assuredly, no accident that the physician—that is, "the technical expert who by special training and experience, and by an institutionally validated status, is qualified to 'help' the patient" (Parsons 1951:439)—is, overwhelmingly, the question-asker in these encounters. Insofar as questions initiate activities that restrict and mandate subsequent grounds for action by their recipients (Frankel in press), physicians' positions in larger order structural arrangements dictate that they, rather than patients, will properly invoke those restrictions and mandates.

Third, we can observe that large-scale institutional arrangements also provide a rationale for patients' evident discomfort while asking doctors questions. For example, one patient, after politely but firmly pressing his physician on reasons for a longstanding back problem, said "*Ah*'m not tryin' duh pla:y doctuh:. Cuz zat's not muh fie::l'." Implicit in his disavowal is the suggestion that asking questions *is* tantamount to playing doctor (and playing doctor may be tantamount to playing God). So, although patients may indeed have pressing practical concerns that would predispose them to query physicians, the very premise on which their relationship is based may discourage patients from using this means to solicit information from their doctors.

In closing, consider the views of one doctor on patient-initiated questions:

> A little learning is not only a dangerous thing. When exhibited by patients, it can also be downright annoying. And more and more patients are exhibiting it. With the growing number of pseudo-scientific articles in the lay press, the physician's word is increasingly being questioned. (Fisher 1977:169)

This physician seems to imply that the very legitimacy of the physician's authority may be threatened by patients' inquisitiveness.

CONCLUSION

In this chapter, I have used work in conversation analysis (Schegloff and Sacks 1973; Sacks et al. 1974; Schegloff et al. 1977; Frankel, in press) in developing a preliminary theoretical framework for analyzing the organization of questions and answers between patients and family physicians during routine visits to the doctor. Insofar as questions and answers do in fact constitute a means of information exchange in medical dialogues, my findings suggest that the information exchanged through these means is not organized in two-way fashion. Explicit comparison of the initiation of questions and answers by physicians and patients reveals an asymmetric distribution of utterance-types, in which patients provide responses and doctors ask the questions. Further, how questions are formulated by physicians and patients in these exchanges gives indication of a preference for this order of interaction between parties to talk.

Whether this is the best or only way to organize interaction between physicians and patients is a matter of heated personal opinion for many. It is also, however, a matter for continued scholarly investigation. For it is only through systematic empirical study of the minutiae of doctor–patient interaction that we can learn what constitutes the alleged communication "gap" between doctors and patients,[10] and how it might be transformed. To know, for example, how to educate patients to ask "better" questions, we first need to know what kinds of questions patients *do* ask. Similarly, in educating physicians to "improve" their rapport with patients, we will benefit by a knowledge of the kind of rapport currently in existence. If communication is the issue here, empirical investigation of the structure of communication itself is surely the first priority.

REFERENCES CITED

AMERICAN MEDICAL ASSOCIATION COUNCIL ON MEDICAL EDUCATION
    1964   Statement. Excerpted in "Teaching old docs new tricks?" Health/PAC Bulletin 80:1–31 (February 1978).
BELSKY, M.S.
    1978   Are you a smart patient? *Cosmopolitan* 185:172–230 (October).
DALY, MARY
    1978   *Gyn/Ecology: The Metaethics of Radical Feminism.* Boston: Boston Press.
FISHER, J.J.
    1977   Who's in charge here, anyway? *Medical Economics* (May 16): 169.
FRANKEL, RICHARD M.
    In press   Talking in interviews: A dispreference for patient-initiated questions in physician-patient encounters. IN *Interactional Competence*, George Psathas and Richard Frankel, Eds. New York: Irvington.
FUNK AND WAGNALLS
    1964   *Britannica World Language Edition of Funk and Wagnalls Standard Dictionary*, Vol. 2. New York: Author.
GALTON, L.
    1979   Often-missed diagnoses: A guide to mystery ailments. *Family Circle* 92:8 + (March).
GOFFMAN, ERVING
    1981   Replies and responses. In his *Forms of Talk*, pp. 5–77. Philadelphia: University of Pennsylvania Press. (Reprinted from *Language* 54: 787–815, 1978).

---

[10] Parsons first made this contention in 1951 (:441). Recently, however, the notion has received a good deal of popular support. *Family Circle*, for example, offers readers "How To Understand Your Doctor" through an alphabetized "Guide to Medical Language" (January, 1979). *Cosmopolitan* features "Are You A Smart Patient?" (October, 1979), stressing important questions patients often forget to ask. Another leading article in *Family Circle* (March, 1979) specifies a dozen or more "Mystery Ailments" potential patients can look for and call to their doctors' attention.

JEFFERSON, GAIL
  1972   Side sequences. IN *Studies in Social Interaction*, D. Sudnow, Ed., pp. 294–338. New York: The Free Press.
  1973   A case of precision timing in ordinary conversation: Over-lapped tagpositioned address terms in closing sequences. *Semiotica* 9:47–96.
KORSCH, B.N.; E. K. GOZZI; AND V. FRANCIS
  1968   Gaps in doctor-patient interaction and patient satisfaction. *Pediatrics* 42:855–870.
LAKOFF, ROBIN
  1975   *Language and Woman's Place*. New York: Harper Colophon.
MEEHAN, A.J.
  1979   Some conversational features of the use of medical terms by doctors and patients. IN *Medical Work, Realities and Routines*, P. Atkinson and C.C. Heath, Eds., pp. 107–127. Farnborough (England): Gower.
PARSONS, TALCOTT
  1951   *The Social System*. New York: The Free Press.
RANDOM HOUSE
  1975   *The Random House College Dictionary*, Rev. ed. New York: Author.
ROY, N.L., AND E.G. WEBB
  1966   Speech duration effects in the Kennedy news conferences. *Science* 153:899–901.
ROYAL COLLEGE OF GENERAL PRACTITIONERS
  1972   *The Future General Practitioner: Teaching and Learning*. For the Royal College of General Practitioners by the British Medical Journal B.M.S. House. London: Lavenham Press.
SACKS, HARVEY
  1966   Unpublished lectures. University of California, Los Angeles.
SACKS, HARVEY; EMANUEL SCHEGLOFF; AND GAIL JEFFERSON
  1974   A simplest systematics for the organization of turn-taking in conversation. *Language* 50:696–735.
SCHEGLOFF, EMANUEL
  1968   Sequencing in conversational openings. *The American Anthropologist* 70:1075–1095.
  1972   Notes on a conversational practice: Formulating place. IN *Studies in Social Interaction*, D. Sudnow Ed., pp. 75–119. New York: The Free Press.
  1981   Discourse as an interactional achievement. Paper presented at the Georgetown University Round Table on Linguistics and Language Studies, March 1981.
SCHEGLOFF, EMANUEL; GAIL JEFFERSON; AND HARVEY SACKS
  1977   The preference for self-correction in the organization of repair in conversation. *Language* 53:361–382.
SCHEGLOFF, EMANUEL, AND HARVEY SACKS
  1973   Opening up closings. *Semiotica* 8:289–327.
SHUY, ROGER W.
  1974   Problems of Communication in the Cross-Cultural Medical Interview. *Working Papers in Sociolinguistics* 19.
WALLEN, J; HOWARD B. WAITZKIN; AND J. D. STOECKLE
  1979   Physicians' stereotypes about female health and illness: A study of patient's sex

and the informative process during medical interviews. *Women and Health* 4:135–146.

WEST, CANDACE

Forthcoming When the doctor is a 'lady': Power, status and gender in physician-patient exchanges. IN *Women, Health, and Medicine*, A. Stromberg, Ed. Palo Alto, Calif.: Mayfield.

APPENDIX
TRANSCRIPTION CONVENTIONS

The transcript techniques and symbols were devised by Gail Jefferson in the course of research undertaken with Harvey Sacks. Techniques are revised and symbols added or dropped as they seem useful to work. There is no guarantee or suggestion that the symbols of transcripts alone would permit the doing of any unspecified research tasks: They are properly used as an adjunct to the tape-recorded materials.

Mary: I don' ⌈know⌉ John: ⌊you⌋ don't	Brackets indicate that the portions of utterances so encased are simultaneous. The left-hand bracket marks the onset of simultaneity, the right-hand bracket indicates its resolution.
A: We:::ll now	Colons indicate that the syllable immediately preceding the colons is prolonged.
A: But-	A hyphen represents a cutting off short of the immediately preceding syllable.
CAPS or *italics*	Both of these are used to represent heavier emphasis (in speaker's pitch) on words so marked.
A: Swat I said = B: = But you didn't	Equal signs are used to indicate that no time elapsed between the objects "latched" by the marks. Often used as a transcribing convenience, it can also mean that a next speaker starts at precisely the end of a current speaker's utterance.
(1.3)	Numbers encased in parenthesis indicate the seconds and tenths of seconds ensuing between speaker turns. They may also be used to indicate the duration of pauses internal to a speaker's turn.
(#)	Score sign indicates a pause of about a second that it wasn't possible to discriminate precisely.

(word)	Single parentheses with words in them indicate that something was heard, but the transcriber is not sure what it was. These can serve as a warning that the transcript may be unreliable.
((softly))	Double parentheses enclose "descriptions," not transcribed utterances.
A: I (x) I did	Parentheses encasing an "x" indicate a hitch or stutter on the part of the speaker.
A: Oh Yeah?	Punctuation marks are used for intonation, not grammar.
()	Empty parentheses signify untimed pauses.
°So you did.	The degree symbol represents softness, or decreasing amplitude.
.hh, hh, eh-heh, .engh-henh	These are breathing and laughing indicators. A period followed by "hh's" marks an inhalation. The "hh's" alone stand for exhalation. The "eh-heh" and ".engh-henh" are laughter syllables.
(.)	The period encased in parentheses denotes a pause of one tenth of a second.

Structure and Structuring

7

Doctor Talk/Patient Talk: How Treatment Decisions Are Negotiated in Doctor–Patient Communication*

Sue Fisher

Hysterectomies are performed at a higher rate than any other surgical procedure. The National Center for Health Statistics estimates that 794,000 women had hysterectomies in 1976, which represents a 15% increase over the three previous years. In 1976, 10 out of every 1,000 women underwent this surgery. At the current rate, the Center notes, more than half the women in the U.S. will have their uteruses removed before they are 65 years old (National Center for Health Statistics 1976).

The increase in hysterectomies is a major problem. A 1976 congressional subcommittee estimated that in 1974, there were 2.4 million unnecessary surgeries at a high cost to the American public. The costs were more than monetary. Unnecessary surgery caused 11,900 deaths in 1975 ("Cost and Quality of Health Care" 1976). The death rate for hysterectomies is higher than the reported death rate for uterine/cervical cancer (Larned 1977). The American

* Acknowledgment and thanks for providing helpful comments in the preparation of this manuscript go to Hugh Mehan, Sam Wallace, Irving Kenneth Zola, and Donna Eder. This paper was presented at the Society for the Study of Social Problems Annual Meeting, New York, New York, August 1980. An earlier version appeared in *Linguistics and the Professions*, edited by Robert J. Di Pietro, Norwood, N.J.: Ablex, 1982.

Cancer Society estimates that of the 46,000 cases of uterine or cervical cancer reported every year, 12,000 are fatal (Virginia Health Bulletin 1977). For hysterectomies, the fatality rate is 1,000 out of every one million. In addition the Cancer Society claims that the majority of these cancer deaths could be prevented with regular Pap smears and gynecological examinations (Larned 1977; Virginia Health Bulletin 1977).

Yet, these figures do not represent the psychosocial costs of hysterectomies. A 1973 English study found that within three years of having hysterectomies, one-third of the women studied were treated for depression (Caress 1977). Psychiatrists agree that a hysterectomy can often damage a woman's sense of identity. Larned reports Dr. Peter Barglow's findings that

> the hysterectomy is clearly and immediately visualized [by the patient] as an irreversible drastic procedure which removes an organ with high value in the ego's image of the body, as well as with considerable conscious value in the woman's sense of self and identity. Surely, the loss of an organ whose presence was reaffirmed monthly cannot be so easily denied. (Larned 1977:206).

Physicians believe that with adequate counseling, "well-adjusted" women can cope with hysterectomies (Larned 1977).

How are treatment decisions negotiated in practitioner–patient communication? How is the exchange of information in medical interviews organized, and how does that organization produce and constrain the negotiation of treatment decisions? Given the asymmetry inherent in the doctor–patient relationship, medical practitioners not only have technical skills and medical knowledge that patients lack, but they also have the potential to control patients' access to and understanding of the information on which they will make their treatment decisions. This power imbalance increases when practitioners, especially residents, perceive patients as poor and powerless.

This discussion shows how medical practitioners act as gatekeepers, providing options to some that are denied to others. It suggests that medical interviews are social events in which the asymmetry in the practitioner–patient relationship combines with the practical concerns each brings to the examination room or consulting office, which influences therapeutic discourse and the treatment decisions.

THE BACKGROUND CONTEXT

The research discussed here was done in a university teaching hospital. Like most teaching hospitals, the delivery of health care was organized into inpatient and outpatient services. The outpatient services were further divided into two clinical systems. These clinical systems were organized around medical specialties. My research was done in a paired set of clinics in the Department of Reproductive Medicine and the specialty of oncology (cancer).

Because of the organization and staffing of each clinic, I have called them the Faculty Clinic and the Community Clinic. The Faculty Clinic was staffed by professors of reproductive oncology and, for the most part, accepted patients referred by other medical practitioners in the community. The Community Clinic was staffed by residents under the supervision of staff physicians and primarily accepted patients referred by social agencies or other clinics in the hospital's system of community clinics.

Over the course of a nearly two-year period, I followed 21 women with abnormal Pap smears referred to, diagnosed, and treated in the Faculty and Community Clinics. I found, among other things, that women with abnormal Pap smears referred to the Community Clinic were more likely to receive nonconservative treatment (i.e., to have hysterectomies) than were women referred to the Faculty Clinic (see Fisher 1979a).

The sample population was assembled largely for practical reasons. My entry into the hospital had been gained with the help of a staff physician who was a gynecological oncologist. As a consequence, the population was defined as women with cancerous or precancerous problems in their reproductive systems.

As I was interested in patients' careers as well as the negotiation of treatment decisions, I followed patients longitudinally through the diagnosis/treatment/recovery process. Doctor–patient interactions were captured on audiotape. Early in my involvement with patients, I found that I was not prepared to deal with death on a daily basis; thus, no patients with invasive disease were part of the sample population.

To document the organization of doctor–patient communication, I spent nearly two years as a participant–observer. For the first 13 months, I conducted informal interviews with staff physicians, attending physicians, residents, medical students, nursing staff, and other support personnel. I attended lectures for residents, read patients' files, observed in consulting offices and examining rooms, and visited patients in the hospital to talk informally about what they were feeling. For the next eight months, I audiotaped the exchange of information between practitioners and patients.

The analysis in this chapter is drawn from verbatim transcripts of auditoaped practitioner–patient communications, information gathered from medical files, and other ethnographic materials. My background knowledge grew from impromptu interviews with practitioners and was heightened by attending lectures with residents, studying the residents' training manual, and reading appropriate sections of their gynecological textbooks.

To display how medical decisions were negotiated in practitioner-patient communications, I extended the analysis beyond the linguistic boundaries of the transcripts and blended verbatim linguistic data with more impressionistic ethnographic data. Neither practitioners nor patients say aloud all that contributes to their decision making.

For example, patients rarely say aloud that they do not trust their medical practitioners or that they suspect them of trying to manipulate the situation. Similarly, neither staff doctors nor residents say aloud that a patient looks like a poor woman, or that she talks like an uneducated woman. They do not say that how patients talk, look, or dress leads them to believe that the patients are not responsible and will not return for necessary follow-up care. They do not say that these factors contribute to their recommending a less conservative treatment. Neither doctors nor residents say aloud that a particular patient has all of the children she needs or should have because she is on welfare and cannot afford the children she already has. They do not say that hairy underarms and legs, asking too many questions or being too quiet, acting too passive or too aggressive, or wanting children (or more children) contributes to the treatment they recommend. Residents do not say aloud that they need surgery experience or that a particular patient is a good candidate for a hysterectomy (even though a hysterectomy is not absolutely necessary on medical grounds). Although not said aloud, my observations suggest that these factors (and others like them) contribute to the negotiation of treatment decisions.

THE MEDICAL CONTEXT

Women with abnormal Pap smears provided an ideal population to study the negotiation of differential decision making. Pap smears are preventive health measures, They are recommended for most women once a year as a screen for cervical cancer.

The results of Pap smears traditionally come in five classes. Class 1 is normal, and class 5 is the most abnormal and may indicate invasive disease. Classes 2, 3, and 4 represent a gray area between normal cells and invasive disease. They often indicate dysplasia, or abnormal changes in cells that, although not cancerous, may be precursors to cervical cancer.

Pap smears in the gray area give medical practitioners the widest latitude in their decision making. When a Pap smear is abnormal, the medical task is to ensure that the whole area of abnormal cells can be visualized to rule out the possibility of invasive disease. Once the extent of the lesion and the degree of abnormality have been determined, treatment decisions are based on two separate but interrelated goals: (a) to protect the patient from developing more extensive disease (cancer), and (b) to preserve, where possible, the patient's reproductive functions.

During my study, I observed three treatment options routinely used to treat women with Pap smears in the range between normal and invasive disease: cryosurgery (freezing), cone biopsy or conization, and hysterectomy.

Cryosurgery is an office procedure that retains a woman's reproductive capacity. Cone biopsy or conization is a hospital procedure done under anesthetic. A thin, cone-shaped slice is cored out of the endocervical canal and examined. Cone biopsies can be either diagnostic or therapeutic. If the upper limits of the cone sample are free of abnormal cells, then this diagnostic procedure becomes an effective therapeutic one. It threatens, but does not terminate, reproductive capacity and has been demonstrated to be as effective in treating dysplasia as has the hysterectomy. Hysterectomy is the surgical removal of the uterus.

The manual prepared for residents further stipulates how treatment decisions are to be made. It says that when the limits of the lesion are seen and there is no evidence of invasive disease, treatment should be based on the patient's wish. If she wishes to retain her reproductive capacity, conservative measures like cryosurgery may be used. If she requests sterilization, hysterectomy is the treatment of choice. According to the manual, hysterectomies are indicated only when conservative techniques fail, when there is evidence of invasive disease, or when a patient requests a hysterectomy for sterilization.

These seem rather clear criteria for medical decision making. Yet, based on my observations, treatment decisions are not as clear as they seem. On purely medical grounds, it is hard to explain why no patients in the Faculty Clinic received hysterectomies. Or, even though there was no evidence of invasive disease, why 7 out of 13 women in the Community Clinic were given hysterectomies.

Given the parameters just outlined, we could speculate that perhaps the women in the Community Clinic requested hysterectomies for sterilization. However, I was in the examining room while treatment decisions were reached; and during the two years of my research, these patients never requested sterilization.

THE SOCIAL CONTEXT

If treatment decisions are not made on medical grounds alone, how, then, are they made? Much of the literature of medical sociology (cf. Ehrenreich and Ehrenreich 1970; Freidson 1970; Mechanic 1968; Navarro 1973; Stevens 1966; Waitzkin and Waterman 1974) suggests that medical decisions are made using social criteria.

Still, the medical decisions made in the study cannot be justified solely on social grounds. Social criteria like referral patterns, organization of the setting, and such demographic factors as age, ethnicity, number of children, and social class did not completely account for the distribution of treatment decisions. When social criteria were considered, a trend emerged. Young, Caucasian, single or divorced women with few or no children who are referred by private physicians or social agencies to the Faculty Clinic are more likely to receive conservative treatment. Older, Mexican, or Mexican-American women, married or divorced with multiple children, referred from within the system of Community Clinics or by social agencies to the Community Clinic are more likely to receive less conservative treatment (i.e., to receive hysterectomies).

These social factors are important, yet they are not explanatory. An analysis of the medical and social factors that underlie treatment decisions focuses on the product of a decision. Once products, or treatment decisions, are tabulated and grouped together, all instances of a given treatment are treated the same. This kind of analysis leaves several questions unexplored. Chief among them are as follows: How do practitioners and patients gather information from each other to reach decisions? What input do practitioners and patients make into the decision-making process? Given the practitioners' specialized medical knowledge and technical skill and the asymmetry inherent in the relationship, how do practitioners decide what treatment to recommend? Once they have decided, how do they convey that information to patients, and what are the consequences, in terms of treatment outcomes, of how information is exchanged?

These questions shift the focus from an exclusive concern with products to an analysis of process as it occurs in organization contexts. It displays treatment decisions as produced and constrained by the exchange of information in medical interviews.

THE ANALYTIC CONTEXT

When listening to conversation, one is impressed with the variety of ways that information is exchanged. When analyzing discourse, one is equally impressed with its organized character. Theory and research in several disciplines suggest that language is a social production in which different linguistic arrangements are visible in different situations and in which there is a relationship between the words spoken, the actions performed, and the structure of talk. More recently, language has been analyzed as discourse—a naturally occurring, locally organized, social production.

Hymes (1962) states that one of the goals of an "ethnography of speaking" is to capture naturally occurring talk, do a detailed analysis of it, and display it as socially produced. The sociolinguistic concepts of "communicative competence" and its methodological counterpart, an "ethnography of speaking," (Hymes 1962, 1972, 1974) have been the foundation of many studies that examine the properties of natural language use (cf. Bernstein 1971; Ervin-Tripp and Mitchell-Kernan 1977; Halliday and Hasan 1976; Labov 1972; Philips 1972; Shatz 1975; Shatz and Gelman 1973; Shuy 1983).

Labov and Fanshel (1977) demonstrate Hymes's (1962) claim that discourse is a social or speech event organized around an exchange of information. As a speech event, therapeutic discourse is a routinized form of behavior with well-defined boundaries. It is an interview structured by who initiates the event and who is helped by it.

Labov and Fanshel found the speech event in therapeutic discourse to be asymmetrical. The participant who initiates the event and is helped by it (the client/patient) is in a subordinate position. In addition, they demonstrated that the asymmetry is socially produced and structures the exchange of information between participants.

The asymmetry Labov and Fanshel discuss is similar to Waitzkin and Waterman's (1974) "competence gap." Waitzkin and Waterman claim that socioeconomic factors cause doctors and patients to enter a therapeutic interview with different resources. This produces an inherent asymmetry, which affects health care delivery.

In a discussion of medical interviews, Shuy (1982) suggests that a great deal hinges on small features of the interview that are normally taken for granted by medical practitioners and only recently have come under investigation by social scientists. He points out that medical interviews are like other conversations in that they are structured, predictable, and organized around topics. He also demonstrates that medical interviews are different from normal conversation.

In normal conversation, there is an expectation of balanced participation. Participants talk, introduce topics, and respond to topics in about the same quantities. Not so in medical interviews. Shuy further claims that the differences in medical interviews have an impact on patient's participation and understanding. Others also have argued that how information is exchanged has an impact on how it is understood (cf. Chafe 1976; Cicourel 1974, 1975; Keenan and Schieffelin 1976; Kuno 1976).

THE DECISION-MAKING CONTEXT:
THE MEDICAL INTERVIEW

An analysis of the practitioner–patient communication through which treatment decisions are negotiated provides information not available when only the medical and social criteria underlying medical decision making are considered. These criteria are, in many ways, external and constraining "social facts" that produce and inhibit the decision-making process. Yet, treatment decisions are also affected by the participants' interactional activities and, as such, are socially produced in the setting. An analysis of the strategic use of language in medical interviews displays how treatment decisions are accomplished within the contextual framework provided by medical and social factors.

Medical interviews are social events oriented toward the specific end of a treatment decision. In this event, practitioners have, and use, quite a wide latitude of choice in recommending treatment options. In analyzing how language is strategically used to accomplish treatment decisions, I do not intend to characterize the field of medicine as a whole or to praise or criticize particular medical practitioners. Rather, it is my intention to demonstrate that medical practitioners and patients have different practical concerns that organize how they exchange information. This organization has consequences in terms of the decisions reached.

Patients enter medical interactions from a position of relative weakness. For example, they have an abnormal Pap smear and feel threatened by the possibility of a cancer-related medical problem. They enter unfamiliar surroundings in which all of the other participants seem to share a common language. This language is, for the most part, unintelligible and frightening to them.

Medical practitioners, on the other hand, are in their "home court" in the medical setting. They understand and have some control over the workings of the hospital and clinic bureaucracies. The special medical jargon is their professional lexicon. They have knowledge and skills that are usually mysterious to patients. It is from this position of relative strength that practitioners greet patients and the medical interview begins.

Medical practitioners, in addition, are very busy. Their time is budgeted and oriented toward making a diagnosis and recommending treatments. For practitioners, the diagnostic/treatment process is a general concern. Their focus is on how, within certain parameters, to treat a specific medical problem. The patient is one among many with similar problems.

For residents, the diagnostic/treatment process includes an additional concern. They need surgical experience if they are to become competent practitioners. This creates a dual focus for them: (a) providing adequate medical care, and (b) producing maximum opportunities for surgery experience.

In addition, medical practitioners are not as able to separate themselves from death as I had been. The relationship between abnormal Pap smears, cancer, and the kind of death most cancer causes may contribute to the practitioners' treatment recommendations. This may be especially true when they treat lower-class, minority women, who practitioners may view as immature, irresponsible, and unlikely to return for the necessary follow-up care.

The practical concerns are not the same for patients. Patients are not interested in making a diagnosis. They cannot recommend treatments, do not need surgery experience, and have not faced death on a daily basis. Their time is not measured into equal increments to be divided among a maximum number of patients. For patients, the focus is on the meaning of their medical problem and how it will affect their everyday lives. Time is measured as time away from school, job, or family; time until they find out the results of laboratory tests or treatments to be recommended; time as a bomb ticking away precious moments before the suspected cancer explodes and takes over their lives. Patients are interested in finding out what their abnormal Pap smears mean, whether they indicate cancer, and what needs to be done. They are afraid of the unknown, worried about the possibility of having cancer, and fearful that their lives, reproductive capacities, and value as women may be at risk (Fisher 1979b).

Both the practitioner and patient have information that is necessary to the decision-making process of the other. To gain access to this information, they exchange information organized around topics by requesting and providing information to each other. During the exchange, language functions strategically to move the decision-making process closer to a treatment decision. On some occasions, requests for information function as "questioning strategies." Both the practitioner and patient request specific information and provide access to less specific information. For example the question, "What did Karen tell you about your Pap smear?" is a request for specific information. It is also a way to gain less specific information about the woman's competence as a patient.

Both practitioners and patients use questioning strategies. They are used by medical practitioners during talk about reproduction to gain access to information that only patients can supply. Patients use questioning strategies during talk about treatment options to gather information about the necessity of a recommended treatment. When used by residents and staff physicians, they are used differently and these differences impact upon the decision-making process.

On other occasions, information is provided in ways that function as "presentational" and "persuasional" strategies. Both strategies are negotiating mechanisms. They provide information while *suggesting* or *specifying* how the information should be understood.

Presentational strategies are "soft sells." They provide information while *suggesting* how patients should make sense out of it. For example, a practitioner would say, "We usually treat this by freezing." This presentation provides the patient with information about a treatment option while suggesting that it is the "usual" or "normal" way to treat her condition.

Persuasional strategies are harder sells. They provide information while *specifying* how it should be understood. For example, a practitioner might say, "What you should do if you don't want any more children is have a hysterectomy. No more uterus, no more cancer, no more babies, no more birth control, and no more periods." This presentation provides the patient with information about what treatment she should have while specifying why she should have it (no more uterus, no more cancer, etc.).

Only practitioners use presentational and persuasional strategies. And, again, the strategies are used differently by residents and staff physicians. They are used when talking about cancer and treatment options to provide information about what treatment decision the patient should make.

Questioning, presentational, and persuasional strategies are interactional mechanisms that accomplish treatment decisions. They are the strategies through which the information necessary to negotiate treatment decisions is exchanged.

THE COMMUNICATION CONTEXT:
NEGOTIATION MECHANISMS

An analysis of the strategic use of language suggests that practitioners have power that patients lack, a power manifested and reflected in how practitioners present information to patients. Although patients do not have the same kind of power practitioners do, they too have input into the decision-making process. They can ask questions that can redirect talk about treatment options and that can affect how the treatment decision is reached.

The discussion of how language is strategically used takes the analysis beyond the linguistic bounds of the transcript and embeds it in its ethnographic context. A comparison across settings, participants, and treatment decisions provides a view of how treatment decisions are negotiated and accomplished in the situated actions of the participants and in specific organizational contexts.

Medical Practitioners' Use of Questioning Strategies

Questioning strategies provide a slot for patients to display their competence.[1] Marrianna, for example, was diagnosed and treated in the Faculty Clinic. She was a 21-year-old Anglo woman; a student at a local university; had never married; and had been pregnant once and had had an abortion. She was referred to the junior oncologist in the Faculty Clinic by a women's health care specialist. A routine Pap smear taken in this clinic was returned with the notation that it contained abnormal cells; and because of the professional relationship between the women's health care specialist and the new doctor in the hospital (the junior staff oncologist), she was referred to the Faculty Clinic.

On her first visit, the doctor twice requested information in a strategic manner. He said, "Now did Karen explain to you the abnormal, what this abnormal Pap smear business is?"

The patient answered, "She [the women's health care specialist] explained that the cells looked abnormal...the cells are in a dysplastic condition."

The doctor continued by asking, "Dysplasia, what's your understanding of that?"

To which she responded, "Well, what's anyone's understanding of it? They're abnormal and you don't know why and they don't know if it leads to cancer."

In both of these requests for information, Marrianna responded by providing the information requested, and in so doing, presented herself as a competent young woman.

In the next case, the same doctor asked similar questions, but the patient did not display herself as competent. The patient, Anelen, was a 30-year-old Anglo

---

[1] In this discussion *competence* is not intended to index the patient's overall ability, but rather it indexes the patient's ability to display herself as appropriate within the doctor's medical framework.

woman. She had been married once, divorced, been pregnant once, and given the child up for adoption. She was referred by the same women's health care specialist.

During the interview the doctor asked a question that functioned strategically. He said, "Do you know that the Pap smear, do you understand what the Pap smear means? What it does?"

The patient responded by saying, "Uhmm, Karen explained a little, but I'm not sure of the possibilities. I don't even know what all those are but she told me not to worry yet."

Anelen's response neither provided the information requested nor made her appear as a competent woman. To be sure that Anelen had the necessary information to understand her medical problem and reach a decision, the doctor followed this exchange by providing information about her Pap smear and about the diagnostic and therapeutic procedures used to manage it.

In the third example, no slot was provided for the patient to display her competence. Marvi, a 23-year-old Mexican-American woman, was married, the mother of three small children, and was referred to the Community Clinic from the Primary Care Clinic where a postpartum checkup and routine Pap smear disclosed abnormal cervical cells. At the time of Marvi's visit to the Community Clinic, she was pregnant with an unwanted pregnancy, which led to an abortion. Although this was her first abortion, it was not the first time her birth control had failed. Given these factors, it is not surprising that the practitioner had recommended a hysterectomy. What is more surprising is that she did not have a hysterectomy. Marvi is the only woman in the sample population with multiple children who was treated with cryosurgery.

The bureaucratic organization of the Community Clinic contributed to Marvi's treatment with cryosurgery. At the Community Clinic, Marvi was discouraged from having a tubal ligation for sterilization. Instead, a hysterectomy was recommended to treat her medical problem and for sterilization. When the patient was referred to another clinic for abortion counseling, that clinic did not discourage a tubal ligation. Marvi, then, had an abortion and a tubal. When she returned to the Community Clinic, there were no longer any medical grounds on which a hysterectomy could be performed, and so she was treated with cryosurgery.

The exchange of information in Marvi's case took place differently from the exchange in Marrianna and Anelen's case. Marrianna and Anelen were treated in the Faculty Clinic by a professor of medicine—a staff physician. In each case, the physician asked questions that functioned strategically. These questions provided a slot into which patients could respond—displaying their competence in the process.

On the other hand, Marvi was treated in the Community Clinic by a resident who did not use questions in a strategic manner. Thus, Marvi did not have an opportunity to show herself to be a competent patient. When the resident questioned her, he used very specific questions about her birth control practices. Because she had come to the clinic with an unwanted pregnancy, it was quite clear that Marvi had not been a competent user of birth control. It is interesting to speculate on why the resident did not use more general questions, which might have allowed Marvi to display her competence as a patient. I suspect that he had already judged her to be incompetent on grounds that are not displayed in the verbal communication between them. These assumptions structured the exchange of information that followed and had an impact on the treatment recommended.

Patient's Use of Questioning Strategies

Patients also ask questions. They ask them in response to information provided by medical professionals during a discussion of treatment options. When asked by patients, questions have the potential to change the direction of the treatment decision, as shown in the following examples.

When Anelen returned to the Faculty Clinic to discuss the results of her tests and make a treatment decision, she asked a question during a discussion of treatment options. On her previous visit Anelen provided the information that she did not want to have any more children. The doctor responded by recommending a hysterectomy as a permanent method of sterilization and to treat her abnormal Pap smear.

On the second visit, the exchange opened with a discussion that reviews what had transpired on the previous visit and during a previous phone conversation. The doctor reminded Anelen that he has recommended a hysterectomy, and Anelen asked a question that redirected the talk about treatment options and affected the final treatment. She said "Have a hysterectomy and that, I'm that, if there's an alternative. I'm terrified of operations." The doctor responded, "Uh, okay, well, there certainly is an alternative, yeah, we can treat this by just freezing it here in the office and that usually will take care of it about 90% of the time." The discussion of options and the treatment performed was redirected after the patient raised a question. She was treated with cryosurgery.

The next patient, Lucy, was diagnosed and treated in the Faculty Clinic after being referred from a social agency staffed by native Spanish-speaking workers. Lucy was a 42-year-old, bilingual, Mexican-American woman. She was married and had three children. Her diagnosis and treatment in the Faculty Clinic was related to her being a poor, bilingual Mexican-American woman, and to my participation as both a researcher and translator.

The patient had a medical problem for which she went to her private physician. He recommended surgery, and she did not have the money to pay for it. In her search for less expensive medical care, a friend referred her to the outreach clinic staffed by native Spanish-speakers. At the clinic, Lucy received advice about how to apply for MediCal (the California equivalent of Medicaid) and was referred to the junior staff oncologist at the Faculty Clinic.

When the doctor and patient met to discuss treatment options, he informed her that the extent of her lesion had not been visualized, told her that she needed to have a conization biopsy as the next diagnostic step, and talked about a hysterectomy. Lucy was concerned about how she would pay for hospital care and confused by the letter she had received from MediCal. She asked the doctor to clarify the letter and he was unable to do so (which does not speak well for MediCal's style of communication).

To provide the information Lucy requested, the doctor called the billing office. While he was on the phone, Lucy turned to me and asked, in Spanish, if the doctor had said he was going to take out her uterus. I explained, in Spanish, the difference between conization biopsy and hysterectomy and confirmed that the doctor had been talking about removing her uterus. She asked if that would be necessary and I suggested that she ask the doctor.

Two things particularly struck me about our exchange. First, because Lucy spoke English so well, both the doctor and I assumed she understood it equally well. She did not. After reviewing the transcript, I was not surprised. When talking about treatments, the doctor had used several words interchangeably: *womb, uterus, cervix,* and *hysterectomy*. I was also struck by the consequences of our exchange. At the next opportunity, which occurred during a discussion of treatment options, the patient requested information that functioned strategically, changed the direction of the discussion of options, and affected the treatment performed.

While talking about how long the patient would have to be in the hospital, the doctor explained that the longer stay was because they would be taking out her uterus. The patient then asked, "Is that necessary?" The doctor responded, "Well, it isn't absolutely necessary; it may or may not be..." For much of the remaining exchange of information, the doctor worked to move the patient toward a treatment decision of hysterectomy. In each instance, the patient responded by asking if it was necessary or by saying that if it was not necessary, she did not want it. She was treated with a conization biopsy.

Another patient, Pat, asked questions, but did not change the direction of the discussion of options or the treatment performed. Pat, a 32-year-old Anglo woman, had been married, divorced, pregnant five times, and had three children. Although she was an American citizen, she married and had lived most of her adult life in Ireland. Her children still lived there with their father. When she returned to the Community Clinic to discuss her treatment options, she was told that the extent of the lesion had not been visualized, asked if she wanted more children, and told that a conization biopsy followed by a hysterectomy was the best treatment for her.

During the discussion of treatment options and in response to information that the resident was presenting, she made a request for information, a request that functioned strategically. She said,

> Well, for this way now would you say, for instance, you're talking about there could be surgery, if, uh, there is an advancement of cancer there, a sign of cancer. Well, also the fact that you asked me did I want any more children, there's another way of doing it too, but it also means that it could travel, is that it, the cancer could spread, say for instance, if I don't have a hysterectomy, is that the idea?

The doctor responded, "Well, if you have cancer, then it has to be treated because it can spread, right?" The talk about treatment options did not change the direction of the discussion of options or the treatment performed. This patient was treated with a vaginal hysterectomy.

The communication in this case between practitioner and patient is different from that with the two previous patients (Anelen and Lucy). Pat is the only patient who added information to the "facts" provided by the medical practitioner. She added the notion that cancer could spread if not treated with a hysterectomy. It was this information the resident picked up and used to justify his treatment recommendation. Pat's question is also not as clear or as strong as those used by the other two patients. She did not ask if there were alternatives or if a hysterectomy was necessary. In addition, she asked two questions during the same utterance. The resident avoided discussing alternatives entirely. And he answered only part of the second question. He did not address whether the abnormal cells would spread if she did not have a hysterectomy. Instead, he answered a hypothetical question that she had not really asked. He answered the question, If it is cancer, would it spread without a hysterectomy? He did not tell her that if she did not have cancer, there were other alternatives.

In Anelen's, Lucy's, and Pat's cases the medical professional's presentation of information provided a slot into which the patient could request information that functioned strategically. In each case, the medical professional's response to the question was different. In addition, the medical professionals themselves elicited information from patients differently in each case. With Anelen, the doctor asked questions to request specific information and to provide a slot for her to display her competence. In response, she neither provided the information he asked for nor displayed her competence. In Lucy and Pat's cases, no questions were asked. Neither patient was given an opportunity to display her understanding of her medical problem or her competence as a patient.

It is interesting to speculate why Lucy and Pat were not given the opportunity to display their competence, as Anelen was; or why neither Lucy nor Anelen were given a hysterectomy, as Pat was. On closer inspection, Lucy shares features with both Anelen and Pat. Although Lucy and Anelen were both treated in the Faculty Clinic by the same staff physician, their referral patterns had been quite different. Anelen had been referred by a women's health care specialist with whom she had a long-standing relationship. This relationship provided an outside advocate who could hold the medical practitioner in the hospital accountable. Neither Lucy nor Pat had an outside advocate. Lucy had been referred from an outreach clinic staffed by native Spanish-speakers, and Pat had been referred from within the system of community clinics. In each case, neither the interest of the referring medical practitioner nor the organization of the bureaucracy provided the kind of support Anelen had developed with the women's health care specialist.

It seems reasonable to speculate that both Lucy and Pat were judged as less powerful than Anelen on grounds that are not immediately apparent in their verbal communication. This judgment structured the exchange of information between practitioner and patient and had an impact on the treatment decision reached. Although in each case the medical practitioner provided a slot for the patient to request information that functioned strategically, he responded to the questions patients inserted into these slots differently.

At first glance, then, it would be reasonable to assume that Lucy and Pat, denied the opportunity to display their competence and perceived as less powerful, would be treated with hysterectomies and Anelen would not. My observations suggest two reasons this was not the outcome. First, Lucy was treated in the Faculty Clinic by a staff physician and Pat was treated in the Community Clinic by a resident. Staff physicians do not have the same "need" to perform hysterectomies as do residents, who must have the surgical experience to become fully qualified doctors. Second, Lucy, unlike Pat, used a strong questioning strategy and kept returning to it each time the doctor suggested a hysterectomy. Pat used a weaker questioning strategy and did not return to it, even when her questions were not fully answered. Thus, Pat's impact on the decision-making process was weak, and she was treated with a hysterectomy.

Medical Practitioners' Use of Presentational and Persuasional Strategies

Although both practitioners and patients ask questions, doctors do so during exchanges of general information to gather the details of patients' reproductive history and desire. Patients, by contrast, ask questions during discussions about treatment options. In addition, there are differences in how medical practitioners present information to patients when discussing cancer and treatment options. They use presentational and persuasional strategies to provide patients with the information necessary to reach treatment decisions and with ways of understanding or making sense out of that information.

In each of the previous three cases, the medical professional's response to patients' questions provided specific information and suggested how that information should be understood. In Anelen's case, the doctor responded by saying, "There certainly is an alternative . . . " and by providing the information that cryosurgery is an alternative that is 90% effective. He provided specific information, and by the tone of his presentation, made the choice of cryosurgery perfectly acceptable.

In Lucy's case, the doctor responded by saying, "Well, it isn't absolutely necessary . . . " The statement that "it isn't absolutely necessary" frames the medical information to suggest a preference: Although a hysterectomy is not absolutely necessary, it certainly is preferable.

In Pat's case, the resident avoided directly answering the patient's question. By answering only a small part of what was asked, he suggested that the answer to the whole was contained within the part; that is, that a hysterectomy was a necessary procedure.

In Anelen's, Lucy's, and Pat's cases the medical practitioners used presentational strategies to suggest how information should be understood. In the next case, information is presented in a way that does more than suggest how to make sense out of it. Persuasional strategies are used to specify the grounds on which understanding is to be based. In presenting the options to Marvi the resident said the following:

> What I was going to tell you is that there are two ways this can be treated. Okay? One is for dysplasia that we could do a hysterectomy and just remove the uterus. That means no more babies in the future and so you know, as a form of contraception also, okay? The second is to freeze the cervix and then follow you with the understanding that that should cure it, but that you need to be followed in the future and that you could have children in the future if that's what your plans include.

The resident presented information about a hysterectomy as the means to have no more babies and as a method of contraception. To a woman who is pregnant with an unwanted pregnancy and who has had repeated birth control failures, this is a particularly persuasive presentation. He continues by saying that she could be treated by freezing the cervix but she could still have children and would have to be followed. Again, a very persuasive presentation. This is a poor woman who does not want more children and does not have either the time or the money to return to the hospital for frequent follow-up care. In addition, the resident presented the hysterectomy option first, and then presented cryosurgery as an option. This order suggested that the less conservative treatment (hysterectomy) was somehow preferable. Later in the exchange, the resident summed up his position using another persuasional strategy. He said, "Absent uterus, no periods, no cancer, no babies."

Similarly, in Pat's case, when the resident presented her with an informed consent form to sign, he said,

Even though with this form that I have before me that the government requires you to sign, it's a request for a hysterectomy for sterilization, even though it says here that you have no problems which require a hysterectomy and we know that you do, the hospital and state require me to ask you to sign this so that you understand that what we're talking about is permanent sterilization with no possibilities of future pregnancies.

This, again, is a particularly persuasive presentation. The patient in no way requested a hysterectomy for sterilization. She had been referred to the clinic with a class 5 Pap smear. During a discussion about treatment options, a hysterectomy was recommended as the most appropriate treatment. The grounds for this recommendation were specified as follows: "It [cancer] could come back, " and " . . . for somebody your age, that's had your family, you're sure that you don't want children, I'd recommend a hysterectomy." To a woman who has had a class 5 Pap smear and is already afraid that she has a life-threatening medical problem, this is a particularly persuasive presentation. It heightens the emotional impact of the abnormal Pap smear by stressing that "it" could come back. The "it" being referred to is, of course, cancer. In addition, it is the resident, not the patient, who links the need for a hysterectomy with the patient's age, her childbearing history, and her lack of desire for additional children. To a woman who lived many of her childbearing years in a Catholic country and has had three children and two abortions, this again is a very persuasive presentation.

The persuasive overtones were strengthened when the resident gave her the informed consent to sign and told her that although the form said that she had no problems requiring a hysterectomy, "We know that you do." He brings all of the authority of his medical role to bear in this statement. As a man, as a medical practitioner, and as her physician, he is telling her what to do and implying dire consequences if she does not comply.

There is an additional issue involved in this presentation. The resident told the patient what he was required to by law and then suggested that she ignore it. This amplifies the power and authority of his medical role and his use of it to manipulate her decision-making process. One might ask, What kind of informed consent procedure does this represent?

ACCOMPLISHING THE TREATMENT EVENT

Caress (1975, 1977) suggests several reasons for the explosion of hysterectomies in recent years. First, she argues, gynecologists and obstetricians are surgeons. As the birth rate continues to level out, these doctors face reduced opportunities to practice their surgical skills. Second, many physicians have united their professional skills and their political ideals. As a result, poor, minority women are bearing the brunt of unnecessary hysterectomies. Finally, she claims, hysterectomies are good money makers.

Other reasons for increased hysterectomies have also been discussed. Once reproduction is over, many doctors agree that the uterus is a useless organ. John Morris, M.D., told a congressional subcommittee that, "An arm is a useful structure. Breasts have cosmetic advantages. However, there are certain organs that are absolutely useless. One such is your appendix, another is the uterus after childbearing" ("Important Cost and Quality Issues" 1977:354).

The uterus, seen as a useless organ past childbearing, is also depicted as a potentially dangerous organ. As Dr. R. C. Wright wrote in a 1969 issue of *Obstetrics and Gynecology* "The uterus has but one function: reproduction. After the last planned pregnancy the uterus becomes a useless, bleeding, symptom-producing, potentially cancer-bearing organ and therefore should be removed" (Larned 1977:199).

Ninety-seven percent of all gynecologists in the U.S. are men. As men, to some extent their attitudes toward women reflect current views of women in society (Larned 1977). As Scully and Bart (1973) point out, these attitudes are magnified and reinforced in medical school. Medical students and residents learn to view the uterus and the women who have them negatively. To quote from a widely used gynecological textbook:

> No drastic results are found following the removal of the uterus . . . Indeed, it should be not construed as callous if many gynecologists feel that, in the woman who has completed her family, the uterus is a rather worthless organ. (Novak et al. 1970:26)

This attitude has been described as quite common: "This is indeed the attitude of most gynecologists. While it may seem harsh and ill-phrased, it is a logical viewpoint and one with which I personally agree" (Paulshock 1976:26). Scully (1980) points out, and the data in this article supports, that these attitudes provide the basis on which residents learn and use a regular "sales pitch" for hysterectomies.

SUMMARY

As I pointed out, no patients in the Faculty Clinic received hysterectomies, while 7 out of 13 women in the Community Clinic did receive hysterectomies. It is logical to deduce, as Caress (1975, 1977) and Larned (1977) suggest, that if doctors believe that hysterectomies are in women's best interest, the number of hysterectomies will continue to increase.

It is likely that staff physicians and residents bring different sets of practical concerns into the examining room that affect how language is used and how treatment decisions are reached. It is also reasonable that patients referred from the private sector to professors of medicine in the Faculty Clinic are less likely to be treated with hysterectomies than are patients referred from the public sector to residents in the Community Clinic. The Faculty and Community Clinics provide very different settings in which to deliver and receive medical care.

Faculty and Community Clinics were organized in different ways, to serve a different population of patients and were staffed in a different manner. The Faculty Clinic was staffed by gynecological oncologists who were professors of medicine. There were no residents rotating in and out of the clinic; thus, there was a kind of continuity of care not normally found in teaching settings. The physical layout honored the humanness of patients. There was a separation of public and private space. The waiting room was separated from the backstage medical area. Examining rooms were separated from consulting offices.

The Community Clinic, on the other hand, was staffed in a rotating fashion. Everybody rotated—residents, support personnel, and supervising staff, thus heightening the lack of continuity of care. Assignment to the Community Clinic, the narrow definition of the medical problem under their care, and the constant rotation also increased the fragmentation of the care delivered. In addition, the physical layout of the clinic did not honor the humanness of patients. There was no separation of public and private space. There was no waiting room. Patients sat in the hall outside of the examining room overhearing medical talk that frightened them. There were also no consulting offices. All talk with patients occurred either in the halls (in the presence of other patients) or in the examining rooms. I suspect that it is a very different experience to sit across from a doctor, fully clothed, discussing your medical problem from having a similar discussion with a resident while you are sitting undressed on the examining table.

The data discussed in this chapter support the view that although the doctor–patient relationship is an asymmetrical one, the asymmetry increases when patients are perceived as poor and powerless and medical practitioners are residents rather than staff physicians. It seems that the need for surgery experience and the lack of an outside advocate plus internal norms of medical adequacy contribute to the differential outcomes in the Faculty Clinic and Community Clinic. It follows, quite naturally, that these structural and organizational features of the delivery of health care are manifested during medical interviews in the exchange of information between participants, negotiated through the use of linguistic strategies, and have consequences for the treatment decision reached.

The linguistic and ethnographic data discussed here further suggest that the medical interview is organized in predictable ways. A detailed examination of how language is used and treatment decisions are negotiated provides information not available in an analysis of the medical and social facts underlying medical decision making. It displays the processes through which treatment decisions are jointly accomplished. First, medical practitioners and patients, exchanging the information necessary to reach treatment decisions, use language strategically, thus doing communicational work. In addition to specifying how treatment decisions are negotiated in the activities of participants, this kind of an analysis suggests that the communicational work of the participants is oriented toward the specific end of a treatment decision, thus linking interaction (or communication) to outcomes (or treatment decisions). Finally, this kind of analysis places the decision-making process in a specific organizational context.

By placing linguistic phenomena in their social context and analyzing how that context organizes linguistic structures, three levels of analysis (structural, organizational, and interactional) that are normally treated separately are linked. The detailed analysis of the communicational process through which treatment decisions are negotiated displays how the negotiation of hysterectomies is produced and constrained by structural, organizational, and interactional contexts and accomplished through the communication between participants.

There are theoretical, methodological, and practical ramifications inherent in the documentation of the communicational work through which treatment decisions are reached. Theoretically and methodologically, a systematic analysis of the communicational strategies used to accomplish treatment decisions provides insights not normally available when the subtleties of the practitioner–patient relationship are not examined. These insights can have practical consequences for medical education, resident training, and the creation of informed consumers.

In an era in which both medical practitioners and patients are displaying increasing dissatisfaction with the way things are—the high costs of medical care, the increasing performance of unnecessary medical procedures, the difficulties with patient compliance, the problems with informed consent, and the use and possible abuse of medical malpractice procedures—awareness of the processes used to communicate hold the potential for improving communication and improving the delivery of health care.

REFERENCES CITED

BERNSTEIN, BASIL
    1971   *Class, Codes and Control.* London: Routledge & Kegan Paul.
CARESS, BARBARA
    1975   *Sterilization.* Health/PAC Bulletin #62, January/February, pp. 1–13.
    1977   *Womb-boom.* Health/PAC Bulletin, July/August.
CHAFE, WALLACE L.
    1976   Givenness, constrastiveness, definiteness, subjects, topics and point of view. IN *Subject and Topic*, Charles H. Li, Ed., pp. 25–56. New York: Academic Press.
CICOUREL, AARON V.
    1974   Interviewing and memory. IN *Pragmatic Aspects of Human Communication*, Colin Cherry, Ed., pp. 51–82. Dordrecht: Reidel.
    1975   Discourse and text: Cognitive and linguistic processes in studies of social

structure. To appear in *Versus*. (Portions presented at 1975 American Sociological Association Meetings.)

1976   Cost and Quality of Health Care: Unnecessary Surgery Report by the Committee on Oversight and Investigations of the Committee on Interstate and Foreign Commerce, House of Representatives, Ninth Congress Second Session, January, 1976. YN.IN 8/4 H 34/35.

EHRENREICH, BARBARA, AND JOHN EHRENREICH

1970   *The American Health Empire*. Health-PAC Book. New York: Vintage.

ERVIN-TRIPP, SUSAN, AND CLAUDIA MITCHELL-KERNAN

1977   *Child Discourse*. New York: Academic Press.

FISHER, SUE CAROLE

1979a   The Negotiation of Treatment Decisions in Doctor/Patient Communications and Their Impact on Identity of Women Patients. Doctoral dissertation, University of California, San Diego, California.

1979b   Mirror, mirror on the wall; Women's identities and women's role. Paper presented at annual meetings of the Mid-South Sociological Association, Memphis, Tennessee, November 1979.

FREIDSON, ELIOT

1970   *Profession of Medicine*. New York: Dodd, Mead.

HALLIDAY, MICHAEL A., AND RUQAIYA HASAN

1976   *Cohesion in English*. London: Longmans.

HYMES, DELL

1962   The ethnography of speaking. IN *Anthropology and Human Behavior*. Washington, D.C.: Anthropological Society of Washington.

1972   Models of the interaction of language and social life. IN *Directions in Sociolinguistics: The Ethnography of Communication*, John J. Gumperz and Dell Hymes, Eds., pp. 38–71. New York: Holt, Rinehart and Winston.

1974   *Foundations of Sociolinguistics*. Philadelphia: University of Pennsylvania Press.

1977   Important Cost and Quality Issues of Health Care Hearings before the Subcommittee on Oversight and Investigations of the Committee on Interstate and Foreign Commerce, House of Representatives, 95 Congress/First Session, April 25 and 29, May 2 and 9, 1977. V/4 IN8/4:95–32.

KEENAN, ELINOR OCHS, AND BAMBI B. SCHIEFFELIN

1976   Topics as a discourse notion: A study of topic in the conversations of children and adults. IN *Subject and Topic*, Charles N. Li, Ed., pp. 335–384. New York: Academic Press.

KUNO, SUSUMU

1976   Subject, theme, and the speaker's empathy—a reexamination of relativization in phenomena. IN *Subject and Topic*, Charles N. Li, Ed., pp. 417–444. New York: Academic Press.

LABOV, WILLIAM

1972   *Sociolinguistic Patterns*. Philadelphia: University of Pennsylvania Press.

LABOV, WILLIAM, AND DAVID FANSHEL

1977   *Therapeutic Discourse: Psychotherapy as Conversation*. New York: Academic Press.

LARNED, D.

1977   The epidemic in unnecessary hysterectomy. IN *Seizing Our Bodies: The Politics of Women's Health*, Claudia Dreifus, Ed. New York: Vintage Books.

MECHANIC, DAVID
   1968   *Medical Sociology*. New York: The Free Press.
NATIONAL CENTER FOR HEALTH STATISTICS
   1976   Surgical operation in short-stay hospitals, US, 1973. IN *Vital and Health Statistics*, Series 13, No. 21. Washington, D.C.: Author.
NAVARRO, VICENTE
   1973   *Health and Medical Care in the U.S.: A Critical Analysis*. Farmingdale, N.Y.: Baywood Publishing Co.
NOVAK, E.R. ET AL.
   1970   *Novak's Textbook of Gynecology*. Baltimore: Williams and Wilkens.
PAULSHOCK, B.Z.
   1976   What every woman should know about hysterectomy. *Today's Health* 54(2) (February):23–26.
PHILIPS, SUSAN
   1972   Participant structures and communicative competence: Warm Springs children in community and classroom. IN *Functions of Language in the Classroom*, Courtney Cazden, Vera John, and Dell Hymes, Eds., pp. 370–394. New York: Teachers College Press.
SCULLY, DIANA
   1980   *Men Who Control Women's Health: The Miseducation of Obstetricians-Gynecologists*. Boston: Houghton Mifflin.
SCULLY, DIANA, AND P. BART
   1973   A funny thing happened on the way to the orifice: Women in gynecological textbooks. *American Journal of Sociology* 78(4):1045–1050.
SHATZ, MARILYN
   1975   Towards a Developmental Theory of Communicative Competence. Doctoral dissertation, University of Pennsylvania.
SHATZ, MARILYN, AND ROCHEL GELMAN
   1973   The Development of Communication Skills; Modifications in the Speech of Young Children as a Function of Listener. *Monographs of the Society for Research in Child Development* 38.
SHUY, ROGER W.
   1983   Three types of interference to an effective exchange of information in the medical interview. IN *The Social Organization of Doctor-Patient Communication*, Sue Fisher and Alexandra Dundas Todd, Eds., pp. 189–202. Washington, D.C.: The Center for Applied Linguistics.
STEVENS, ROSEMARY
   1966   *Medical Practice in Modern England: The Impact of Specialization and State Medicine*. New Haven: Yale University Press.
VIRGINIA DEPARTMENT OF HEALTH
   1977   Uterine cancer and the Pap test. *Virginia Health Bulletin* 29, Series 2, Number 3. Richmond, Va: Author.
WAITZKIN, HOWARD B., AND BARBARA WATERMAN
   1974   *The Exploitation of Illness in Capitalist Society*. Indianapolis: Bobbs-Merrill.

8

A Diagnosis of Doctor–Patient Discourse in the Prescription of Contraception*

Alexandra Dundas Todd

Women in our society are obviously and importantly unique in their physical ability to reproduce the species. The social and cultural consequences of this characteristic have been discussed by both feminist and nonfeminist scholars. Yet in this century, the medical profession has been given sole legal authority and cultural recognition for dealing with the physiological aspects of reproduction.

Throughout the United States, women regularly visit gynecologists' offices to ask questions about their reproductive systems. Because the two individuals— doctor and patient—have access to different information on the subject, an exchange is necessary between them (see Davis 1963). The woman has asked the original question, or she would not have initiated the interview. Yet ironically, as we shall see, the doctor dominates the dialogue in the interview and not simply its diagnostic outcome.

The doctor–patient relationship has been discussed widely in writings on medical sociology and the recent literature on women's health. Although theoretical frameworks for understanding this relationship have been proposed, the actual interaction and discourse between participants in the medical setting have received less sociological attention. The systematic study of language, until

* Grateful acknowledgment is made to Hugh Mehan, Sue Fisher, and Will Wright for their helpful suggestions and comments. This is a revision of an earlier paper entitled "The Prescription of Contraception: Negotiations Between Doctors and Patients," in *Discourse Processes*.

recently, has been left to other disciplines. Several notable exceptions have been Fisher (1980), Mehan (1979), Cicourel (1975), Zimmerman and West (1975, 1980), and Sacks, Schegloff, and Jefferson (1974), who bring sociological analysis to linguistic data. My purpose here is to contribute to this literature by examining the discourse between doctors and patients to see the process whereby power is manifested in the interaction and how expression of this power in face-to-face communication follows a scientific medical model.

A second goal is to integrate theory with empirical data. Throughout the history of sociology, arguments about the importance of context for understanding human behavior have abounded. Context has been interpreted as historical, cultural, and social, with each of these areas subject to many subinterpretations. Similarly, differing opinions have been expressed about the importance of empirical data. The question centers on how to ground the study of the social world—whether in historical evidence, in the theorizing of scholars, or in data-driven empirical work. I will address this question sporadically throughout this analysis.

The data for this study were derived from in-depth observations and audiotaped recordings of doctor–patient interactions gathered in two gynecological settings during a two-and-a-half year period that I spent in a city in Southern California. The first setting was a women's health clinic in a general community health center. This setting employed gynecological residents (doctors in training) from local teaching hospitals. The three doctors I observed in the clinic, Smith, Jones, and Long, rotated their work hours and were paid by the hour. They were assisted by volunteers who took patient histories, dispensed medications, and performed similar work. The second setting was the office of Dr. Masters, a gynecologist in private practice who conducted all medical interactions with the patients. Dr. Masters is a prominent doctor of long standing in the area and a member of the clinical faculty at a nearby medical school.

My data include 20 audiotaped medical interviews, 10 from each setting, each about 10 minutes long. Discussion of these data reflects my observations in the settings as well as the taped information, broadening the context for interpretation. The taped interactions provide still shots of the wider observed database.

My context should be understood as a spiral, moving from interactional situation, through organizational setting and theoretical, structural milieu, and back to interactional situation. Although I propose no causal link between the data and context (at the moment sociology is primitive in this regard), I base my analysis on the assumption that interaction, here discourse, does not occur in a vacuum. It is micropolitical, as communication is influenced by and is a reinforcer of the cultural values of the society in which it takes place.

I will examine the organization of the doctor–patient interviews in three ways. Part 1 uses distributional analysis to present an overview of all of the interactions. Speech act theory offers a means to break the flow of talk into discrete parts. Part 2 provides insight into the interaction between doctor and patient by focusing on the sequential properties of the medical interviews. Turn-taking analysis combined with consideration of the distribution of speech acts contributes to a broader view of the data than was permitted by the distributional information in Part 1. Part 3 introduces a topical analysis, placing the talk in two "frames," one contextual and the other medical. Some consequences of the interaction described by the distributional, sequential, and topical analyses are discussed in Part 4.

PART 1: DISTRIBUTIONAL ANALYSIS

The examination of social speech acts and their contexts has become both a methodological and a theoretical tool in sociology for linking the larger, institutional levels of social order to everyday interaction and behavior (see Cicourel 1980; Streeck 1980). Speech act theory, as outlined by Austin and Searle,[1] is helpful theoretically for sociological analysis. Speech act theorists, however, do not address a cultural, or contextual, sociological analysis. The basic unit of analysis used is the self-contained action unit rather than the interaction unit, where context and the role of all of the participants are important (Streeck 1980).

D'Andrade has developed a system for the classification of speech acts derived from a sociocultural framework. His work belongs in the tradition of several writers who in recent years have applied speech act analysis to actual conversations (Cole, Dore, Hall, and Dowley 1978; D'Andrade, n.d.; Gelman and Shatz 1977; Labov and Fanshel 1977; Måseide, n.d.). Figure 1 lists D'Andrade's six categories for speech acts: statements, questions, expressives, directives, reactives, and commissives. I have adapted these categories to my own data, abridging the system in the process to fit the specific needs of the medical interview. I excluded expressives and commissives; although these actions take place in the medical setting, they do so subtly and in the form of statements, questions, and directives. Strong emotion is not considered appropriate in the gynecologist–patient relationship, and actions such as vowing and exasperation tend to be played down and absorbed into other acts. I have further subdivided reactives into two categories: reactives and answers. Speech acts will be considered answers when they provide a substantive response to a question.

---

[1] Chomsky's (1968) view of linguistics addressed the relationship between linguistic form and meaning in syntactic terms, with the sentence as the unit of analysis. Searle (1969) differs from Chomsky by distinguishing between the proportional content of utterances and locutionary force, or intention to act on the world. Austin (1962) and Searle (1969) shifted the focus from the linguistic emphasis on syntax to the relationship between language and action (also see Streeck 1980). For example, the utterances "I command" display *and* accomplish the act of commanding.

DOCTOR: You've just finished your period?
PATIENT: Uh hum.
DOCTOR: Okay.

As the display shows, the doctor first states/asks information about the patient. I have coded the doctor's sentence as a question because of its questioning tone and because the doctor receives an answer from the patient (second) that provides substantive information regarding her period. (I have determined the meaning of these conversational acts on the basis of their function in speech rather than their inherent grammatical form.) Third, the doctor acknowledges the patient's answer with a reactive. The classification system used for these data thus consists of statements (S), questions (Q), reactives (R), answers (A), and directives (D) applied to conversations between the doctor (D) and the patient (P).

Using the categorization features of D'Andrade's model, I have collated an aggregate of the speech acts in the 20 interviews. Table 1 outlines the types of

A. *Statements* (expositives,
    representatives, assertions)
  reports
  quotes
  instantiations
  claims
  stimulations (?)
  inferences

B. *Directives* (request, orders,
    exercitives)
  suggest/request/order
  request object
    agrees as to truth
    expression of approval/
      sympathy/support, etc.
    commitment
    direct action
  direct/indirect

C. *Questions*
  wh-form
  yes/no form
  tag form
  intonation-only form
  information-only versus
    other uses

D. *Reactives* (various kinds of
    agreement or disagreement
    with what has previously
    been stated)
  agree as to truth versus disagree
    as to truth
  give attention
  accede (agree to commit, or
    actually do) versus refuse

E. *Expressives*
  give approval versus disapproval
    (sympathy, regret, exasperation,
    etc.)
  direct versus indirect
    (accusations, disagreements, etc.)

F. *Commissives*
  promise, offer, vow, etc.

FIGURE 1   D'Andrade's Preliminary Speech Act Category System

TABLE 1   Aggregate of Speech Acts

Speech Acts	Statement D	P	Question D	P	Answer D	P	Reactive D	P	Directive D	P	Subtotal D	P	Total
Clinic													
N	210	92	251	45	42	244	220	123	69	0	792	504	1296
%	70	30	85	15	15	85	64	36	100	0	61	39	100
Dr. Masters Exam													
N	123	69	105	8	3	96	66	86	85	1	382	260	642
%	64	36	93	7	3	97	43	57	99	1	60	40	100
Consult.													
N	125	53	80	8	6	71	73	139	73	0	357	271	628
%	70	30	91	9	8	9	34	66	100	0	57	43	100
Total													
N	248	122	185	16	9	167	139	225	158	1	739	531	1270
%	67	33	92	8	5	95	38	62	99	1	58	42	100

utterances made by doctors and patients during gynecological care involving the prescription of contraception.

Analysis of the data in Table 1 disclosed several differences between the community clinic and the private practitioner's office.

1. The gap between questions asked by doctors and questions asked by patients was greater in Dr. Masters's office than in the clinic. More questions were asked by doctors and patients in the clinic. Very few questions were asked by patients in Dr. Masters's office.

2. The same was true of answers to these questions. The patients in Dr. Masters's office asked fewer questions and received fewer answers. Further, the patients in Dr. Masters's office received fewer answers to questions asked than did the patients in the clinic.

3. In the clinic the doctors uttered more reactives than the patients. The reverse was true in Dr. Masters's office.

4. Directives were used more frequently by Dr. Masters than by the clinic doctors.

The analysis also revealed a number of similarities in the two settings.

1. The doctors asked more questions than the patients did. In the clinic the doctors asked approximately 5.6 times as many questions as the patients. Dr. Masters asked approximately 11.5 times as many questions as the patients.

2. The patients provided more answers than the doctors—in the clinic, approximately 5.6 times more. Dr. Masters's patients provided approximately 19 times as many answers as the doctor.
3. The doctors made more statements than the patients. The clinic doctors and Dr. Masters made approximately twice as many statements as the patients.
4. Doctors (with one exception) made all the directives.

These findings give us important information about who says what to whom and how (see Hymes 1972). Speech act tabulation provides an overview of the data in the form of a distributional analysis that divides talk into discrete pieces, showing the similarities and differences in the structure of the discourse between the two settings and between doctors and patients. Comparisons suggest a preliminary view of the distribution of power in the medical interview. As informative as this view is, we must keep in mind that speech act analysis masks how doctors and patients act in concert, influencing each other in the course of their interaction.

Although cultural influences are used to assign meaning, the theory in and of itself does not display the interconnection of speakers in conversation and thus does not provide the basis for a thorough consideration of power relationships. The sequential flow of events that takes place in the talk between the doctor and the patient, presented in the next section, broadens our understanding of the medical interview.

PART 2: SEQUENTIAL PROPERTIES

The doctor–patient discourse takes place in the institutional setting of health care delivery. In this system, doctors have power both as experts (Ehrenreich and English 1979) and often as men (Scully 1980). The patient participates in an exchange that is structured by the sequencing of questions and answers and by the institutional setting, which constrains the form of the interaction. The discourse and the organization thus display a dialectic relationship.

Discourse analysis has revealed a two-part structure in conversation between equal participants in everyday settings, but researchers have found that dialogue between individuals in insitutional settings is organized differently.[2] The

---

[2] Sacks, Schegloff, and Jeffersons' turn-taking analysis (1974) assumes talk occurring in natural, everyday interactions between equals in contexts where turn taking is spontaneous and turn allocation is open. Sacks et al. describe a two-part structure in which a question receives an answer or a greeting receives a return greeting, and when it is not interrupted by side or insertion sequences, this response takes place in the next immediate turn at talk, providing a sequential organization of conversation. Labov and Fanshel (1977) have provided a structural outline of the medical interview as an interactional event involving the exchange of information in a routine manner with defined boundaries and expected behaviors.

difference seems to be a consequence of the asymmetry between participants (West forthcoming), which produces a third part to the conversation. In the educational setting, this third part is an evaluation act: the teacher, in an institutionalized role, evaluates the work the students are doing (Mehan 1979). The utterance of the third pair-part in the doctor–patient interaction links the institutional, sociopolitical context and the actual, situated discourse (Fisher 1980; Todd 1982).

In the doctor–patient interactions that I discuss, the third part is a reactive used by the doctor, in turn, to maintain control of the floor. The doctor initiates a request for information, receives information from the patient, and acknowledges the answer with a reactive (see Figure 2).

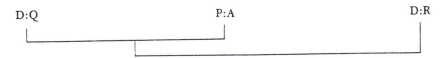

D:Q   P:A   D:R

FIGURE 2   Three-Part Structure of an Interaction

The doctor's reactive serves two purposes. The doctor initiates the interaction with a question. In so doing, the doctor also controls the topics discussed in their relation to the patient's presentation. The reactive serves, first, to end the interactional segment and the topic, and the second, to bring control of the interaction back to the doctor, allowing the doctor to end that frame and to initiate a new one (see Figure 3).

In the sequence shown in Figure 3, the words *all right* acknowledge the patient's reply, while control of the floor conversationally returns to the doctor. The doctor is now in a position to change the topic and the structure of the speech act by introducing a statement that interprets the problem. The patient acknowledges the information with a reactive, and in turn is acknowledged by a reactive from the doctor. This final reactive allows the doctor to proceed with the questioning (see Figure 4).

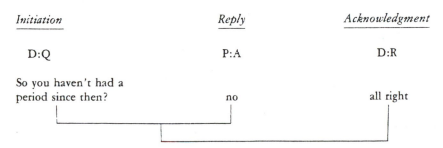

Initiation	*Reply*	*Acknowledgment*
D:Q	P:A	D:R
So you haven't had a period since then?	no	all right

FIGURE 3   Diagram of an Interaction

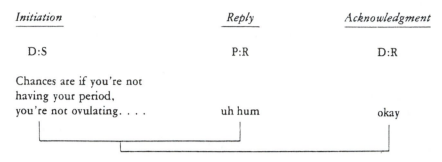

Initiation	*Reply*	*Acknowledgment*
D:S	P:R	D:R
Chances are if you're not having your period, you're not ovulating. . . .	uh hum	okay

FIGURE 4   An Interaction With Two Reactives

Throughout, my data indicate that the doctor initiates the sequence, directs the conversation, and initiates the next sequence. The patient's conversation also displays reactives; the patient's reactives, however, differ from those of the doctor in that they occur in single speech act turns. The patient does not usually, in her turn, utter a reactive and continue. Rather, she utters the reactive as both the initiation and the end of her turn and in response to the doctor's utterance.

The use of reactives in the two institutional settings indicates subtle and not so subtle organizational and interactional influences on discourse. In both settings the doctor's conversations exhibited how reactives provide the means to change topics, swerve the talk back into the doctor's turn, and maintain control of the conversation, thereby manifesting medical institutional power. The difference in the settings—Dr. Masters used fewer reactives than clinic doctors and his patients used more reactives than clinic patients—exhibits interesting patterns in the discourse. Dr. Masters changed topics abruptly, often "talking over" the patient with a directive.

The more abrupt changes in topic account in part for the fewer reactives and the greater number of directives displayed in Dr. Masters's interviews. Dr. Masters also uttered directives at a far higher rate than did the clinic doctors in instructing patients about treatment decisions. Examples 1 and 2, involving Dr. Jones and Dr. Masters, respectively, concern two patients who both suffer from amenorrhea, cessation of menstruation. Both ask for renewals of prescriptions for birth control pills. The clinic patient wants to resume use of the birth control pill after a lapse of several months. The patient seen by the doctor in private practice has come for a routine renewal of her prescription. The discourse shows the very different styles of the two doctors. In the clinic, Dr. Jones is attempting to explain the problem to the patient, using statements as the major form for imparting instructions and information. Dr. Masters is much freer with directives, using them both to mention new aspects of the problem and to impart instructions.

Example 1

(S)	Dr. Jones:	I discussed your problem with one of the head doctors at General, uhm, he knows more about this than I do, about amenorrhea, not getting your period, and he seemed to think, uhm, he seemed to agree with me that it would probably be a good idea to give you a test dose of this progesterone to see if you have a withdrawal bleeding. I assume that this is probably what you were injected with earlier this summer, that was the injection, progesterone, that's a hormone in your body that makes your uterus shed its lining and you bleed, okay, and it works, progesterone is a normal hormone that works in regular cycles. Now, uhm, since you don't have any strong desires to get pregnant at this point, since you did come here for
(R)	PATIENT:	right
(S)	DR. JONES:	contraception, uhm, we both seem to think that it would be, uhm, the best idea to give you the progesterone for five days, have a withdrawal bleed, and then start you on the pill.
(Q)		Okay?
(R)	PATIENT:	Okay
(S)(D)	DR. JONES:	And if you don't get a withdrawal bleed with progesterone, it's a pill which you'll take for five days, if you don't, call us and then we'll see you and we'll have to give you—we'll have to go through another test before we start you on something.
(Q)		Okay?
(S)		Now, uhm, just judging from what, you know, from your story, you told me that you did have a little spotting
(R)	PATIENT:	uh hum
(S)	DR. JONES:	from the injection, it sounds like you, you just haven't been ovulating so this could be a problem when you do try to get pregnant, you know, when you do want to get pregnant again, we'll have to get you on regular cycles where you're ovulating in order for you to get pregnant.
(Q)		Okay?
(Q)	PATIENT:	Now, this time if I take it for five days, what happens if I just start bleeding?
(A)	DR. JONES:	That's—even the slightest amount is okay.
(Q)		Okay?
(S)		Even if it's just a little spot. It doesn't have to be like a real period, just, you know, a little spot here and there. You might want to wear a mini pad or something.
(R)	PATIENT:	Okay.

Example 2

Note: The clinic was organized around a single doctor-patient interaction in the examination room; in contrast, Dr. Masters's interview started with the exam and was followed by a consultation in the office after the patient had dressed.

Exam:

(D)	Dr. Masters:	Look,
(S)		what I think is happening, that your pills are not strong enough,
(Q)		you know?
(S)		I've put you on a very low pill as you know
(R)	PATIENT:	right
(S)	DR. MASTERS:	and sometimes this will cause [swallows word]. Now what I would like to do is when you finish your pills. Let's see, you're on the 28 days. [long pause]
(R)	PATIENT:	Right
(S)		Uh, 21 day.
(R)	DR. MASTERS:	21 day, all right.
(D)		When you finish your pills, and if you don't menstruate within 5 to 6 days, come in.
(S)		I'll give you an injection to get you started.
(R)	PATIENT:	Okay
(D)	DR. MASTERS:	If you do menstruate, come in then.
(S)		I won't charge you anything if I don't have to do anything and I will give you a prescription for a different kind. I want to see what you're going to do. I also want you to report back on this.
(R)	PATIENT:	Right, uh hum.
(Q)	DR. MASTERS:	Okay?
(R)	PATIENT:	Oh, okay

Consultation:

(D)	DR. MASTERS:	Now, look,
(S)		what I want you to do, you understand now, all right, you have X number of tablets,
(D)		then you finish the package,
(Q)		right?
(R)	PATIENT:	Right
(R)	DR. MASTERS:	Right.
(D)		Finish them wait four to five days. If you flow, come in then while you're flowing and I'll, uh, uh, and I'll give you more pills. [long pause]
(R)	PATIENT:	Okay
(S)	DR. MASTERS:	I won't charge you.
(D)		If you don't flow, call me,
(S)		then I will give you an injection,
(D)		don't take any more tablets then.
(R)	PATIENT:	Uh hum.
(S)	DR. MASTERS:	I'll give you an injection and I'll, uh, get you started with your menstruation and I'll give you a different type of pill. [long pause]
(R)	PATIENT:	Okay
(Q)	DR. MASTERS:	Okay?
(R)	PATIENT:	All right.

(D)   DR. MASTERS: But meanwhile, stay on the pills. Don't you get into trouble.
(R)   PATIENT: Right.

These examples indicate, first, that Dr. Masters's directives provide him with control of the floor much as reactives provide control for the clinic doctors and, second, that the doctor in each setting did most of the talking about the patient's concerns (also see Table 1); the doctors uttered multiple speech acts per turn in both examples, while the patients uttered one or occasionally two speech acts per turn. The distribution of questions and answers in the doctor–patient interviews in both settings shows the doctor asking more questions with the patient providing more answers. In addition, Dr. Masters more often demands a response from patients. Although the clinic doctors did use tag questions and expectant looks to elicit reactives from patients, they never, in my observations, insisted on a response. In fact, they so often rushed through tag questions in their talk that the patient was scarcely able, let alone required, to respond. Dr. Masters, however, used tag questions and/or long pauses accompanied by a piercing, direct gaze to accomplish patient recognition, in some cases repeating this procedure for emphasis. In Example 2 Dr. Masters states, "I also want you to report back on this," emphasizing the words with very direct eye contact. The patient responds with a double reactive, "right, uh hum," to reassure him that she will do her part. Dr. Masters responds with a tag question "Okay?", for further emphasis, eliciting reassurance from the patient in the form of another reactive, "oh, okay."

These examples show the asymmetry of power between the doctor and the patient in the medical interview. The floor is controlled by the doctor, thus the topics are initiated by the doctor, not the patient. Dr. Masters exemplified this tendency even more than Dr. Jones in that he directed the interaction in a more authoritarian style. In general, the patient brings the problem to the doctor's office with some knowledge about her body and her situation, but the doctor does most of the talking (multiple speech acts), and the patient merely responds to the doctor's management in the interview.

The difference in power between doctor and patient can also be seen in how Dr. Masters demanded attention from patients using his social, often jocular comments as well as responses based on responsibilities with regard to medical treatment. The following is taken from field notes.

Example 3
The doctor turned his attention to the patient and started examining her breasts, which were quite large. As he was looking at her breasts, she was flat on her back staring at the ceiling. Dr. Masters said, "Yes, this is all girl," and smiled at the patient. No one in the room—the patient, the medical assistant, or myself—acknowledged the doctor's remark. The room was unusually quiet as the doctor started checking the patient's other breast. He slowly and measuredly started

talking while looking around at each one us, "I *said*, this is all girl." At this point the patient smiled wanly, the medical assistant chuckled, and I smiled. With our responses the doctor's good humor returned and he told the patient to "get dressed like a good girl" and he would give her "some more happy pills."

In this example Dr. Masters exerted power in two ways. First he demanded and received attention from everyone present regarding a topic irrelevant to the patient's health needs. Second, while performing the breast exam, he implied that having large breasts made the patient "all girl," as small breasts could not (incongruous with the purpose of screening the patient for cancer). The growing literature on doctors' differential treatment of male and female patients suggests that male patients would not be subject to similar observations about their anatomy (Schiefelbein 1980).

The differences between the settings in Examples 1 and 2 (and their similarities) can, in part, be attributed to differences in the organizational features of a community clinic and the office of a private practitioner. Dr. Masters, a private practitioner, has and exerts more power in his interactions with his patients than do the clinic doctors and, in his office with its large desk and prestigious diplomas, he is the major and often only event in the patient's visit. Nothing happens in this office that Dr. Masters does not know about, organize, and control. The patient interacts solely with Dr. Masters concerning her reason for visiting a doctor. Her power lies in her freedom to choose not to come, not to return, or to ignore the doctor's instructions. In my observations, the strongest reaction that women showed Dr. Masters in the interaction was silence.

The clinic doctors, in contrast, display no possessiveness toward the patients. Clinic patients are seen by rotating doctors in an atmosphere in which it is acknowledged that the patient has other resources, such as health educators and counselors, if she is dissatisfied with or confused by the doctor's information. Whereas Dr. Masters exercised sole control, the clinic doctor is only one possible step of a number of steps. Interestingly, Dr. Master's patients asked fewer questions than did patients in the clinic; it is possible that patients felt less active and more dominated in Dr. Masters's office.

A large sociological literature discusses the institutional level of health care organization and delivery as it is structurally defined and observable, across settings, in traditional medical care in our society (Conrad and Kern 1981). The discourse that I recorded between doctors and patients reflects the institutional power of the physician as it has been discussed and criticized theoretically. The doctor dominates the conversation in an active manner, as we have seen; the patient, whose reproductive life and health are the topic of the interview, remains passive.

Lazare (1979) found in his work with psychiatric outpatients that the doctors dominate the interaction to the extent that the patients' requests are often never mentioned and thus are not heeded. He advocates eliciting the patient's interpretation and requests from the very onset of the interview so that the interaction becomes a negotiation between two active participants. Interactions such as those I recorded display an irony: The patient has come to question the doctor, but the doctor asks all the questions.

PART 3: SOCIAL AND MEDICAL FRAMES

An analysis of the sequential properties of the doctor–patient interview provides a framework for expanding the speech act distribution to reveal institutional dimensions in the conversation between doctors and patients and in the structure of the interaction. Examination of this interface between the micro level of discourse and the macro level of institutionally designated power offers insights useful for further study of the doctor–patient interview and health care delivery.

In conversations that take place in everyday life and in institutional situations, information is arranged by topic. Neither the distributional nor the sequential properties analyzed in the literature have addressed this order in the medical interview. My data suggest that the doctor and patients framed their conversations in different ways—the former in medical, technical terms and the latter in more social, biographical terms. The doctor–patient interviews I observed and taped present primarily technical conversations centered around a biologically treated and defined issue (e.g., the need for prescription renewal or amenorrhea and its possible connection to use of the birth control pill).

Birth control, however, has more than technical significance for women (Luker 1975; Todd 1982). The choice and use of contraceptives interrelate with sexual relationships, contextual circumstances, and life options. Therefore, whereas the doctor speaks from a technical, biological standpoint, the patient's speech is often social and contextual. As I noted earlier, the doctors have more control in the interaction than do the patients, so that the exchange of information is primarily technical. When patients do take control of the floor, their topics center on their social understanding of their health and their bodies, as exhibited in Example 4.

Example 4
(S)   PATIENT: Uh, I haven't been here lately because I had to, uh, switch to
                      Kaiser for financial reasons and I've been on a leave of absence
                      and they can't take me back for a while.
(R)   DR. MASTERS: Uh huh.
(Q)   What pills are you on now?

The patient in Example 4 has visited the clinic for birth control pill renewal and has introduced several topics: (a) failure to visit the doctor, (b) an alternative health plan, (c) financial matters, (d) leave of absence, and (e) loss of work. The doctor reacts to the patient's comments and then immediately changes the topic to the birth control pill that the patient is presently using. The conversation in Example 4 fails to strike a balance between the topics of concern to the patient and the doctor's more technical response (see Halliday and Hasan 1976). The patient is talking in a social/contextual mode about her health care and her life. The doctor responds with a medical, prescription-oriented question. The patient considers her social/contextual understandings of her life circumstances relevant to her health care; financial matters and the change of health care facilities combined with a leave of absence and loss of work are important variables in her contraceptive maintenance or she would not have mentioned them in this interview. Evidently, since he does not probe, the doctor does not regard these issues as worthy of consideration.

The interchange in Example 5 takes place during a routine pelvic exam and gynecological checkup for renewal of a prescription for birth control pills.

Example 5

(R) DR. SMITH:	Okay,
(S)	I'm going to take a little bit of your secretion to look at it to make sure you don't have an infection, too.
(R)	Okay,
(S)	coming out, you're doing fine.
(D)	Stay right there, now.
(Q)	Doing all right, Norma?
(A) PATIENT:	I feel uneasy tonight.
(S)	I don't know why.
(R) DR. SMITH:	Well,
(S)	we're almost done.
(D)	Relax.
(R)	Okay,
(S)	your cervix's right there. Right behind your pelvic bone's your bladder.

The patient has reported a vaginal discharge. Throughout the interaction she has appeared depressed and has expressed dissatisfaction with the birth control pill. In this brief excerpt the patient tentatively makes a social statement about her mood. The doctor's response incorporates this statement into a technical model relating to the exam and directs the patient to relax, changing the topic, in turn, back to the physiological explanation.

The insertion of a social topic into the medical discourse occurs frequently enough in the data to require explanation and infrequently enough to constitute a breach in the normal interactional flow (Table 2).

In some instances the social utterance produced an exchange between the doctor and patient based on shared contextual knowledge, an example of

TABLE 2   Aggregate of Speech Acts Divided Into Medical and Social Frames

Speech Acts	Statement D	P	Question D	P	Answer D	P	Reactive D	P	Directive D	P	Subtotal D	P	Total
CLINIC													
Frame dominant													
Medical	181	62	229	39	35	214	204	108	67	0	716	423	1139
Social	29	30	22	6	7	30	16	15	2	0	76	81	157
Percentage of speech acts													
Medical frame	16	5	20	3	3	19	18	10	6	0	63	37	100
Social frame	19	19	14	4	4	19	10	10	1	0	48	52	100
DR. MASTERS													
Frame dominant													
Medical	197	67	141	12	5	126	119	194	146	1	608	400	1008
Social	51	55	44	4	4	41	20	31	12	0	131	131	262
Percentage of speech acts													
Medical frame	19	7	14	1	1	13	12	19	14	0	60	40	100
Social frame	19	21	17	2	2	16	7	12	4	0	49	51	100

"particularistic co-membership" (Erickson 1975). In one instance, Dr. Jones's comment on a patient's New England accent triggered a discussion of the doctor's medical school years in Massachusetts. For the most part, however, social comments were isolated remarks embedded in or eliciting a change back to a medical, technical frame. Sequences in the discourse show a weaving back and forth between social and medical topics, with social topics in the minority.

The sequences also display a difference in the way doctors and patients talk about social issues. Occasionally, especially in Dr. Masters's office, the social talk was an equal exchange of information regarding a patient's trip or a subject unrelated to the current reason for the patient's visit. The majority of the social utterances in both settings, however, were distinctly different for the doctor and the patient.

When the patient talked of social issues, they were particularistic and contextual, impinging on her life in ways she considered relevant to the discussion of her body, as in Example 6.

Example 6

DR. JONES: Okay, push back and sit up. Sometimes after you go off the pill, you cannot have your period for a while and that's not abnormal, to not have a period.

PATIENT: Uhh, before I had my daughter my husband was stationed, or no, it was after I had Sally, he was stationed overseas and I went off the pill and my period started like six weeks after.

In this sequence the doctor presents general medical knowledge as it explains why menstrual periods cease after a woman stops taking birth control pills. The patient responds with a particularistic, social statement indexing her own body's cycles with contextual, family information. The sequence in Example 7 displays a similar medical/social distinction between the doctor's questions and the patient's answer, and Example 8 similarly exhibits the patient's contextual understanding of her body and reproductive functions during a visit to Dr. Masters's office. This patient's "happiness" is embedded in her information regarding her sexual life.

Example 7

DR. JONES: Yeah. When was the last time that it did something like this, was late [menstruation]?

PATIENT: I missed one once right before my wedding. That was in September, but that was because I was so nervous, I mean we were moving all around so

Example 8

DR. MASTERS: Your pregnancy test is negative.

PATIENT: Okay, doctor.

DR. MASTERS: That makes us happy.

PATIENT: It makes me happy, especially since I broke up with him three months ago.

When the doctors did make social comments regarding the patients' reproductive circumstances, they reflected stereotypical attitudes. The doctors voiced an abstract, social understanding, triggered by the specific situation of the topic being discussed. In the sequence given in Example 9, Dr. Masters directed the patient not to have intercourse for two to three weeks, as she was still recovering from childbirth.

Example 9

PATIENT: Don't worry, I keep telling you people I could take it or leave it, preferably leave it.

DR. MASTERS: Look, honey, you have a husband don't you.

PATIENT: Yeah, I know [resignedly].

This patient expressed her disinclination for sexual activity at the present, and Dr. Masters volunteered a stereotypical comment on women's responsibilities as a sexual partner in marriage. (He did not probe for information about her current sexual problems or initiate discussion of ways for her to understand her present situation.) In Example 10 Dr. Masters, in lecturing a woman on taking her pills properly and the risks of missing them, exhibited a traditional attitude toward marriage and pregnancy.

Example 10
DR. MASTERS: You know, and you're going to, uh, particularly since you're not married, you're going to take care of it [baby] and you're going to have all the problems.
PATIENT: [nods head]

Dr. Masters here displayed the assumption that marriage comes before pregnancy and drew on it when he urged the patient to use birth control properly.

Similar views of women's reproductive roles can be seen in the clinic interactions. As shown in Example 11, Dr. Smith discouraged a patient from using an intrauterine device (IUD) for several reasons, including the possibility that she would jeopardize her future fertility, and encouraged her to use the birth control pill. (All of the doctors observed in my study very much opposed the IUD.)

Example 11
Note. Emphasis added.
DR. SMITH: I, I have a very negative opinion of the IUD, *particularly for young women who haven't had their family yet*, because if
PATIENT: Uhm, they give it to girls who have abortions and miscarriages. Why, why is that?
DR. SMITH: I think that's just because it's, the, the women don't feel that they could take the pill, and it's some, it's some form of birth control, at least. For women who just can't remember to take the pill or won't, that need protection, then the IUD is some [pause], you know, is second best. But you're really taking a big chance of infection. We're seeing at least I'd say five in a hundred IUDs that we put in are coming back with some, some sort of infection, often not serious, but it can be very serious. It can mean hospitalization and antibiotics into your veins, and some of them even have their organs operated on or removed because they get so infected, it can even result in death, then, you know, so it's, again, a remote possibility the same as blood clots are with birth control pills, although it's not as remote as that. It happens, it really, you know, much more frequently. *Uhm, I think the scariest thing, even if, you know, you don't get an overwhelming infection, with the IUD is that we don't know what we, what your future fertility would be like.* The IUD works by causing a little infection inside your uterus and it can climb up inside the tubes and it may destroy the normal structure of the tubes enough so that the egg, which is very small, and the tube, which is also very small, don't fit, and they can get hung up. There's a
PATIENT: I see.
DR. SMITH: higher incidence of ectopic pregnancy, tubal pregnancies, when the egg stops in the tube and then tries to grow into a baby there, with women who've had IUDs.
PATIENT: Oh, I see.

DR. SMITH: So I, I really think, unless you're really adamant and you, you're willing to take all those chances, I really wouldn't tend, wouldn't recommend it.
PATIENT: [laugh] Okay, that answers
DR. SMITH: So it sounds like maybe the pill really is the right thing.

In Example 11, the doctor voiced a primarily technical but emphatic warning about the dangers of the IUD and concomitantly promoted the birth control pill.[3] This patient and doctor would assert that the patient had chosen her birth control method herself. This is true, but she had help in the decision-making process. The social assumptions of the doctor in this example center around the "future" fertility of the young, single patient who seeks contraception. There is an assumption, first, that the patient will one day want children, and second, that despite possible infection, surgery, and death, the IUD is more to be feared as a potential cause of infertility. The discussion implies that for a young woman who already had a family, the potential dangers of infection, surgery, and death would not be quite as serious. In Example 12 (the same speakers as in Example 1) Dr. Jones comments on women's reproductive roles when discussing amenorrhea with a recently divorced, single mother who in this interview has shown no interest in having more children and has stated that she is not presently sexually active.

Example 12
Note. Emphasis added.
DR. JONES: *You know, when you do want to get pregnant again*, we'll have to get you on regular cycles, where you're ovulating, in order for you to get pregnant, okay?
PATIENT: [nods head and changes topic]

Doctors from both settings assumed the role of protector of reproductive function (Examples 11 and 12) and discourager of reproductive carelessness (Example 12). In the social talk, the doctors also engaged in "keeper-of-the-moral-order talk" (Fisher 1980). To a white middle-class married woman, Dr. Masters said in a friendly, chatty manner, "Now look Susan, uh, this is the third time [abortion]. I'm talking as a friend to you as well as your doctor, okay?" In Example 13 Dr. Masters spoke with a young, single black woman receiving state medical aid.

---

[3] Fisher (1982 and this volume) discusses how gynecological residents promote hysterectomies to women patients. She asserts that the doctors' selling techniques reflect self-interest rather than concern for the patient. Scully (1980) outlines the ways gynecological obstetric residents learn to persuade patients to accept treatment procedures.

Example 13
DR. MASTERS: Look, you already had two abortions, at seventeen.
PATIENT: I know this.
DR. MASTERS: Well!?!
PATIENT: But the next time I become pregnant, I'm gonna keep it.
DR. MASTERS: Yeah, but I mean at seventeen and being single, do you want to be pregnant?

The doctor was far sterner in talking to the unmarried black patient about her reproductive history and future than he had been with the married, white woman. Dr. Masters strongly disapproved of pregnancies among young, single women and in conversations with me referred to women in this group who become pregnant as "stupid" and generally beyond rationality.

The clinic doctors were rarely so explicit in their advice.. Dr. Long, in treating a 21-year-old single woman for postabortion pain did not discuss her failure to use birth control until the end of the interaction. As he was concluding the exam and preparing to leave the room, he rather grimly directed her as follows: "Okay, well, use your diaphragm. Use it every time, remember to take it out every time."

Throughout the exam, Dr. Long's patient had evidenced intense pain. The doctor had ignored her signals and moans. As the doctor and I left the examining room, he rolled his eyes at me and said, "She acts like she's 14 years old." Both settings include such social interpretations. In the office of Dr. Masters they form part of the discourse between doctor and patient. In the clinic they tend to receive subtler expression in the doctor–patient discourse and to be voiced among staff members.

To distinguish between the social/contextual and medical/biological modes of discourse, I drew in my analysis on the concept of "frames"—forms in speech that reference conceptual levels of understanding in an interaction. Frames indicate the parameters for each social or medical topic, and as topics discussed in the interviews invariably had both social and medical components, I used a dominant/residual continuum to avoid the need for a sharp break between the two.

My data indicate that patients talk *within* the medical frames but do not initiate medical topics (Todd 1982). When a patient did initiate a topic, it was social. The doctors' social talk, in contrast, was more abstract and tended to be embedded in the medical talk.

Like the distributional and sequential analyses, analysis of the frames showed that the doctor exerted more power and control in the interaction than the patient. The doctors' power was used in part to reinforce traditional stereotypes of women and their life options, stereotypes that have been increasingly questioned in the past decade. In addition, the doctors' focus on technical information and relative exclusion of contextual information reveals more general conceptions of the purposes and proper domain of science, a matter that I shall consider at greater length in Part 4.

PART 4: CONSEQUENCES

In the data I collected, several patterns were consistently evident: (a) the doctor's reasoning or interpretation took priority over the patient's, (b) the doctor expressed condescension toward the patient, and (c) social and medical topics introduced by the doctor generally prevailed, while the doctor either ignored the patient's social talk or used it to return the discourse to a medical topic. Let us consider the three patterns in sequence.

1. In Example 14, from the clinic, a woman complains of dizziness, bloating, tiredness, and general dissatisfaction that she feels is caused by a five-year course of birth control pills. Dr. Smith is skeptical that the birth control pill is the cause of these problems and dominates the ensuing interchange.

Example 14

DR. SMITH: Do, do your legs swell, is that part of your problem or do you just feel kinda bloated?

PATIENT: My, I don't know, my stomach just feels really, like it's out here, you know, very

DR. SMITH: uh hum. Sometimes things get blamed on the pills that aren't always the pills' fault so, like

PATIENT: what?

DR. SMITH: women who say they gained weight because they're taking the pills when ordinarily they're expecting to gain weight, so maybe they eat a little bit more, and uh, then they gain weight and say, oh, look at the pill made me gain weight.

PATIENT: But it makes me hungry. When I'm not on the pill, I don't feel hungry.

DR. SMITH: I've never heard that one before [laughs].

Although the doctor laughs off the patient's concerns about the birth control pill, the patient is not unreasonable to question this method of contraception. Seaman (1969) and Seaman and Seaman (1977) stressed the numerous potential health hazards of hormonal tampering. Congress has conducted hearings on the dangers of oral contraceptives.

Ehrenreich and English (1979) discussed how doctors as experts control women's reproduction, despite growing evidence that many of the prescribed medical treatments have negative effects. Although the birth control pill may, in fact, be useful to the patient in Example 14, depending on her contextual needs to avoid pregnancy, the concerns she expressed are legitimate and deserve careful consideration. In Example 15, an interchange between Dr. Masters and a patient of several years, the doctor makes recommendations to her about medical coverage, racing over her financial worries and defining her needs. (Interestingly, when I interviewed the patients quoted in Examples 14 and 15, I learned both had accepted the advice of the doctor. The clinic patient explained to me that her swelling and dizziness were the result of her diet rather than her use of birth control pills. Dr. Masters's patient was nervous about possible medical expense for office visits but decided to keep the Blue Cross medical insurance.)

Example 15

DR. MASTERS: Uh, Nancy, anything you need, you know that from previous times, you just see me, you know, anything medical, you know. And what I would suggest, now you have a choice between Kaiser and Blue Cross, I think [pause]

PATIENT: Uh hum.

DR. MASTERS: take Blue Cross. You don't need anything for office calls. You're not going to go broke on that; you know that. [pause]

PATIENT: Uh hum.

DR. MASTERS: Uh, but you should have some hospital and surgery, so if you want to stay with me, you know, and, uh, I would suggest that you just take Blue Cross on the hospital and surgical, you know, uh, then you can come to me.

PATIENT: Okay.

DR. MASTERS: You know, since you feel that strongly about it, you know.

PATIENT: But does Blue Cross cover like examinations when you have a physical?

DR. MASTERS: Honey, this is what I'm trying to tell you. Look, yes

PATIENT: I don't think they do.

DR. MASTERS: Some do, some don't. But that basically is not what you need. Now, you're not going to go broke by coming once or twice a year for a pelvic examination.

PATIENT: Yeah

2. The doctor's condescension to patients was observable in sequences throughout the interviews. The doctors in the clinic were more likely than Dr. Masters to explain to a patient what they were doing, but still they often seemed to be talking "down," as if to a child. The exchange in Example 16 was particularly common in the clinic when the patient observed her cervix during the exam by using a mirror.

Example 16

DR. JONES: You can hold the mirror and you can just kind of angle it in and see it [cervix]. Can you see it?

PATIENT: Oh, yeah.

DR. JONES: It's like a little pink doughnut?

PATIENT: Uh huh.

DR. JONES: It's got a little hole.

PATIENT: Uh huh.

DR. JONES: That's where the baby comes out.

The doctors used the diminutive "little" in many of their explanations—in such statements as the one in Example 16; in initiating an exam ("I'm just going to do a little exam"); in applying medication to vaginal warts ("a little bit on that one and a little bit on this one"); and in teaching women breast self-examination ("just march your little fingers...").

Dr. Masters examined patients without explaining his actions. He often showed a condescending attitude toward patients, however, in demanding a response while revealing a suspicion that they would not follow his instructions. Statements to a Mexican-American woman regarding her usage of birth control: "Okay, I've given it to you in English and Spanish. Now you better mind it, okay?" In Example 17, Dr. Masters addresses a woman who has run out of birth control pills and must wait until her next cycle to resume taking them.

Example 17

DR. MASTERS: Okay, now, honey, look, so that you don't get pregnant again, I want you to get this foam, okay?

PATIENT: Uh hum.

DR. MASTERS: You go to the drugstore and get it, and then here are the instructions. Read it. Now it's very simple. [This woman has not been pregnant recently.]

Dr. Masters's "honey" and the step-by-step instructions were typically uttered slowly and carefully, as if to a small child, with favorite expressions that included "Have you been a good girl?" meaning "Have you used contraception with intercourse?" and "Here are your happy pills," meaning birth control pills. These phrases generally elicited nervous laughs and twitches from the patients.

3. It should be noted that doctors' control of social and medical topics may jeopardize the outcome of medical treatment. If the patient is in a passive position, she will often refrain from making requests (Lazare 1979). If topics related to contraception are not discussed, as a result, the consequences for her health and life might be serious. In Examples 4 and 5, the doctor shifted the patient's social topic to a medical one. When the doctor wanted to pursue social topics, however, the transition was accomplished with ease. (In demanding a reactive from the patient and staff while performing a breast exam, Dr. Masters required compliance from the patient, even when she was reluctant.)

Thus, the question of immediate importance from the sociological viewpoint is, Why are such doctor-patient encounters so systematically repeated? What could hold such a system together? Why are women compelled to allow entire life experiences and biographies to be erased from the arena of consideration? And why should doctors efface them in the first place?

Sexism and elitism are certainly involved, and feminist theories invite consideration of reproduction as a political and social phenomenon. But a full description of oppressive and exploitative aspects of the encounter does not completely explain the structure of doctor-patient interaction. Why does Dr. Jones in Example 7, with the best of intentions, consider the patient's marriage irrelevant to her reproductive concerns? Why does Dr. Smith in Example 5 assume in a kindly way that the patient is uneasy about the pelvic exam, when the patient has specifically stated she is uneasy "tonight"—a night, in fact, when she is considering a change of contraceptive method? Why does Dr. Masters in Example 4 ignore the patients economic situation when prescribing contraception?

The discussion that I have presented here incorporates three foci apparent in current literature on medical interaction. Critical medical social theory provides a wide range of analyses for understanding the power relationships in the present American medical system (see Conrad and Kern 1981; Ehrenreich and English 1978; Friedson 1970; Navarro 1976; Waitzkin and Waterman 1974). The literature emphasizes study of the organization and institution of health care for understanding medical inequality and dominance of the doctor-patient relationship by physicians. Recent feminist scholarship has contributed complementary writings on women's health care needs in modern medical treatment, concentrating on the effects of patriarchal society on reproduction. A third group of writers uses conceptual analysis of the influence of a scientific–biological model for understanding issues of health (McKeown 1976; Todd 1982; Wright 1982). Such analysis, which delves into the world view arising out of the scientific revolution of the sixteenth and seventeenth centuries, has received less attention than the other two, but in my opinion makes an essential contribution to understanding of interactions such as those that I recorded.

The doctors' exclusion of the realms of life to which the patients refer has origins that predate the sixteenth and seventeenth centuries, but advances associated with the scientific revolution are probably chiefly responsible for this exclusion. Certainly the scientific revolution institutionalized the "scientific" notion that the conscious mind can be understood as separate from the mechanical body, an idea that has particularly influenced medical theory and practice (McKeown 1976). The medical system assumes a health care delivery service based on the understanding that illness is a biological function of individuals or individual organs.

Merchant (1980), in her historical work on the rise of modern science, discusses how the image and control of nature and reproduction changed from female to male, active to passive, holistic to mechanical parts, contextual to context-free, and subjective to objective with the discovery of scientific laws of external forces and a natural order beyond human control. Shifts in human understanding of nature are also reflected in institutional attitudes toward human beings. Medicine defines patients as passive entities divided into mechanical bodily parts. The contextual aspects of patients' lives and their subjective understandings are negated in favor of objective, technical, medical control. This separation has gone unexamined by modern medicine, for the most part, and by the doctor and the patient in the interaction, as well as by most social scientists who study the health care delivery system.

CONCLUSION

Conversations between the doctor and the patient in the medical setting provide significant evidence that linguistic data can be useful for sociological inquiry. In the actual discourse, the sociologist can observe situated interaction, organizational features, institutional structures, conceptual definitions, and cultural assumptions of reproduction.

The doctors' position in the interaction is exhibited in the breakdown and use of speech acts. Their medical knowledge is surrounded by an aura of reverence, which turns that knowledge into an interactional tool for the wielding of socially defined and accepted power as indicated by the doctors' use of language. Medical institutional power in both settings was reflected in the domination by the doctors of the questioning and directive strategies. Furthermore, the doctors controlled the sequencing of turns in the interaction.

The topical analysis of social and medical frames and their use by the doctor and the patient in conversation affords additional insights. The doctor, although conforming to acceptable standards within the medical model, truncates the patient's social understandings with clinical, technical definitions and with stereotypical social definitions of women's proper roles (when and how to be sexually active, when and how to be reproductive, and when and how to use birth control).

The doctor and the patient are implicitly in conflict in this interaction. The patient asks the doctor for help in understanding how to adjust her body to her social life. The doctor's technical answer assumes that the patient should adjust her social life to her body, because the doctor does not consider information about the patient's social life theoretically relevant to health care delivery. Biological issues of health and illness have been defined as treatable separate from contextual concerns, but such a division is problematic for reproductive cycles, which normally involve social and contextual—and not merely biological—activities in women's lives.

As I have noted, doctors do use social information and interpretations in these interactions. The social frames display views of women, sexuality, and reproductive function—attitudes that have been questioned, criticized, and broadened in the past decade. Although traditional roles are related to larger societal and cultural values, expression of them by the medical profession is important because it is the primary institution in control of reproductive processes in this society. Doctors' assumptions can play a powerful role, defining women's definitions of self as well as influencing their health (Ehrenreich and English 1979; Fisher 1980; Todd 1982, in press).

The study of language—its use and structure—in discourse thus provides varied sociological insights. In talk itself are observable the situated event of the interaction, the organizational arrangements, the institutional structures, the conceptual scientific definitions, and the cultural assumptions of women's reproductive roles, all of which interrelate.

Analysis of medical discourse can also lead to improved health care. One might argue that the present system is adequately arranged. Yet some findings indicate (Fisher 1982; Todd 1982) that when women patients do not have access to interactional and communicational channels in the medical interview, they often receive inappropriate reproductive care, which affects their life options. Shuy (1974) has also discussed the inadequacies in doctor-patient relationships involving highly technical physicians and cross-cultural or minority patients, or both.

Some evidence suggests, then, that health care delivery is inadequate today. The benefits of further research, whether for medicine or for sociology, will require, I think, increased awareness of empirical data in their relationship to larger theoretical issues. Empirical data enlighten theory and thereby lead to improved hypotheses. In addition the data, in this case doctor-patient interviews, are illuminated by theory—critical medical writings, feminist scholarship, and research into the evolution of the scientific world view—and in fact cannot be understood without it. Theory and empirical data thus operate in tandem. Together they can suggest potential strategies for improved medical interactions between doctors and patients. It is in the interests of doctors—and of all concerned with improved health care—to broaden current definitions of health and the roles of the participants in medical settings.

REFERENCES CITED

AUSTIN, J.L.
   1962   *How to Do Things With Words*. Cambridge, Mass.: Harvard University Press.
CHOMSKY, NOAM
   1968   *Language and Mind*. New York: Harcourt Brace Jovanovich.
CICOUREL, AARON V.
   1975   Discourse and text: Cognitive and linguistic processes in studies of social structure. *Versus: Quaderni de Studi Semiotici* 12:33–84.
   1980   Three models of discourse analysis: The role of social structure. *Discourse Processes* 3:101–132.
COLE, MICHAEL; J. DORE; W. S. HALL; AND G. DOWLEY
   1978   Situation and task in young children's talk. *Discourse Processes* 1:119–176.
CONRAD, PETER, AND ROCHELLE KERN, EDS.
   1981   *The Sociology of Health and Illness: Critical Perspectives*. New York: St. Martin's Press.
D'ANDRADE, ROY A.
   n.d.   A tentative cultural classification of speech acts. Manuscript, Department of Anthropology, University of California, San Diego.

DAVIS, FRED
   1963   *Passage Through Crisis: Polio Victims and Their Families*. Indianapolis: Bobbs-
          Merrill.
EHRENREICH, BARBARA, AND DEIRDRE ENGLISH
   1979   *For Her Own Good: 150 Years of the Experts' Advice to Women*. Garden City,
          N.Y.: Doubleday, Anchor Books.
ERICKSON, FREDERICK
   1975   Gatekeeping and the melting pot: Interaction in counselling encounters.
          Harvard Educational Review 45:44–70.
FISHER, SUE
   1980   The Context of Medical Decision-Making: An Analysis of Practitioner/Patient
          Communication. *Working Papers in Sociolinguistics* 75.
   1982   The negotiations of treatment decisions in doctor/patient communication. IN
          Linguistics and the Professions, Robert Di Pietro, Ed., pp. 51–82. Norwood,
          N.J.: Ablex.
FREIDSON, ELIOT
   1970   *Professional Dominance*. Chicago: Aldine.
GELMAN, ROCHEL, AND MARILYN SHATZ
   1977   Appropriate speech adjustments: The operation of conversational constraints on
          talk to two-year olds. IN *Interaction, Conversation and the Development of
          Language*, M. Lewis and L. Rosenbaum, Eds., pp. 27–61. New York: John
          Wiley and Sons.
HALLIDAY, MICHAEL A., AND RUQAIYA HASAN
   1976   *Cohesion in English*. London: Longmans.
HYMES, DELL
   1972   Models of the interaction of language and social life. IN *Directions in
          Sociolinguistics: The Ethnography of Communication*, John J. Gumperz and
          Dell Hymes, Eds., pp. 38–71. New York: Holt, Rinehart and Winston.
LABOV, WILLIAM, AND DAVID FANSHEL
   1977   *Therapeutic Discourse: Psychotherapy As Conversation*. New York: Academic.
LAZARE, AARON, ED.
   1979   *Outpatient Psychiatry: Diagnosis and Treatment*. Baltimore: Williams &
          Wilkins.
LUKER, KRISTIN
   1975   *Taking Chances. Abortion and the Decision Not To Contracept*. Berkeley:
          University of California Press.
MÅSEIDE, PER
   n.d.   Cognitive-linguistic approaches to analyses of social interaction: An analysis of
          clinical talk. Manuscript, Department of Sociology, University of California,
          San Diego.
MCKEOWN, THOMAS
   1976   *Medicine: Dream, Mirage, or Nemesis?* London: Nuffield Provincial Hospitals
          Trust.
MEHAN, HUGH
   1979   *Learning Lessons: The Social Organization of Classroom Behavior*.
          Cambridge, Mass.: Harvard University Press.

MERCHANT, CAROLYN
1980   *The Death of Nature: Women, Ecology, and the Scientific Revolution*. San
       Francisco: Harper and Row.
NAVARRO, VINCENTE
1976   *Medicine Under Capitalism*. New York: Prodist.
SACKS, HARVEY; EMANUEL SCHEGLOFF; AND GAIL JEFFERSON
1974   A simplest systematics for the organization of turn-taking in conversation.
       Language 50:696–735.
SCHIEFELBEIN, SUSAN
1980   The female patient: Heeded? hustled? healed? *Saturday Review* 3:29.
SCULLY, DIANA
1980   *Men Who Control Women's Health: The Miseducation of Obstetrician-
       Gynecologists*. Boston: Houghton Mifflin.
SEAMAN, BARBARA
1969   *The Doctors' Case Against the Pill*. New York: Avon.
SEAMAN, BARBARA, AND GIDEON SEAMAN
1977   *Women and the Crisis in Sex Hormones*. New York: Rawson Associates.
SEARLE, JOHN R.
1969   *Speech Acts: An Essay in the Philosophy of Language*. Cambridge: Cambridge
       University Press.
SHUY, ROGER W.
1974   Problems of Communication in the Cross-Cultural Medical Interview. *Working
       Papers in Sociolinguistics* 19.
STREECK, JURGEN
1980   Speech acts in interaction: A critique of Searle. *Discourse Processes*
       3:133–154.
TODD, ALEXANDRA DUNDAS
1982   The Medicalization of Reproduction: Scientific Medicine and the Diseasing of
       Healthy Women. Doctoral dissertation, University of California, San Diego.
In press   Women's bodies as diseased and deviant: Historical and contemporary
       issues. IN *Research in Law, Deviance, and Social Control*, Vol. 5, Steven
       Spitzer and Rita Simon, Eds. Greenwich, Conn.: JAI Press.
WAITZKIN, HOWARD B., AND BARBARA WATERMAN
1974   *The Exploitation of Illness in Capitalist Society*. Indianapolis: Bobbs-Merrill.
WEST, CANDACE
Forthcoming   When the doctor is a 'lady': Power, status and gender in physician-
       patient exchanges. IN *Women, Health, and Medicine*, A. Stromberg,
       Ed. Palo Alto, Calif.: Mayfield.
WRIGHT, WILL
1982   *The Social Logic of Health*. New Brunswick, N.J.: Rutgers University Press.
ZIMMERMAN, DON H., AND CANDACE WEST
1975   Sex roles, interruptions, and silences in conversations. IN *Language and Sex:
       Difference and Dominance*, Barrie Thorne and Nancy Henley, Eds., pp.
       105–129. Rowley, Mass.: Newbury House.
ZIMMERMAN, DON H., AND CANDACE WEST, EDS.
1980   Language and social interaction. *Sociological Inquiry* 50(3–4).

Power and Resistance

9

Policing the Lying Patient: Surveillance and Self-Regulation in Consultations with Adolescent Diabetics

David Silverman

I don't believe a thing
Who do we believe in this clinic?

(NT: 18.9)

We want to give you the correct advice
but we don't want to tell you what to do.

(NT: 15.1)

INTRODUCTION

The treatment of illness inevitably occurs within a moral framework. In the care of diabetic patients, as with other chronic illnesses, there is a perceived need for sufferers to show that they are doing their best to contain their disorder. Where deviance may be willful, there is an investigative potential present in the consultation and the corrective strategy may be to address the deficiencies in the socialization of the deviant. A recently instituted measure of blood-glucose level (glycosylated hemoglobin) can be used as a means of policing, as observed in this study of 47 consultations with adolescent diabetic patients attending two out-patient clinics. This measure provides a form of surveillance which finds truth inside the patient rather than as conversationally constituted. The implications of this practice will be considered and alternative strategies discussed.

Diabetes mellitus is the most common metabolic problem in childhood (Rosenbloom 1984). In the United Kingdom it affects 7 out of every 10,000 children (Jones 1983). Like many other chronic diseases, it presents a problem to medical staff in that no "cure" can be offered to the patient, only a continuing routine of hospital visits and, in this case, a life-long regime of invasive, self-administered tests and injections and control of diet. This self-administration creates a special problem in itself for it demands a degree of activity from the patient that is very different from the common model of the passive patient and the active physician (Szasz and Hollander 1956). Not surprisingly, it is reported that in a study of nearly 4000 out-patients from a typical diabetic clinic only about fifteen percent were "well controlled" (Gillespie and Bradley 1983).[1]

Medicine has responded in two kinds of ways to this situation. The dominant biological model of health and illness has led to extensive research to improve measurement and control of blood-sugar levels. Although this has produced improved testing and therapy, a recent review of the literature is forced to conclude that "strict diabetes control remains theoretical because of our inability to mimic the pancreatic beta-cell response with intermittent insulin injection" (Rosenbloom 1984). The author goes on to note that widely accepted therapies, like twice-daily injections, have not been supported in controlled studies. This "seat of the pants" character of diabetes treatment has led one sociologist to emphasize how faith, optimism and ritualistic elements enter into medical practice in this area (Posner 1977).

A second kind of medical response has arisen from the pediatric "whole person" model of the patient and also perhaps from the "chronic disease" model which stresses the role of "motivation...as a major problem in long-term disorders" (Gillespie and Bradley 1983). This has led to a number of studies of patient and family response to diabetes (Cerreto and Travis 1984; Lavoie and Barker 1980; and Ory and Kronenfeld, 1980). The "chronic disease" model goes beyond purely biological versions of health and illness. It is prepared to treat diabetes as "about people not pancreases" as one doctor has put it (Newton, 1985). The most recent work also allows for process and change (Bradley et al. 1984). Motivation is now seen as "a changing interpersonal and cognitive process" (Gillespie and Bradley 1983).

---

[1] This relates to the continuing medical concern with patient "compliance" which extends over a wide range of treatments and illnesses. Gerry Stimson has suggested that it is worth considering why compliance is treated as less of an issue in certain types of treatment, e.g., patients at drug clinics get a urine test to measure compliance but not GP patients taking antibiotics. Of course, drug clinics take patient policing to further lengths than normally observed in diabetic clinics. Patients are nearly always assumed to lie about their condition and a urine test has a purely policing function because self-regulation is not tolerated.

Such "liberal" or "humanistic" imperatives avowedly owe a great deal to the discovery of the "social" and the "psychological" realms by the human sciences. One of the themes of this chapter, however, is that knowledge is never neutral and that "enlightenment" is invariably double-edged. The focus on anatomy produced an organic medicine which was at once (arguably) more efficient at treatment than the earlier medicine of "essences" but, also more authoritarian. The still later discovery of the "social" made medicine less authoritarian but also more intrusive. I will return to this issue later.

SETTINGS AND METHODS

The study began as a result of a chance meeting with a consultant pediatrician who worked at a General Hospital in a new town some 30 miles from London. Having described my previous work to him, I was invited to observe his monthly clinic with adolescent diabetics. As I later learned, this clinic was held for "problem cases." The more routine cases were dealt with by the registrar. In a sense, however, all adolescent diabetics are problem cases, combining the expectation of psychological problems already discussed in this chapter and the kinds of conflicts between medical expertise and the perceived need for self-regulation that I have just been considering. After observing several clinics, the doctor concerned readily accepted my comparison of diabetics with alcoholics. From the medical point of view, both represent "no-win" situations. Medical expertise is relevant insofar as patients are prepared to perceive that they have a problem and to become actively involved in its treatment. Unlike much medical practice, the patient's active involvement in decisionmakng is basic to success. Consequently, often sometimes reluctantly, doctors feel compelled to get involved in what for them are murky, intractable psychological and social issues.

At this clinic, the patients see the health visitor before the consultation begins. The clinic used to do a blood test (via a fingerprick) and, sometimes, engage in health education through a discussion of diet, often using teaching materials such as models of different foods. These activities would take place in a small room which, like the consulting room, is located next to a children's ward. Consequently, the waiting area is filled with small children's seats, as well as larger adult ones, and has a play area containing a slide as well as a number of toys.

After seeing the health visitor, there is often a few minutes' wait before it is time to see the doctor. The consultant sits at the side of a desk at the far side of the consulting room. Against the wall nearest the door there are scales and a device for measuring height. Under a window is an examination couch which is rarely used for these patients. The patient, health visitor and researcher arrange themselves in a semi-circle of chairs facing the doctor. Apart from new patients, who seem always to be accompanied by parents, many patients are unaccompanied. Where parents bring their child to the clinic, they do not enter the consulting room if it is established that the child does not want them to be present. Overall, of the 10 patients seen more than once during my observation of the clinic, 5 always had their consultations without their parents being present and 4 had their parents absent from at least one consultation. Only one patient had a parent present at all consultations.

In order to allow some comparison, I obtained access some months later to another diabetic clinic held in a General Hospital in a suburb of London. The consultant there is also a pediatrician but the clinic differs in a number of ways. All children attend—there is no special adolescents' clinic—and are seen either by the consultant or his registrar according to the time they arrive. I observed only those consultations involving patients aged between 11 and 18. At the time I was observing there was no health visitor present (although one had recently been appointed). Before the consultation, patients see a dietitian and have their weight and height recorded by a nurse. They may also chat to a voluntary worker, herself a mother of a diabetic child, who attends all clinics, keeps tabs on patients and their problems, and organizes a parents' group. Although there is a sideroom, mostly used by mothers and young children, most teenage diabetic patients wait with other adult nondiabetic patients, seated on chairs placed along the walls of a waiting area, with doctors' rooms on each side.

I observed consultations and made notes. After an initial period of observation, all consultations were tape-recorded with patients' and parents' permission. Due to a lack of resources, however, only three consultations were transcribed in their entirety. The initial aim of the analysis was to establish recurrent interactional forms within a version of the "ceremonial order of the clinic" (Strong 1979). Since I had no access to patients' own accounts outside the consultation, my interest was in what all parties were *doing* in these encounters rather than in what they *thought* about what they were doing. More specifically, I became interested in the kind of medical dilemmas over patient autonomy and medical control that I have already described.

I sought to find patterns across all consultations, using analytic induction to generate categories and strengthening my analysis via the pursuit of deviant cases (Mitchell 1983) and the use of simple methods of counting where appropriate (Silverman 1985, Chapter 7). The analysis came to focus on four areas:

1. A description of the distinctive interactional forms found in these consultations and the dilemmas created for the parties.
2. An illustration of the working out of these dilemmas taking advantage of my longitudinal data on several consultations with the same patient.
3. An attempt to depict different medical 'styles' in the consultation centering around the balance between autonomy and control.
4. An assessment, in the light of this analysis, of a number of practical suggestions to reform diabetic clinics.

TABLE 1   The Data

Clinic	'New Town'	'Suburban'
Period of observation	10 months	3 months
Number of clinic sessions observed	10	3
Number of doctors	1	3
Number of consultations	33	14

I observed the first (new town) clinic over a much longer period than the suburban clinic as shown in Table 1.

As shown in Table 2, consultations at the new town clinic last, on average, twice the length of those at the suburban clinic. The longest consultation at the new town clinic was with a new patient and her parents and the shortest was with an educationally subnormal patient who, unusually, had turned up without his mother. The shortest consultations at the suburban clinic were seen by an elderly locum with no previous knowledge of the patients or their patients.

INTERACTIONAL FORMS

This account is based, almost entirely, on the "new town" clinic data because of the far larger database derived from 33 consultations held by a single doctor. Many aspects of these forms are seen in the "suburban" consultations although, as I suggest later in a discussion of medical styles, there is a tendency here to stick closer to a medical model of patient passivity with lip-service only being given to the complex issues involved in self-regulation of care. This is reflected in the far shorter consultations in the suburban clinic—although it must be kept in mind that, unlike the new town clinic, this is not a clinic for "problem" patients, and that dietary issues are dealt with outside the consultation.

It will be helpful if I locate the forms I have identified in the chronology of events in which they unfold. This chronology is taken from the "new town" clinic. After the patient enters, she is weighed and measured by the health visitor while the doctor reads the notes.[2] Following standard pediatric practice, the

TABLE 2   Length of Consultations

Clinic	'New Town'	'Suburban'
Mean length of consultation (in minutes)	24	12
Shortest and longest consultations	14–31	6–16

---

[2] All four doctors that I observed were male. The patients were both male and female. As a convention, then, I have used "she" to describe the patient group.

child's height and weight are then plotted against a normal distribution. The variation between the curve and the actual measurement can be an occasion for compliments—"you are doing very well." Sometimes it is used to warn—"You are putting on too much weight"—and sometimes to encourage. Teenage boys are assured that, if they can control their diabetes, they will grow taller. A link between weight and control is regularly used with girls.

The doctor then moves on to the main business of blood-sugar levels. He inspects the results of today's blood and/or urine test and, if available, the more reliable results of the test measuring long-term glycostylated hemoglobin. The patient is told whether the figures have moved up or down since the last visit and may be asked to account for such movements.[3]

At this point, the doctor will ask to see the child's own blood and urine test results. These are supposed to be recorded several times a day in a little book provided by the clinic. Two kinds of issues arise from these sets of figures: the levels of blood-sugar recorded and the frequencies of tests. Where the former is high and the latter is low it will be seen as a problem.

The rationale behind the testing program is to provide information for the patients, so that they can become more aware of variations in blood-sugar levels due to diet, exercise, or time of day and adjust their injections accordingly. Nonetheless, both sides treat the figures as an occasion for medical judgment leading to praise, blame, or excuses, as appropriate. In turn, the testing figures are often more complete in the days immediately preceding the clinic visit. Frequently, the doctor will turn back a page and remark on "all the empty spaces."

A parallel is with a visit to the dentist when you may look after your teeth particularly carefully immediately before. As with the dental visit, although both parties theorize the condition of your teeth or blood-sugar level as your own problem to be assessed and acted upon yourself, nonetheless, the practitioner's judgment will be treated as crucial, asserting the moral worth or otherwise of your performance. So both diabetic and dental patients hope to be "let off lightly" by the practitioner. Once again, the dilemma of the balance between autonomy and professional control is neatly illustrated. Being responsible for your own health, the cherished aim of much health education literature, *may* amount to little more than becoming a target for the degradation ceremonies that are feasible in character work.

As a result of the evaluation of these figures, a series of things may happen. The doctor may suggest a new program of testing which may be more realistic in light of the patient's past behavior. Diet may be discussed in the same terms, calling upon the health visitor's knowledge of meal preparation at home. This

---

[3] Linnie Price has pointed out the similarities with obstetrics where "objective measures" may be used to displace the mother's account. In both cases we can observe the use of the natural world to support the definitions of one set of actors (see Callon 1986).

may lead to a teaching session where the child is asked to say what would happen with hypothetical changes in diet or insulin dosage. The aim here is to check the patient's competence in the self-regulation of her condition. The sites of injections may also be examined for the same reason and advice given on varying them. Finally, again drawing upon the inside knowledge of the health visitor, some attempt may be made to explore family relations.The issue of "nagging" by anxious parents often surfaces. It parallels the way in which health professionals may also be constituted as authority figures by these children. This kind of problem is something of which this doctor was only too aware. I will examine shortly his "negotiating" strategy for handling it.

Disposals usually center around a newly negotiated program of diet, testing or insulin dosage. A follow-up appointment, usually of three to four months, is arranged, with the child sometimes being asked to attend earlier for a glycosylated hemoglobin test so that the results are available at the next consultation. Only in two cases was admission as an in-patient considered. In one case, the child's control had been consistently very poor; in the other it was suggested that he might be admitted to be given a "hypo" under proper care. The aim was to overcome his fear of "hypos" which had prevented him from raising his insulin dosage when appropriate.

In the context of this chronology of the consultation, I have identified a number of interactional particulars which distinguish diabetic clinics from other adolescent clinics. I will call these as follows: attributions of theoreticity, locating actions in a moral framework, discussing family relations, discussing the patient's psychology and, finally, negotiating outcomes. Some of these features have been identified in other clinics for adolescents—attributions of theoreticity seem to be a central feature of cleft-palate clinics (see Chapter 7). Others are less common: a serious discussion of family relations would not normally seem to be appropriate in many other clinics given the predominance of the rule of "politeness is all" (Strong 1979); a moral framework might be central to parents' conceptions of their behavior or to doctors working in such areas as drug-abuse or alcoholism but it would not usually arise in discussions of purely physical disorders. What is important here, however, is the combination of these five elements into a 'ceremonial order' (Strong 1979) which reveals the double-edged nature of appeals to patient autonomy and responsibility.

1. Theoreticity

It is standard practice in diabetic care to encourage patients to understand and to treat their disease. This is reflected in the educational process that occurs during the in-patient stay after diabetes has been identified. It is recognized that the parents—usually the mother—will be centrally involved up to, say, the age of ten. However, as the child enters her teens, she is treated quite openly as the person to whom medical encounters are directed and the person who should be making the decisions regarding her health care. "Theoreticity," then, refers to the attribution of the capacity of rational thought, including the ability to perceive and choose between alternative courses of action (McHugh 1970).

In the early stages, there will be an attempt to wean the child away from dependence on parents. For instance, in the case of Rajiv, a boy of 14:

(NT:17.7)
HV = Health Visitor; M = Mother
HV: Rajiv, you're doing the testing?
M: Sometimes
HV: Rajiv, it's *your* urine. [*To mother*] He's a young man now. Come on Rajiv do your own wees. It's a bit undignified. It's not your Mum's job.

The issue of the responsibilities of age again surface in a consultation with Murray (M), aged 15, who lives in a Children's Home where the staff are reluctant to vary his dosage of insulin:

(NT:15.1)
D: What do you feel about making the decisions?
M: I'm getting to know a lot.
D: So it may be time for you to make the decisions. You're fifteen and a half now. But if you're in doubt you could ask P (the health visitor)...
D: You're old enough to tell when to put it up.

Overall in 23 out of the 33 consultations observed at the new town clinic, overt attributions of theoreticity were made. A typical exception was a consultation with a 12-year-old, attending for the first time, where management of the diabetes was largely treated in terms of an alliance between the child, her parents, and the doctor. Also the educationally subnormal boy of 13 was sometimes not granted theoretic status, the discussion taking place largely between his mother and the doctor. Even he, however, was reminded on one occasion by the health visitor that he must eventually take charge of his testing: "You're growing up. You're going to have to do it" (NT:16.10).

In these clinics then, for quite understandable reasons, patients will tend to be treated as theoretic actors whether they like it or not. The assumption was that making decisions and considering their consequences was for the patients' own good as in this further comment to Murray:

(NT:18.9)
D: Do you know that you're doing the testing for you rather than for me. So you can adjust your insulin. If you only adjusted your insulin every time you came here it wouldn't make sense.

2. The Moral Framework

Once the patient is defined as an active decision maker, she gains autonomy at the cost of being morally responsible for her actions. If rewards and sanctions are the means of maintaining discipline with young children, then the production of feelings of guilt is a subtle means of control when they are granted autonomy, as these two instances show:

(NT:11.9)
D: So long as you know that smoking is not good for diabetic people
(NT:16.10)
HV: So we won't nag you. Unless you do it you won't be growing right

Failing to carry out tests and their results when done lead to implicit moral charges and to expressions of disappointment likely to be associated with the production of guilt. For instance, after a poor blood-test result:

HV: Over 22
M: Oh (looks glum)

And later:

D: Yes, I was hoping that you would have had the (glycosylated) test done
     [*Murray's testing book is examined*]
D: Yes, it's just that you've done no urine test since December and we haven't had any
     early morning tests (NT:15.1).

Blame can however turn into praise—the doctor later says that Murray's testing program is "not going too badly." Another example of praise, this time within more explicit moral framework ("reformed character"), later leads into implied moral charges:

(NT:11.9)
J = June
D: So no sugar in the urine
HV: No, she's a reformed character
     [...]
D: Are you keeping to a reasonable diet or do you just go free?
J: No I'm keeping to it a bit better now
     [...]
D: What about your testing? Have you got any tests for us?
J: No
D: When was the last time you did a test?
J: Not since I was on holiday

Sometimes the interrogation on the blood-test results leads to an attempt to get the patient to condemn herself out of her own mouth:

(NT:18.9)
S = Sylvia M = Mother
D: Well, you've got the record today. 22 percent
       [...]
D: Would you say the control's good?
S: I don't know
D: Come on!
M: It was good but it's gone off lately
       [...]
D: Well the control's a bit up and down isn't it?
S: Yes

The contrast between the patient's own test results and what is known from hospital-administered tests provides an important moral lever for medical staff. A very powerful moral charge in this context is cheating via "cooking the books." The possibility of such cheating is mentioned in this statement after a big difference has been found between home and hospital test figures:

(NT:20.11)
HV: It's not that we don't believe you, Christine. Some children I wouldn't believe

The following examples of comments made after other patients have left the consulting room show such nonbelief:

(NT:16:10)
D: He used to invent results. I find him very frustrating to deal with

(NT:18.9)
D: His voice is getting very guilty. He was caught out
HV: I don't believe a thing

The only case of an implied charge of lying being made, clarified by the child's father (F), arises in this consultation with Alan (A), a boy of 14:

(NT:16.10)
D: Alan, these (figures) look too good to be true. Is that right Alan?
A):   No
F: What he means is have you been making them up?
       [no response]
       [...]
D: Does anybody check them with you?

A: Sometimes
D: Well I think all we can say is that it's unlikely that the results really indicate your
      control
      [*Alan is fiddling with his sweater*]

In fully 28 out of these 33 consultations some sort of moral framework is used in the interpretation of test results. Most of the deviant cases are easily explicable: the 12-year-old new patient is barely accorded theoreticity and so cannot be held fully responsible for her actions yet. Again a later consultation with June occurs after she has had a hypoglycemic attack the day before and reassurance rather than evaluation of her actions follows.

More frequently, however, the moral framework employed comes to constitute the consultation as a kind of trial for the patient in which she is to be held accountable for her actions. It should be stressed that the medical staff here are aware of the possible negative consequences of interrogating their patients as this brief comment to a 16-year-old makes clear:

(NT:15.1)
D: How would you like us to carry out these clinic visits? Sometimes we feel like
      policemen

The medical staff become policemen as an unintended consequence of their desire to recognize their patients' autonomy, while being committed to their professional role of the detection and treatment of disease. A technical advance, in the form of the glycosylated hemoglobin test, has highlighted the potential conflict between self-regulation of diabetes and medical control. On the surface, the test gives useful information about blood-sugar levels over a two-month period. In practice, it underlines the ability of medical staff to "see through" patients' behavior and to dispense praise or blame.

3. Family Relations

As Strong (1979) has argued, most British NHS consultations take on a "bureaucratic" format in which doctors limit themselves to highly specialized functions. In this format, the "body" is an appropriate topic for medical discourse, family relations are not. This split between public and private realms helps to explain why, until recently, casualty doctors seemed reluctant to enquire too deeply into the causes of children's injuries.

In these clinics, family relations were topicalized in 14 out of 33 consultations. This breaching of the bureaucratic format seems to arise because of the recognition by medical staff that their inadvertent "policing" of patients may mirror, on a smaller scale, what is happening in the home. While doctors *can* limit their involvement with their patient to purely bureaucratic forms, no such space is available to parents. Cultural norms of parental responsibility, revealed most clearly when they are infringed (as in child abuse cases), are given an added twist by the issues of diet, testing, and injecting that are the responsibilities of the diabetic child/parent. When children stray from "the straight and narrow" responsible adults must intervene:

(NT:16.10)
D: If Tessa is going on the straight and narrow, we'll see her again in four months

Being responsible means sternness and policing when appropriate:

(NT:18.9)
[*Discussion of health visitor's daughter's work, checking up on Youth Opportunity Scheme participants*]
D: So your daughter has to act as a policeman
HV: Just like Mum
M: Sometimes you do have to be a bit stern

In such circumstances, the space that society demands be given for teenagers to develop their autonomy can be circumvented by the fulfillment of proper adult responsibilities. The uneasy tension between these conflicting demands is neatly brought out in this exchange:

(NT:16.10)
[*The doctor is considering what to do about Tessa, aged 15, whose control "isn't so good"*]
M: She's a big girl
D: She's in-between. There's a bit of her wanting you to take an interest
M: Oh I do. For her own sake. She's growing up fast

Using the insight he has gained in trying to walk the tightrope between autonomy and control, the doctor here tries to act as a kind of honest broker. This sometimes involves elliptical attempts to ask teenagers about family relations:

(NT:17.7)
J = June
[Doctor has just gone out to speak to June's mother after June had said she didn't want her to attend the consultation]
D: Sounds like you're having a tough time with your Mum
J: She keeps me in
      [...]
D: I'm going to talk to your Mum about not getting on to you about your diabetes

An alternative strategy is to encourage the patient to negotiate an agreement with the family, while the doctor keeps out of the picture. For instance, after Martin (M) has conceded that his poor control might be because he is "digging in his heels" with his Mum:

(NT:15.1)
D: So would it be worth having an agreement with your Mum and Dad about your diabetes?
M: Yes, it doesn't work when they start the discussion
     [...]
D: OK so I think the most important thing to do is to discuss this with your parents
     [...]
D: I think the best thing is for us not to have any communication with your parents, not to go behind your back plotting to get the better of you

In cases like this, the doctor moves entirely beyond the limits of a purely organic version of medicine, surveying and interviewing in family relations. Ironically, just like parents he must find a middle ground between futile nagging and what society would see as an "irresponsible" laissez-faire attitude.[4]

4. Psychology

It is likely that doctors generally prefer to stay with an organic version of medicine partly because it is their own safe territory and also because of the intractable problems of the social and psychological world protected, as it is, by the British norm of politeness. This doctor goes further than most by enquiring into family relations. However, total surveillance would require investigation of the teenager's psychology. Only rarely is this explored here—understandably, given the lack of response shown in this example with Rajiv (R), aged 14:

(NT:19.1)
D: Do you like coming here?
R: No
D: Why not?
     [*Rajiv shrugs his shoulders*]
D: Is it because we embarrass you?
     [*No response and the doctor changes the subject*]

---

[4] Phil Strong has noted that, in American hospitals, adolescents are not seen alone and it is normal for parents to attend until the age of eighteen. Hence, a doctor–parent alliance may be much more common in American practice.

At the suburban clinic, where there is barely any questioning of patients' motives, an exception arose when one patient, Joan (J) aged 14, was visibly very miserable, having been told that her insulin dosage was to be increased. The doctor tries to elicit some explanation without success and changes the subject:

(S:12.2)
M = Mother J = Joan
D: You don't look so happy about it. What's the matter?
J: [*looking down*] Nothing
D: Any hypos at all?
      [*no response*]
D: Are you a bit cross about the number of tests you're having to do recently?
J: No
      [...]
D: The blood sugar is really too high
      [*Joan looking miserable*]
M: We have to fight this all the way
D: One or two units, does this really upset you?
      [*Joan is looking down and fiddling with her coat*]
D: All I want to do is to increase your morning Monotard to 28 and the evening we'll just increase the Actrapid. That'll just get things over. Make them a little smoother
      [*Joan is crying*]
D: Is it the volume in the needle?
      [*Joan is still crying*]
D: [*discusses injection sites with Joan's mother*]

As Joan's mother says, "we have to fight this all the way." When it comes to understanding teenagers, or still worse, encouraging particular courses of action, doctors and parents may make little progress. In this situation, it is tempting to treat the norm that encourages teenagers' own autonomy ("learning by experience") as an escape clause freeing adults from the responsibility of intervening in the child's life.

5. Negotiations

One way of balancing the demands of autonomy and responsibility is to negotiate a "contract" based on balancing the patient's perceived needs with the adult's knowledge of the consequences of courses of action (or inaction). Earlier, we saw the doctor in the new town clinic suggesting that his patient come to such an "agreement" with his parents. In a majority of these consultations, 18 out of 33, a negotiating format is used to work out the patient's own treatment of their diabetes, particularly their program of testing. In this case, a contract looks very much like a last resort:

(NH:17.7)

J = June

D: What should we do about your diabetes? Because you've not been doing your
      testing
      [*no response*]

D: I know at the moment you're feeling sad all this altogether

J: Don't know

D: Would it help if we got off your back?
      [*no response*]

D: Can we make a deal? If you will do some testing twice a week for two weeks. If at
      the end of that four lots of testing P (health visitor) can see you

It is unclear here whether June is a partner to this agreement. In this other
example, Tessa seems actively opposed:

(NT:16.10)

T = Tessa

D: I think you ought to have a realistic plan. Twice a week, three times a day. What do
      you think? Isn't that a bit more realistic for you?

T: [*shrugs*]

D: I'm being generous

Only in one case is the testing program genuinely self-imposed:

(NT:18.1)

M = Martin

D: Well, what sort of testing would you like to do? Something that's realistic to you

M: Well I could do . . . (suggests testing routine)

D: OK so you think that's reasonable

I will shortly look at the policy implications of patient-defined or negotiated
programs. Compared to the built-in conflict between purely formal assertions of
the patient's autonomy or theoreticity and consultations which come to take on a
policing function, negotiation seems to offer one practical solution to the doctor's
(and parents') dilemma.

Given these dilemmas, how do the doctors I have observed cope? Table 3
shows the varying policy directions used by a New Town doctor with four of the
patients on whom I have data from several consultations. In all cases, "control"
improved during the period of the study, although I would make no claims about
the representativeness of these four cases. In each case, some attempt at
negotiation of testing or treatment was made but this sometimes occurred side-
by-side with a policing role. Despite great efforts, little seems to have been
achieved, from the doctor's point of view, in improving family relations or in
understanding the patient's motives.

TABLE 3: Medical Interventions over Several Consultations

Patient	Age	Consultation Number	History	Form of Intervention
Murray	14½	(1)	Lives in Children's Home Poor glycosylated hemoglobin test results	Interrogation about conflict with Murray's own test figures.
	15	(2)	Better glycosylated hemoglobin result Doing more testing	Statement that diabetes Murray's own problem Negotiation of testing program Modest congratulations
Aidan	13	(1)	ESN but has come on own today Poor control	Short consultation Aidan leaves in tears after refusing blood test Attempts to convince Aidan to do more testing
		(2)	Mother present Control still poor	Persuades reluctant mother to increase insulin amounts Attempts to convince Aidan to do more testing
		(3)	Been in casualty after a hypo Control better	Negotiates admission to Ward
		(4)	Mother concerned about his mental and physical well-being	
Martin	16	(1)	Problematic control Lack of regular testing	Interrogation Statement that diabetes is Martin's own problem Suggests Hg test
		(2)	Glycosylated hemoglobin test result poor	Exploration of Martin's feelings and of family 'nagging'—suggests Martin discusses it with them Negotiation of testing program
		(3)	Glycosylated hemoglobin result slightly better Family relations not improved	Encouragement of Martin to change his insulin dose himself Re-assurance about hypos
June	16	(1)	God control but poor testing Rows with mother	Negotiates testing program Encouragement to adjust dosage herself
		(2)	Just had hypo More rows with mother	Exploration of eating habits Negotiation of revised testing program Unsuccessful attempt to explore family relations
		(3)	Glycosylated hemoglobin test indicates better control Not kept to testing 'contract'	Encouragement to adjust insulin dosage herself Re-assurance about hypos

STYLES OF DIABETES CARE

The "negotiating" style just discussed was unique to the new town clinic. I will conclude this description of the clinics with an attempt to depict three contrasting styles of diabetes care which I observed in both clinics. Each may be seen as an attempt to cope with the dilemmas just considered.

1. Policing

Here the emphasis is on getting good data about the patient's control through investigating the "truth" of the patient's own figures. An attempt is made to impose rules of good behavior. Two consultations with Gordon, aged 15, illustrate this policing style. Although Gordon has taken the initiative to vary his own insulin levels between consultations, the doctor concentrates on criticizing him for his smoking habit and pointing out his poor blood test results. The following sequence about Gordon's testing program illustrates well the investigative stance that the doctor takes. Although Gordon is not actually accused of lying, the doctor's skepticism will be readily apparent:

(NT:19.3)
G = Gordon
D: Are you doing them one a day or are you doing them...
G: Two or three a day
D: Two or three *every day*?
G: Well not *every* day
D: Hh hmm
G: You know something like (2.0 second pause) one day, miss a day and then again (1.00 second pause)
D: Uh I mean I'm impressed. I've not er been critical er been impressed if you've been doing these

2. Avoidance

Another way of handling the dilemmas of caring for these patients is to stay largely in the traditional organic realm of medicine, to concentrate on diagnosing and prescribing and to avoid recognizing psychological and social issues. The consultation at the suburban clinic tended to take this form. As Table 4 shows, the distinct interactional forms present in the new town clinic were found much less frequently here.

Three factors may explain these contrasting figures. First, unlike the new town consultations, they were not part of a "special" clinic set aside for problem cases. It may have been, then, that the patients seen here did not have the kinds

TABLE 4   Interactional Forms at Two Clinics

Form	Suburban Clinic (n = 14)	New Town Clinic (n = 33)
Attribution of theoreticity	4	23
Moral framework	6	28
Discussion of family relations	0	14
Discussion of patient's psychology	1	3
Negotiating format	2	18

of problems that would justify a departure from the normal (limited) medical role. Certainly, as already noted, the mean length of consultations was only half that at the new town clinic. Second, there was no separate adolescents' clinic here. Given a patient load where a baby may be followed by a 17-year-old, it may be difficult for doctors to switch to a more open-ended role. Finally, during the period of observation, three different doctors (a consultant, a registrar, and a locum) saw patients. Consequently, as is often the case in hospital practice, doctors lacked continuous contact over time with patients. This may have led to an imperfect overall picture of the patient's circumstances which would already have been limited by the lack of a health visitor with home contact with the families. The consultation with Joan (on p. 226) is a good example of how doctors at the suburban clinic do not pursue family and psychological issues to a very great extent. Even with some evidence of problems in this area, the consultation lasts the standard 12 minutes, during which there is only a limited attempt to explore the source of these problems. (Note that this is not to imply that this is necessarily a flawed consultation. Quite apart from the dubious politics of surveillance, there is little evidence that the greater involvement of the new town doctor in these matters has any outcome which the suburban doctor would regard as positive.)

3. Self-Regulation

Although the usually stated aim of diabetes care is patient self-regulation, we have already seen the dilemmas that this can create for doctors. Nevertheless in one or two consultations we see the doctor attempting to allow the patient to define her own version of the "problem and its management." Where the discussion is based on the patient's expressed needs, then policing ceases to be appropriate.

Tessa, aged 15, has poor control of her diabetes. At the first consultation I observed an attempt was made to get her to suggest a program of testing that she could live with. Six months afterwards, it was not clear that she had kept to it and her control was still not good. Although there is little attempt to check the veracity of the figures recorded in her book, the consultation concentrates on asking Tessa to specify her feelings about her control and about what she would like to do about changing her monitoring pattern and dosage. It becomes clear that Tessa would like to do more but she is scared to alter her dosage on her own. Consequently, Tessa (T) requests help:

D: But you need to get some information to help you make the decision eh love?
T: I'd rather someone help me so I'd know what I was doing

and a little later:

(NT:2.4)
HV: Wouldn't it be worth you finding out for yourself which bit needs putting up?
T: It would yeah (2.0 seconds pause) but I'm still gonna need help.

Here medical control is re-established but on the basis of the patient's own request. The patient is encouraged about the prospects of successful control and a new testing program is negotiated on the basis of options offered by the doctor. The consultation lasts 27 minutes, slightly longer than the average for this clinic.

REFORMING THE CLINIC?

Despite my emphasis on the dilemmas and problems in these consultations, it is important to stress that, by the standards of the literature, the new town clinic is an example of good practice. In particular, the style of "self-regulation" follows very closely the approach recently recommended by two U.S. pediatricians, offering:

realistic, direct discussions...between the health professional and the teenager, discussions that empathize with the adolescent, acknowledge his feelings of difference (and) encourage appropriate experimentation with the regulation of his own therapy program. (Cerreto and Travis, 1984:706).

Moreover, the negotiating format we have observed fits neatly with psychological theories of compliance, as advocated by Rosenbloom (1984). By offering realistic goals, rather than by making unrealistic demands, a vicious circle of resistance is avoided and compliance, he maintains, is more likely (Figure 1).

Outside the consultation the new town clinic offer a support system which is fully in accord with current medical thinking. In particular, the use of a health visitor (cf. Jones, 1983) who maintains a link between the hospital and the home and who coordinates an educational program for her clients (cf. Cerreto and. Travis, 1984). This offers not only essential information on diet and the

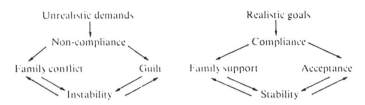

FIGURE 1   Consulting Styles and Patient Response (adapted from Rosenbloom, 1984: 112–13)

practicalities of testing and injecting but competitions and holidays organized through the British Diabetic Association.

Up till this point, it would appear that we are faced with an easy choice between two practices. This may be simply illustrated in Figure 2.

Practice A looks like the "old-fashioned" version of organic medicine. It treats the patient as passive and seeks to impose medically defined outcomes. Conversely, Practice B has excellent "progressive" credentials. It represents a newly emerging "whole person medicine," based on the latest psychological thinking, which respects patients' own expertise and self-knowledge.

It would now follow that the difficulties and conflicts generated in the new town clinic arise from the imperfect adoption by the doctor of Practice B. If only he could remove the traces of "old-fashioned" organic medicine from his questions, he would avoid these conflicts and offer a self-maintained form of diabetic control. This, indeed, was the doctor's response to reading a first draft of this chapter. At subsequent clinics, he was observed to stick much more consistently to the "progressive" line. Instead of announcing test figures and querying patients' accounts, he was much more likely to stick to a negotiating format in which patients were actively involved in requesting information and making decisions.

Unfortunately, there are at least two reasons why matters are not quite so simple. First, medicine is constituted by a distinctive (albeit changing) body of knowledge associated with a set of clinical routines. To ask of medicine that it

Practice A		Practice B
Moral charges	versus	Emphasizing patient's choices
Policing/the search for truth	versus	Negotiating contracts
Surveillance	versus	Self-regulation

FIGURE 2   Two Styles of Medical Intervention

should cease to survey objectified bodies or give up its search for hidden truths concealed in organic processes is to demand that medicine should dissolve itself. This, of course, would be unacceptable not only to doctors but also to lay people who demand of medicine precisely that it should provide such truths. This, then, is why, against all his best intentions, traces of what I have called Practice A remained in the new town doctor's behavior. Despite all the latest psychological texts that lined his consulting room, despite what he took to be the advice of a researcher offered access for that very purpose, he could not constitute doctoring entirely as nondirective therapy.

The second complication arises from a problem I have already noted. I pointed out that attributions of theoreticity are doubled-edged. On the one hand, the theoretic subject is free to respond and choose. On the other, she if *forced* to respond and to choose and is held accountable for those responses and choices. So the greater involvement of the patient in the consultation is both emancipating and constraining. The mistake is to treat surveillance purely as a function of professionals treating patients as *objects* of the clinical gaze. Surveillance works no less efficiently when we are constituted as free *subjects* whose freedom includes the obligation to survey ourselves. A brief return to one consultation will, I hope, illustrate what I mean.

THE NORMAL, FREE SUBJECT

We are in the society of the teacher–judge, the doctor–judge, the educator–judge, the "social-worker"–judge; it is on them that the universal reign of the normative is based; and each individual, wherever he may find himself, subjects to it his body, his gestures, his behavior, his aptitudes, his achievements. (Foucault 1979:304).

What Foucault calls "the universal reign of the normative" refers to how effects of power are least visible when free subjects define and assess themselves through professionally defined bodies of knowledge. In the consultation discussed below, the patient volunteers versions of his behavior and motivation based on socially approved standards. Moreover, the doctor largely avoids overt policing. Instead, he offers the opportunity for the patient himself to produce the professionally desired response which the doctor then supports and reinforces.

Gordon, aged 15½, is one of the "problem patients" seen in the new town clinic. He lives with his divorced mother and during the consultation reveals that his older brother—also a diabetic—has left home and cannot be traced. His diabetic control has been defined as poor. Here is an extract from early on in the consultation following three minutes of assessment and discussion of Gordon's (G) height and weight:

(NT:19.3)

D: OK (4.0) When we (0.5) did your blood test last time in September (0.5) the level
      was (0.5) *not* terribly good. I mean it wasn't (0.5) the worst level we've seen but it
      could be better

G: Yes

D: That's why and we made some changes with your doses last time

G: Yeah

D: And I thought it would be useful to check it again to see whether there's been any
      improvement. Okay?

G: Yeah

*D: Do you think the control's better?

*G: Yes I do

In *Discipline and Punish*, Foucault (1979) describes how the "individual"
emerged past the threshold of description. For modern medicine (law, prison
administration, social work), each individual becomes a "case" and the case:

> is no longer, as in casuistry or jurisprudence, a set of circumstances defining an act
> and capable of modifying the application of a rule; it is the individual as he may be
> described, judged, measured, compared with others, in his very individuality.
> (Foucault 1979:191)

So the details of Gordon's blood sugars must be carefully measured and his
individual needs for insulin closely assessed. But surveillance and expert
decision making are alone insufficient. This version of modern medicine "not
only alllows the patient to speak as an experiencing person but needs, demands
and incites him to speak" (Arney and Bergen 1984:46). Gordon himself must
speak about his diabetic control. All the clinical tests in the world are
insufficient without Gordon's own participation and self-assessment (in the
asterisked exchange). So Gordon is not pounded into submission or silenced;
rather he is incited to speak. He is not repressed; rather he is provided with, and
encouraged to demonstrate, his own aptitudes and skills. External surveillance
still takes place but not in order to impose purely external standards. In the
discussion of smoking, which immediately follows the previous extract, it is
clear that, as in Bentham's panopticon, all aspects of the individual are to be
made visible. But the strategy is normalization rather than repression. The
panopticon works most efficiently when the prisoner turns the warder's gaze
upon himself. Here is the relevant passage:

D: OK. Um (2.0) are you still smoking?

G: Well (1.0) not really now

D: You were smoking three or four a / day in /September

G: /yeah/yeah

D: About the same still or

G: Well (1.0) hardly ever now

D: Why?
G: I don't know, I've just stopped
D: /(   )
*G: /(   ) Well I don't get much money and I haven't got enough money to waste (0.5) really
*D: Yeah (0.5) Well I , I agree with you it is a waste and
G: Mm
D: I wouldn't it's not particularly healthy particularly for you (1.0) So you mean you smoke other people's cigarettes or (0.5) or are you, have you an occasional one of your own
G: Occasional one of me own, if someone gives me one
D: If someone else
G: Yeah (1.0) two (   ) after school (3.0)

Notice how the doctor makes no moral judgment on the "facts" as reported by Gordon. Instead, he pursues why Gordon "hardly" ever smokes. But Gordon's initial response ("I don't know, I've just stopped") does not satisfy the doctor. Gordon must provide a reason for his change of behavior and this reason must demonstrate Gordon's self-surveillance according to the appropriate moral standards. Only when (in the asterisked passage) Gordon refers to spending money on cigarettes as "a waste" does the doctor start to make moral judgments. But his moralizing draws attention to and embellishes Gordon's own formulations.

This consultation took place after the new town doctor had read an earlier draft of this chapter. As I have already noted, this was followed by an emphasis in his consultations on self-regulation (Practice B) rather than policing (Practice A). But policing does not disappear entirely. The extract concludes with an attempt by the doctor to establish the "real facts" about Gordon's smoking behavior which his earlier statement ("hardly ever") glosses over. However, Gordon's further elaboration, vague as it is, does not lead to an additional interrogation. What seems to be most important is that Gordon should speak about his smoking rather than that the "real facts" should finally be established. In what Foucault has called "the politics of truth," the facts of individual behavior are less important than the discovery and *self-recognition* of the person behind the behavior.

The doctor now elicits Gordon's current dose of insulin and expresses surprise at the amount. It appears that Gordon has adjusted his dosage himself in a reportedly successful attempt to stop bed wetting. In light of Gordon's poor control of his diabetes, the doctor implies that the dosage of one form of insulin may now be too low. But Gordon's own change of dosage is not criticized. These encounters are seen by such doctors as being concerned with encouraging self-regulation by the patient. When, towards the end of the consultation, the doctor suggests an increase in insulin, Gordon is asked to assess himself ("if you find that they've not been satisfactory"). All he is expected to do is to call the health visitor to discuss "how you're going to change them again."

Immediately after Gordon's revelation of his self-assessed change of insulin dosage, the doctor learns that Gordon has left behind his testing book containing the results of his home tests of blood and urine.

D: Um (0.5) have you got some tests there?
G: I left them at home this morning because I was doing I *done* an exam today and I was in a bit of a panic
D: Oh dear what exam was that?
      [*discussion of exam and Gordon's performance in it*]

Unlike many of the earlier consultations, there is no suggestion that the doctor is policing the patient. Gordon's account goes completely unchallenged, despite the already stated medical view that patients' records are unreliable and likely to be "cooked." Instead, the doctor simply asks for Gordon's own recollection of his test results (in a passage a part of which was discussed earlier):

D: *Okay* (0.5) so what sort of results are you getting then?
G: Well ( ) average between ten and six (1.0) not too bad
D: Blood blood sugars you're talking/about?
G: /Yeah blood sugars
D: When when are you doing them mostly?
G: *Well* I'm doing them before my breakfast, before my tea and er (   ) now and again I'm doing them before bed and weekends I'm doing them at dinner time and that
D: Are you doing them one a day or are you doing them
G: Two to three a day
*D: Two or three *every day*?
G: Well not *every* day
D: Hh hmmm
G: You know something like (2.0) one day miss a day and then again (1.0)
*D: Uh I mean I'm impressed. I've not er been critical er been impressed if you've been/doing these (   )
G: / well I realised (0.5) if I done as I've been told and that then I feel a lot better inside
D: Do you? Do you/really?
G: /yeah
D: Feel more energetic
G: Better than, it's better than / feeling
D: /Mm. But er so the results are all between six what did you say?
G: Between six and ten but sometimes it goes over ten /it depends
D: /Mm
G: What I'm doing really

In the asterisked utterances, the doctor clearly does revert to the policing role found in his earlier consultations. Gordon's story of his testing regimen is closely interrogated ("if you've been doing these"). However, the interrogation melts away with Gordon's revelation that "I feel a lot better inside" if "I done as I've been told." The doctor cannot restrain his admiration ("Do you? Do you really?"). Gordon is saying that he has internalized the medical model: he surveys himself.

I am reminded of Foucault's statement of the major effect of the panopticon:

> to induce in the inmate a state of conscious and permanent visibility that assures *the automatic functioning of power*. So to arrange things that the surveillance is permanent in its effects, even if it is discontinuous in its action; that the perfection of power should tend to render its actual exercise unnecessary; that this architectural apparatus should be a machine for creating and sustaining a power relation independent of the person who exercises it; in short, that the inmates should be caught up in a power situation of which *they themselves are the bearers'*. (Foucault 1979:201; my emphasis).

PRACTICAL IMPLICATIONS

At this point, we seem to have come full circle. Reforming the clinic merely appears to reinstate new and, perhaps more subtle, strategies of power. This can be underlined by a brief review of each of the three areas where reforms in diabetic care have been suggested: namely, changing doctors' consulting styles, broadening the care team, and introducing patient support groups.

1. Changing Consulting Styles

I have already noted the new town clinic doctor's change from a "policing" to a "self-regulating" style. This is fully in accord with the suggestions made by the psychologists Gillespie and Bradley (1983). They reject what they call "the traditional confrontational interview" where the patient is told the problem and the solution(s): if the patient fails to comply, then he is defined as "at fault." Gillespie and Bradley call instead for a "motivation enhancing interview." Here, for instance, the doctor enquires what problems the patient herself has perceived with her diabetes, what she proposes to do about it, and whether she would like to see the results of laboratory tests.

Unfortunately, this returns us again to Foucault's "power situation of which they (in this case the patients) are the bearers." For discipline as a modality of power is not geared to repression but to the inculcation of aptitude and skills (Foucault 1979: Part IV, Chapter 3). It is precisely concerned with the person behind the act and is economical and subtle in its functioning. Indeed it is in just such a disciplinary framework that one would expect doctors and psychologists to carry out experiments to alter behavior and to correct and train individuals. The modern clinic, like the modern prison, is very much a laboratory of power and Gillespie and Bradley's well-meaning proposals resemble those of laboratory experimenters.

2. Broadening the Care Team

There is a broadening conventional wisdom that chronic patients, such as diabetics, need support outside the clinic setting. For instance, Aiken (1976) argues that doctors tend to focus on immediate symptoms and give less attention to the long-term care and adjustment needs of chronically ill patients. She proposes that nurse practitioners can play a useful supporting role, visiting patients in their home to offer a friendly ear and serving as a patient-advocate in the clinic.

The work of the health visitor in the new town approximates this model. Her role did not seem to be defined as intrusive by either patients or families and she was observed to function as the kind of ombudsman suggested by Aiken. Certainly, the kind of role is less contestable than the suggested involvement of child psychiatrists (Smith et al. 1984) or the practice of family therapy (Cerreto and Travis 1984), both of which seem to constitute diabetic people as a deviant or problem group. However, friendly home visitors also clearly function as part of the medical team. They are both patient-advocates and also an additional clinic eye and ear. Broadening the care "team" also therefore broadens the surveillance of the patient inside and outside the consulting room.

3. Support Groups

An alternative program would seek to minimize professional involvement and to maximize self-help using peer-group support. One example is provided by the Young Leaders scheme used in Edinburgh (Steel 1985): Patients with good control are offered an adventure holiday together and asked to offer support to their peers when they return.

As Arney and Bergen (1984) note, the support group offers a face of medicine as "unobtrusive, humane, even liberating" (p. 107). At the same time, however, it synthesizes all aspects of the techniques of normalization. It allows individuality to be aired without judgment and enables experts, armed with knowledge of "the trajectories that constitute the good life," to make the anxieties of the patient inert through normalization and positive imagery. For Arney and Bergen, then, following Foucault, the support group is not an alternative to medical power, it is the new form of medical power:

> the form that ties together the two lines of modern medical thought—that which
> individualizes and that which maps—and the form that joins together the

individual, with his or her unique special concerns and problems, and the expert whose knowledge is redemptive. (pp. 107–168)

By now, readers with a practical involvement in diabetic care may be more than a little frustrated. Is any attempt to change care doomed to undermine professional power?

The social control functions of the old-style medicine of "policing" are immediately apparent. Yet it is now being argued that the new-style psychology of autonomy and self-expression creates a more subtle practice of "normalization." So the links between knowledge and power do not go away but merely take different forms.

This is not, however, just an account of how two pediatricians happen to run their clinics. The practices we have observed here are the end-product of a network of historical and institutional processes. Doctors are expected to be concerned about, say, kidney failure or blindness in diabetic people because their task, in part, is surveying objectified bodies. Especially where these patients are young, we demand that doctors act responsibility towards them. For instance, even the most noninterventionist strategies of diabetic care (e.g., Kinmonth 1985) draw the line when the patient's life is threatened. It is wrong, then, to criticize medicine as a form of social control when that is partly what it is.[5] Similarly, if we expect that "adolescents" or "young adults" should replace their parents as the source of accounts and opinions, it is because of widely diffused assumptions about the rights attached to advancing years.

The strains between Practice A and B in the new town clinic are the outcome of such historically sedimented factors. On the one hand, the doctor has to be responsive to the psychological development and well-being of his patients. As in education's "child-care" pedagogy (Walkerdine 1984), pediatrics wants to concern itself with the "monitoring...and facilitation of individual psychological capacities" (p. 162). On the other hand, modern high-technology medical practice must be receptive to "objective" assessments like the GHg test and to their implications for treatment.

It is not, then, as if doctors face a choice between such practices. Although the new town doctor may give rather more emphasis to overtly psychological strategies than the suburban doctor, both constitute their work through notions of responsibility *and* autonomy.

It would be entirely wrong, however, to view such notions and strategies as ideologies which should be stripped away to allow all concerned to express themselves more "authentically." Real subjects are constituted in discourses and these discourses, in turn, are predicated on institutionalized practices in medicine and education. As Walkerdine has put it in relation to the child-centered pedagogy:

---

[5] I am grateful to Robert Dingwall for this way of expressing the argument.

Neither the child nor the individual can be liberated by a medical stripping away of the layers of the social. Such a model assumes a psychological subject laid bare to be reformed in the new order. But if social practices are central to the very formation of subjectivity the laying bare is an impossibility...there is no pre-existent subject to liberate. (1984:195)

So the dilemmas of medical practice are not to be resolved by constructing a new counter-discourse without any grounding in institutions or subjects. Nor does it pay to assume that any one existing discourse, such as "child centeredness," is intrinsically more liberating than any other.

It is always a questions of the relation between discourses which, in themselves, have no intrinsic value. As Foucault recognized, challenges to strategies of power arise within the very subject positions (or voices) that such discourses create. So a patient can interrupt a discourse of autonomy by a discourse of responsibility, demanding advice rather than self-expression as in the following exchange considered earlier:

HV: Wouldn't it be worth you finding out for yourself which bit needs putting up?
T: It would yeah (2.0) but I'm still gonna need help.

Here Tessa unknowingly follows Deleuze and Guattari's (1981) injunction: She makes a line not a point, she does not sow but grafts.

REFERENCES CITED

AIKEN, L.H.
    1976   Chronic illness and responsive ambulatory care. *Medicine* 239–251.
ARNEY, W., AND BERGEN, B.
    1984   *Medicine and the Management of Living.* Chicago: Chicago University Press.
BRADLEY, C., ET AL.
    1984   Psychological aspects of diabetes. IN *Diabetes Annual, 1984*, K. Alberti and L. Krall, Eds. Amsterdam: Excerpta Medica.
CALLON, M.
    1986   Some elements of a sociology of translation. *Sociological Review* 32: 194–233.
CERRETO, M., AND TRAVIS, L.
    1984   Implications for psychological and family factors in the treatment of diabetes. *Pediatric Clinics of North America* 31(3): 689–710.
DELEUZE, G., AND GUATTARI, F.
    1981   Rhizomes. *Ideology and Consciousness* 8: 49–71.
FOUCAULT, M.
    1979   *The History of Sexuality* (Vol. 1). London: Allen Lane.
GILLESPIE, C. AND BRADLEY, C.
    1983   *Motivation and the person with diabetes.* Unpublished paper, Nottingham Postgraduate Centre, University Hospital.

JONES, M.
1983   Survey of diabetic children in the Yeovil area. *Health Visitor* 5(10): 378–379.
KINMOUTH, A.-L.
1985   Children into young adults. *Practical Diabetes* 2(4): 21–22.
LAVOIE, J., AND BARKER, M.
1980   Psychology of juvenile diabetics. *Union Medical of Canada* 109(2): 199–211.
MCHUGH, P.
1970   Commonsense conception of deviance. IN *Recent Sociology* (No. 2), H.P. Dreitzel, Ed. New York: Macmillan.
MITCHELL, J.C.
1983   Case and situational analysis. *Sociological Review* 31(2):187–211.
NEWTON, R.
1985   Social integration of the adolescent diabetic. *Practical Diabetes* 2(4): 25–28.
ORY, M., AND KRONENFELD, J.
1980   Living and juvenile diabetes mellitus. *Pediatric Nursing* 6(5): 47–50.
POSNER, T.
1977   Magical elements in orthodox medicines: Diabetes as a medical thought system. IN *Health Care and Health Knowledge*, R. Dingwall and C. Heath, Eds. London: Croon Helm.
ROSENBLOOM, A.
1984   Primary and subspecialty care of diabetes mellitus in children and youth. *Pediatric Clinics of North America* 31(1): 107–117.
SILVERMAN, D.
1985   *Qualitative Methodology and Sociology.* Aldershot, England: Gower.
SMITH, M., STRANG, S., AND BAUM, J.
1984   Organization of a diabetic clinic for children. *Practical Diabetes* 1(1): 8–12.
STEEL, J.
1985   Evolution of adolescent diabetic care in Edinburgh. *Practical Diabetes* 2(4): 29–30.
STRONG, P.
1979   *The Ceremonial Order of the Clinic.* London: Routledge.
SZASZ, T., AND HOLLANDER, M.
1956   A contribution to the philosophy of medicine. *A.M.A. Archives of Internal Medicine* 47: 585–592.
WALKERDINE, V.
1984   Developmental psychology and the child-centered pedagogy. IN *Changing the Subject*, H. Holloway, Unwin, Venn, and V. Walkerdine, Eds. London: Methuen.

10

Nice Doctors and Invisible Patients: The Problem of Power in Feminist Common Sense*

Kathy Davis

INTRODUCTION

Despite the obvious centrality of power for understanding gender relations, its conceptualization can be an endeavor fraught with problems. In this chapter, I shall be exploring some of the difficulties involved in conceptualizing power, taking my own field of inquiry; namely, the interaction between women and men in medical encounters, as a case in point (Davis 1988b). I will be dealing with problems with power on three levels:

1. *Power as a conceptual problem* or how power should be theorized in interaction, in general, and medical consultations, in particular.
2. *Power as an empirical problem* or the way power works in the interaction between male doctors and female patients.
3. *Power as a problem for feminist theory* or how power works in gender relations.

---

* I would like to thank Willem de Haan for his helpful comments on various drafts of this chapter, and Sue Fisher and Alexandra Todd for waiting so patiently for it to arrive.

After taking a critical look at how power is conceptualized within social theory as well as feminist studies on interaction between the sexes, I shall direct my attention at two specific difficulties I encountered in trying to uncover the workings of power in medical consultations between male doctors and female patients; namely, the problem of the Nice Doctor and the problem of the Invisible Patient. By showing what made these instances problematic for the analysis of power in medical consultations, an attempt will be made to clarify some more general issues involved in conceptualizing power at the level of interaction. Finally, I will show how what might be called our feminist common sense not only facilitates, but also sometimes gets in the way of understanding how power works in gender relations. Some suggestions will be made for how this common sense might be elaborated to provide more adequate feminist accounts of power asymmetries in encounters between the sexes.

CONCEPTUALIZING POWER: "ANYTHING GOES"

For any (feminist) social scientist interested in power, it might seem a reasonable first step to take a look at how others have tackled the subject. However, even the briefest of looks will be enough to convince her that contemporary social theory on power is in a state bordering on utter confusion. Despite massive theorizing concerning the "nature of the beast," there appears to be little agreement as to how it should be defined. As Stephen Lukes (1982), himself a leading theorist on power, has noted: When it comes to power, one is left with the unavoidable impression that "anything goes."[1]

What does this mean for our feminist social scientist wanting to investigate power in some specific area of social life and hoping to find some assistance from social theories on power? For starters, she will be in for a rude awakening. Expecting theoretical clarification about the nature and workings of power, she will encounter instead a veritable conceptual jungle—from the classic theorist on power Hobbs or, a bit later, Weber and Marx, to the more modern scholars Parsons, Ahrendt, Foucault, Bourdieu, Habermas, Giddens, and Lukes. The list is dizzyingly long and, whereas each theory has much to say for itself, the issue of what power actually is remains to be resolved. Power is and presumably will

---

[1] For example, power is something which is possessed; it can only be exercised; it is a matter of authority. Power belongs to the individual, to collectivities; it doesn't belong to anyone, but is a feature of social systems. Power involves conflict; it doesn't necessarily involve conflict; it usually involves conflict, but it doesn't have to. Power presupposes resistance; it is primarily involved in compliance (to norms); it is both. Power is tied to repression and domination; it is productive and enabling. In short, power is bad, good, demonic, or just routine. For a good discussion of different conceptions of power, as well as a laudable attempt to make some sense out of the confusion, the reader is referred to Lukes (1974, 1979, 1982).

always be an "essentially contested concept" (Lukes 1979),[2] which means that the debate about power can be expected to continue indefinitely.

From the heatedly debated difficulties around the conceptualization of power, here are three which I was also confronted with in my own particular inquiry into how power works in medical consultations between male doctors and female patients.

First of all, most social theories provide disembodied conceptions of power— conceptions which are devoid of any connection to concrete social contexts or the actual situated social practices of the people involved. Take, for example, Foucault's famous definition of power:

> Something which circulates, . . . something which only functions in the form of a chain. It is never localized here or there, never in anybody's hands, never appropriated as a commodity or piece of wealth. Power is employed and exercised through a net-like organization . . . individuals circulate between its threads; they are . . . the vehicles of power, not its points of application. (1980:98)

A set of general features is provided, describing what power is all about. What is neglected, however, is how this "something which circulates" or its "net-like organization" is to be located in the empirical world. Foucault is, by no means, an exception. Although theorists on power are notoriously adept at displaying the merits of their own conception of power *vis à vis* other conceptions of power, these all-important theoretical differences do not provide secure guidelines for deciding which conception will meet the requirements of an investigation into power in a specific setting. And, even if the investigator is lucky enough to find something resembling one of the available definitions of power, she may still wonder how she should proceed to analyze it.

A second problem is that power tends to be treated as an exclusively "macro" issue (Knorr-Cetina 1981); that is, something belonging to social structures, institutional orders, professional pyramids, or social movements, rather than everyday encounters or the more routine occurrences of social life. If power is about individuals at all, it's about heads of state, corporate managers, or prison wardens, rather than housewives, grandmothers, or cashiers. Power is rarely viewed as having to do with the more humble particulars of everyday life.

---

[2] Borrowing from Gallie's (1956) formulation of concepts which are essentially open to dispute, Lukes says of power: any given interpretation or conception of it is inextricably tied to further background assumptions which are methodological and epistemological, but also moral and political assumptions, which themselves partly govern which reasons count in favor of one conception rather than another. Thus it is that there can be disputes about the proper use of the concept of power which are both "endless" and "perfectly genuine," different uses serving "different though of course not altogether unrelated functions" for different social groups, and contending positions "sustained by perfectly respectable arguments and evidence." (1979:262)

These two theoretical problems, that is, the conceptualization of power as a disembodied and as a macro-phenomenon, give rise to a third, methodological problem. Even those social scientists who do believe that power is not simply "out there" in the social order, but can be discovered at the level of face-to-face interaction as well, will find themselves confined to methodologies which are not amenable to the study of power. A case in point is conversation analysis. Studies within this tradition have been concerned with mundane reasoning processes and how ordinary people engage in social practices using talk as a medium (Sacks, Schegloff, & Jefferson 1974; Atkinson & Heritage 1984; Heritage 1985). Whereas conversation analysis provides the methodological tools for the microanalysis of social life, power is rarely included among the topics deemed suitable for investigation.[3] Social interaction tends to be viewed as an essentially orderly and harmonious enterprise—a cooperative co-production, involving the activities of all participants. These participants, otherwise referred to as "members," are regarded as having access to the same kinds of interactional resources for engaging in social interaction. As peers in the interaction game, they do not seem to have a gender or any of the other accouterments of asymmetrical power relationships.

Given these theoretical and methodological difficulties, the conclusion is unavoidable that the problem of how power should be conceptualized in interaction or, for that matter, in encounters between the sexes, cannot be solved in advance. However coherent theories of power may be on paper, they simply do not provide the necessary guidelines for locating and delineating power in the concrete contexts of everyday life. Methodologies for analyzing social interaction are not much help in this respect either. Thus, the would-be analyst of power may find herself having little choice but to tackle the problem of power in the empirical analysis itself.

POWER IN INTERACTION BETWEEN THE SEXES

Various feminist scholars have drawn attention to power inequalities in the interaction between men and women in diverse social contexts: private conversations between couples and mixed groups (Zimmerman & West 1975; Henley 1977; Fishman 1978), the public arena of television talk shows and meetings (Trömel-Plötz 1984), and institutional settings like medical consultations, psychotherapy, courts, and classrooms (Fisher & Todd 1983, 1986; West 1984; Davis 1986; Fisher 1986; Todd 1989). What they discovered, quite

---

[3] In fact, Harvey Sacks, the well-known founder of conversation analysis, launched his new method of inquiry by warning social scientists to stay away from what he called the "big issues" of the social sciences if they wanted to get really objective descriptions of talk (Sacks 1984). Power apparently fell under that heading.

simply, was that where gender was a part of the interaction, power was soon to follow. An explicit attempt was made to uncover how the asymmetrical power relations between men and women were being constructed within and through their talk.

In most cases, this was accomplished by studying the sequential organization of the conversations and by showing how women and men do not have equal access to the interactional resources for ordering that talk. The findings will come as no great surprise. It would seem that men have a tendency to hog the conversational floor. They get their topics initiated and talked about more often, interrupt with equanimity, and are notably reticent about performing the "interactional shit-work" (Fishman 1978) which is necessary for any conversation if it is to proceed in a pleasant and well-oiled fashion. Just as unsurprisingly, women seem to have considerable difficulty getting the floor. Once they do, their topics tend to get broken off mid-stream or are taken over by others. They are subject to constant interruption and are rarely the recipients of "interactional shit-work," but rather the ones who do it.

Whereas these studies are very different in terms of their subject matter and their theoretical underpinnings, they have primarily two things to tell us about power in the face-to-face interaction between the sexes.

First, conversational power is something that men have and women do not.

Second, power relations between the sexes in conversational contexts have as their most distinguishing feature control, restraint, and repression.

In other words, the model of power and gender relations being employed in feminist studies on interaction is a top-down, repressive one.

At this point, the reader, particularly if she is a feminist, may be inclined to ask: So, what's wrong with that? In fact, this model of power and gender relations does bear considerable resemblance to women's interactional experience. It would almost seem to be their conversational lot. Moreover, it is a model which has stood women in good stead as they have attempted to uncover the inequities faced in the various contexts of their everyday lives. It is also the model which I used as I embarked on my own research into the workings of power in consultations between male doctors and female patients. Whereas I do not believe that this model is entirely wrong, it has some rather serious drawbacks for explaining how power works in gender relations, including, but not limited to, the level of face-to-face interaction between the sexes.

I shall now illustrate this using two specific power problems, which I encountered in my own research.[4] The first problem will be called the problem of the Nice Doctor, and the second the problem of the Invisible Patient. Both of these problems fall under a more general category of conceptual power problems:

---

[4] For a complete account of my research, including a much more detailed empirical analysis of power than is possible in this chapter, the reader is referred to Davis (1988a, 1988b).

namely, the problem that, with power, appearances can be deceiving or that nice doctors and invisible patients, upon further examination, are not what they seem. After showing how the experience of grappling with these contradictory appearances is itself crucial for understanding how power works, some conclusions will be drawn for conceptualizing power in institutional, gendered interaction.

THE PROBLEM OF THE NICE DOCTOR

My inquiry was concerned with how women's complaints are defined, diagnosed, and treated in consultations with male general practitioners, and how asymmetrical relations of power are produced, maintained, and/or undermined in that process. The physicians were not particularly representative, being younger and better educated than the run-of-the-mill Dutch general practitioner[5]. This possible lack of representativity did not seem problematic to me at the time. I firmly believed that power asymmetries between male physicians and female patients could not be reduced to the (evil) intentions of the individual practitioner, but would be an integral feature of any encounter between the sexes. As I began listening to recorded consultations for instances of power, I expected to find the kinds of phenomena so abundantly and convincingly described in feminist literature on women and health care: physicians undermining women's control and authority over their reproduction (Arms 1975; Culpepper 1978; Ehrenreich & English 1979; Oakley 1979; Fisher 1986; Martin 1987; Todd 1989), making moralistic statements about women's roles as wives and mothers or about their sexuality (Scully & Bart 1973; Lorber 1976; Fidell 1980; Scully 1980; Standing 1980; Fisher & Groce 1985), not taking their complaints seriously (Homans 1985; McPherson 1988), finding lots of psychological disorder in even the most harmless complaint (Lennane & Lennane 1973; Davis 1986), prescribing tranquilizers at the drop of a pin (Cooperstock 1978), and so on.

Much to my surprise, however, I discovered that the GPs were behaving in an undisputedly friendly and benevolent fashion. They displayed an unflaggingly sympathetic interest in their patients' problems, even the most trivial ones. They had obviously received social skills training and were familiar with the more holistic approaches to medicine. Whereas they did prescribe quite a few tranquilizers for their female patients, it was only with great hesitancy and reluctance. In fact, it was almost as though I had wandered into a conversation

---

[5] A large corpus of audiotaped general practice consultations was made available to me by the Institute for General Practice at the Free University in Amsterdam, The Netherlands. Most of the general practitioners had received vocational training, which has only been mandatory in The Netherlands since 1973.

between two friends, rather than an institutional encounter. It did not look anything like an arena for a power struggle.

In order to allow the reader to judge for herself, however, I shall now take a closer look at one of these "nice doctors" in action.[6] It is just one example from the many others like it, which made me, as feminist analyst of power, throw up my hands in despair.

The GP in this consultation is in his early thirties and the patient is a middle-aged woman, married with two children. Upon entering the GP's office, she straightforwardly announces:

P: Sore throat and headache, that's the only thing that /(laughs)/ I h-have-

The GP proceeds to examine her throat. Upon examination, however, he is unable to find anything. The patient is perplexed ("*How* can that be, when it feels so strange" and "I wake up during the night from it, there's such pain here") and begins to elaborate on how painful her sore throat is, how long it's been going on, and how she has even been in the hospital for it. The GP listens encouragingly, as in the following segment:

P: And I think, oh well, I'll just stop *smoking* then maybe it'll go away but that doesn't work any more either ((laughs))
D: So, you've stopped smoking too?
P: Yeah. Yeah. I *don't* do that any more. Well, yeah, once and awhile one. ((distinct)) Bu- but last week, I didn't do it all week, but it ((soft)) didn't help at all, not even a little bit.
D: No?
P: Yeah.
D: Does that make you *anxious*, that feeling?

Although the GP has not been able to find anything causing the sore throat, he shows no signs of trying to get rid of the patient. On the contrary, by asking questions, he gives her the opportunity to talk about her problems, including how she feels about them. In particular, his final query opens the floor for talk about the psychological dimension of the complaint. Few modern Dutch general practitioners would leave an unidentified bodily complaint without taking at least a cursory look at the patient's psychological well-being, and this GP is no exception. And, quite right he is, as the following excerpt just a bit later, demonstrates:

---

[6] The original consultation was in Dutch, as were the transcripts from which the analysis was made. Since my point in this chapter is of a more theoretical nature, I have not analyzed this particular consultation in a detailed way here.

D: Yeah. But that you have the feeling uhh- that uhhh- god, is there something- there- or
     some-
P: -yeah I do sometimes. Because my father ((laughs)) had it in his throat, too. I think
     well, maybe I've got it, too. Do you understand, he had throat cancer, too, so I
     think, God, maybe that's what I have too, you know what I mean ((laughs))?
D: Well- after all it's a uhh- an understandable thought.

Not only does the GP seem perfectly willing to lend a sympathetic ear to the
patient's various physical symptoms, but he encourages her to dwell on any
"understandable" fears she might have that her problem is more serious than
"just" a sore throat. Moreover, he is clearly an advocate of patients' taking some
responsibility for their own health and well-being, as the following example
demonstrates:

D: What do you think? I just can't find anything unusual. When I examine you I don't
     find anything unusual. I can't see anything.
P: No. You can't see anything. No.
D: Do you just want to wait awhile?
P: Yeah?
D: Or uhh- yeah. Would you like a *pill* or something, uhh you know - if you're really
     nervous-
P: Yeah
D: uhh something - something uhh for the *nervousness*?

It is the patient's decision: She can either wait until her sore throat goes away
on its own, or she can try tranquilizers for her nervousness. Whereas the choice
is, ultimately, hers to make, his hesitant speech indicates that he himself is not
overly enthusiastic about prescribing psychotropic drugs.
   This elicits a whole new round of troubles-telling on the part of the patient
where she provides all sorts of reasons for being nervous: her children are sick,
she has to find a nursing home for her mother-in-law, and her invalid brother-in-
law calls her on the phone all the time. Whereas her husband complains about
the situation, he doesn't seem to have much to offer in the way of help other than
the suggestion that she see a doctor about her headache. The patient is having to
fit caretaking responsibilities for her own family and her husband's relatives in
with her job, and on top of all this, with a headache and sore throat. Throughout
this ongoing tale of woe, the GP clucks sympathetically ("yeah" and "Oh?"),
even trying to reassure her:

D: Yeah. You're a little ashamed about it, I get that impression.
P: Yeah. I think well uhhh-
D: Yes, but there's a difference between- between *nervousness*-
P: Yeah-
D: -and if you really have something something
P: Yeah-

D: -have a *problem*, right?-
P: -yeah, have a problem
D: -like you have that uhhh- that family member who is-
P: -yeah-
D: -seriously ill, after all.

The patient is told not to worry about being "nervous"—not with "real" problems like these. After asking whether she can talk to her husband about her current difficulties, the GP produces the following, as a final condolence:

D: Yeah. Well. You can tell your husband that it really isn't uhh-
P: -not uhhh-
D: isn't *physical*-
P: Oh.
      ((pause))
D: ((clears throat)) No. I really thought that uhhh- the *problems*-
P: -yeah, that-s what I thought too-
D: ((clears throat))-were just getting caught in your *throat*-

And, on this sympathetic note, the consultation comes to a close.

In view of such friendly interaction, the reader can probably imagine that the feminist researcher begins to wonder what happened to her research object. Power seems to have vanished altogether from this medical encounter. The GP bears little resemblance to that omnipotent and villainous representative of the male medical establishment, gracing the pages of critical feminist literature on women and health care. At this point, I might have abandoned my inquiry altogether, concluding that the problem of medical sexism no longer existed. Perhaps the exposure of male physicians to more than a decade of feminist critique had finally paid off.

I am a skeptic, however. I was not convinced that health care for women had changed that much and, indeed, I soon discovered that the niceness and empathetic concern had another, somewhat less benevolent, side as well. For example, I began to ask myself how it was possible for a patient to announce at the outset of a consultation that she had a sore throat and a headache ("the only thing I've got"), but leave with a prescription for tranquilizers just seven minutes later. Why were problems like balancing the caretaking of a family and various relatives with physical illness, the demands of a job, and a husband who wasn't providing much support a matter of her nervousness (instead, for example, of her husband's laziness)? And, finally, how was it possible for a GP, who couldn't find anything at the beginning of the consultation, to still manage a diagnosis of sorts ("problems having gotten stuck in your throat") and even a prescription by the time the consultation closed? All of this smacks of medicalization and social control; that is, the expanding jurisdiction of medicine over people's everyday lives (Ehrenreich & Ehrenreich 1978; Conrad & Schneider 1980; Riessman 1983). Women's problems with the oppressive exigencies of their lives are channeled into the safer paths of psychological disturbance (Ehrenreich & English 1979; Showalter 1985; Hearn 1987), and this seemed to be an instance of just that phenomenon.

This was enough to convince me that my feminist common sense, which told me that power would be involved in any encounter between the sexes, had not left me in the lurch after all. Armed with this conviction, I proceeded to place my "nice doctors" under the microscope, analytically speaking. This revealed all sorts of not-so-nice practices, which both supported, but also elaborated the feminist critique of how women fare in consultations with male physicians.

The very quality, which made this consultation and other consultations like it seem to be devoid of power at the beginning of the analysis, turned out to be what power was all about. Power in gender relations is not simply a matter of overt repression or coercion. On the contrary, it can have a friendly face. In fact, it is precisely this friendly face which makes power continually seem to be something else, thereby enabling a control far more extensive, subtle and, ultimately, effective than would have been possible with more obvious authoritarian means.

Having discussed some of the difficulties involved in investigating the power practices of "nice doctors," I shall now direct my attention to the second power problem which emerged in the course of my inquiry; namely, the problem of the invisible patient.

THE PROBLEM OF THE INVISIBLE PATIENT

Current studies on medical interaction tend to take the vantage point of the professional (Mishler 1984), even when the analyst is of a critical or feminist persuasion. The analysis focuses primarily on the dominant party in the interaction; that is, the doctor, with the patient taking a secondary position on the sidelines of the interaction. Her interactional activities seem to be orchestrated by the doctor. For example, she is depicted as the one supplying the "answers" to the physician's "questions" (Heath 1981; Hughes 1981, 1982; West 1984), or interrupted at the physician's convenience (West 1984). The physician controls the topicality of a consultation, with the patient, at best, producing what sociolinguists like to call a "patient-initiative" (Bliesener & Siegrist 1981). As the term itself suggests, this rarely gets beyond the most fragmentary beginning.

When the patient is a female, this pattern is aggravated by asymmetries based on gender. For example, decisions on contraception or abortion tend to be shaped by the physician, often in accordance with his stereotypic views on women (Fisher & Todd 1983, 1986; Fisher & Groce 1985; Fisher 1986; Todd 1989). The patient seems to have very little effect on what happens in the medical interview. She emerges as the inevitable recipient of his not-so-benevolent ministrations. The only time she may exercise any control over the decisions being made in the consultation is when she is "allowed to" do so by the physician. This is the case, for example, when she is middle-class and conforms with his cultural assumptions of what constitutes a "good woman" (Fisher & Groce 1985).

Although these analyses are quite different from the studies which treat power asymmetries as part of the "normal appearances" of medical talk,[7] they have one thing in common. In their commitment toward uncovering power imbalances in medical interaction, feminist investigators have focused on the physician as the locus for delineating how asymmetrical power relations are produced and reproduced in consultations with female patients. The patient's activity becomes—almost automatically, it would seem—more shadowy and less well-defined. Although the cause for this subordinate position in the interaction is attributed to "oppression" rather than "incompetence" (Hughes 1981), the outcome in terms of patient visibility is, in fact, similar. The patient's contribution to the encounter is obscured.

When I began my own analysis, I also expected the GPs to be in charge, just as physicians in these other studies had been. And, in one sense, they were. They definitely decided which topics got talked about, the form that talk would take, and, without exception, they had the last word about what was wrong with the patient and what should be done about it. They had more access to different resources and conversational sanctions than the patients and, more to the point, these resources were more powerful in terms of influencing what happened in the consultations. Even when the patients employed similar resources, the result was not the same. For example, GPs could use their knowledge in medical matters as a resource for getting a diagnosis established. The same resource, when used by a patient, had an entirely different effect. She was told that she didn't know what she was talking about and put abruptly in her place. So much for patient autonomy.

This was, however, only part of the picture. The fact that the patients did not, when all was said and done, come out on top in the interactional power struggles did not mean that they went down without a fight. In fact, I discovered that just as male doctors could be nice and friendly while exercising control, patients were often surprisingly recalcitrant and rebellious. In fact, the patients routinely exercised power in all sorts of subtle, sneaky, and even somewhat unorthodox

---

[7] It should be noted here that these studies were part of a pioneering endeavor to reconnect socially structured relations of power and gender inequality to the study of medical talk as an interactional accomplishment. They have also provided valuable insights into many of the difficulties faced by women in medical encounters. My criticisms refer to the—often implicit—way that power seems to be conceptualized in feminist studies of medical interaction, including, just parenthetically, my own (Davis 1986).

ways. Although the consultations were conducted in a cooperative and—as previously mentioned—friendly fashion, patients could engage in activities that served to undermine the physician's authority over their problems as well as what was to be done about them. These power practices were not dramatic, but rather microscopic attempts to shift the power imbalance in favor of the patient.

As an illustration, let us return to the patient with the sore throat and headache. Upon learning from the GP that her throat is "normal," she immediately lodges a vehement protest:

P: *How* can that be...when it feels so strange. I wake up during the night from it, there's such pain, here, over here, on the left side ((groans))

By drawing upon physical sensations to which the GP has no access, she is able to cast some doubt upon the accuracy of his findings.

Or, a bit later in the consultation, the same point is made in a somewhat different form. By citing an earlier experience with the Health Service, the patient highlights the failure of the medical profession, in general, to discover the source of her current distress[8]:

P: But fourteen days ago I was at home for a week. I had such a headache then. Well, I just couldn't *work*-
D: Yeah-
P: -you know? but then I started up *again* and then that doctor from uhh- what's it called uhhh- the Health Service, right? - ours, he took my blood pressure but he says, it's *all just fine*, so uhhh- but I had *such a headache*. I just couldn't even *walk* from the headache.
D: Yeah- ((pause)) yeah, oh well, you've just uhhh-

By means of the utterly mundane activity of complaining, the patient can demonstrate just how debilitating her headache is. Not only is it difficult to get a word in edgewise, but who can counter such a rendition, replete with convincing sound effects (the occasional groan for emphasis) as well as colorful descriptions of the pain, how long it has been going on, and the various circumstances under which it occurs? Without disagreeing with the doctor's assessment in-so-many-words, the patient succeeds in maintaining her version of her problem as something meriting serious attention.

The patient not only has her own ideas about her physical complaints, but she provides her own reading of her so-called "nervousness" as well. When the GP suggests that she might want some tranquilizers to still the anxiety she feels about her sore throat, the patient replies:

---

[8] Of course, the GP might have felt relieved that he was not alone in his inability to dispatch his professional duties with success, which only goes to show that the power practices of patients may have a friendly face as well.

P: I do - yeah. And I am ((laughs)) a little bit nervous.
D: Yeah.
P: We have so many uhhh- strange things at the moment.
D: -then shall I-
      ((pause))
      Yeah? At the moment, lots of uhhh-
P: Yeah: ((complaining)) I've got my mother-in-law, and my brother-in-law, everything, and whether I'm also making myself *nervous*, that I don't know-

Although she agrees that she may well be "a little bit nervous," she is quick to indicate what she sees as the source of her distress. Who wouldn't be nervous with all these problems?

At first glance, patients may seem to go amicably along with the GP's expert assessment of their current complaint, when, upon closer examination, it appears that they were not in agreement at all. This is accomplished with a compliant "yes," followed by a "but" and a counterexample which directly contradicts what the doctor had been saying (the "yes, but..." strategy).[9] Another minuscule form of protest entails not laughing at paternalistic jokes (Davis 1988a). In some cases, the patient may even take the offensive by casting doubt, subtly but unmistakably, on the GP's competence as a medical expert.

Take, for example, the "nervous" patient. When the GP asks her whether she can talk to her husband about all these problems, she says, sweetly:

P: *Sure, yeah*, right, yeah sure.
      ((pause))
      But my husband says, just go to the doctor ((laughs))
      with that headache.

Generally speaking, patients go along with the doctor's orders, but indicate, at the same time, through irony, silence, or subtle criticism, that the ideological wool has not been pulled over their eyes. Compliance does not necessarily mean total agreement. Although some patients exercise power with a rather heavy hand,[10] the majority of the power practices are of an ordinary and routine sort: a continual picking away at the bases of the GP's authority.

Having provided a cursory look at some of the power practices of my not-so-invisible patients, the question now becomes: What can we learn from them in terms of how power should be conceptualized in medical interaction or, more

---

[9] This is also a favorite in therapy conversations. See, Davis (1986).

[10] For example, one patient managed to keep her GP occupied for a good 30 minutes with a seemingly unending supply of complaints. When he tried to round the consultation up (with—what else—a prescription for valium), she produced a veiled suicide threat and, ultimatley, staged a hyperventilation attack, thereby avoiding having to leave the doctor's office for another 10 minutes (Davis 1988b). Whatever one's feelings about the desirability of such methods, there can be no doubt that they belong to the category of potential power practices which can be exercised by patients.

generally, in gender relations? To begin with, a top-down model of power relations will simply not do. If the investigator's attention is focused exclusively on dominant parties, whether physicians, men, or that doubly powerful combination of the two—the male physician—she may find herself losing sight of the less-powerful party in the interaction. This means missing out on all the microscopic and often sneaky power practices, which actors routinely, ongoingly, and sometimes even successfully employ to undermine relations involving domination and subordination. Or she may risk passing over how subordinate parties manage to display some degree of power even when they are unable or unwilling at that particular moment to do something to alter the course of events.

A final word of caution is in order. Giving the subordinate party, whether woman or patient, a place of honor in a (feminist) analysis of power does not mean ignoring the fact that medical interaction does not involve equals. Doctors and patients as well as men and women do have asymmetrically structured access to resources for influencing what happens in any encounter. Nevertheless, no analysis of how asymmetrical relations of power are interactionally produced and reproduced is complete without taking into account all the ways participants also go about undermining them.

In conclusion, the question concerning how power should be conceptualized at the level of interaction cannot be answered at a strictly theoretical level. Coming to terms with the complex and elusive workings of power requires an ongoing interaction between our theoretical notions about power and the situated social practices of the social actors we are investigating. Using the Nice Doctor and the Invisible Patient as case in point, I have demonstrated just how difficult it can be for the would-be analyst of power to confront her research object at the level of face-to-face interaction. At the same time, however, it is precisely the empirical confrontation with the refractoriness of power practices in actual social contexts which provides the guidelines needed in order to develop adequate theories on power at the level of interaction as well as, more generally, in gender relations.

With this in mind, I shall now return to the problem raised at the beginning of this chapter; namely, what this might mean for feminist theory on power in gender relations.

FEMINIST COMMON SENSE AND POWER

Historically, feminist scholarship has displayed a certain ambiguity towards the phenomenon of power. On the one hand, power is regarded as a pivotal issue in understanding relations between the sexes. On the other hand, despite its centrality to feminist thinking, power has not been subject to much explicit theorizing. For feminists, gender relations have always been about male domination and female subordination. By focusing on the subordinate position of the women, oppression became a kind of female experience par excellence. By linking power to relations involving domination, it could hardly be anything but coercive, oppressive and, of course, negative for women. In short, the feminist conception of power in gender relations was originally top-down and repressive.

During the past two decades, this model has enabled feminist scholars from various disciplines to uncover patterns of gender inequality in a multitude of social, cultural, and historical contexts. Through these efforts, gender, together with class and race, could take its place as one of the three axes along which the major power inequalities in contemporary society could be organized (Scott, 1986). Gender inequality also became the red thread uniting the experiences of otherwise highly dissimilar women (and men) as a central topic of concern, thereby giving the feminist scholar her *raison d'être*.

Whereas power is crucial for understanding what makes relations between the sexes worthy of attention, it has not received much attention within feminist theory. Questions remain unanswered concerning the specific features of power in gender relations at the various levels of social life or, for that matter, the exact nature of the relationship between power and gender. For example, should gender be regarded as a central organizing principle of social life, including power relations? Or can gender relations best be understood in terms of power, similar to other relations between dominant and subordinate groups? Are there specifically gendered forms of power or does power operate in much the same fashion in any asymmetrical relation? In short, are power and gender linked in any absolute sense or are they simply contingent in much of social life as we know it?

The conceptual relationship between gender and power has not been clarified and, with the notable exception of Hartsock (1983), we have yet to see a specifically feminist perspective on power. The lack of explicitly feminist theory on power is problematic for various reasons and it goes well beyond the scope of this chapter to discuss them all. I will, however, be dealing with one particular difficulty; namely, the reification of a top-down, repressive model of power into a kind of feminist common sense on relations between the sexes. I will be arguing that this feminist common sense, which has stood us in good stead in the past, is, ultimately, neither complex nor dynamic enough to enable us to come to terms with many of the everyday encounters between the sexes.

To begin with, common sense encompasses what we need to know in order to make sense of what we and others are doing in the course of our everyday lives. For women, common sense will include our experiences with oppression and exploitation, born of myriad everyday encounters with sexual inequalities. Every woman will come equipped with notions about these experiences, enabling her to make sense of and get along in the routine and ongoing power struggle between the sexes (Stanley & Wise 1983). One of the original tasks of feminism was to articulate these often-tacit perceptions and beliefs about our own experiences and those of other women into a kind of feminist common sense. Within this feminist common sense, women emerged as the oppressed victims of male supremacy as exercised by individual men or male-dominated institutions, depending on one's political affiliations. In any case, power was clearly something that men "had" and women did not. Although women might—and hopefully did—engage in "resistance" from time to time, our relation to power was that of the disapproving outsider. In our relations with one another, power was even something of a dirty word, conjuring up images of competitive, career-oriented females, stepping over the backs of their less fortunate sisters or hob-nobbing with men for a piece of the pie. It had no place in the egalitarian women's communities we envisioned for ourselves. This model of power as a fundamentally top-down and repressive phenomenon informed feminism as a social movement and provided the implicit foundation upon which most feminist studies were built. For the most part, it was not subjected to critical reflection, but was treated as the taken-for-granted background knowledge for feminist endeavors.

Unfortunately, common sense, including feminist common sense, is not infallible.[11] Just as our beliefs are founded and implicated in our day-to-day activities, they also stand to be corrected by these same activities. Although our feminist common sense is essential for keeping us on track in our investigations into the workings of power in gender relations, it is also in need of revision when it proves inadequate for coming to terms with what we see happening in the situated social practices of the men and women we are investigating. In other words, a reflexive relationship between feminist common sense and the situated practices of men and women is required.

As an illustration of how this reflexive relationship might work, I shall return to those two aspects of feminist common sense which proved problematic in my own analysis of power in gender relations in medical encounters; namely, power as a top-down phenomenon and power as synonymous with domination. Having shown some of the limitations of this model for understanding the power practices of not-so-nice male doctors and not-so-invisible female patients, I shall now take a look at some of the theoretical and methodological implications to be drawn for feminist theory on power.

I shall begin with the notion that power between the sexes can best be viewed as *top-down*. Feminist studies of interaction in gender relations have generally drawn from the tradition of interpretative sociology (ethnomethodology, con-

---

[11] The distinction that Giddens (1984:336) makes between "mutual knowledge" and "common sense" is useful here. The former refers to what members, including social scientists, need in order to make their way in everyday life. Since it accounts for our even being able to engage in practical social activities in the first place, it cannot be subject to correction. "Common sense," on the other hand, refers to propositional beliefs, which, though founded and implicated in day-to-day activities, do sometimes prove wrong on the basis of those very activities and, subsequently, need to be altered.

versation or discourse analysis, phenomenology or symbolic interactionism) in order to describe the workings of gender inequality at the level of face-to-face encounters. One of the main contributions of interpretative sociology was to break radically with mainstream Parsonian sociology and its treatment of the individual as "cultural dope" (Giddens 1976). The social actor was no longer regarded as blindly driven by social forces beyond her control and a valiant attempt was made to retrieve her as basically competent and knowledgeable. Early studies in the field were devoted, in fact, to displaying just how—often surprisingly—able members were at finding their way about in social life. Social interaction was always and everywhere viewed as a human accomplishment, actively and knowledgeably negotiated by the participants themselves.

Ironically, this stance of uncovering how ordinary people "do social life" and giving them at least a little credit for knowing what is going on seems to disappear as soon as the participants turn out to have a gender. Suddenly, the man does all the interacting, almost negotiating the encounter by himself, while the woman sits helplessly on the sidelines, at best a shadowy respondent. It would seem that one of the unintended consequences of introducing gender inequality to the interactional scene is that women become transformed into that "cultural dope" we used to be so interested in avoiding.

This is more than a methodological inconsistency, however. It has political implications as well. It goes almost without saying that feminist scholars have always been especially interested in how women fare in the various contexts of their daily lives. If the original concern was with domination or "systems of male control and coercion," there has been a growing emphasis in recent years on how women themselves "participate in setting up, maintaining, and altering the system of gender relations" (Gerson & Peiss 1985:322). The idea is not to deny the fact that structured asymmetries exist in the resources available to men and women for exercising control over what happens in any encounter; nor to blame women for their own oppression. It is, however, important to delineate how relations of power are being negotiated; that is, the process by which relations involving domination and subordination are ongoingly produced and reproduced, but also transformed.

This requires, among other things, being particularly alert to how women exercise control, even when their resources are limited or when they don't, when all is said and done, come out on top. It also involves directing our attention at the often microscopic and sometimes even trivial ways that women routinely undermine asymmetrical power relations or display some degree of penetration of what is going on, despite being unable or unwilling at that particular moment to do anything to alter the course of events.

It is this concern with the "boundaries"—how women and men delineate their relations at any given time or place—that is essential for coming to terms with processes of change. Uncovering how they "make and reshape their social worlds" (Gerson & Peiss 1985:321) enables us, ultimately, to explain how and why these boundaries change or, more to the point, might be changed at some future date.

In short, an adequate feminist analysis of gender relations requires replacing a top-down model of power with a model which treats power relations as something to be negotiated by parties who both have access to some resources, albeit unequal ones.

I shall now turn to the second notion inherent in feminist common sense concerning power; namely, that power is inevitably *linked to domination* and subordination. The implication of this linkage is that power is basically a nasty business, employed by men for the sole purpose of keeping women down, silencing them, or otherwise preventing them from acting, thinking, or feeling as they would chose to when left to their own devices. There are several difficulties with such a conception of power.

First, if we want to investigate power, we will be forced to look for it in situations which involve overt and authoritarian forms of control by men over women. This eliminates interaction between the sexes which is friendly, pleasant, or intimate. Since much of the interaction between men and women could be characterized in precisely this way, however—including the interaction between the male GPs and female patients in my own study—then obviously a model of power is required which will enable us to investigate it anywhere. In other words, we need a model of power relations which can also deal with power as it is exercised in friendly or intimate encounters.

Second, if power relations are strictly of the coercive or repressive kind, it is difficult to account for why women continue to go along with them. The only possible explanation becomes that they are, indeed, powerless to do anything about them or, more probably, the misguided victims of what used to be dubbed "false consciousness." This, once again, relegates women squarely to the position of "cultural dope," that passive and unenlightened victim of circumstances beyond their control.

Third, if power is equated with domination and subordination, it is difficult to see how we as feminists could ever develop forms of social action and interaction which are something different than that. What would our feminist alternative be? We can criticize, but we are unable to come up with anything better. Thus, we are forced by our own conception of power into a kind of political nihilism. In our own best interests, we clearly need a feminist account of power which can link it both to domination as well as potentially positive or enabling relations.

In conclusion, a model of power in gender relations needs to be elaborated to meet the following requirements (at least):

1. Power must be treated as an integral feature of social life, operating in all contexts and at all levels. This means that even the most insignificant or routine encounter between the sexes can be investigated for how power

works within it, even when—at first glance—it appears to be a highly cooperative, harmonious, or intimate affair.

2. Power needs to be conceptualized in a way which is complex and subtle enough to account for relations involving domination, coercion, or repression as well as relations which are positive, productive, or enabling. Understanding asymmetrical power relations will often entail sorting out just how these two dimensions are intertwined within concrete instances of interactions as well as interactional outcomes.

3. We need a feminist conception of agency—that is, a way of reinstating women to the position of agent without falling into the concomitant stance of blaming them for social inequities. This requires a dialectical approach to power, which delineates how both women and men attempt to influence the course of events in their interaction.

Finally, a few words of a more general nature are in order concerning the relationship between feminist common sense and theorizing. In many ways, it is old hat to claim that theories need to be located in an ongoing and reflexive exchange between theory and empirical data. This seems to be nothing more than another rendition of that old familiar Glaser and Strauss (1967) tune about the necessity of grounding our theoretical notions empirically. All social scientists, whether feminist or not, will use their common sense to generate research problems, help them find their way into their material, and interpret what is going on. Although common sense is an essential part of research practice, it can, however, be wrong. It is in the context of this fallibility that our reflexive relationship between our theories on power and power practices located in our empirical data needs to be elaborated.

This has two consequences for how we should use our feminist common sense: First, our common-sense notions about male domination and female subordination provide the foothold we need in unraveling the often elusive and contradictory workings of power in gender relations. Our belief that power will inevitably belong to any encounter between the sexes can keep us on the track, providing us with an ongoing sensitivity of the "I-smell-a-rat" variety. It is this same uneasy sense of something being wrong without being able to articulate or immediately put a finger on its source, which can be found in the social practices of the women we are investigating. As feminist scholars, we need to make welcome use of this practical awareness of gender inequality, both our own as well as that of the women who are the objects of our inquiries, in our accounts of power in relations between the sexes. Second, we must accept that common sense, including our feminist common sense, is bounded. It is not only productive, but will sometimes block our vision as we try to understand asymmetrical gender relations. Just as the social activities of women (and men) are constrained by conditions over which they have no control, or are only partially aware, our own common-sense beliefs can be faulty or incomplete. For this reason, feminist common sense needs to be subject to correction by what we see happening in the various institutional and gendered contexts of everyday life. It is only by employing our (feminist) common sense in this doubly reflexive sense that we will be able to generate feminist theories which are sophisticated enough to come to terms with the complexity of power asymmetries in gender relations.

REFERENCES

ARMS, S.
  1975   *Immaculate Deception.* New York: Bantam Books.
ATKINSON, J.M., AND J. HERITAGE, EDS.
  1984   *Structures of Social Action.* Cambridge: Cambridge University Press.
BLIESENER, T., AND J. SIEGRIST
  1981   Greasing the Wheels: Conflicts on the Rounds and How They Are Managed. *Journal of Pragmatics* 5: 181–204.
CONRAD, P., AND J.W. SCHNEIDER
  1981   *Deviance and Medicalization.* St. Louis: The C.V. Mosby Co.
COOPERSTOCK, R.
  1978   Sex differences in psychotropic drug use. *Social Science & Medicine* 12B: 179–186.
CULPEPPER, E.
  1978   Exploring menstrual attitudes. IN *Women Looking at Biology Looking at Women*, M.S. Hennifin, Ed. Cambridge, Mass.: Schenckman Publishing Co.
DAVIS, K.
  1986   The process of problem (re) formulation in psychotherapy. *Sociology of Health and Illness* 8(1): 44–74.
DAVIS, K.
  1988a   Paternalism under the microscope. IN *Gender and Discourse: The Power of Talk*, A.D. Todd and S. Fisher, Eds. Norwood, NJ: Ablex Publishing.
DAVIS, K.
  1988b   *Power Under the Microscope. Toward a Grounded Theory of Gender Relations in Medical Encounters.* Dordrecht: Foris Publishing Co.
EHRENREICH, B., AND J. EHRENREICH
  1978   Medicine and social control. IN *The Cultural Crisis of Modern Medicine*, J. Ehrenreich, Ed. New York: Monthly Review Press.
EHRENREICH, B., AND D. ENGLISH
  1979   *For Her Own Good.* London: Pluto Press.
FIDELL, L.S.
  1980   Sex role stereotypes and the American physician. *Psychology of Women Quarterly* 4(3): 313–330.
FISHER, S.
  1983   Doctor talk/patient talk: How treatment decisions are negotiated in doctor-patient communication. IN *Social Organization of Doctor-Patient Communication*, first edition S. Fisher and A.D. Todd, Eds. Washington, DC: Center for Applied Linguistics Press.

FISHER, S.
   1986   *In the Patient's Best Interest. Women and the Politics of Medical Decisions.* New
           Brunswick, N.J.: Rutgers University Press.
FISHER, S., AND A. DUNDAS TODD, EDS.
   1983   *The Social Organization of Doctor-Patient Communication.* first edition Wash-
           ington, DC: Center for Applied Linguistics Press.
FISHER, S., AND A. DUNDAS TODD, EDS.
   1986   *Discourse and Institutional Authority: Medicine, Education and Law.* Nor-
           wood, NJ: Ablex Publishing.
FISHER, S., AND S.B. GROCE
   1985   Doctor-patient negotiation as cultural assumptions. *Sociology of Health and
           Illness* 7(3): 342–374.
FISHMAN, P.
   1978   Interaction: The work women do. *Social Problems* 26: 397–406.
FOUCAULT, M.
   1980   *Power Knowledge: Selected Interviews and Other Writings, 1972–1977.* New
           York: Pantheon.
GALLIE, W.B.
   1956   Essentially contested concepts. *Proceedings of the Aristotelian Society*:
           167–198.
GERSON, J.M., AND K. PEISS
   1985   Boundaries, negotiation, consciousness: Reconceptualizing gender relations.
           Social Problems 32(4): 317–331.
GIDDENS, A.
   1976   *New Rules of Sociological Method: A Positive Critique of Interpretative
           Sociologies.* London: Hutchinson.
GIDDENS, A.
   1984   *The Constitution of Society.* Cambridge: Polity Press.
GLASER, B.G., AND A.L. STRAUSS
   1967   *The Discovery of Grounded Theory: Strategies for Qualitative Research.* New
           York: Aldine Publishing Co.
HARTSOCK, N.
   1983   *Money, Sex, and Power. Toward a Feminist Historical Materialism.* New York:
           Longman.
HEARN, J.
   1987   *The Gender of Oppression. Men, Masculinity, and the Critique of Marxism.*
           Brighton: Wheatsheaf Books.
HEATH, C.
   1981   The opening sequence in doctor-patient interaction. IN *Medical Work. Realities
           and Routines*, J.M. Atkinson and C. Heath, Eds. Westmead, Farnborough,
           Hants: Gower.
HENLEY, N.M.
   1977   *Body Politics. Power, Sex and Non-Verbal Communication.* Englewood Cliffs,
           NJ: Prentice-Hall.
HERITAGE, J.C.
   1985   Recent developments in conversation analysis. *Sociolinguistics* 15(1): 1–18.
HOMANS, H., ED.
   1985   *The Sexual Politics of Reproduction.* Hampshire, England: Gower.

HUGHES, D.
 1982   Control in the medical consultation: Organizing talk in a situation where co-
        participants have different competence. *Sociology* 16(3): 359–376.
KNORR-CETINA, K.D.
 1981   Introduction: The micro-sociological challenge of macro-sociology: Towards a
        reconstruction of social theory and methodology. IN *Advances in Social Theory
        and Methodology: Toward an Integration of Micro- and Macro-Sociologies*,
        K.D. Knorr-Cetina and A.V. Cicourel, Eds. Boston: Routledge & Kegan Paul.
LENANNE, K.J., AND J. LENANNE
 1973   Alleged psychogenic disorders in women—A possible mainfestation of sexual
        prejudice. *New England Journal of Medicine* 288(6): 288–292.
LORBER, J.
 1976   Women and Medical Sociology: Invisible professional and ubiquitous patients.
        IN *Another Voice. Feminist Perspectives on Social Life and Social Science*, M.
        Millman and R. Moss Kanter, Eds. New York: Octagon Books.
LUKES, S.
 1974   *Power, a Radical View*. London: MacMillan Press.
LUKES, S.
 1979   On the relativity of power. IN *Philosophical Disputes in the Social Sciences*,
        S.C. Brown, Ed. Sussex: Harvester Press, Ltd.
LUKES, S.
 1982   Panoptikon. Macht und Herrschaft bei Weber, Marx, Foucault. IN *Kursbuch 70*,
        K.M. Michel and T. Spengler, Eds. Berlin: Rotbuch Verlag.
MARTIN, E.
 1987   *Women in the Body*. Boston: Beacon Press.
MCPHERSON, A., ED.H
 1988   *Women's Problems in General Practice*. Oxford: Oxford University Press.
MISHLER, E.G.
 1984   *The Discourse of Medicine*. Norwood, NJ: Ablex Publishing.
OAKLEY, A.
 1979   A case of maternity: Paradigms of women as maternity cases. *Signs* 4(4):
        607–631.
RIESSMAN, C.K.
 1983   Women and medicalization. A new perspective. *Social Policy* 14(1): 3–19.
SACKS, H.
 1984   Notes on methodology. IN *Structures of Social Actions*, J.M. Atkinson and J.C.
        Heritage, Eds. Cambridge: Cambridge University Press.
SACKS, H., E. SCHEGLOFF, AND G. JEFFERSON
 1974   A simplest systematics for the analysis of turn-taking in conversations.
        Language 50: 696–735.
SCOTT, J.
 1986   Gender: A useful category of historical analysis. *American Historical Review*,
        91: 1053–1075.
SCULLY, D.
 1980   *Men who Control Women's Health*. Boston: Houghton Mifflin.

SCULLY, D., AND P. BART
  1973   A funny thing happened on the way to the orifice: Women in gynecological
         textbooks. *American Journal of Sociology* 78: 1045–1050.
SHOWALTER.
  1985   *The Female Malady.* London: Virago Press.
STANDING, H.
  1980   Sickness is a woman's business? Reflections on the attribution of illness. IN
         Alice Through the Microscope, The Brighton Women and Science Group, Eds.
         London: Virago Press.
STANLEY, L., AND S. WISE
  1983   *Breaking out: Feminist Consciousness and Feminist Research.* London: Rou-
         tledge and Kegan Paul.
TODD, A.D.
  1989   *Intimate Adversaries: Cultural Conflict Between Doctors and Women Patients.*
         Philadelphia: University of Pennsylvania Press.
TRÖMEL-PLÖTZ, S.
  1984   *Gewalt durch Sprache.* Frankfurt: Fischer Taschenbuch Verlag.
WEST, C.
  1984   *Routine Complications: Troubles with Talk Between Doctors and Patients.*
         Bloomington: Indiana University Press.
ZIMMERMAN, D.H., AND C. WEST
  1975   Sex roles, interruptions and silences in conversation. IN *Language and Sex:
         Difference and Dominance*, B. Thorne and N. Henley, Eds. Rowley, Mass.:
         Newbury House.

11

Exploring Women's Experiences: Power and Resistance in Medical Discourse*

Alexandra Dundas Todd

DOCTOR: Where is the drape [cloth used to cover women patients during a gynecological pelvic examination]?
NURSE: She did not want one.
DOCTOR: (to the nurse) The patient doesn't have anything to say about it. She's going to use one. She might bleed and get everything about, uh on her clothes, then she's going to squawk.
NURSE: Okay.
DOCTOR: (to the patient) In this office we always use a drape. Honey, maybe you'll start bleeding. You're going to soil your clothes and everything else[1].

*This chapter is a revision of "L'ascotto della voce delle donne: potere e resistenza nel colloquio medico," in *Asimmetrie Comunicative: Differenze di genere nell' interazione medico-paziente*, Franca Pizzini, ed. Milano, Italy: Franco Angeli.

I would like to thank Sue Fisher, Stephen Fox, Franca Pizzini, and Nicole Rafter for their comments on this article.

[1]These examples are taken from a two-and-a-half year study of a gynecological clinic and private gynecologist's office in the United States. Twenty patients were audiotaped in their interactions with doctors and interviewed later in their homes. The next section of this chapter is revised from part of Chapter 4, *Intimate Adversaries: Cultural Conflict Between Doctors and Women Patients*, Alexandra Dundas Todd, University of Pennsylvania Press (1989). For methodological elaboration on expansion of texts, see pages 77-82 in this book.

The doctor talks, the nurse and patient listen; the doctor orders, the nurse and patient obey. Within much of the literature on the doctor–patient relationship, this is the scenario that seems to prevail most often. Subtler signs of negotiation also appear and have been duly noted, but the conclusions are that the doctor is more likely to raise and direct topics, and control the flow of communication; the others present merely respond. In sum, the doctor holds the power.

In the late 1960s and early 1970s, when women again began articulating the limitations of women's roles in society, the emerging interpretation of women rendered them passive. Women were lumped together in one group and seen as oppressed. They were defined as pawns in a man's game, be he father, husband, or doctor. Today researchers question whether patients are *really* this passive, this victimized.

As the women's movement grew internationally with a concomitant change in expected gender roles, and as women have become, in the 1980s, increasingly active in public and private spheres, the interpretation of women's roles has shifted slightly. To define women as passive recipients of society's and/or male dictates is seen as misrepresenting and underestimating women's strengths. Women, whether involved in a struggle for social change or accepting of traditional values, are redefined as active participants in their own lives, even in their own oppression (albeit unwittingly). In other words, better to have been an active participant in the arrangement of one's life (regardless of how problematic) than to be a passive being. Furthermore, today, the group "woman," the all-inclusive category, is shifting ground. Differences and diversity among women are seen as pivotal to feminist analyses, regardless of one's stance in the active-passive debate. Race, class, ethnicity, sexual preference, as well as individual difference, make for many groups among women whose experiences and interests are embedded in a multitude of contexts.

These directions are part of current concerns that ask us to delve deeper, to look at contexts within contexts, to come up with more complicated understandings of social relations, power, and resistance to that power. It is assumed that where there is power, there is also resistance, and it is this active resistance which we need to focus on (see Foucault, 1980, for a discussion of the social relations of power and resistance).

For me these debates are both intriguing and dangerous. Yes, women have many strengths; yes, women are not passive victims lying on examining tables waiting to take whatever comes; yes, women have some power, however subtle, to resist and redefine their lives; but...and it is the "but" that worries me, women as a group are still oppressed in varying degrees. For example, domestic violence, acquaintance rape, and incest, primarily against women, appear commonplace; single mothers and their children are the poorest people in America; a man with an eighth-grade education has equal earning power with a college-graduate woman—the list goes on and on. The powers that be move slowly, if at all, toward basic equity issues (decent daycare, etc.), and South Africa remains the only industrialized nation with a more deplorable family policy than the United States.

Such examples indicate that the majority of women in America, albeit differently, are subordinates. We are in the position of responding to or resisting events rather than creating them. In American health care, for example, doctors do still often stride into examining rooms telling nurses and patients what they should and should not do. The flow of communication is not usually determined or controlled by women patients.

How can we think about these questions of gender, power, and resistance? What do these dynamics look like? How can we incorporate diversity into our understandings without forfeiting a common bond and power base? How can we see women as strong, active agents in the organization of their lives and health without losing sight of oppression? How can we keep the former without making the latter an illusion?

My interests, in this chapter, are to look at doctor–patient communication and interviews with women patients as a move in the ongoing discussion of these questions. How are the active-passive debates, power-resistance dynamics, and commonality-diversity questions manifested in medical interactions and in women's lives? The answers, of course, are elusive. Seemingly clear categories turn fuzzy. However, what I suggest in this chapter is the need for balance rather than dichotomies—a continuum rather than a too eager pendulum.

METHODOLOGICAL APPROACHES

Feminist scholarship, concerned with contextualization and variety, has a long tradition of listening to women's voices as a way to explore differing perceptions. These voices are a place to start, a way to avoid the great men and great movements, or as Carroll Smith-Rosenberg remarked, "the noble and public" (1985:17) traditions that have so often left women invisible. Dorothy Smith (1974), always ahead of her time, discussed the centrality of women's experiences when developing theories and methods for the study of gender. Listening to women's voices allows glimpses into women's lives, providing ways to rethink the complexities of gender.

> There are and must be different experiences of the world and different bases of experience. We must not do away with them by taking advantage of our privileged speaking to construct a sociological version which we then impose upon them as their reality. . . . Our conceptual procedures should be capable of explicating and analyzing the properties of their experienced world rather than administering it. Their reality, their varieties of experience must be an unconditional datum. (Smith 1974:12)

Elaine Showalter (1985), too, in her critique of historians of madness calls for a new database, an alternative set of cultural artifacts to ground more sophisticated gender analyses.

> In order to supply the gender analysis and feminist critique missing from the history of madness, we must turn to a wholly different set of cultural sources: inmate narratives, diaries, women's memoirs, and novels. These other accounts of insanity, by women from Florence Nightingale to Mary Barnes, as well as the writings of those women practitioners who commented, albeit from a marginal position, on the development of the psychiatric profession itself, offer an indispensable perspective on the diagnosis, treatment, and theory of the female malady from those who were more often the subjects of psychiatric discourse than its theorists and shapers. (Showalter 1985:6)

Not only do Smith-Rosenberg, Smith, and Showalter seek to avoid overgeneralizations about gender, but by grounding theory in women's experiences, they also provide a method to begin sorting out the active-passive debate. First, by virtue of women's stories being taken seriously in the research process, women's participation becomes clearer. Rather than passive subjects, we can see active participants. Second, in careful textual analysis—be it conversational, literary, historical, or cultural—we can see women's oppressions as well as their strategies for resistance.

The above writers, while calling for an expanded database, see this database as a method, not as an end in itself. Lived experiences, memoirs, and so forth, while sources for methodological investigation and for theory construction, are not verbatim truths by themselves. As Alison Jaggar (1983) points out,

> Those who construct the standpoint of women must begin from women's experience as women describe it, but they must go beyond that experience theoretically and ultimately may require that women's experience be redescribed. (Jaggar 1983:384)

Attention to women's experience is not new in feminist scholarship. What *is* new here is that the ways of thinking, the ways of knowing are shifting. We are being encouraged to move from looking at the universal oppression of the female sex under a monolithic, capitalist system and/or patriarchal culture, to a closer scrutiny of the different experiences of women. Yes, women share life in a world that denigrates them, but they do so embedded in a profusion of oppressions and multitude of resistances, in endless diversity. The examination of cultural artifacts and women's voices provide for a different kind of analysis of women's lives—an analysis that highlights the "endless variety and monotonous similarity" (Rubin 1975:160). Discourse, like textual analysis, becomes a methodological strategy—a strategy used in the next section to analyze doctors and women talking to each other and women talking with me about their health care and their lives.

THE DOCTOR–PATIENT DISCOURSE AND EXPANSION OF THE TEXT

The following doctor–patient conversations display interactional productions of power and resistance. These interactions are expanded upon with information from interviews with women patients about their experiences. I present five examples which highlight different patterns of women talking with their doctors about contraception and health needs. These discussions illuminate diverse instances of subtle or attempted resistance (see Footnote 1).

Ms. Martinez

Ms. Martinez is 26, married, and has a tired air about her which can easily turn to animated interest if her sense of humor is aroused. She has four children ranging in age from six months to 11 years, and a varied contraceptive history. While the clinic rarely recommends the IUD (intrauterine device) for birth control, it has been recommended to Ms. Martinez because she has four children and the clinic feels this is enough for a low-income (government aid) family. She also has had a history of an unexpected pregnancy which places her in the clinic's category of an inept contraceptor. Ms. Martinez has agreed, somewhat reluctantly, to this birth control method. Her past experience with the IUD has not been satisfactory. On this visit she comes to the doctor for the standard pre-IUD check-up, and an appointment is made for insertion of the IUD in two weeks time.

Doctor(D)–Patient(P) Discourse

P: It won't hurt will it?
D: Oh, I doubt it.
P: I'm taking your word (laugh).
D: I haven't had anybody pass out from one yet.
P: The last time/
D: (cuts patient off with a joke, both patient and doctor laugh)
P: The last time when I had that Lippes Loop, oh, God/
D: (interrupts patient)/You won't even know what's going on. We'll just slip that in and you'll be so busy talking and you won't know it.

In the doctor–patient discourse, Ms. Martinez asks a direct question about possible pain. In two subsequent turns she tries to raise her past and painful experience with the IUD. Each time she is interrupted and cut off by the doctor. She attempts to raise the topic three times. This makes her an assertive patient. Most patients in this study did not so actively try to raise topics.

Medical literature supports the view that women experience pain with insertion of the IUD rather than after it is in place. The doctor seems to assume this to be the case here as well. This was not Ms. Martinez's concern. My follow-up interview provides an expansion of what Ms. Martinez was trying to express.

Expansion of the Text

P: I tried an IUD...I got an IUD put in, a Lippes Loop, (Interviewer(I): uh huh) and I got that put in and I had that in August, for four months and I couldn't take it.

I: Well, what was it like using the IUD?

P: Oh, God, it was the most awful, terriblest, uncomfortable, it was awful. I hated it...I had it taken out 'cause I couldn't hack it...

I: How come?

P: I, it, it killed me. I was, oh, oh, that's why I'm so scared with this one, the one I'm going to get...I remember the pain, yeah, it was awful.

I: When it was put in?

P: No, when it was put in it didn't hurt...It was okay all month long until I started my period, like the day before I started my period, my God in heaven, I'd be on the bed crying in pain...I even started taking pain killers.

I: Why did you keep it?

P: Because when I went, I went to the Public Health, ...and they just said...you'll have a little cramp and that's it. And you know that actually it didn't hurt a bit getting it in. (*I*: uh huh). It didn't bother me a bit, but it was just that I was so scared and so tense, (*I*: uh huh), and nobody would tell you, relax, and, you know, take it easy, or anything like that. Let you just freak out, you know, you just, then it was fine, you know, nothing bothered me. Went back to school that day and everything. And then the next month when my period started, well, the doctor had told me, "now don't be a baby and come back because you get a little pain." (*I*: uh huh). "Don't be a big baby and come back and say you want it out. You gotta give it a couple of months chance." So I kept saying, oh, it's just getting adjusted, it's just getting, the first time, it's just, you know, just the pain, it's just going to get adjusted. (*I*: oh). The next month, it was "don't be a baby Maria," they said "don't be a baby; hmm, hmm, hmm."

The doctor made an assumption regarding Ms. Martinez's concerns based on a generalized understanding of IUD use. Ms. Martinez's experiences, however, are particularistic, based on her own history of pain after insertion. Conflict in perspective and the doctor's more powerful position to control the discourse leave the patient's concerns unaddressed. In turn, the fears the doctor assumed she was addressing (pain on insertion) are lightheartedly dismissed. But signs of resistance are present in the interaction. They are overruled, well-intentionally, but nonetheless effectively. The doctor's power here is by no means that of a curmudgeon. Rather he relies on his (medical) belief system that he is the knower, overlooking and overtalking Ms. Martinez's perceptions of her situation. In two weeks time she does not show up for her IUD-insertion appointment. She tells me in a telephone follow-up interview that she is too frightened and decides not to return. Like Ms. Conrad, the next example, she ultimately turns her back on the medical profession.

Ms. Conrad

Ms. Conrad is a divorced woman in her late twenties. She has short blond hair, is shy, and tentative in her speech, as if she is never quite sure she is saying the right thing. She is presently working as a dental assistant to support herself and her four-year-old daughter, Jenny. Ms. Conrad has come to the clinic in December for two reproductive-related concerns. Although now sexually inactive, she wants birth control in case she might need it, and she has not had a menstrual period since the previous January (amenorrhea).

Doctor–Patient Discourse

D: Okay, and your last period was when?
P: Uhm, In January...
D: You haven't had a period since then?
P: No, I, I went to a doctor, I think it was in July, and he gave me a shot to get it started and I had some spotting but it only lasted for a half a day and that was it...
D: Uhm, we could give you birth control pills to try to regulate your period.
P: Well, I tried that, too, the doctor suggested it and I took them and they didn't, it didn't start either...
D: Uhm (pause).
P: In January my husband and I were having difficulties and then we separated at the end of February/
D: (interrupts) /Okay. But it's been almost a year/
P: /Yeah, I know/
D: /now since you had a period....

The doctor leaves the room to consult with another doctor.

D: ...It would probably be a good idea to give you a test dose of this progesterone to see if you have a withdrawal bleeding. I assume that this is probably what you were injected with earlier this summer....it would be uhm, the best idea to give you the progesterone for five days, have a withdrawal bleed, and then start you on the pill... .

Ms. Conrad has not menstruated for almost a year, since she and her husband "were having difficulties." She raises this with the doctor who brushes over the topic with a statement which implies a year is long enough to recover from a divorce. While there may or may not be a causal link between Ms. Conrad's marital upset and her amenorrhea, her tentative raising of the issue expresses this as a concern. The doctor ignores this information and offers technical solutions in the form of progesterone and birth control pills—solutions that were to fail this time as they did in the past.

Expansion of the Text

P: Most of the time even before I had Jenny, I stayed at home because we did move a lot and we, or he would take leave and so we could just pack up and travel, (I: uh huh), so I never worked . . . And then when he came back from overseas, we came out here and for the first six months that we were out here, we were very happy and content, and then after that, I just wanted to have another child, but he kept saying no, but never gave me any reasons, (I: uh huh). And then after a long time it finally came to him, and he said he didn't love me any more and wanted a divorce.

I: Uh huh, and so how was, how did you feel about that?

P: I was rather upset. I, you know, I never expected it. He was going through a change, I noticed last fall and winter, but he was in the service for ten years and got out this April, and I thought it was just, uh, all the decision of getting out, going on to school, going on to medicine, you know, and there were financial concerns, and I thought that's his major cau . . . or worry, (I: uh huh), at that time, (I: uh huh), but then he finally came to me and said he didn't know how he felt about me any more. He thought he didn't love me . . . .

I: And did he have any reasons for, for this change toward you . . . ?

P: Well, he really wouldn't talk about it, . . . He just said he was going through a change . . . the way I was brought up in the, in the community or my father and mother's, (I: uh huh), relationship, because I was brought up in the Midwest and it seems like people back there are more family oriented and I was like programmed, you know, when you grow up, you're going to get married and have your family . . . uhm, I'm very happy to be in the home situation, the family around me, and I enjoy doing things for someone special . . . .

I: Yes, uh huh. So you, you mentioned something about stopping your periods. You want to talk a little bit about that?

P: Okay, in January of this year my, I was on the pill at the time, and my period stopped.

I: Even while you were on the pill?

P: Right. And then in February I still didn't get one and we separated and so finally in March, I went in and had a pregnancy test run just to make sure [it was negative] . . . .

Once again we see a patient volunteering information about her life that she feels is pertinent to her health. She is a woman who holds traditional values, she has been divorced unexpectedly without understanding why, and a year later she is no happier with this decision than when it took place. Ms. Conrad makes a tentative connection between her reproductive processes and her social circumstances. Her doctor, well trained in the conventional biomedical model, focuses on biological processes severed from the social events of her life. Both of these women represent a pattern in medical encounters where the patient has a story to tell but is not allowed to tell it. Both try in the discourse to resist the biomedical definitions of their bodies and lives, but to little avail. Ms. Conrad, like Ms. Martinez, leaves the clinic and doesn't look back.

Ms. Adams

Ms. Adams is a college senior at a large university, majoring in environmental design. She is 21-years-old and is affiliated with a popular sorority on campus. Her appearance, full of youthful exuberance, brings to mind "now generation" television advertisements. She has come to her private practitioner for a routine checkup and a birth control pill prescription renewal.

Doctor–Patient Discourse

D: Pills are doing all right?

P: Yup. . . .

D: Uh, Amanda, I'm going to give you a six months supply . . . Uh, look, if I shouldn't be here or something then you're stuck, always when you start the last package, uh get in touch. . . . You're taking these twenty-one days, you prefer those to the twenty-eight?

P: Yeah.

D: How do you buy your pills? Do you buy just one at a time?

P: Two months, two months at a time.

D: When you get the last two [birth control pill packages], you know, then on the last one, take a red pencil and mark across it, across, and then you know this is my last package, you know . . . Here are your happy pills. Don't miss them. Anything unforeseen, you let me know, you know. You know, you read the pamphlet, you know the potential risks are minimal but you are aware of them.

P: Uh hum.

Ms. Adams comes to the doctor's office, goes through a gynecological examination, tells the doctor the pills are doing fine, and leaves with a renewal prescription. This doctor prescribes the birth control pills as the best contraceptive method for the majority of women and assumes, as would any observer, that Ms. Adams concurs. Given this premise the doctor prescribes "happy pills" for the patient, leaving little opening for a discussion to emerge on alternative methods.

Expansion of the Text

P: I want to get off of it [the pill] for the time being let my body system take over for a while and let it get back on its own because I'm scared something could happen ...

I: /What kinds of things?

P: Oh just, having problems when you do want to get pregnant, (*I*: uh huh), because your body won't ovulate when you, you know, when it's supposed, you know what I mean, it's it's triggered...

I: So you're going to, you're thinking of getting off of it for a while?

P: Yeah....I plan to get off of it because I'm kinda ify-ify but I do think there's side effects to it when you stay on it too long...Especially now since Bill and I aren't really going out that much anyways.

I: Yeah, and what kind of birth control method do you think you would use then?

P: I have no idea, I have no idea. I have no background and I'd have to find out.

I: ...and have you talked to Dr. M about that?

P: No....I just feel strange talking to him. It's just the way I was brought up, you know, a male...I, I've honestly wished, I could find a lady gynecologist and when I do I hate to say it, but I will transfer, not because he's not a good doctor because he's an excellent doctor, (*I*: uh huh),...[But] you just don't let a male see you like that, you, until you're fully dressed, and so this, after that being pounded into my head for twenty-one years, this, it's just not...I mean he just makes me feel uncomfortable...

I: Uh hum, and you feel that that's true, would be true of any male doctor, or/

P: /Yeah, obviously, yeah.

Ms. Adams finds herself in the paradox of needing information she is too uncomfortable to elicit from the place authorized to dispense it. The expansion reveals, first, that she is nervous about her health and future fertility on the pill, second, that the relationship with her boyfriend, Bill, has slowed down and she finds she does not need constant birth control, and third, that she has no idea about what method she would use in place of the pill. Because the doctor is a man she is uncomfortable asking him for information. Her efforts to find a woman doctor yielded little help. The number of female gynecologists is still relatively small in America; the ones she did call had long patient waiting lists or were taking no new patients. When I suggested the university clinic which would be free and available, Ms. Adams was appalled. To go to a school-affiliated office might allow others to know about her sexual activity—an activity she did not reveal to her friends or sorority.

Ms. Adams exemplifies a dilemma many women face in the gynecologist's office. Society says good women keep their bodies to themselves until marriage (or sexual intimacy). Sexual organs are not to be revealed to strangers of the opposite sex. Yet doctors are often strangers or, at best, office acquaintances. Joan Emerson (1970) discusses strategies doctors and their staff use to manage this breach in social rules. However, even with careful management, this discomfort can add yet another dimension to the distance and communication gap between doctor and patient.

This doctor, like the ones above, wields benevolent direction, "friendly persuasion" (see Fisher and Todd 1986), never considering that patients may have some power of their own—the power not to come back, as in the first two examples, or, as in this case and the next, to choose not to comply with the advice given.

Ms. Barrett

Ms. Barrett is a woman in her mid-twenties, assistant manager of a bank, married with no children and no immediate plans to have any. She has come to the private practitioner for a post-abortion checkup and for birth control. The doctor gave her a birth control pill prescription at the time of her abortion and today he gives a renewal prescription for the next three months.

Doctor–Patient Discourse

D: You take your pills?
P: Uh hum, I still have some, maybe a week's worth.
D: ...I'm going to give you today a prescription for three months.
P: Okay.
D: Then I want you here when you start on the last package.
P: Okay....
D: Okay? Do you read the pamphlet uh in the, well, which comes with the pills, huh?
P: Okay (nodding head).
D: And, you know, there are certain risks but you're at risk when you cross the street too.... All right, you dress, come and see me. I will give you a prescription, you know, and everything is fine.

But everything is not fine. As in the previous case, the doctor prescribes a method of contraception to a patient, who, it turns out, is reluctant. If one were to witness this doctor–patient interaction or to listen to a tape of it, one would surmise that Ms. Barrett was using an oral contraceptive. Her view of this method does not emerge in the encounter. Rather, she purposefully withholds information from the doctor, whom she has come to and is paying for a service, to avoid an old and repeated confrontation about her reproductive control. This is evidence of a form of active participation and resistance on the patient's part, albeit in an unequal relationship.

Expansion of the Text

I: ...What was it like using the pill during that, that time?

P: It was all right. I didn't, the only physical side effect I had at that point was uh the splotchy skin, the colasma....Uhm, I hated those and I got them pretty bad....

I: Where were the, where were the blotchy, the blotch skin?

P: On my face...It was my own personal vanity. They were pretty dark and they were pretty definite, and it looked like I had a moustache and, (*I*: uh huh), uh, it looked, I had them around on my cheeks and they were pretty definite. My, I didn't, make-up wouldn't cover them up or anything like that, and I never had very good skin to begin with and I didn't need to add something like that to it...

I: Okay, and uhm why did you switch to the diaphragm?

P: I think it was, my sister-in-law was using a diaphragm at the time....I thought I'd give it a try, (*I*: uh huh, okay), and I'm still using it....

I: And when you were at Dr. M's office...he talked to you about being on the pill...and you didn't mention the diaphragm?

P: Yeah. He's pretty strong hearted and uh about that, and uh/

I: /About what?

P: Taking the pill...He's been after me to take it for a while and every time that I say no, he just looks at me ...he's uh, he's set in his ways and so uh, the, we've had the same discussion over and over.

I: And have you tried telling him, talking to him about the fact that you, you just aren't going to use it?

P: Yeah, uhm, and he'll ask my concerns, (*I*: uh huh), and he assures me that my age, uh is a safety factor there. Uhm, I don't know,...that it's good. There's a lot of things that have come up about oh, clotting of blood and different things and there's a lot being tested that's so unknown, you know...I think he's a good doctor, but instead of working with me, uh with the diaphragm, he'd rather see me take the pill...and so instead of getting into confrontations with him, because he's pretty strong willed,...but uh he's doing it for my own good.

Like Ms. Martinez, Ms. Barrett has been labeled a "birth control failure" (she has had an abortion) which could account for the doctor's adamance about the pill. However, when this doctor (like the majority of American gynecologists) prescribes and recommends the pill as the most effective nonsurgical form of birth control for women, the tendency is to minimize the dangers with such statements as "you're at risk when you cross the street too"—a statement often mirrored in patient's discourse. But Ms. Barrett is concerned about the safety of the birth control pill and has suffered ill effects from it in the past.

Interestingly, while Ms. Barrett would rather the doctor work with her on using the diaphragm, she still feels he is generally a good doctor who looks out for her best interests. This is a good example of the basic conflict between trying to hold onto a trust for the doctor while concomitantly refusing his advice.

Ms. Long

Ms. Long is a single woman in her mid-30s. She runs the "one-girl" office for her father's construction firm and takes night classes in Spanish and real estate at the local community college. She was originally put on the birth control pill in her teens to regulate her periods, and in her late twenties when she became sexually active she resumed taking the pill as a contraceptive method. She has come to her private practitioner in September for a check-up because her menstrual periods stopped in June, and for a renewal prescription for the pill.

Doctor–Patient Discourse

D: So you haven't menstruated since June.
P: Yeah, I don't think I did in July. I'm pretty sure I didn't...
D: Okay, you haven't missed any pills?
P: No.
D: Look, what I think is happening, that your pills are not strong enough, you know? I've put you on a very low pill as you know...and sometimes this will cause (swallows word). Now what I would like to do is when you finish your pills, let's see, you're on the twenty-eight days. (long pause)
P: Right, Uh, twenty-one day.
D: Twenty-one day, all right. When you finish your pills, and if you don't menstruate within five to six days, come in. I'll give you an injection to get you started.
P: Okay.
D: If you do menstruate, come in then...I will give you a prescription for a different kind...
P: Right, uh hum...

The doctor suggests as a solution to Ms. Long's amenorrhea an injection (progesterone) and a stronger birth control pill. Ms. Long seems to accept this treatment plan unquestioningly . The doctor and patient seem to agree. Despite this agreement there is argument in the medical community as to the safety and efficacy of this treatment for amenorrhea[2], as well as a disinclination for the stronger hormonal content pills—information that does not emerge in this encounter.

Expansion of the Text

I: ...Uhm, do you talk to, have you ever talked to someone about birth control?
P: Not besides the doctor, no...

---

[2] The treatment for amenorrhea is a point of conflict in gynecology. Research shows that to give hormones (in the pill) to women with amenorrhea may temporarily solve the problems. However, over the long term this treatment can aggravate the problem by overwhelming the pituitary gland, decreasing the chances for normal recovery.

Later in the interview discussing the amount of information received from doctors on contraception:

P: Not a lot. Uhm, a little bit with Dr. M. but not, you know, not a, specific.

I: And how did you decide on using the pill as a method?

P: Uh, it's the most convenient and it's most reliable.

I: Do you ever worry at all about the health side effects or any of/

P: /Well, it's a concern but I uhm, I've never had any side effects at all from it, (*I*: uh huh). And I go in, I go in to the doctor twice a year and I know he knows what he's doing, so, you know, I feel reasonably safe, you know . . . safe with it. I'm sure there's a chance but there is with anything . . . .

I: Okay, and how about any long term, have you had any long term experiences, relationships with men?

P: Ah, let's see, not really long term.

I: How about the man you were talking about that you broke up with in December?

P: Well, we were together for about six weeks but that was the time he was here . . . I haven't had a boyfriend, you know, an actual boyfriend, I mean I've had occasionally, you know, had something, someone that just didn't work out but I haven't had a boyfriend since then.

I: Uhm, so have you ever had sexual relations on a regular basis?

P: Well, when I've got a boyfriend, yes.

This is an interesting example (and quite typical) in that nowhere, unlike the previous examples, is there any sign of resistance, either in the conversation with her doctor or in the interview. It could be argued that there is no struggle here to resist. Analysis of the discussions, however, shows otherwise.

What the expansion provides is a picture of a woman who for nine months has had very sporadic sexual activity, no regular "boyfriend," and no anticipation of regular sexual activity on the horizon. Given the medical controversy over appropriate treatment for amenorrhea, the medical questioning of the high estrogen dosage in the stronger birth control pills, and Ms. Long's present reduced sexual activity, a fuller discussion of the range of contraceptive options is called for. Alternative methods are never discussed and Ms. Long's stated reasons for using the pill mirror almost exactly Dr. M's choice of words when recommending this method to new patients. This is not to say that Ms. Long should *never* use oral contraception, but her decision should be an informed one. While an alternative contraceptive method might have helped Ms. Long's health, neither the doctor nor the patient brought it up as a possibility. Is this the equal responsibility of the two participants? I think not. Doctors have historically fought to be the dispensers of knowledge on health, in general, and contraception, in particular. Given the asymmetry in the relationship at this time, the greater responsibility in our model of health care falls on the doctor. This responsibility is reflected in Ms. Long's reliance (perhaps overreliance) on her doctor as her sole source of contraceptive information.

DISCUSSION OF THE DATA

The pictures that emerge from the data address the questions raised earlier—questions of oppressions and oppressed, the active-passive debate, monoliths or multitudes of power and resistance, and commonality and diversity among women.

In the pattern displayed by Ms. Martinez and her doctor, there are signs of resistance inside and outside the doctor's office. Ms. Martinez tries to raise her own experiences and is continually interrupted. Her experiences, in fact, fall within the parameters of the biomedical model, relevant by medical definition to the discussion. Her topics are of pain and menstruation with the use of a medical device. She herself firmly believes her information is important and persists in trying to speak to the topic, but to no avail. Ms. Conrad's attempts highlight a slightly different type of resistance. She raises an explicitly social topic—divorce—a topic that this doctor makes very clear does not belong here. It is not medically defined as relevant to the body, the physiological explanations of the problem. In this case the woman is able actually to raise the topic, but is so decisively corrected that the subject is dropped.

While these examples of resistance take slightly different forms in doctors' offices, they look very similar once outside. Both Ms. Martinez and Ms. Conrad lose confidence in the medical profession's capacity to help them at the moment and do not return. Their response is a common one. J. H. Lavin (1983) found that women are more likely to change their doctors than men, and while there are no hard data, my discussions with alternative, holistic practitioners suggest that women more than men turn to unconventional methods of healing.

Ms. Adams and Ms. Barrett display a very different pattern of resistance. In their interactions with doctors they appear compliant. Once outside the office, however, they each find themselves in different but resistant positions. Ms. Barrett discusses in the interview how on previous visits she has tried to insert her views into the medical discussion. She concludes, however, that her doctor is "set in his ways and so uh, the, we've had the same discussion over and over." She does not choose to leave this doctor. She finds him "a good doctor." Her resistance comes in the form of continuing in his care for check-ups and gynecological help, but seeking contraceptive advice elsewhere (her family, another practitioner). In terms of this doctor, she is noncompliant in her rejection of the birth control pill.

Similarly, Ms. Adams, compliant in the doctor's office, is dissatisfied with the information and care given. She is too embarrassed to question her doctor and thus, unlike with Ms. Barrett, there is no sign here of any history of interactional resistance. Neither has she found satisfaction elsewhere. She is noncompliant without benefit of alternative help.

All these women show signs of active resistance in varying forms to medical authorities. Each of the women represents patterns where the idea that "the doctor knows best" is being questioned. The lives and perspectives of each woman in some way conflict with conventional medical wisdom, and each tries (with varying degrees of consciousness and success) to resolve this conflict.

Ms. Long, however, represents a very different pattern—a pattern of nonresistance. She does correct her doctor when he misstates the type of birth control pill she is using, but throughout the rest of the discussion she agrees with everything he says. In the interview later in her home, she has only praise for her doctor, her only source of contraceptive information. "I go in, I go in to the doctor twice a year and I know he knows what he's doing." Here is a woman who is completely satisfied with her medical care even though some would argue whether she should be. How do we account for this? Are Ms. Long and women like her to be blamed for not being more assertive and knowledgeable? Or are they the poor things earlier feminists were talking about? Are they oppressed people, moved along on a conveyor belt from one authority to the next?

There is another way to understand the lack of resistance in this example as well as the lack of resistance elsewhere in society—an understanding that arises out of cultural values and belief systems. Ms. Long and her doctor share a belief system in the authority of doctors, the medical model, biomedical definitions of women's health, and in a larger context, the scientific world view and the role of the expert (Todd 1989). She is not a passive person, someone who cannot think for herself. Rather she, like all of us, both reflects and reinforces cultural expectations and values unquestioningly in some parts of her life.

CONCLUSION

After this search for resistance, I am still intrigued *and* worried. In the detailed analyses of the data, very different women with very different concerns emerge. Yes, there is resistance and yes, all the women, resistant or not, are active participants in the shaping of their lives. But, and the but is still very evident, resistance and power are enacted in unequal relationships. The *consequences* for all of the women are problematic. Ms. Martinez and Ms. Conrad resist, but do not receive the health and reproductive care they need. Ms. Barrett and Ms. Adams come to the doctor for a service, pay him a considerable fee, and find they have to withhold information to have his cooperation. These two women covertly resisted the doctor's power. The doctor's overt control in the interaction goes uncontested. This type of interaction is the antithesis of what good reproductive health care should be. Women's health and quality of life are at stake in all these examples. Similarly, with Ms. Long, while she is compliant with the recommendation for stronger birth control pills, one doubts that she should be. She is given a controversial remedy without an explanation or discussion that the medical community is in conflict over this approach. By overemphasizing the role of activity and resistance, are new trends in feminist theory running the danger of overlooking inequalities and the very real power women, like those above, face in their daily lives?

Showalter raises a relevant warning in understanding the history of women and madness:

> It is certainly possible to see hysteria within the specific historical framework of the nineteenth century as an unconscious form of feminist protest, the counterpart of the attack on patriarchal values carried out by the women's movement of the time. . . . Such claims, however, come dangerously close to romanticizing and endorsing madness as a desirable form of rebellion rather than seeing it as the desperate communication of the powerless. (1985:5)

As feminist scholars, writing about women's lives, speaking for women, we need to carefully seek balance. First, to fragment women and power runs the risk of conceptually diluting both. It is important to remember that women, whether understood to be passive or active, have generally *responded to* (as illustrated above) rather than *created* societal expectations. This does not mean that women do not strive and succeed in society, but that women are survivors in a tough game. Second, while the essentialist label "woman," used to include all women regardless of differences, is problematic, it is important not to go so far as to drift into fragmentation rather than solidarity. The women discussed above are all different, with different problems. But they have commonalities, shared anxieties about their health and reproductive control. Their ultimate strength lies in their differences *and* their similarities. For oppression, power, and resistance are complicated relationships, embedded in contexts that include historical, cultural, and societal as well as group and individual variations. People are neither solely active nor passive. Rather, different people behave differently in diverse situations and under various conditions.

Feminist theorist, Biddy Martin, sums up these complexities well. On the one hand, rather than seeing power "as originating outside of and independent of concrete social interactions and their natural effect" as something that is held and wielded by "a clearly identifiable and coherent sovereign group," we need "to get at the operations of power at their most material and concrete," to ground our theorizing in "ways of living, style, behavior, personal interaction, sexual relations, language and gender," to see women's lives as "paradigmatic enactments of . . . struggles over meaning." I would add to this that we need the same careful analysis of the ways women resist—to ground operations of resistance at their most material and concrete. To do this we must consider women's experiences.

On the other hand, Martin also warns that "there is a danger in too virulent a critique of the notion of oppression."

> The question of woman, like all questions of meaning, must be particularized, localized, specified and robbed of the mystical and ontological. However, if we fail

not to assert the category woman from our own shifting and open ended points of view, our oppression may easily be lost among the pluralities of new theories of ideology and power. There is a danger that Foucault's challenge to traditional categories, if taken to a 'logical' conclusion, if made into imperative rather than left as hypotheses and for methodological provocations, could make the question of women's oppression obsolete. (Martin 1988:17)

The "Woman Question" has been replaced with "women questions." This is a significant gain. Intellectually and practically it is important for feminist theorists to depict women diversely, situated in many contexts. It is equally important not to lose sight of shared experiences among women. Similarly, there are significant gains in recognizing both that power is not a monolithic force, whether patriarchal or capitalistic, and that where there is power, there is resistance. But, once again, it is critical not to so relativize power, make it so diffuse, that it disappears altogether.

In sum, it is problematic to lump women into one group and define them as static, passive pawns. Such passivity and inability to resist or create leave women without a voice and change becomes impossible. But it is also problematic to let the pendulum swing too far in the opposite direction in our enthusiasm for women's variety and contributions. To do so blurs the picture, hindering the very activity being sought.

REFERENCES

EMERSON, JOAN
   1970 Behavior in private places: Sustaining definitions reality in gynecological examinations. IN *Recent Sociology* (No. 2), H.P. Dreitzel, Ed., New York: MacMillan.
FISHER, SUE AND A. D. TODD
   1986 Friendly persuasion: The negotiation of decisions to use oral contraceptives. IN *Discourse and Institutional Authority: Medicine, Education and Law*, S. Fisher and A.D. Todd, Eds. Norwood, NJ: Ablex Publishing.
FOUCAULT, MICHEL
   1980 *The History of Sexuality, Volume I: An Introduction*. (R. Hurley, trans.). New York: Vintage Books.
JAGGAR, ALISON M.
   1983 *Feminist Politics and Human Nature*. Totowa, NJ: Rowman and Allanheld.
LAVIN, J.H.
   1983 Why 3 out of 5 patients switch. *Medical Economics*: 11-17.
MARTIN, BIDDY
   1988 Feminism, criticism, and Foucault. IN *Feminism and Foucault: Reflections on Resistance*, I. Diamond and L. Quinby, Eds. Boston: Northeastern University Press.

RUBIN, GAYLE
  1975   The traffic in women. IN *Toward An Anthropology of Women*, R.R. Reiter, Ed.
         New York: Monthly Review Press.
SHOWALTER, E.
  1985   *The Female Malady: Women, Madness, and English Culture, 1830–1980*. New
         York: Pantheon Books.
SMITH, DOROTHY
  1974   Women's perspective as a radical critique of sociology. *Sociological Inquiry*
         4:7–13.
SMITH-ROSENBERG, CARROLL
  1985   *Disorderly Conduct: Visions of Gender in Victorian America*. Oxford: Oxford
         University Press.
TODD, ALEXANDRA DUNDAS
  1989   *Intimate Adversaries: Cultural Conflict Between Doctors and Women Patients*.
         Philadelphia: University of Pennsylvania Press.

12

Reflections on Gender, Power and Discourse*

Sue Fisher

Gender, power, and discourse are topics that have been and continue to be at the center of my work. I have a longstanding interest in how we understand gender and power, as well as in the role that discourse plays in the social accomplishment of them as in-the-world realities and as sociological constructs. In this chapter I address the following kinds of questions: (a) Are power and gender rooted in the cultural and/or the structural arrangements of society? If so, does this mean that individuals lack agency, are passive victims of a repressive model? (b) Are power and gender socially accomplished in interaction or through discourse? If gender and power are socially accomplished as people interact and/ or communicate with each other, does this mean that interaction and/or communication are shared resources equally available for all, regardless of the context—organizational, structural, and/or cultural?

In the social sciences, these two research questions are usually posed in an either/or fashion, engendering debate. The first question is most often posed in terms of a cultural or a materialist analysis. Here power and gender are either relatively stable features of a common culture or they flow from the economic organization of society. The second question is posed in terms of an interactional analysis. Here people are actively accomplishing the social reality of their gender and/or power. In my work to date I have argued that we need to reconceptualize the way we discuss these questions. Rather than posing social structure and social interaction as disparate theoretical perspectives and engaging in an either/or debate, we need to see them as reflexively related to each

* Paper presented at Hartford Medical Sociology Association April 25, 1989.

other, to explore how cultural, structural, and institutional arrangements shape the interactional accomplishment of social realities, such as gender and power, as well as how the interactional enactment of these realities help sustain the cultural, structural, and institutional arrangements of society.

It is this reflexive relationship between social structure and social interaction that has been at the center of my work. In focusing on a reflexive relationship between social structure and social interaction, cultural and materialist conceptions informed methodological investigation of how power and gender are interactionally accomplished as doctors and patients communicated over the course of a medical encounter, and these methodological investigations both informed an ongoing process of theory construction and displayed how the participants interactionally accomplished the social realities of gender and power. In this way discourse data reflexively linked social structure and social interaction, linked what Knorr-Cetina and Cicourel have called macro- and micro-sociologies (Knorr-Cetina and Cicourel 1981).

While I have argued that the patient is an active interactional participant, the method of argument—moving as it does from cultural and materialist conceptions to interactional accomplishment and back—orients us more to the ways the patient is oppressed than to the ways the patient resists. Enter a different reading.

Drawing from my past work on the doctor–patient relationship, first I will talk about the reflexive relationship between social structure and social interaction—the method of analysis I have been using—then I will reexamine some of the same data to see how resistance works interactionally. I will finally discuss what these ways of looking mean and whether they might be combined to enrich our understanding of gender, power, and resistance?

SOCIAL STRUCTURE AND SOCIAL INTERACTION

To demonstrate the method of analysis I have been using, I draw from a paper: *Friendly Persuasion: Negotiating Decisions to Use Oral Contraceptives.* In this paper, Alexandra Todd and I argue that to understand how doctors persuade women to use oral contraceptives, you need to understand that one of the organizing features of the medical profession is its autonomy (Friedson 1970). "Autonomy combines with a professional monopoly and state support to give physician top position in the medical hierarchy" (Fisher and Todd 1986:5), and to leave patients with few resources other than to be dependent on their doctor's advice. You also need to understand why doctors persuade women patients to use oral contraceptives. The medical model on which the delivery of health care rests is organized to treat dysfunctional body parts, to provide a technical fix for acute or chronic disease. We argue that women seeking reproductive control do not fit easily into this biomedical model. Birth control is not a treatment, if anything it is a preventive measure. Women seeking reproductive control are not diseased. They are not just looking for a technical fix for a biological problem. Reproductive control is as much a psychosocial issue—an issue rooted in the context of women's daily lives—as it is biomedical. "[A] technical fix for social problems engenders a conflict, one which has the potential to have an enormous impact on women's lives" (Fisher and Todd 1986:5). Yet in the context of the medical model, doctors are oriented towards the technical—the medical— almost to the exclusion of the psychosocial—the patient's life world (Todd 1989; Mishler 1984). Medical interactions about contraception occur in this context.

To make this argument we examined doctor–patient communication during the medical interactions through which decisions about contraception were reached, and discussed how these interactions were characterized by a style we called friendly persuasion—a style which we claimed linked social structure and social interaction. The data were gathered in five settings in two disparate geographical regions across a combined period of six years. Regardless of the setting, who the practitioners were, what their medical specialty (family practice, obstetrics and gynecology, or reproductive oncology [cancer]) is, or how they were paid, the diagnostic-treatment process was characterized by friendly persuasion in which doctors systematically pushed for the birth control pill, downplayed all other contraceptive methods, while ignoring the potential consequences or "side effects" of the pill. If doctors gave information using their directive power to persuade or withheld information, the consequences for patients were all too often the same: Patients were systematically denied the kind of information they needed to participate actively in contraceptive decisions, decisions that were very important in their daily lives. Sarah is a case in point[1]:

She is a quiet-spoken, shy Caucasian woman dressed in a conservative, middle-class style. At 23, she is unmarried and only recently has become sexually active. While her stated reason for coming to the family practice clinic is for a Pap smear and a pelvic examination (her first), it quickly becomes apparent that her motivation for coming to the clinic includes a prescription for birth control. She asks,

PATIENT: Would you be able to prescribe an oral contraceptive for me, since you don't know my family history?

DOCTOR: Well, I was going to talk to you about that. See, you want a birth control pill for birth control?

PATIENT: Uh huh.

DOCTOR: Alright, well we ought to talk a little bit about all the different types of birth control and I could tell you about some of the side effects and what are the good effects. First of all, do you want children?

PATIENT: Yes.

---

[1] The data and discussion here are quoted from *Friendly Persuasion: Negotiating Decisions to Use Oral Contraceptives,* Fisher and Todd, 1986.

The doctor begins with a discussion of the birth control pill.

DOCTOR: OK, well let's go through them all. There is birth control pills which is a little bit over 99% effective. Which is pretty good odds. If you take them right and don't miss your pills you are going to be in pretty good shape. Uhm, and of course everybody uses birth control pills. But as you know, anybody that reads the papers knows, that there are some side effects from them. The short term side effects, the biggest one that everybody worries about is the likelihood of blood clots. It's very uncommon, I haven't myself seen one. I haven't had a patient to have it but, of course, everybody knows somebody who's had a patient who had a blood clot while they were on it and it usually forms in the legs and the reason it's bad is 'cause sometimes it can get into your lungs, cause that kind of problem we see in girls that smoke. Do you smoke?
PATIENT: Uh uh (shakes head no).

After establishing that the patient does not smoke and is not overweight, the doctor continues by discussing the side effects of the pills.

DOCTOR: ...The short term studies look pretty good but//
PATIENT: //What are the short term studies? How long does it run? 5 years?
DOCTOR: 5 to 10 year studies. You know, uh, the, I think the cancer that everybody worries is the endometrial cancer. Not necessarily cervical cancer....it doesn't appear to be related. Now if you told me your mama had cancer of the womb and my aunt had breast cancer, and my grandmother died of female cancer, then maybe we should talk a little bit more. But that sounds like cancer runs in the family. It doesn't sound like uh, you have any, you know, presidposing uh factors with cancer, so you know I think we can feel safe on birth control pills. So they're, they're 90% effective and all side effects short term, but there are a lot of little nuisance problems, some ladies have that we can blame on birth control pills. Some ladies seem to have headaches, uh, that never had headaches before. Uh, but I'm talking about this as what has been recorded and this is not you... (*Patient*: //uh huh.) Uh, that's happened that some ladies get skin rashes. Uh, some ladies complain that they feel different on these, you're in a worse mood. Uh, I guess that's probably the three biggest complaints that there are.
PATIENT: Are those short term, are you just suggesting to me what they are?
DOCTOR: Yeah, usually if you just ride it out in that short term, that means that some ladies get...short-term headaches...headaches are so common and so many people have them, it is hard to say whether or not birth control pills uh, cause, I mean, if you never had a headache and two weeks after you started taking the pill, you get a horrible headache, we got some (headaches) that the birth control pills start and I think if you uh, hang in there a little bit they will go away, and sometimes we can adjust the medication in the pills, try a new one and it doesn't cause them. And we can

do the same thing with the other little problems ladies get// (*Patient*: //Um hum.) and I think every complaint that has ever come up has been blamed, at one time or another on the birth control pills, so we just hang in there, but most ladies that I prescribe birth control pills for, they take them and they go away and they never have problems// (*Patient*: Uh hum.) One thing I will tell you is really not a long-term problem, it's sometimes a short-term problem. When you decide, I want a child, I think its good to get off of them six months before you wanna start trying because there's such a thing called post-pill ammenorhea. Which means after you quit the pill there will be several months interval in some ladies where they don't have a period.

At this point the doctor goes into quite a lengthy explanation about how birth control pills work and what happens physiologically when the patient goes off of them. He then moves on to the next type of birth control, the IUD (intrauterine device):

DOCTOR: The other type of birth control is the IUD. Now what that is a little coil that we put inside of the uterus and...uh, we're not sure exactly how they work...but they are pretty effective, about 99% effective. Now, but, I don't recommend them for anybody that's never had a baby. Their side effect is that they occasionally cause a pelvic infection which can get into your tubes and cause scarring and infertility. So I never recommend it for someone who definitely wants children, too much risk, and I won't use it. Some doctors may use it, but I don't not on// (*Patient*: //when) not on you, someone who wants babies. Now if you had three children and don't want two more, I think it is pretty well worth the risk.

The doctor moves on to a discussion of barrier methods of birth control (the diaphragm and condom).

DOCTOR: OK, now you are down to diaphragms. Diaphragms are reported to be anywhere from 85% to 95% effective and what it is, it's a rubber shield that you put over your cervix. You slip it in before intercourse. It's kinda like a guy wearing a condom. Here what you're doing is blocking the pathway of the sperm way to the cervix. You're keeping it on the outside and keeping the egg and womb on the inside and also you put a little jelly on it that's fairly effective. When somebody is intelligent and that would take time in putting it in. A lot of people won't take the time to put it in, so if it's not in, it's in the drawer next to the bed, it doesn't work, so that's a reasonable form of birth control. Now the birth control pill is safer uhm, and of course you've got condoms, which are very effective as long as they are intact. They are effective, there's no way, uh, just according to you feelings are toward them// (*Patient*: //Uh hum). If it's, intercourse, is just as pleasurable for you and your mate well there's no reason not to use it. It's safe as long as you're sure there's not a hole in it.// (*Patient*: //Uh hum.)

And finally he discusses over-the-counter birth control remedies.

DOCTOR: OK, and then there's foams and jellies and uh they are anywhere from 70 to
85 percent, maybe. I don't think they are as high as 85 and there are a lot of
failure rate on foams and jellies. So I don't recommend them to anybody//
(*Patient*: //uh hum.) I mean if your playing with fire, you might get pregnant
before long, but eventually I think, I think it will catch up with you. Uh,
o.k., so that's it.

PATIENT: OK, let me ask you this, it's kinda a personal question, if your wife had to
use a form of birth control what would you give her? What would you
recommend?

DOCTOR: Well my wife, we uh, have used birth control pills in the past, but she
doesn't use them now. We have a child, and we want some more. We use a
diaphragm. It has been very effective for us// (*Patient*: //Um hum.) and it's
no side effects, and if she got pregnant accidentally it wouldn't be any great
problem, because we want some more children// (*Patient*: //uh hum.) but
then I have one couple uh, whose wife has caesareans and the physician feels
that there's no way that she could have another child . . . and she has used a
diaphragm for 30 years and she is still fertile . . . and I feel safe using that.
You know I never had a lady get pregnant on the diaphragm, course I don't
have a 1000 patients with a diaphragm// (*Patient*: //Um hum.) But you know,
for a short period, I don't see anything wrong with the birth control pills. I
don't like them but I don't hate them. Uh, it's a hard decision to make. You
know that there are a lot of birth control methods round, but they all have
their drawbacks. There's not a perfect birth control yet. Well when you
decide not to have any more children you could have your tubes cut, either a
vasectomy or have a tubal ligation for you// (*Patient*: //Um hum.) that's nice//
(*Patient*: //Would take care of it.) it sure does, but you're really gonna have
to be the one to make your decision on that// (*Patient*: //Uh hum.) You plan to
get married soon, . . .

PATIENT: Uh huh// (Doctor: //OK) it wouldn't be until I get out of school which should
be next summer.

DOCTOR: Well, what would be perfectly acceptable for me, if I wuz in your shoes, is
to be on the birth control pill until next summer for sure, and, uh, that time
see how you did on them and if you don't like them you know you can
always switch over to a diaphragm or he can switch over to condom.

Sarah's interest in contraception coupled with her desire to avoid an unwanted
pregnancy is evident in the transcript. Thus, at first glance, the decision reached
has qualities of an interactional accomplishment jointly produced by doctor and
patient. But while Sarah, and patients in general, do have some input into the
decision-making process, it is the doctor who has the authority to persuade.

Let's take another look. The discussion about contraception begins with the
question, "First of all do you want children?" Why is a question about children
first? Why not ask how much interest do you have in protecting yourself from
possible iatrogenically produced illness? This seems to us to be the more critical

question. Yet neither of us has ever heard it asked. Instead, information is presented selectively. When scientific information is presented, it is discussed in terms of safety and efficiency. The birth control pill and the IUD are both presented as 99% effective—a "fact" many disagree with—however their safety is discussed selectively. The more negative aspects associated with the use of oral contraceptives are systematically downplayed. Blood clots, endometrial and breast cancer are all called "short-term side effects" and their dangers are qualified. Blood clots are declared uncommon. And, while the evidence is not in yet, endometrial cancer and breast cancer are said not to appear to be related to pill use.

A diaphragm is reported to be effective if you are intelligent, if it is used and not left in the drawer, and if it is inserted properly. While the diaphragm is safe, the implication is that most women are neither intelligent nor committed enough to use it effectively.

The condom is okay, if it is intact, and does not interfere with pleasure. Foams and jellies are not recommended. The doctor explains that they are not as effective in preventing pregnancy as the birth control pill.

The messages sent here are subtle and potentially frightening for the patient. She has clearly stated that she wants a safe method of birth control. If the IUD is presented as risky, and the diaphragm, foams, and jellies as less than safe, it is unlikely that she will risk using them. And given the assumption in this society that intercourse with a condom is akin to taking a shower with a raincoat on, she is equally unlikely to risk her partner's pleasure or her own pleasure and reproductive security by using them.

Toward the end of the presentation of information about birth control methods, Sarah asks, ". . . if your wife had to use a form of birth control what would you give her?" In response, the resident recommends birth control pills and grounds that recommendation in the patient's status as an unmarried woman who cannot risk pregnancy. Are we to assume from this recommendation that the risks associated with the pill—blood clots and cancer—are safer than the infertility associated with the IUD or the slightly increased evidence of pregnancy associated with the diaphragm? Whatever our assumptions, this recommendation provides an example of how the doctor, while providing information, also expresses more subtle assumptions about women, family arrangements, childbearing, and birth control.

It is medically well-accepted today that no organ system of a woman's body is unaffected by the birth control pill. The risks associated with the pill take 20 years or more to mature and are too varied to enumerate here. Yet, birth control pills are widely prescribed. Several factors encourage this perspective pattern.

First, the practice of medicine is very time-consuming and most doctors do not spend a lot of time keeping up with the latest developments in their fields. More specifically, they receive most of their information about drugs, such as birth control pills, from drug salespeople and medical journals. The pharmaceutical industry has reaped tremendous profits from the birth control pill. Their salespeople can hardly be considered unbiased teachers. This same kind of bias is evident in medical journals. Most journals are dependent on advertising dollars. The pharmaceutical industry is a heavy advertiser. Editorials and articles as well as advertisements reflect the journal's dependence on the pharmaceutical industry's continued good will.

Historically the American Medical Association and the American College of Obstetrics and Gynecology have been hesitant to explain the side effects and risks of the pill to pill users. It has been argued that to do so would confuse and alarm many women patients, and to have others do so would interfere with the doctor–patient relationship. These are male-dominated, sexist assumptions based on a view of women as emotionally unstable and unable to understand complex explanations. While to a large extent the medical profession lost this battle in Senate hearings, and information about the risks and side effects of the pill are included in each packet of birth control pills, doctors still have the upper hand. As we saw in the data, patients look to doctors as the final arbitrators of contraceptive information, and the manner in which the information is presented functions to persuade. Feminists argue that to the degree discrimination toward women is pervasive in our society, it is also deeply embedded in the field of medicine (Scully 1980; Ruzek 1978; Ehrenreich and English 1978). These materialist values and cultural attitudes are important factors in the medical treatment of women.

In the prescription of birth control, the selective use of information and medical authority legitimates the medical model and sustains the dominance of the medical profession. It also reinforces a technological approach which addresses physiological or biological aspects of health and illness. The technology of reproductive control developed, promoted, and found profitable by the drug companies creates a demand for its use and encourages the prescription patterns and the persuasion strategies we have discussed. Medical providers using the institutional authority of their role provide information in ways that function to persuade, and the birth control pill becomes an institutionalized, self-serving, standard medical procedure. While this persuasion may be friendly, the selective use of authority and the selective presentation of information denies patients the information they need to be active participants in their own health care.

The analysis is informed by cultural, material, and institutional understanding of gender and power, documents their interactional accomplishment, and argues that this accomplishment both reflects and reinforces the cultural, material, and institutional arrangements of society. It is also, at least implicitly, calling for a more humane, patient-centered medical encounter as a way to minimize the asymmetry in the medical relationship and to challenge traditional power arrangements, changes to be brought about through the actions of active, resisting subjects.

RESISTANCE

To demonstrate what resistance of this kind would look like, I draw from the data presented earlier in this book, (see Chapter 7). While I make an argument in this chapter that links social structure and social interaction, I will reinterpret some of the data to show how patients can be seen as acting powerfully and can resist, even in the face of doctors' greater institutional authority.

To restate, questioning, presentational, and persuasional strategies are interactional mechanisms through which the information necessary to negotiate treatment decisions is exchanged. It is these interactional mechanisms that I will examine here.

When patients ask questions, they have the potential to change the direction of the treatment decision, as shown in the following examples.

Anelen was diagnosed and treated in the Faculty Clinic. She was a 30-year-old Anglo woman who had been married once, divorced, been pregnant once, and gave the child up for adoption. When she returned to the Faculty Clinic to discuss the results of her tests and make a treatment decision, she asked a question during a discussion of treatment options. On her previous visit Anelen provided the information that she did not want to have any more children. The doctor responded by recommending a hysterectomy as a permanent method of sterilization and to treat her abnormal Pap smear.

On the second visit, the doctor reminded Anelen that he has recommended a hysterectomy, and Anelen asked a question that redirected the talk about treatment options and affected the final treatment. She said, "Have a hysterectomy and that, I'm that, if there's an alternative. I'm terrified of operations." The doctor responded, "Uh, okay, well, there certainly is an alternative, yeah, we can treat this by just freezing it here in the office and that usually will take care of it about 90% of the time." Here the medical practitioner used a presentational strategy. He provided the information that "there certainly is an alternative" and that this alternative "is 90% effective." This presentation provides information while suggesting how it should be understood.

The next patient, Lucy, was diagnosed and treated in the Faculty Clinic after being referred from a social agency staffed by native Spanish-speaking workers. Lucy was a 42-year-old, bilingual, Mexican-American woman. She was married and had three children. After a hysterectomy was recommended, the patient asked, "Is that necessary?" The doctor responded, "Well, it isn't absolutely necessary; it may or may not be . . . " Again, a presentational strategy was used. The statement that "it isn't absolutely necessary" framed the medical information to suggest a preference: Although a hysterectomy was not absolutely necessary, it certainly was preferable. For much of the remaining exchange of information, the doctor worked to move the patient toward a treatment decision of hysterectomy. In each instance, the patient responded by asking if it was necessary or by saying that if it was not necessary, she did not want it. She was treated with a conization biopsy.

Another patient, Pat, asked questions, but did not change the direction of the discussion of options or the treatment performed. Pat, a 32-year-old Anglo woman, had been married, divorced, pregnant five times, and had two abortions and three children. When she returned to the Community Clinic to discuss her treatment options, she was told that the extent of the lesion had not been visualized, asked if she wanted more children, and told that a conization biopsy followed by a hysterectomy was the best treatment for her.

During the discussion of treatment options and in response to information that the resident was presenting, she made a request for information, a request that functioned strategically. She said, "Well, for this way now would you say, for instance, you're talking about there could be surgery, if, uh, there is an advancement of cancer there, a sign of cancer. Well, also the fact that you asked me did I want any more children, there's another way of doing it too, but it also means that it could travel, is that it, the cancer could spread, say for instance, if I don't have a hysterectomy, is that the idea?" The doctor responded, "Well, if you have cancer, then it has to be treated because it can spread, right?" When the resident presented Pat with an informed consent form to sign, he used a persuasional strategy. He said, "Even though with this form that I have before me that the government requires you to sign, it's a request for a hysterectomy for sterilization, even though it says here that you have no problems which require a hysterectomy and we know that you do, the hospital and state require me to ask you to sign this so that you understand that what we're talking about is permanent sterilization with no possibilities of future pregnancies."

This is a particularly persuasive presentation. The patient in no way requested a hysterectomy for sterilization. During a discussion about treatment options, a hysterectomy was recommended as the most appropriate treatment. The grounds for this recommendation were specified as follows: "It [cancer] could come back," and "...for somebody your age, that's had your family, you're sure that you don't want children, I'd recommend a hysterectomy." To a woman who has had an abnormal Pap smear and is already afraid that she has a life-threatening medical problem, this is a particularly persuasive presentation. It heightens the emotional impact of the abnormal Pap smear by stressing that "it" could come back. The "it" being referred to is, of course, cancer. In addition, it is the resident, not the patient, who links the need for a hysterectomy with the patient's age, her childbearing history, and her lack of desire for additional children.

The persuasive overtones were strengthened when the resident gave her the informed consent to sign and told her that although the form said that she had no problems requiring a hysterectomy, "We know that you do." He brings all of the authority of his medical role to bear in this statement. As a man, as a medical practitioner, and as her physician, he is telling her what to do and implying dire consequences if she does not comply. The talk did not change the direction of the discussion of options or the treatment performed. This patient was treated with a vaginal hysterectomy.

Anelen, Lucy, and Pat all had abnormal Pap smears in the middle range—the gray area between normal cells and invasive disease. Each of them had a hysterectomy recommended. But only Pat received one.

When I analyzed these interactions in the earlier article, I focused on the relationship between social structure and social interaction (Fisher 1983, 1986). I argued, for example, that Anelen and Lucy were treated in the Faculty Clinic by an attending staff physician, a professor of medicine. Pat, by contrast, was treated by a resident in the Community Clinic. Clearly, "staff physicians do not have the same interest in performing hysterectomies as do residents, who must have surgery experience to become fully qualified doctors" (Fisher 1983, 1986)—an interest that can be seen in the strategies used to "sell" hysterectomies. With Anelen and Lucy, presentational strategies were used. The doctor provided information while specifying how it should be understood. With Pat, persuasional strategies were used. The resident provided information while specifying how it should be understood. The force of the "sell" was clearest with the informed consent procedure. Here, the resident "told the patient what he was required to by law and then suggested that she ignore it" (Fisher 1983, 1986).

If I turn my gaze from the institutional authority of the medical provider—an authority that was used to "sell" hysterectomies—to the strategies patients employed to resist the sell, a different picture emerges. From this vantage point we can see that Anelen and Lucy directly resisted the doctor's authority with the questions they asked. Anelen asked if there were any other alternatives to a hysterectomy, saying that she was terrified of operations, and Lucy asked if a hysterectomy was necessary, insisting that if it was not, she did not want to have it done. These are clear, strong questions that challenge the doctor's authority, as they resist the imposition of the treatment that has been recommended. This was not the case with Pat.

Pat was the only patient who added information to the "facts" provided by the medical practitioner. She added the notion that cancer could spread if not treated with a hysterectomy. It was this information the resident picked up and used to justify his treatment recommendation. Pat's question was also not as clear or as strong as those used by the other two patients. She did not ask if there were alternatives or if a hysterectomy was necessary. In addition, she asked two questions during the same utterance. The resident avoided the first question entirely. He did not discuss alternatives. And he answered only part of the second question. He did not address whether the abnormal cells would spread if she did not have a hysterectomy. Instead, he answered a hypothetical question that she had not really asked. He answered the question, "If it is cancer, would it spread without a hysterectomy?" He did not tell her that if she did not have cancer, there were other alternatives, and Pat did not ask. By not asking clear, strong questions, by not insisting that the questions she asked were answered, by not finding the fallacy in the information the resident provided, Pat neither challenged the resident's authority nor resisted the recommended treatment. In fact, the decision to perform a hysterectomy can be seen as a co-production. Pat helped the resident convince her that a hysterectomy was necessary. She provided the "facts" upon which he based his sell.

Have I provided an empirical analysis of how individuals are active, resisting agents? Have I avoided the pitfalls of global, totalizing theories which tend to portray one group of people—in this case women patients—as passive victims of a repressive model? If I have, if women patients have been portrayed as actively resisting, as self-conscious agents responsible for their actions within the constraints of an institutional order, then this portrayal would not be without costs.

First, if the analysis rests, as it does here, on the ways patients resist, then Anelen and Lucy have resisted successfully and Pat has not. This seems to come perilously close to blaming the victim. This problem is closely related to the next. I may have located the interactional accomplishment of resistance at the cost of losing sight of how power is produced and constrained in the context of larger cultural, structural, and institutional arrangements. For example, the focus on the institution as a site for the exercise of and the resistance to power leaves no way to factor in how the institution is located in a web of cultural and structural factors. There is no way to consider how the fee-for-service practice of medicine or the organizational structure of medicine, located as they are in a capitalist economic context and a patriarchal cultural context, produce and constrain the kinds of interactions just described, indeed, how they structure the very content of resistance. There is also no way to factor in how medicine as a gendered profession and a gendered way of knowing bolsters the authority of physicians and places all patients at a disadvantage, but especially women patients. Add minority status, lower class, and a host of other oppressions and the disadvantages multiply.

Clearly, resistance as it has been used here is inadequate for the task at hand. There is another theoretical perspective which suggests that the formulation of power and resistance I have been using relies on an essentially liberal conception of the individual as an active, more or less self-conscious agent responsible for resisting within the constraints of an established institutional order.

From this perspective there is a very different formulation of the problem. Here, power, resistance, and gender are not to be found in "the actions of individuals or institutional agents, (n)or in the effects of structures or systems" (Smart 1985:122). Rather, power is rooted in a system of social relations— exercised through tactics, techniques, and strategies—organized from below and, of necessity, accompanied by a multitude of resistances. Foucault (1979) argues explicitly that power does not flow from the state, or from the economic organization of society, nor is it the outcome of constitutive subjects. It is, rather, a "history of the present" where "detailed examination of the connection between forms of human experience and relations of power and knowledge" provide for understanding. From this perspective a system of power relations and the resistance which accompany them socially construct the very categories of doctor and patient.

But if we accept this model of power, what basis do we have for understanding or formulating theoretical or political resistance to the dominant power relations?

Is there a way to engage each theory productively to enrich our understanding of the workings of power and resistance and, if so, on what model of the actor and of society would we rely?

REFERENCES

EHRENREICH, B., AND D. ENGLISH
   1978   *For Her Own Good*. New York: Anchor Press/Doubleday.
FISHER, S.
   1986   *In the Patients' Best Interest: Women and the Politics of Medical Decisions*. New Brunswick, NJ: Rutgers University Press.
FISHER, S., AND A. D. TODD
   1986   Friendly persuasion: The decision to use oral contraceptives. IN *Discourse and Institutional Authority: Medicine, Education and Law*, S. Fisher and A.D. Todd, Eds. Norwood, NJ: Ablex Publishing.
FOUCAULT, M.
   1979   *The History of Sexuality, Vol. 1: An Introduction*. London: Allen Lane, Penguin Press.
FREIDSON, E.
   1970   *Profession of Medicine*. New York: Dodd, Mead.
KNORR-CETINA, K., AND A.A. CICOUREL, EDS.
   1981   *Advances in Social Theory and Methodology: Toward an Integration of Micro- and Macro-Sociologies*. Boston: Routledge & Kegan Paul.
MISHLER, E.
   1984   *The Discourse of Medicine: Dialectics of Medical Discourse*. Norwood, NJ: Ablex Publishing.
RUZEK, S.B.
   1978   *The Women's Health Movement*. New York: Praeger.
SCULLY, D.
   1980   *Men Who Control Women's Health*. Boston: Houghton Mifflin.
SMART, B.
   1985   *Michel Foucault*. London and New York: Ellis Horwood, Ltd.
TODD, A.D.
   1989   *Intimate Adversaries: Cultural Conflict Between Doctors and Women Patients*. Philadelphia: University of Pennsylvania Press.

Author Index

A

Abelson, R.P., 36, *46*
Aiken, L.H., 238, *240*
Arms, S., 8, *11*, 248, *262*
Argyle, M., 79, *99*
Arney, W., 234, 238, *240*
Atkinson, J.M., 75, *99*, 246, *262*
Austin, J.L., 3, *11*, 185, *207*

B

Barker, M., 214, *241*
Barker-Benfield, H.J., 7, *11*
Bart, P., 8, *13*, 178, *182*, 248, *265*
Bateson, G., 34, 35, *45*
Baum, J., 238, *241*
Beller, E., 111, *126*
Belsky, M.S., *154*
Bergen, B., 234, 238, *240*
Bernstein, B., 166, *180*
Bliesener, T., 252, *262*
Boyle, C.M., 19, *30*
Bradley, C., 214, 237, *240*, *241*
Bruhn, J.G., 77n, *99*
Bryan, T.E., 32, *45*
Bucher, R., 41, *45*
Byrne, P.S., 111, *126*

C

Callon, M., 218n, *240*
Caress, B., 162, 177, 178, *180*
Cassell, E., *99*
Cerreto, M., 214, 231, 238, *240*
Chafe, W.L., 36, *45*, 167, *180*
Chance, M., 79, *99*
Chomsky, N., 3, *11*, 185n, *207*
Churchill, L., 109, *126*
Cicourel, A.V., 10, *11*, 40, 41–42, *45*, 75n, *99*, 167, *180*, *181*, 184, 185, *207*, 288, *299*
Cole, M., 185, *207*
Collins, R., *11*
Condon, W.S., 85n, *99*
Conrad, P., 194, 205, *207*, 252, *262*

Cook, M., 79, *99*
Cooperstock, R., 248, *262*
Culpepper, E., 8, *11*, 248, *262*

D

Daly, M., 5, *11*, 152, *154*
D'Andrade, R.G., 64, 65, *66*, 185, *207*
Davis, F., 183, *208*
Davis, K., 243, 246, 247n, 248, 253n, 255n, 262
Dean, J., 79, *99*
Delaney, J., 8, *11*
Deleuze, G., 240, *240*
Dore, J., 185, *207*
Douglas, J.D., 75, *99*
Dowley, G., 185, *207*
Dreifus, C., 8, *11*
Durkheim, E., *99*

E

Eakins, B.W., 9, *11*
Eakins, R.G., 9, *11*
Ehrenreich, B., 4, 5, 7, *12*, 165, *181*, 188, 202, 205, 206, *208*, 248, 252, *262*, 299
Ehrenreich, J., 4, *12*, 165, *181*, 252, *262*
Eisenberg, L., 72n, *99*
Emerson, J., 78n, *99*, 276, *284*
Engel, G.L., 72n, *99*
English, D., 4, 5, 7, *12*, 188, 202, 205, 206, *208*, 248, 252, *262*, 299
Erickson, F., 75n, 86, *99*, 196, *208*
Ervin-Tripp, S., 166, *181*
Exline, R., 79, *100*

F

Fabb, W.E., 32, *45*
Fabrega, H., 72, *100*
Fanshel, D., 109, *126*, 166, *181*, 185, 188n, 208
Fidell, L., 8, *13*, 248, *262*
Fisher, J.J., 153, *154*

Fisher, S.C., 8, 9, *12*, 163, 169, *181*, 184, 189, 200, 206, 207, *208*, 246, 248, 252, 253, *262*, *263*, 277, *284*, 288, 289, 296, 297, *299*
Fishman, P., 246, 247, *263*
Forester, J., *12*
Foucault, M., 233, 234, 237, *241*, 245, *263*, 268, *284*, 298, *299*
Frake, C.O., 35, *45*
Francis, V., 128, 139, 150, *155*
Frankel, R.M., 80, 86n, *100*, 128, 129, 136, 137n, 139, 151, 153, *154*
Friedson, E., 4, *12*, *165*, *181*, 205, *208*, 288, *299*

G

Gallagher, E.B., 32, *45*
Gallie, W.B., 245n, *263*
Galton, L., *154*
Garfinkel, H., 3, *12*, 75n, 81, *100*, 110, *126*
Gelman, R., 166, *182*, 185, *208*
Gerson, J.M., 259, *263*
Giddens, A., 258n, *263*
Gillespie, C., 214, 237, *241*
Glaser, B.G., 261, *263*
Gleitman, H., 39, *46*
Gleitman, L.R., 39, *46*
Goffman, E., 33, 35, 41, *46*, 110, *126*, 130, 133, 151, *154*
Goodwin, C., 80, 90n, 93, *100*
Gordon, L., 8, *12*
Gozzi, E.K., 128, 139, 150, *155*
Green, J., 33, 34, 46, *47*
Griffin, P., 9, *12*
Grimes, J.E., 50, *66*
Groce, S.B., 248, 252, 253, *263*
Guattari, F., 240, *240*
Gumperz, J.J., 32, 34, 35, *46*
Gunter, R., 113, *126*

H

Haberman, P.W., 19, *30*
Habermas, J., 9, *12*
Hall, W.S., 185, *207*
Halliday, M.A., 166, *181*, 196, *208*
Hartsock, N., 257, *263*
Hasan, R., 166, *181*, 196, *208*
Hearn, J., 252, *263*
Heath, C., 252, *263*
Hefferman, M.W., 32, *45*
Henley, N., 7, 9, *12*, *13*, 246, *263*

Heritage, J., 246, *262*, *263*
Hollander, M., 214, *241*
Homans, H., 248, *264*
Howell, M.C., 8, *12*
Hughes, D., 252, 253, *264*
Humphrey, F., 9, *12*
Hymes, D., 3, *12*, 166, *181*, 188, *208*

I

Ickes, W.J., 79, *100*

J

Jaggar, A.M., 270, *284*
Jefferson, G., 27, *30*, 86, 91, 93, *100*, *101*, 109, *126*, 128, 130, 131, 132, 134, 135, 138, 153, *155*, 184, 188n, *209*, 246, *264*
Jellison, J.M., 79, *100*
Jones, M., 214, 231, *241*
Jones, L.K., 50, *66*

K

Kahneman, D., 63, *66*
Kennan, E.O., 167, *181*
Kendon, A., 79, 85n, 89, *100*
Kern, R., 194, 205, *207*
Kimball, C.P., 19, *30*
Kinmoth, A.-L., 239, *241*
Kleinman, A., 32, 34, *46*, 72, *100*
Knorr-Cetina, K.D., 245, *264*, 288, *299*
Korsch, B.N., 128, 139, 150, *155*
Kronenfeld, J., 214, *241*
Kuno, S., 167, *181*

L

Labov, W., 3, *13*, 109, *126*, 166, *181*, 185, 188n, *208*
Lakoff, R., 9, *13*, 130, *155*
Larned, D., 161, 162, 178, *182*
Lavin, J.H., 281, *284*
Lavoie, J., 214, *241*
Lazare, A., 194, 204, *208*
Lenanne, J., 248, *264*
Lenanne, K.J., 248, *264*
Liberman, R., 77n, *100*
Long, B.E., 111, *125*
Lorber, J., 248, *264*
Luker, K., 195, *208*
Lukes, S., 244, 245, *264*
Lupton, M.J., 8, *11*

M

Martin, B., 283–284, *284*
Martin, E., 248, *264*
Måseide, P., 185, *208*
McHugh, P., 220, *241*
McKeown, T., 5, 6, *13*, 205, *208*
McPherson, A., 248, *264*
Mechanic, D., 165, *182*
Meehan, A.J., 137n, *155*
Mehan, H., 9, 10, *13*, 75n, *101*, 184, 189, *208*
Merchant, C., 205, *209*
Merton, R.K., 44, *46*
Miller, C., 9, *13*
Minsky, M., 36, *46*
Mishler, E.G., 111, *126*, 252, *264*, 289, *299*
Mitchell, J.C., 216, *241*
Mitchell-Kernan, C., 166, *181*
Mons, C., 111, *126*

N

Navarro, V., 4, *13*, 165, *182*, 205, *209*
Newport, E.L., 39, *46*
Newton, R., 214, *241*
Novak, E.R., 178, *182*

O

Oakley, A., 248, *264*
Ogston, W.D., 85n, *99*
Ory, M., 214, *241*

P

Paget, M.A., 119, *126*
Parsons, T., 128, 153, *155*
Paulshock, B.Z., 178, *182*
Peiss, K., 259, *263*
Philips, S., 166, *182*
Phillips, W., 32, *45*
Pollner, M., 76, *101*
Pomerantz, A., 116, *126*
Posner, T., 214, *241*
Prather, J., 8, *13*

R

Reichman, R., 50, *66*
Reiser, S.J., 7, *13*
Reissman, C.K., 252, *264*
Rosenbloom, A., 214, *241*
Roy, N.L., 151, *155*
Rubin, G., 270, *285*
Rumelhart, D.E., 36, *46*, 51, *66*
Ruzek, S.B., 7, *13*, *299*

S

Sacks, H., 75, 86, 91, *101*, 109, *126*, 128, 130, 131, 133, 134, 135, 153, *155*, 184, 188n, *209*, 246, *264*
Schank, R.C., 36, *46*
Scheflen, A., 88n, 89n, *101*
Schegloff, E., 86, 91, *101*, 109, *126*, 128, 130, 131, 132, 133, 134, 135, 136, 138, 153, *155*, 184, 188n, *209*, 246, *264*
Schenkein, J., 108, *126*
Schiefelbein, S., 194, *209*
Schieffelin, B.B., 167, *181*
Schneider, J.W., 252, *262*
Scott, J., 257, *264*
Scully, D., 4, 7, 8, *13*, 178, *182*, 188, *209*, 248, *265*, *299*
Seaman, B., 4, 8, *13*, 202, *209*
Seaman, G., 4, 8, *13*, 202, *209*
Searle, J., 3, *13*, 109, *126*, 185, *209*
Shatz, M., 166, *182*, 185, *208*
Showalter, E., 252, *265*, 270, 283, *285*
Shultz, J., 75n, *99*
Shuy, R.W., 19, 27, *30*, 109, *126*, 130, 151, *155*, 166, 167, *182*, 207, *209*
Siegrist, J., 252, *262*
Silverman, D., 216, *241*
Smart, B., 298, *299*
Smith, D., 269, *285*
Smith, M., 238, *241*
Smith-Rosenberg, C., 269, *285*
Standing, H., *265*
Stanley, L., 257, *265*
Steel, J., 238, *241*
Stelling, J.G., 41, *45*
Stevens, R., 165, *182*
Stimpson, C.R., 5, *13*
Stoeckle, J.D., *14*, 111, *126*, 128, 139, 151, *155*
Stone, G.C., 72n, *101*
Stone, P., 32, *45*
Strauss, A.L., 261, *263*
Streek, J., 185, *209*
Strang, S., 238, *241*
Strong, P., 216, 219, 223, *241*
Swift, K., 9, *13*
Szasz, T., 214, *241*

T

Tannen, D., 33, 34, 35, 41, 43, *46*, *47*, 56, *66*
Thorne, B., 9, *13*

Todd, A.D., 5, 6, *13*, 189, 195, 201, 205, 206, 207, *209*, 246, 248, 252, *263*, *265*, 267n, 277, 282, *284*, *285*, 288, 289, *299*
Toth, E., 8, *11*
Travis, L., 214, 231, 238, *240*
Tromel-Plotz, S., 246, *265*
Tversky, A., 63, *66*

V
Van Egeren, L., 72n, *100*
Van Hooff, J.A.R.A.M., 77n, *101*

W
Waitzkin, H.B., 4, *14*, 111, *126*, 128, 139, *151*, 165, 167, *182*, 205, *209*

Walkerdine, V., 239, 240, *241*
Wallat, C., 33, 34, *46*, *47*, 56, *66*
Wallen, J., 128, 139, 151, *155*
Waterman, B., 4, *14*, 165, 167, *182*, 205, *209*
Webb, E.G., 151, *155*
West, C., *101*, 142, *156*, 184, *209*, 246, 251, *265*
Wise, S., 257, *265*
Wittgenstein, L., *14*
Wright, W., 5, 6, *14*, 205, *209*

Y
Yellin, A., 79n, *100*

Z
Zimmerman, D., 76, *101*, 184, *209*, 246, *265*

Subject Index

A

Ambulatory care
and communicative interaction, 73–74

B

Birth control prescription, 195–206, 271–280, 289–294
Buffer language, 43

C

Cone biopsy (conization), 165
Context, 2–7, 184
and culture, 5–7
and language, 2–3
Conversation, elements of
anaphora, 20
sequence markers, 20, 27–29
topics, 20–21
Cryosurgery, 165

D

Diabetes, adolescent
background of treatment, 213–217
policing, 223, 229
reforming clinic practices, 231–233, 237–238
self-regulation, 217–219, 220–223, 230–231, 233–237
styles of care, 229–231
support for, 238–239
Diagnosis, 108; *see also* Treatment decisions
role of questions in, 108–111, 123–125

F

Feminist studies, 7–9, 204–205
of gender relations, 267–270
of power, 244–246, 256–262, 283–284
Frames theory, 35–42, 201–202
elicitation frames, 42
registers associated with frames, 39–42
shifting frames, 37–39

G

Gaze
in physician–patient interaction, 84–96
relationship to speaking, 79–81
and touch, 92–93
violating rules of, 81–84
Gender relations
feminist studies of, 267–270
in physician–patient interaction, 269–280
and power, 246–248, 256–262

H

Health-care delivery system
organizational structure of, 4–5
and sexism, 4, 7–9; *see also* Gender
relations in physician–patient
interaction
Hysterectomies
and depression, 162
increase in, 161–162, 177–178
options to, 165
treatment decision making, *see* Treatment
decisions

J

Jargon, 18–19
code switching, 18
receptive competence, 19

L

Language
sociological approaches to, 2–5, 183–184
Linguistics and medicine, 17–21
cultural differences, 19–20
jargon and vocabulary, 18–19
structure of discourse, 20–21
Looking, *see* Gaze

M

Motherese, 39, 40

P

Patient autonomy vs. medical control, 216,
    218–219
  family relations, 223–225
  and moral responsibility, 221–223
  negotiations, 226–227
  psychology, 225–226
  support groups, 238–239
  theoreticity, 219–220
Physician–patient conversation
  emotional demands, 42–44
  gaze in, 84–96
  and gender relations, 248–256, 269–280
  vs. normal conversation, 21, 22ff, 188n
  phase transitions, 85–87
  and power, 248–256
  questions in, 110–123, 141–149
  role of modern science in, 205–206
  social topics in, 195–202
  touch in, 87, 92–93
Power
  conceptualization of, 244–246
  in doctor–patient interaction, 248–256
    doctor, 248–252
    patient, 252–256
  and gender relations, 246–248, 287ff
  feminist perspective on, 256–262
  and resistance, 271–*284*, 295–298
Primary care defined, 71n
Progress notes, 51–56
  recoding, 51, 55, 64–65

Q

Questions
  and answers, 129–138
  definition of, 129–131
  and diagnosis, 108–111, 123–125
  physician-initiated vs. patient initiated,
      139–149, 187–188
    analysis of, 149–153
  requests for confirmation, 136–137
  requests for repair, 134–136
  strategies, 169–175
    medical practitioner's use of, 170–172
    patient's use of, 172–175

S

Sequence marking, 27–29

closings, 28
openings, 27–28
transitions, 28–29
Social structure and social interaction,
    288–294
Sociological theories of language, 2–5
Speaker-based rules, 93–94
Speech acts, 3
  categories of, 185, 186
  queries as, 93
  theory, 185–188
Stuttering, 147–149
Suicide
  Durkheim's study of, 75–76

T

Tokens
  of acknowledgment, 136
  of disapproval, 116
  lax, 27
Topic
  criteria for identification of, 21
  introduction, 22–24
  response, 24–27
  sequence marking (cohesion), 27–29
Treatment decisions (for hysterectomies),
    164–175, 295–298
  criteria for
    medical, 164–165
    social, 165–166
  presentational/persuasional strategies, 169,
      175–177, 293–294, 297
  questioning strategies, 169
    medical practitioner's use of, 170–172
    patient's use of, 172–175
  role of medical interview, 167–169
  unspoken factors in, 164

V

Vernacular Black English, 19–20

W

Work Group on Education for the Health
    Professions, 74–75
World view, effect of on behavior, 5–7